Scholarship in the Digital Age

Scholarship in the Digital Age
Information, Infrastructure, and the Internet

Christine L. Borgman

The MIT Press
Cambridge, Massachusetts
London, England

For information about special quantity discounts, please e-mail <special_sales @mitpress.mit.edu>.

This book was set in Sabon by SNP Best-set Typesetter Ltd., Hong Kong.
Printed and bound in the United States of America.

Library of Congress Cataloging-in-Publication Data

Borgman, Christine L., 1951–
Scholarship in the digital age : information, infrastructure, and the Internet / Christine L. Borgman.
    p. cm.
Includes bibliographical references and index.
ISBN 978-0-262-02619-2 (hardcover : alk. paper)
1. Communication in learning and scholarship—Technological innovations. 2. Scholarly electronic publishing. 3. Information technology. 4. Learning and scholarship—Social aspects. I. Title.
AZ195.B67   2007
001.2—dc22
                                                                2006036057

10 9 8 7 6 5 4 3

For Cindy

Contents

Detailed Contents

Preface

Scholars in all fields are taking advantage of the wealth of online information, tools, and services to ask new questions, create new kinds of scholarly products, and reach new audiences. The Internet lies at the core of an advanced scholarly information infrastructure to facilitate distributed, data- and information-intensive collaborative research. These developments exist within a rapidly evolving social and policy environment, as relationships shift among scholars, publishers, librarians, universities, funding agencies, businesses, and other stakeholders. Schol arship in the sciences, social sciences, and humanities is evolving, but at different rates and in different ways. While the new technologies receive the most attention, it is the underlying social and policy changes that are most profound and that will have the most lasting effects on the future scholarly environment. This is an opportune moment to think about what we *should* be building.

This book is grounded in developments of the twenty-first century, set in both a social and historical context. Today's initiatives in cyberinfrastructure, e-Science, e-Social Science, e-Humanities, e-Research, and e-Learning emerged from a tumultuous period in scholarly communication in which technological advances converged with economic and institutional restructuring. Every stage in the life cycle of a research project now can be facilitated—or complicated—by information technologies. Scholars in the developed world have 24/7 access to the literature of their fields, a growing amount of research data, and sophisticated research tools and services. They can collaborate with other individuals and teams around the world, forming virtual organizations. Data have become an important form of research capital, enabling new questions to be asked by leveraging extant resources. With the mass digitization of books now under way, previously unforeseen possibilities arise to compare literary themes, extract details of events, improve machine translation, and compile extensive indexes and directories. Text and data mining promise everything from drug discovery to cultural enlightenment.

These wondrous capabilities must be compared to the remarkably stable scholarly communication system in which they exist. The reward system continues to be based on publishing journal articles, books, and conference papers. Peer review legitimizes scholarly work. Competition and cooperation are carefully balanced. The means by which scholarly publishing occurs is in an unstable state, but the basic functions remain relatively unchanged. Research data are another matter entirely. While capturing and managing the "data deluge" is a major driver for scholarly infrastructure developments, no social framework for data exists that is comparable to that for publishing. Data can be discrete digital objects, but their use is embedded deeply in the day-to-day practices of research. Scholarly infrastructure also must be understood in the context of legal, policy, and economic arrangements. The "open-access movement" to expand the availability of scholarly publications, data, and other information resources is grounded in several centuries of Western thought about "open science." Open science, in turn, is based on economic principles of public goods. The ethos of sharing that is fundamental to open science and scholarship is threatened by the expansion in scope and duration of copyright protection and patents. These tensions, in turn, are reflected in new forms of publishing and licensing, such as the "information commons" or "knowledge commons." The many stakeholders in scholarly information infrastructure are addressing their own territories, whether technical, legal, economic, social, or political, or in individual research domains, but few are taking a big-picture view of the interaction of these factors. The integrative and inter-disciplinary analysis presented here is intended to provoke a conversation among the many parties whose interests depend on a rich and robust scholarly environment.

The argument is laid out in nine chapters, grouped thematically into three parts. The first three chapters frame the issues. The next five chapters identify the problems to be solved if the vision of an ideal scholarly information infrastructure is to be achieved. Chapters 4 and 5 compare the stability of the scholarly communication system to the instability of the current scholarly publishing system. Chapter 6 compares the role of data in scholarship to that of publications, explicating notions of "data." Chapter 7 explores the social, behavioral, and policy context of data and documents in more depth, set in the context of information infrastructure. Chapter 8 provides an extensive analysis of the scholarly artifacts, practices, and incentive structures of the sciences, social sciences, and humanities, assessing how infrastructure issues are playing out in each discipline. Chapter 9 concludes the book by synthesizing the issues and laying out a research agenda.

My previous book in this series, *From Gutenberg to the Global Information Infrastructure: Access to Information in the Networked World* (MIT Press, 2000), examined social, technical, and policy issues of information infrastructure with a particular emphasis on digital libraries and the role of libraries as institutions. That book provides a point of departure for this one. It is not assumed that readers will be familiar with the earlier book, although it offers useful background on developments through the 1990s and information infrastructure issues outside the realm of scholarship.

This book draws on literature from many different disciplines and specialties. Each reader will be familiar with some of these sources, but familiarity will vary by community. In the interest of expanding the conversation beyond individual specialties and stakeholders, I have provided an extensive set of references. A permanent Web page associated with this book is located at <http://snipurl.com/BorgmanDigitalAge>.

Let the conversation begin.

Christine L. Borgman
Los Angeles, California
June 2007

Acknowledgments

As with many books, this one has had a long gestation period, making it impossible to recall all of the provocative conversations, pointers, shared documents, and many other influences on the final product.

The book proposal and the bulk of the first draft were written during a wonderful sabbatical year (2004–05) at the Oxford Internet Institute of the University of Oxford. Bill Dutton, director, my officemates Ted Nelson and Paul David, and many other OII colleagues including Alex Caldas, Stephen Coleman, Corinna diGennaro, Helen Margetts, Gustavo Mesch, Ralph Schroeder, and Yorick Wilks offered many occasions for stimulating discussions, public and private. Alex, Stephen, and Ralph also read and commented on early drafts of this book. Other Oxford colleagues were equally generous with their time and ideas, including Peter Burnett, Matthew Dovey, Paul Jeffries, Marina Jirotka, Marlene Mallicoat, Anne Trefethen, and Steve Woolgar. My time in Britain provided opportunities to engage UK colleagues Elizabeth Davenport, Susan Eales, Jessie Hey, Monica Landoni, Liz Lyon, Cliff McKnight, Jack Meadows, Peter Murray-Rust, Ann O'Brien, Charles Oppenheim, Norman Paskin, Rob Procter, Malcolm Read, Stephen Robertson, Seamus Ross, Chris Rusbridge, Karen Sparck Jones, and Norman Wiseman, among many others. Paul David was an essential source on economic issues, Ann O'Brien on knowledge organization and access, and Peter Murray-Rust on chemistry information.

I am especially privileged to have had continuing conversations about the nexus of technology, policy, and social aspects of scholarly infrastructure with Dan Atkins, who chaired the U.S. Blue Ribbon Panel on Cyberinfrastructure and now heads the Office of Cyberinfrastructure at the National Science Foundation, Stephen Griffin, program officer for Digital Libraries at the National Science Foundation, and Tony Hey, who headed the UK e-Science Program from its inception through June, 2005, and is now the vice president for technical computing at Microsoft. All have been generous with their time, introductions to other people, and recommendations of resources. Steve Griffin also gave permission to reproduce the infrastructure slide he created as part of joint U.S.-UK initiatives.

Many colleagues in the United States, Canada, Europe, and Asia helped me explore these issues in discussions, by sending papers or references, or by offering speaking invitations, including Maristella Agosti, Lluis Anglada, Tatiana Aparac, Sandra Ball-Rokeach, Michael Buckland, Nadia Caidi, Jose Canos-Cerda, David Clark, Julie Cohen, Gregory Crane, Blaise Cronin, Susan Dumais, Ed Fox, Peter Ingwersen, Srecko Jelusic, Brewster Kahle, Noriko Kando, Michael Lesk, Gary Marchionini, Cathy Marshall, Sara Miller McCune, Bill Paisley, Jenny Preece, Edie Rasmussen, Boyd Rayward, Tefko Saracevic, Ben Shneiderman, Marc Smith, Diane Sonnenwald, Shigeo Sugimoto, Elaine Svenonius, Leigh Star, Helen Tibbo, John Unsworth, Herbert Van de Sompel, Catharine van Ingen, Irene Wormell, Paul Wouters, and Ann Zimmerman.

Clifford Lynch, executive director of the Coalition for Networked Information, gave the most magnanimous contribution of time and intellect to my writing of this book. He provided thoughtful critique and extensive written commentary on the book proposal and penultimate draft, complemented by many hours of discussion. Geoffrey Bowker, director of the Center for Science Technology and Society at Santa Clara University, helped me think through critical issues in a series of conversations during my writing and also reviewed the penultimate draft. He gave me access to the manuscript of his book, *Memory Practices in the Sciences*, which he was finishing just as I was beginning this one. Gary and Judy Olson greatly enhanced my understanding of collaborative research, and provided comments on the penultimate draft of chapter 8. They were starting their book as I was concluding mine, and thus the cycle continues.

The three large research projects in which I have been involved between the writing of two books gave rise to many of the themes explored here. The Alexandria Digital Earth Prototype Project examined the use of research data and resources for teaching purposes, raising many issues of data use and reuse. My ADEPT faculty colleagues, Anne Gilliland, Gregory Leazer, Richard Mayer, and Terry Smith, and the many student researchers who participated over a period of six years, produced a rich interdisciplinary mix of ideas and results. Four years as a member of the National Research Council panel that wrote *Signposts in Cyberspace* yielded substantial knowledge of Internet technology and policy. Many hours were spent in conversation with John Klensin, Patrik Faltstrom, and Hugh Dubberly about Internet navigation and information retrieval. Roger Levien, who chaired the panel, kindly gave permission to reproduce one of the many figures he drew that did not appear in the final publication. Since 2002, I have been a co-principal investigator of the Center for Embedded Networked Sensing (CENS), a National Science Foundation Science and Technology Center. It is my work with CENS that provoked a deep interest in scientific data and the changing nature of scientific practices associated with new forms of instrumentation. CENS is a truly interdisciplinary collaboration, populated by scholars who thrive on finding common problems with people in other specialties. Deborah Estrin, CENS director and principal investigator, Gregory Pottie, Paul Davis, Michael Hamilton, Mark Hansen, Thomas Harmon, Philip Rundel, and William Kaiser are among the many science and engineering collaborators at CENS who have contributed to my understanding of science practices. Our work on data management at CENS also involves William Sandoval, Noel Enyedy, Jonathan Furner, and Jillian Wallis. Present and former students working on CENS data issues include Alberto Pepe, Matthew Mayernik, Stasa Milojevic, Eun Park, and Kalpana Shankar (as a postdoctoral fellow). Jillian provides the continuity on data management research while I multitask. Possessing a rare combination of scientific and artistic skills, she also redrew figure 2.1. Yang Lu, a University of California at Los Angeles (UCLA) doctoral student, meticulously verified and updated every reference in this book.

Other projects have yielded additional forms of guidance. Bernard Frischer, formerly of UCLA and now director of the Institute for Advanced Technology in the Humanities at the University of Virginia, with whom I collaborated on some of the cultural virtual reality research, has been a fountain of knowledge on digital research in the humanities. Paul Uhlir of the National Academies of Science, who directs the U.S. National Committee for CODATA (Committee on Data for Science and Technology), on which I serve, has patiently answered many questions about legal and policy issues associated with scientific data and pointed me to rich troves of reading. Marc Rotenberg, executive director of the Electronic Privacy Information Center, on whose advisory board I serve, keeps me current on technology and privacy issues.

My UCLA colleagues are a reliable source of enlightening conversation. Phil Agre, Alfonso Cardenas, Michael Curry, Jim Davis, Jonathan Furner, Anne Gilliland, Jerry Kang, Leah Lievrouw, Gary Strong, Sharon Traweek, and the late Chris Foote were particularly influential on matters addressed in this book.

My husband, George Mood, edited many drafts of chapters, as he has edited all my publications for nearly thirty years. He deserves far more credit for the result than he will accept. He and Ann O'Brien have been my muses throughout this project, serving as sounding boards for ideas good and bad, day and night. I offer much thanks and appreciation to all listed herein. I hope that those not mentioned here will forgive my neglect and know that they were part of the process nonetheless.

1

Scholarship at a Crossroads

The Internet is now an integral component of academic life. Faculty and students alike rely on Internet connections for interpersonal communication, access to information resources in support of research and learning, access to administrative resources, entertainment, and day-to-day tasks such as driving directions, dictionary and phone lookups, and restaurant reservations. In a few short years, we have gone from "logging on" to do specific tasks to "always on," where the Internet is the communication channel of first resort for a growing array of activities. As wireless connectivity continues to improve, we have gone from desktop to laptop for Internet access, and are quickly moving to palmtop, phone, and various combinations of information appliances yet to be imagined.

Content and Connectivity

As Internet penetration and bandwidth increase, so has the volume and variety of content online. Much of it is just "stuff"—the unverified and unverifiable statements of individuals, discussions on listservs and Web logs ("blogs"), questionable advertisements for questionable products and services, and political and religious screeds in all languages, from all perspectives.

But a substantial portion of online content is extremely valuable for scholarship. Daily newspapers from around the globe are available on the Internet, usually free, enabling rapid access to breaking news more quickly and from more viewpoints than ever before. Scholarly journals frequently are available online before they are available in print, if they are printed at all. Preprints and penultimate drafts of scholarly articles may be posted online well before the official release, depending on the policies and practices of the scholarly field. Government agencies, research institutions, private foundations, and other entities often distribute their reports only on the Internet. If these documents are available in print, it is with more delay and more cost to the reader. Many forms of content exist only in digital form, such as numerical data, dynamic models, and interactive databases that produce customized results on demand. Their print equivalents would be nearly useless.

An Opportune Moment

The technology now exists to enhance scholarship and learning through online access to information, data, tools, and services. Building the technical framework and associated services will take many years, but progress is well under way. Governments, research funding agencies, and private industry are making massive investments in Internet-based technologies. Policymakers view these investments as opportunities for economic growth and international competitiveness in research and education. Many in the academic community see the alignment of technical and policy goals as a "once in-a-generation opportunity to lead the revolution in science and engineering" (Atkins et al. 2003, 32).

These are not small, local technologies that will be replaced quickly. Rather, they are large-scale international investments in an infrastructure that is expected to be in place for a long time. Once built, it will not easily be changed. History reveals that early decisions in technology design often have profound implications for the trajectory of that technology. Now is the time to determine what we *should* be building.

These are exciting and confusing times for scholarship. The proliferation of digital content allows new questions to be asked in new ways, but also results in duplication and dispersion. Authors can disseminate their work more widely by posting online, but readers have the additional responsibility of assessing trust and authenticity. Changes in intellectual property laws give far more control to the creators of digital content than was available for printed content, but the resulting business models often constrain access to scholarly resources. Students acquire an insatiable appetite for digital publications, and then find on graduation that they can barely sample them without institutional affiliations. New social, legal, and technical frameworks for access to scholarly content are arising, but have yet to find long-term business models.

This is a critical juncture in building the next generation of scholarly information infrastructure. The technology has advanced much more quickly than has our understanding of its present and potential uses. Social research on scholarly practices is essential to inform the design of tools, services, and policies. Design decisions made today will determine whether the Internet of tomorrow enables imaginative new forms of scholarship and learning—or whether it simply reinforces today's tasks, practices, laws, business models, and incentives.

Scholarship in Social and Technical Contexts

As Jim Gray, an oft-quoted U.S. computer scientist, said, "May all your problems be technical" (*Computer Science* 2004, 95). Building a technical framework for scholarship is much easier than understanding what to build, for whom, for what purposes, and how their usage of the technologies will evolve over time. People will adopt new technologies if they perceive a sufficient advantage over the present methods to justify the costs and efforts involved. Once adopted, they will continually adapt those technologies to their practices. With experience, people identify new and unforeseen uses of tools, products, and services. Often neither the designers nor the potential users of a technology can anticipate its value—or lack thereof—months or years into the future. Scholarly information and practices, which are the focus of this book, do not exist in a vacuum. Social, economic, technical, and political trends all influence the environment for scholarship.

Social factors can have profound influences on how technologies are developed and deployed. Internet technologies that are still in place, such as TCP/IP (Transmission Control Protocol/Internet Protocol), were formulated at a time when the network was used and managed by a closed community consisting largely of researchers and their associated technical support staff (Cerf and Kahn 1974). Trust and reciprocity within the community could be assumed. As the Internet became a more open system with access allowed by anyone and from anywhere, these assumptions were no longer viable. In these days of terrorism, identity theft, computer hacking, viruses, spam, and denial of service attacks, security and authentication become important design considerations.

Attitudes toward the dissemination and use of information on the Internet also have changed significantly since the early years. Initially, the Internet was viewed as an open frontier that would broaden democracy, freedom of speech, and access to information, with little need for formal regulation. "Information wants to be free" was the rallying cry of the early days online. Now that phrase is the title of a librarian's blog. The information environment of the Internet consists of a complex mix of content for free and for fee, for public good and private profit, whose quality ranges from the best-of-the-best to worst-of-the-worst.

Commercial scholarly publishing has consolidated into a few large players and many small ones. "Bundles" of "information products" are leased to libraries in place of journal subscriptions. The music industry has found viable business models to sell its products online, but remains aggressive in prosecuting those who distribute copyrighted music via the Internet. Intellectual property laws promoted by the entertainment industry apply equally to scholarly content, severely limiting the educational protections of "fair use" and "first sale."

Economic and regulatory frameworks for digital information have unbalanced traditional relationships among authors, readers, publishers, and librarians. Concerns about the notion of information as intellectual "property" and the deterioration of the public domain are leading to alternative publishing methods. The information commons approach of "some rights reserved" offers a legal framework to distribute scholarly information and other works. Open access models of publishing are intended to make scholarly content more freely available. However, "open access" encompasses a wide range of mechanisms, from "author-pays" journal publishing to posting preprints on personal Web sites. Similarly, institutional repositories offer a means for universities and consortia to capture the scholarly products of their members. These also operate under models that range from current access to permanent preservation.

Economic and political trends can influence the adoption of technologies in unpredictable ways. Some products, such as mobile phones, became ubiquitous once they dropped below a certain price point. Wired broadband, such as cable modems and DSL (digital subscriber lines), has not yet achieved a comparable level of adoption, despite predictions of massive growth. Economists and policymakers debate the relative influence on the take-up rate of high prices, lack of demand, and inadequate quality of service. Meanwhile, wireless technologies for Internet access may make wired broadband unnecessary. Some cities are installing wireless broadband, despite the objections of cable and telephone companies. Cellular telephone technology obviated the need to install wired telephony throughout Central and Eastern Europe after the end of the cold war. Africa and other parts of the developing world also leapfrogged past wired telephony and went straight to mobile, wireless communications technology (*Broadband* 2002; Dutton et al. 2003; Odlyzko 2003).

Embedded in the debates about the present and future use of broadband are decades-old telecommunications policy issues about the role of common carriers. For example, discussions of "net neutrality" in the United States center on whether Internet service providers (ISPs) must continue to deliver all bits on a first-come, first-served flat-price basis, or can offer premium services such as video and voice at higher prices. The basic architecture of telecommunications and the Internet differs with respect to the neutrality with which they deliver traffic. Telecommunications architecture is an "intelligent network" with sophisticated internal capabilities to manage traffic. The Internet, in contrast, was deliberately designed as a "dumb network" on the end-to-end principle that all intelligence should be at the edges of the network (in clients and servers) so that the network itself does not need to know anything about the contents of the bits. Specific definitions of net neutrality vary widely, as do proposed resolutions. Arguments about innovation, network congestion, capacity, equity, and quality of service abound. Those in favor of neutrality include major content providers such as Google, Yahoo, and Microsoft, while those opposed include major U.S. telecommunications and cable companies such as Verizon, Comcast, and AT&T. These policy issues are being addressed in many other countries and international arenas (Bachula 2006; David 2001; Duguid 2005; Goldsmith and Wu 2006; Keep the Net Neutral 2006; Saltzer, Reed, and Clark 1984; Web's Worst New Idea 2006; van Schewick 2007; Wu 2005).

The Data Deluge: Push and Pull

The volume of scientific data being generated by highly instrumented research projects (linear accelerators, sensor networks, satellites, seismographs, etc.) is so great that it can only be captured and managed using information technology. Social scientists are analyzing ever-larger volumes of data from government statistics, online surveys, and behavioral models. Humanities scholars, similarly, are producing and analyzing large bodies of text, digital images and video, and models of historic sites. The amount of data produced far exceeds the capabilities of manual techniques for data management. This "data deluge" (Hey and Trefethen 2003) is pushing efforts to build an advanced information infrastructure for research and learning. At the same time, the availability of fast, high-capacity computer networks and sophisticated instruments to produce data are pulling scholars toward using them. Data, models, and visualizations can be incorporated into journal articles, conference papers, and other scholarly products. Scholarly documents are becoming larger, more complex digital objects. New tools and services are needed to produce, publish, distribute, and manage these objects.

Problems of Scale

Data and information always have been both input and output of research. What is new is the *scale* of the data and information involved. Information management is notoriously subject to problems of scale (Belew 2000; Korfhage 1997; Lesk, 2005). Retrieval methods designed for small databases decline rapidly in effectiveness as collections grow in size. For example, a typical searcher is willing to browse a set of matches consisting of 1 percent of a database of one thousand documents (ten documents), may be willing to browse a 1 percent set of ten thousand documents (one hundred), rarely is willing to browse 1 percent of one hundred thousand documents (one thousand), and almost never would browse 1 percent of 1 million or 10 million documents. The larger the database, the more fine-grained the retrieval methods, ranking algorithms, postprocessing capabilities, and visualization tools required. The scholarly digital repositories of today and tomorrow may contain hundreds of millions of records. Today's search engines are effective at discovering text on the World Wide Web, but this is only a small portion of the formats and sources of content useful to scholarship. Information retrieval mechanisms must continue to adapt to the size, rate of growth, and heterogeneity of collections.

Scaling affects the management of both research data and the information products that result from analyzing and contextualizing those data. When small amounts of data are collected, such as field research recorded by hand in notebooks, documentation can be flexible and adaptable to the immediate problem. As the volume of data collected and the number of researchers involved increases, data management tends to become more automated. Automated data collection is less flexible, as decisions must be made in advance about what data elements are to be captured and how those elements are to be described. If the data are contributed to a repository, compared with other data, or shared with colleagues outside the research team, then the choice and description of data elements must be standardized even more, and therefore be even less flexible. But once collected and documented, they may be used and reused with a variety of data analysis and visualization tools.

Requirements for the description of research documents also vary by scale. Authors often provide coarse topical categorization on their personal Web sites or add a few keywords to conference papers, but few are willing to catalog their entire oeuvre in a specified format, whether for a promotion review or contribution to an institutional repository. Making massive amounts of scholarly output accessible via institutional or disciplinary repositories will require better tools for indexing, markup, and description at the time of input, and better retrieval mechanisms at the point of output.

Preservation and management of digital content are probably the most difficult challenges to be addressed in building an advanced information infrastructure for scholarly applications. The same technology that generates such a wealth of research data also puts those data at risk. If cared for properly, books and journal articles printed on paper can survive in libraries for several hundred years. Digital data have a much shorter life span. They must be migrated to new forms of technology on a regular basis, or else they soon become unreadable due to failure of the medium or the lack of available devices to read the medium. Relatively few disciplines have data repositories, and many of those are funded on fixed-term research contracts. Rarely are they established as permanent institutions on a par with libraries and archives, and charged with responsibility for the historical record. Models for managing and funding long-term digital preservation are a growing policy concern (*Long-Lived Digital Data Collections* 2005; Lord and Macdonald 2003).

Influences on Scholarship and Learning

The data deluge is affecting scholarship and learning in ways both subtle and profound. Producing great volumes of data is expensive, whether by scientific instruments or from national or international surveys. Larger teams of researchers are collaborating to produce these data sets. More funding agencies, journals, and conferences expect researchers to make their data available for others to mine. Sharing data is seen as a way to leverage investments in research, verify research findings, and accelerate the pace of research and development. In some fields, the data are coming to be viewed as an essential end product of research, comparable in value to journal articles or conference papers. While the sharing of data is made possible by the technology of digital libraries and the Internet, it runs counter to practice in many fields. Researchers often are reluctant to share data with others until they have finished mining them and publishing the results. Ownership rights in data may not be clear or intellectual property laws may vary across the multiple jurisdictions in which data are held.

Another trend is the blurring of the distinction between primary sources, generally viewed as unprocessed or unanalyzed data, and secondary sources that set data in context, such as papers, articles, and books. Data sets are being listed as scholarly publications in academic vitae and cited as bibliographic references in scholarly articles. Scholarly publications may contain embedded data sets, models, moving images, and sound files, and links to other documents, data sets, and objects. Systems to manage scholarly documents now must accommodate much more than text, tables, and figures.

Scholarly objects are available online in multiple forms and places. Articles may be described by several indexing and abstracting services, and their full content may exist in more than one database. Authors submit papers to repositories organized by their disciplines, institutions, and funding agencies, in addition to submitting them for publication and posting them on their own Web sites. Multiple versions of journal articles exist online concurrently, sometimes identical and sometimes different in important ways, thus confusing the reader and confounding the scholarly record.

The proliferation of digital content is part of the evolution, revolution, or crisis in scholarly communication, depending on the perspective taken. Authors, libraries, universities, and publishers are wrestling with the trade-offs between traditional forms of publisher-controlled dissemination and author- or institution-controlled forms of open access publishing. At issue are the forms of peer review, the speed of dissemination, the ease of access, the cost, who pays the cost (e.g., the author, library, or reader), and preservation. While these battles are under way, variant forms of documents proliferate, and the librarian's ideal of "universal bibliographic control" slips ever further away. Whether that ideal can be abandoned in favor of better retrieval mechanisms is a matter of much debate in the library community (Ekman and Quandt 1999; Harnad 2001; 2005c; Hawkins and Battin 1998; Oppenheim, Greenhalgh, and Rowland 2000; *Rethinking How We Provide Bibliographic Services* 2005; *Universal Bibliographic Control* 2003; Waters 2006; Willinsky 2006).

Primary and secondary information sources long have been treated as a dichotomy, with different strands of research on each. Sociologists of science study the context in which primary data are produced, while data archivists are concerned with how those data are captured, managed, and preserved. Researchers in the fields of information studies and communication investigate how scholarly publications are written, disseminated, sought, used, and referenced. Librarians select, collect, organize, conserve, preserve, and provide access to scholarly publications in print and digital form. Little research has explored the continuum from primary to secondary sources, much less the entire life cycle from data generation through the preservation of the scholarly products that set those data in context.

Once collections of information resources are online, they become available to multiple communities. Researchers can partner across disciplines, asking new questions using each other's data. Data collected for policy purposes can be used for research and vice versa. Descriptions of museum objects created for curatorial and research purposes are interesting to museum visitors. Any of these resources may also be useful for learning and instruction.

Nevertheless, making content that was created for one audience useful to another is a complex problem. Each field has its own vocabulary, data structures, and research practices. People ask questions in different ways, starting with familiar terminology. The repurposing of research data for teaching can be especially challenging. Scholars' goals are to produce knowledge for their community, while students' goals are to learn the concepts and tools of a given field. These two groups have different levels of expertise in both disciplinary knowledge and the use of data and information resources. Different descriptions, tools, and services may be required to share content between audiences (Borgman 2006a; Borgman et al. 2005; Enyedy and Goldberg 2004).

Networks of Data, Information, and People

Scholarly data and documents are of most value when they are interconnected rather than independent. The outcomes of a research project could be understood most fully if it were possible to trace an important finding from a grant proposal, to data collection, to a data set, to its publication, to its subsequent review and comment. Journal articles are more valuable if one can jump directly from the article to those it cites and to later articles that cite the source article. Articles are even more valuable if they provide links to data on which they are based. Some of these capabilities already are available, but their expansion depends more on the consistency of data description, access arrangements, and intellectual property agreements than on technological advances.

The networking of individuals and information resources is essential for those involved in joint research projects. These projects must be coordinated over time and distance, which requires access to communication channels and content. Individuals may collect and contribute data to a project from multiple, distributed locations. Others may describe, analyze, and augment those data. Teams hold meetings or discussions via e-mail, chat, phone, or videoconference, often while viewing the same documents on local screens. Agreements about access to data before, during, and after a project are an essential negotiating point in establishing collaborations.

The networking of distributed data and documents requires the interoperability of systems and services, which in turn requires standards. In the mid-1990s, the research agenda for interoperability of digital libraries appeared to be clearly established (Lynch and Garcia-Molina 1995). When that research agenda was revisited seven years later, it appeared that the right set of issues had been identified, but the assumptions had been incorrect. The Internet of the mid-1990s was a much friendlier place than it later became; most of the content then online was authoritative, and was described by librarians or other information professionals. Workshop participants in 1995 did not anticipate the "messiness" of today's content environment or changes in copyright laws that created barriers to interoperability. Standards and practices for interoperability of digital libraries now must incorporate the means to authenticate senders, receivers, sources, data, and documents, and to determine copyright and access permissions. Finding ways to address these requirements while facilitating open access to information, ease of use, and adaptation to local practices is among the grander challenges of constructing an information infrastructure (Agre 2000, 2003; Borgman 2002; Lynch and Garcia-Molina 2002).

2

Building the Scholarly Infrastructure

The initiatives of the late twentieth and early twenty-first centuries to build national and global information infrastructures are hardly the first grand visions to unite the world of information. Notions of a "global information system" originated in the fifteenth century, as intercontinental sea routes opened and printing technology advanced (Neelameghan and Tocatlian 1985). Paul Otlet's bibliographic networks of the 1930s were a precursor to hypertext (Rayward 1991, 1994; Rayward and Buckland 1992; RieussetLemarie 1997). "Memex," as envisioned by Vannevar Bush in 1945, anticipated the development of personal computers, indexing tools, hyperlinking, and visualization software. That vision was instrumental in launching U.S. postwar investments in science and technology (Bush 1945a, 1945b). J. C. R. Licklider's 1965 models for networking information and library services in the 1960s are referenced as inspirations for current investments in Internet-based scholarly infrastructure.

The transformative potential of technology, as evident in public discourse about digital scholarship, reflects a set of values and expectations. Computerization movements are a form of "systems movements" (Hughes 1994, 2004) that emphasize the beauty of the human-built world, and may have religious overtones, suggesting that humans are empowered to improve the physical world.

Systems movements need champions, of which digital scholarship has many. Grand visions are fragile. It is difficult to maintain coherence when faced with the practical realities of research and development. Visions are fragmented into pilot projects and proofs of concept. Volunteers must be recruited to test and evaluate unproven and unstable technologies whose capabilities may be miniscule in proportion to the grandiose promises made. Years of investment in basic technical infrastructure may be required before the payoffs to daily practice can be achieved. The discourse of digital scholarship already is creating high expectations, raising concerns about whether these expectations can be met in a reasonable period of time. Achieving the vision is by no means inevitable, and history has shown that the best technology, in any objective sense, does not necessarily win in the marketplace.

Technologies of Information Infrastructure

Technologies that are core to digital scholarship—such as the Internet, the World Wide Web, computing grids, and digital libraries—exist in social and political contexts, and have evolved over time. Brief explanations of these technologies will provide a context for programmatic initiatives in scholarly information infrastructure. Subsequent chapters will refer back to the definitions and policy issues introduced here.

The Internet

An authoritative definition of the Internet is supplied by the U.S. National Research Council: "a diverse set of independent networks, interlinked to provide its users with the appearance of a single, uniform network. . . . The networks that compose the Internet share a common architecture (how the components of the networks interrelate) and software protocols (standards governing the interchange of data) that enable communication within and among the constituent networks" (*Internet's Coming of Age* 2001, 29).

The above definition captures the essential aspect that the Internet is a network of networks, interconnecting an array of public and private networks around the world. Individual users gain access to the commodity Internet through commercial Internet Service Providers such as AOL or MSN, or from local telephone or cable companies that provide the telecommunications capacity, such as AT&T or Time Warner in the United States and BT or Virgin in the United Kingdom. Research institutions and universities also are ISPs for their communities. Universities support digital scholarship applications with higher-capacity, higher-speed networks than those available to the general public.

No single entity controls or governs the Internet. Even the definition of "Internet governance" is hotly contested (Collins 2004; MacLean 2004; *United Nations Working Group* 2005). The "appearance of a single, uniform network" (*Internet's Coming of Age* 2001, 29) is made possible by technical standards and protocols that are invisible to most users. These include the Domain Name System (DNS), simple mail transfer protocol (smtp), hypertext transfer protocol (http), file transfer protocol (ftp), and Internet protocol (IP, as in IPv4 and IPv6, not to be confused with IP as a common abbreviation for "intellectual property"). While some of the low-level technical specifications that make the Internet operate are formal technical standards, many of them have the less formal status of "Request for Comment (RFC)." The motto of the Internet Engineering Task Force, which develops and administers these protocols, is "rough consensus and running code." The task force is a volunteer organization, and the informal means by which core Internet technology is developed and managed is worrisome to some government policymakers (Levien et al. 2005).

The Domain Name System, the "name space" for computer locations on the Internet, was implemented in the early 1980s to provide human-readable, memorable names in place of numerical codes. The DNS is administered by the Internet Corporation for Assigned Names and Numbers (ICANN), whose role in Internet governance also is controversial. Given the number of local and international jurisdictions covered by the Internet, and the complex array of purposes for which the Internet is used, debates about Internet governance will not be resolved anytime soon. Rather, they will be a continuing concern of international policy.

The World Wide Web

Despite the frequency with which the Internet and the World Wide Web (WWW or Web) are conflated in the popular press, they are not coextensive. The WWW is a specific application for providing access to documents in a linked network and incorporates a broad set of technical standards. Responsibility for the development of technologies and the maintenance of these standards lies with the World Wide Web Consortium (*World Wide Web Consortium* 2006). The Web was developed at the European Organization for Nuclear Research in Geneva and launched in 1991 (*What Are CERN's Greatest Achievements?* 2006). It incorporated many, but by no means all, of the capabilities of extant technologies for navigating the Internet such as Gopher, ftp, and Wide Area Information Servers (WAIS), and proposed technologies such as Xanadu (Nelson 1987, 2004; Schwartz et al. 1992). The most significant advance of the World Wide Web was in browsers, which were far more intuitive user interfaces for navigation (Levien et al. 2005). Mosaic, Netscape, and later Internet Explorer, Safari, Mozilla Firefox, and other browsers made it easy to view documents and images formatted with the Hypertext Markup Language (HTML).

Another consequence of the WWW was to make domain names visible in the form of Uniform Resource Locators (URLs) and thus valuable as identifiers. When the Web was much smaller than it is today, users frequently navigated by guessing at domain names. Great commercial value existed in having an easily guessed domain name, such as United.com for United Airlines or Ford.com for the Ford Motor Company, or a generic name such as business.com or sex.com. Intellectual property disputes proliferated, "cybersquatters" bought any domain name that had potential value to anyone, and domain names were bought and sold at high prices.

Guessing domain names declined in effectiveness as the WWW grew in size, which is another example of the scaling problems of information retrieval. Moreover, guessing domain names became risky with the emergence of "phishing" sites that masquerade as trustworthy businesses. Such sites attempt to acquire sensitive information, such as passwords or credit card numbers, for fraudulent purposes. This is an example of the unintended consequences of technologies. Search engines became more widely available, sophisticated, trustworthy, and essential for navigation. As Web content grows in volume and variety, search engines are in a continual race to maintain effectiveness at the next level of size. They also are on guard for new forms of fraud and unethical behavior. Web services provide the architecture for many digital scholarship applications.

Partly in response to the scaling problems, the World Wide Web Consortium (W3C) began to develop the "Semantic Web." The Semantic Web is an ambitious venture to incorporate richer descriptions of documents, more complex vocabulary structures, and intelligent agents to execute tasks on behalf of human clients (*Semantic Web Activity* 2006).

The Grid

In the most general sense, a computing grid is analogous to an electric power grid, which provides pervasive access to electricity. "Grid" also can refer to specific software for accumulating unused computer capacity from networks (Foster 2000, 2003; Foster and Kesselman 2001). Just as the Internet is a "network of networks," the grid can be viewed as a "grid of grids" (Fox 2004). Each community of users might have its own grid, and thus an information infrastructure for research and education might consist of interacting grids for science, social science, humanities, education, and the individual communities therein. Grid computing is one of several technical architectures that will underpin digital scholarship.

Digital Libraries

Since it was first coined, the term "digital libraries" has been an oxymoron: "if a library is a library, it is not digital; if a library is digital, it is not a library" (Greenberg 1998, 106). Early on, Clifford Lynch (1994) noted that the phrase digital library obscures the complex relationship between electronic information collections and libraries as institutions. The concept of digital libraries evolved over the first decade of research and practice to incorporate perspectives from computing, libraries, and archives (Borgman 1999, 2000a).

The comprehensive definition developed by a multidisciplinary group of scholars at a National Science Foundation workshop continues to be cited widely (Borgman et al. 1996):

1. Digital libraries are a set of electronic resources and associated technical capabilities for creating, searching, and using information. In this sense they are an extension and enhancement of information storage and retrieval systems that manipulate digital data in any medium (text, images, sounds; static or dynamic images) and exist in distributed networks. The content of digital libraries includes data, metadata that describe various aspects of the data (e.g., representation, creator, owner, reproduction rights), and metadata that consist of links or relationships

to other data or metadata, whether internal or external to the digital library.

2. Digital libraries are constructed—collected and organized—by [and for] a community of users, and their functional capabilities support the information needs and uses of that community. They are a component of communities in which individuals and groups interact with each other, using data, information, and knowledge resources and systems. In this sense they are an extension, enhancement, and integration of a variety of information institutions as physical places where resources are selected, collected, organized, preserved, and accessed in support of a user community. These information institutions include, among others, libraries, museums, archives, and schools, but digital libraries also extend and serve other community settings, including classrooms, offices, laboratories, homes, and public spaces.

This definition includes both data and documents as contents of digital libraries, signifying an early concern for viewing primary and secondary sources as a continuum. Distributed collections that contain a mix of media usually are called digital libraries, whether they contain scholarly, instructional, or other types of content (e.g., Alsos Digital Library for Nuclear Issues 2006; Cuneiform Digital Library Initiative 2006; Digital Library for Earth System Education 2006; National Science Digital Library 2006; Perseus Digital Library 2006). Institutional frameworks for providing access to digital content sometimes use this term. The California Digital Library, for example, provides an array of services to the ten campuses of the University of California, including library catalogs, publisher databases, archival finding aids, archival content, and an institutional repository. While the publisher databases are available only to members of the University of California community due to contractual arrangements, most of the other content is made freely available (California Digital Library 2006).

Collections of primary research data, such as that generated by satellites or networks of embedded sensors, are more often referred to as data archives or repositories. Collections of scholarly documents made freely available under open access publishing models usually are called either institutional repositories (Crow 2002) or archives—for example, e-Prints

Archive (Eprints 2006) and arXiv.org e-Print archive (arXiv.org e-Print Archive 2006; Ginsparg 2001). Generally speaking, if a database contains only primary data that has had minimal processing (usually numeric data), then the word "data" is used as a modifier: data archive, data repository, or even digital library of data.

Information Infrastructure for Scholarship

The infrastructure for digital scholarship is being built in many places, under many names. An explanation of the evolving terminology provides a useful background to the national and international initiatives under way.

Terminology

Information infrastructure is used here as a collective term for the technical, social, and political framework that encompasses the people, technology, tools, and services used to facilitate the distributed, collaborative use of content over time and distance. Definitions of information are deferred until chapter 3 and further definitions of infrastructure, which are many, are deferred to other forums (Borgman 2000a, 2000b, forthcoming; Bowker and Star 1999; Friedlander 1995a, 1995b, 1996a, 1996b, 2005; Star 1999; Star and Ruhleder 1996).

Research and development programs for scholarly information infrastructure typically use either an "e-" prefix, such as e-Science, e-Social Science, e-Humanities, or e-Research, or a "cyber-" prefix such as cyberinfrastructure or cyberengineering. The United States tends to use "cyberinfrastructure," while Europe, Asia, Australia, and elsewhere tend to use "e-Science," although the forms often are intermingled. The term "i-Science," where the i- prefix means interactive, is found occasionally (Woolgar, 2003). Linguistics is partly to blame for the proliferation of terms. English usage often makes artificial distinctions between science, social sciences, and humanities. German usage incorporates all of these disciplines under the term *Wissenschaften* (Nentwich 2003, 3). However accurate, the term *cyberwissenschaften* is unlikely to be adopted widely. Michael Nentwich, writing largely about European developments, resorts to using "cyberscience" as the collective term. He also uses "cyber-social-sciences" and "cyber-humanities" in narrower contexts.

Neither the e- nor the cyber- prefix is used exclusively within the research and learning communities, complicating matters further. The e- prefix has a long history of meaning "electronic," as in e-mail, e-commerce, and e-business (seen with or without a hyphen). The cyber-prefix echoes the term "cyberspace," popularized by William Gibson in the 1984 novel *Neuromancer*, which in turn launched the genre of "cyberpunk" fiction. The term cyberspace, however, reflects intense legal and social debates over the use of place- and space-based metaphors for the Internet (Cohen 2007; Zook 2006).

When used in the context of technologies to facilitate distributed, collaborative, information-intensive forms of research and learning, the e- and cyber- prefixes to terms such as science, social science, humanities, research, and learning are equivalent. Here "e-" is best understood as enhanced, as the terms "enhanced" and "enabled" frequently appear. e-Science sometimes refers only to scientific applications and sometimes to enhancements of all disciplines. Similarly, cyberinfrastructure sometimes refers only to science and technology, and at other times is used as a collective term, and is often qualified by a discipline, as in "environmental cyberinfrastructure" or "cyberinfrastructure for the humanities." The more inclusive term "e-Research" has begun to encompass scholarly infrastructure for all disciplines. "e-Infrastructure" also can be found as a collective term or a reference to the technical framework. Given the rapid pace with which these neologisms are appearing and disappearing from use, the phrase e-Research is used herein to refer to these funding programs and "scholarly information infrastructure" to the concept. Both terms are qualified by discipline or application in narrower contexts (Atkins et al. 2002, 2003; Enabling Grids for e-Science 2006; T. Hey 2004; Hey and Trefethen 2005; Lord and Macdonald 2003; *Usability Research Challenges in e-Science* 2005; Woolgar 2003).

E-Learning, in its simplest definition, is any means of enhancing learning via the use of information and communication technologies (Kaput and Hegedus 2002; Kellner 2004; Nash, Dutton, and Peltu 2004). Cyberlearning is used in the same sense (*Cyberinfrastructure for Education and Learning* 2005). Thus, e-Learning and cyberlearning are not analogous to e-Research, in that any use of technology is included; no requirements are made for collaboration, networking, or access to information resources.

National and International Initiatives on Scholarly Infrastructure
Major investments in the 1990s to build a generic information infrastructure were instrumental in the expansion and commercialization of the Internet. Massive new investments are being made in the twenty-first century to improve the information infrastructure in support of research and learning. Governments of the United States, the United Kingdom, Europe, the South Pacific, and Asia are investing many hundreds of millions of dollars, pounds, euros, yen, yuan, and other currencies in these efforts. These initiatives are broadly conceived in that they encompass hardware and software, content development, infrastructure technologies, and to lesser extents, sociotechnical and policy research. At the same time, they are narrowly conceived in that they focus largely on the research enterprise, with ancillary concerns for facilitating teaching and learning. Over the long term, these technology investments are expected to have trickle-down effects on the commodity Internet, just as investments in the Arpanet of the 1970s led to the Internet of today (Abbate 1999; Atkins et al. 2003; Brown et al. 1995; e-Science Core Programme 2006; *Europe and the Global Information Society* 1994; G-7 Information Society Conference 1995; Hey and Trefethen 2005; *NSF's Cyberinfrastructure Vision* 2006).

Programmatic research initiatives are political documents, promoting a vision as a means to gain visibility, participation, and funding. Visions must be grand to attract attention and the promised outcomes must be ambitious to attract money. Whether or not the full promise of these programs is achieved, their framing offers insights into the collective goals of the agencies that promulgate them.

UK Infrastructure Initiatives   The United Kingdom was among the first to make large and specific investments in building an infrastructure for information-intensive research. The Research Councils of the United Kingdom (RCUK) announced the e-Science Core Programme in November 2000. Related programs initiated by individual UK funding agencies

include those on e-Social Science and e-Learning, and crosscutting projects such as the Digital Curation Center. The latter was launched in late
2004 (About the UK e-Science Programme 2006; Digital Curation Centre
2006; e-Learning and Pedagogy 2006; e-Learning Strategy Unit 2006;
ESRC National Center for E-Social Science 2006).

The RCUK offers a basic definition of e-Science:

e-Science will refer to the large scale science that will increasingly be carried out
through distributed global collaborations enabled by the Internet. Typically, a
feature of such collaborative scientific enterprises is that they will require access
to very large data collections, very large scale computing resources and high performance visualisation back to the individual user scientists (About the UK
e-Science Programme 2006).

Concern for an impending data deluge is a primary driver of the UK
initiatives. They take a holistic perspective on the cycle of data, information, and knowledge, and also highlight the role of university libraries
in access to and curation of digital data (Hey and Trefethen 2003, 2005).
They recognize sociotechnical aspects of infrastructure via an e-Science
working group on usability, by a complementary program on e-Social
Science with one strand to address the research and development of technology, tools, and data sources for collaborative social science research
and another strand on the social study of e-Science, e-Social Science, and
enhancements to other disciplines (*Specification for the Second Phase
Nodes* 2004; *Usability Research Challenges in e-Science* 2005).

United States Infrastructure Initiatives   The United States has a long
history of investing in research infrastructure such as the Internet and
the supercomputer centers, but it was not the first to establish a formal
program to enhance scholarly infrastructure. The U.S. National Science
Foundation (NSF) released a draft report of the Blue Ribbon Panel on
Cyberinfrastructure about a year after the initial RCUK program launch,
with the final report following a year later (Atkins et al. 2002, 2003).
Multiple references to UK, European Union (EU), and Asian e-Science
initiatives in the U.S. reports reflect their comparable goals. These comparisons note both the need for international collaboration and for the
U.S. to remain competitive in international science.

Cyberinfrastructure is defined only through example, emphasizing
the integrative, collaborative, and distributed nature of new forms of

research: "technology . . . now make[s] possible a comprehensive 'cyber-infrastructure' on which to build new types of scientific and engineering knowledge environments and organizations and to pursue research in new ways and with increased efficacy" (Atkins et al. 2003, 31). Despite the title, *Revolutionizing Science and Engineering through Cyberinfrastructure*, the report explicitly states that the scope of cyberinfrastructure extends to all academic disciplines and education. Cyberinfrastructure programs were established not only within the Computer and Information Science and Engineering Directorate of the NSF, the unit that formed and charged the Blue Ribbon Panel, but also in other directorates, including Engineering, Geosciences, Social, Behavioral, and Economic Sciences, and Education and Human Resources. In 2005, the NSF established the Office of Cyberinfrastructure to coordinate programs across the agency (*Management's Discussion and Analysis* 2005).

Similar concerns for an impending data deluge are evident in the U.S. initiatives. The Blue Ribbon Panel report is one of several calls to build on the ten years (1994–2004) of the NSF's digital libraries initiatives as a core component of cyberinfrastructure. Support for education and concern for collaboration, changing social practices of scholarship, and social and economic factors also are evident in the U.S. cyberinfrastructure initiatives (Atkins et al. 2003; Digital Libraries Initiative Phase II 1999–2004; Digital Libraries 2001; Larsen and Wactlar 2003).

A joint U.S. (NSF) and U.K. (Joint Information Systems Committee (JISC)) working group proposed a model of cyberinfrastructure in which scientific databases and digital libraries form an "information and content layer" above the middleware layer that provides the services and underlying core network technologies (figure 2.1). A similar model, setting digital libraries as an integral component of cyberinfrastructure, was proposed by a U.S. working group that included representatives from the UK, Europe, and Japan (Larsen and Wactlar 2003). These models are consistent with proposals to improve grid services in ways that will enable users to search individual databases and aggregate data from multiple databases (Watson 2003).

Although not part of the federal funding proposals, the American Council of Learned Societies established the Commission on Cyberinfrastructure for the Humanities and Social Sciences, with support

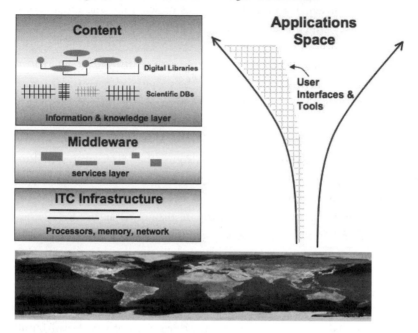

Figure 2.1
Cyberinfrastructure: Layered Model
Reprinted with permission of Stephen Griffin, National Science Foundation.

from the Mellon Foundation. The commission's final report calls for investments in digital resources, tools, services, and training for digital scholarship in constituent fields. Such investments will advance scholarship, and create new audiences for humanities and social sciences content (Commission on Cyberinfrastructure 2006; Unsworth et al. 2006).

International Initiatives   Information infrastructure is inherently international, but funding is organized by political entity. While U.S. researchers typically get their funding from U.S. sources, researchers in Europe often compete for funds from their own countries and multinational agencies. Most projects funded by pan-European sources involve partners from multiple countries. International coordination in e-research initiatives is expanding, especially in connecting computing grid networks and supercomputer centers. Enabling Grids for e-Science

(2006), or EGEE, for example, was established in 2004 by the European Commission to construct a European grid network for researchers in academe and industry. By 2006, it had expanded to serve more application areas and involve more than ninety institutions in thirty-two countries worldwide (Enabling Grids for e-Science II 2006). EGEE, in turn, is built on the EU research network GÉANT, which is funded jointly by the commission and participating countries (GÉANT 2005). GÉANT2, operational from 2004, is the seventh-generation pan-European research and education network. It will connect thirty-four countries through thirty national research and education networks (GÉANT2 2005). Digital library services also are a component of EGEE (*DILIGENT* 2006).

Europe cooperates with the Asia-Pacific region via the TEIN2 network and Latin America through the @LIS network (@LIS 2006). Bilateral links between the grid networks of the United States and China and between the United States and Russia also form part of the global network for e-Research (US, Russia, China link up 2003). Many other countries, including Australia and China, are expanding their national e-Research programs and partnering in international networks to support digital scholarship (Australian Partnership 2006; Zhuge 2004).

Exemplar Projects and Programs   The money being spent to develop and deploy e-Research is spread across many projects, disciplines, and countries. Important research is taking place under the formal e-Science, e-Social Science, and cyberinfrastructure programs. Other research that will contribute to the development of collaborative, multidisciplinary, data- and information-intensive research is occurring under other funding, or occasionally without external research funding. The following is a highly selective sample of projects to give a flavor of the work under way. Most funding agencies maintain lists of active projects, recently closed projects, and calls for future projects on their Web sites.

Each of the comprehensive e-Research initiatives is funding research on core problems of infrastructure such as security, reliability, and interoperability. Crosscutting topics in the European, UK, and U.S. programs include (under multiple names) next-generation cybertools, information infrastructure test beds, collaboratories, information integration, performance measurement, and "cybertrust."

A complementary approach is to organize e-Research centers by discipline or problem. In the United Kingdom, a coordinated national network of e-Science and e-Social Science exists, with universities bidding competitively to establish centers (ESRC National Center for e-Social Science 2006; UK e-Science Centres 2006). At some universities, including Oxford, the e-Science and e-Social Science centers merged into a Centre for e-Research.

In the U.S., a variety of cyberinfrastructure projects are supported by the NSF and other agencies, including the National Aeronautics and Space Administration (Earth Science Data Centers 2006; *NASA's Earth Science Data Resources* 2004). The National Earthquake Engineering Simulation Grid, for example, enables researchers to observe and operate experiments remotely, contribute to and retrieve from a data repository, share computers and analytical tools, and use collaborative tools for conducting their projects (National Earthquake Engineering Simulation 2006). The National Ecological Observatory Network (2006), the Geosciences Network (2006), and the Biomedical Informatics Research Network (2006) are other U.S. national collaborative efforts to share networks, tools, and data. Many of the data repositories associated with these efforts are housed at the San Diego Supercomputer Center in Southern California (Data Central 2006).

e-Research funds are being invested in bottom-up initiatives from individual disciplines or research communities to develop data repositories, digital libraries, tools, and services. The Research Councils of the United Kingdom offer example projects in categories such as astronomy and particle physics, biology and chemistry, engineering, environmental science, finance, and health care (About the UK e-Science Programme 2006). A search for cyberinfrastructure on the Web site of the NSF yields projects scattered across directorates, including the arctic and polar regions, in engineering, the environment, biomedicine, and health care. Most of these topics can be found in the European programs also.

One example project is eDiaMoND, which digitized, collated, and annotated mammograms from multiple hospitals and breast-screening centers throughout the United Kingdom. Its goal was to improve diagnosis of difficult or borderline cases by enabling radiologists to compare their patient mammograms with similar ones from other participating screening centers. The project employed grid technology and federated database services (Breast cancer and the e-Diamond project 2003; Jirotka et al. 2005; Lloyd et al. 2005). An example NSF project is Networked Infomechanical Systems (Batalin et al. 2004; NIMS 2006; Pon et al. 2005; Sutton 2003), which is designing and deploying "self-aware" networks of embedded sensors in habitat environments. The mechanisms can move around in a three-dimensional space using robotic capabilities, sampling and collecting data on temperature, moisture, movement, and other factors. Some data analysis is local and some is remote, as the systems must make probabilistic judgments about what data to collect and what to delete. Substantial amounts of data are generated, which must be transferred to remote data stores. The systems can be operated remotely over the Internet, and multiple research teams can conduct experiments.

International collaborations to share data and instrumentation exemplify e-Research principles, whether or not funded under such initiatives. Astronomy has one of the largest-scale partnerships, involving the U.S. National Virtual Observatory, the UK Astrogrid, the EU Astrophysical Virtual Observatory, and members from many other countries (International Virtual Observatory Alliance 2006). Partners share data, software tools, and services, enabling far more comprehensive access to astronomical knowledge than any one country or continent could gather alone. The Virtual Observatory Alliance has focused more on common standards for data description and access than on building repositories. The Global Earth Observation System of Systems (2006), based at the U.S. Environmental Protection Agency, is another international project to share tools and data in earth science disciplines.

Where Can the Greatest Benefits Be Realized?

The first major investments in scholarly information infrastructure were made in support of science, as were the first investments in advancing the scholarly publication infrastructure of the 1960s. Investments in the social sciences followed in both cases. Data- and information-intensive research in the humanities has emerged in parallel, although with minimal funding directed toward enhancing infrastructure.

Big Science, Little Science, Nonscience

"Big science" is a term used in at least two senses. As originally coined, it refers to the "large-scale, monumental enterprises" through which "societies express their aspirations" (Weinberg 1961, 161). In common parlance, big science refers to projects like space telescopes, sequencing the human genome, and supercolliders for physics that require international collaborations, large number of partners, and vast amounts of computing power and network capacity.

Big science also can refer to mature fields that have formalized their research methods, established international and collaborative projects, and developed invisible colleges of researchers who know each other and exchange information on a formal and informal basis (Taper and Lele 2004). Derek de Solla Price (1963), in his canonical book *Big Science, Little Science*, distinguishes between little and big science not by the size of projects but by the maturity of science as an enterprise—a topic revisited by many others since (Furner 2003). Modern science, or big science, is characterized by international, collaborative efforts and by invisible colleges of researchers who know each other and who exchange information on a formal and informal basis. Little science is the three hundred years of independent, smaller-scale work to develop theory and method for understanding research problems.

Big science, in both senses, encourages standardization of processes and products. Thus, the growth of digital libraries, data repositories, and metadata standards are predictable outcomes of the trajectory. The technical infrastructure of e-Research is especially suited to supporting large-scale international collaborations by providing distributed access to instruments, computational resources, and digital libraries of data. Not surprisingly, science domains such as physics and astronomy were among the first to make these kinds of investments (arXiv.org e-Print Archive 2006; Ginsparg 2001; International Virtual Observatory 2006; Sloan Digital Sky Survey 2006).

Digital libraries for scientific documents and data can promote the progress of science by facilitating collaboration. They also can hinder progress by forcing standardization prematurely. Many scientific research areas continue to be productive without the use of shared instrumentation, shared repositories, or agreements on standards for data description. As less-mature research areas that have relied on handcrafted tools and manual data collection become more instrumented, they are facing many challenges associated with the transition from little science to big science, including what to standardize, when, and for what purposes (Bishop, Van House, and Buttenfield 2003; Borgman, Wallis, and Enyedy forthcoming; Bowker 2005; Fienberg, Martin, and Straf 1985; Taper and Lele 2004; Zimmerman 2003 forthcoming).

Collaboration, especially over distance, has high overhead costs. Teams must devote a considerable amount of time and effort to establishing relationships and to mechanisms for communication and collaboration. In some cases, the overhead is justified by the results of the teamwork; in other cases it is not. Much remains to be learned about the factors that make collaboration more or less successful, and the circumstances under which it is most likely to be worth the effort (Cummings and Kiesler, 2004).

Benefits of digital scholarship are expected to accrue not only to the sciences and technology but also to the social sciences and humanities. They will accrue in different ways, due to the different types of data, research methods, and practices in these fields. The social sciences are becoming more data intensive as they assemble records of computer-based communication and mine databases of demographic and economic data produced by government agencies. The humanities are building large computational models of cultural sites, digitizing archival and museum records, and mining cultural records that are being generated or converted to digital form around the world.

It is essential, however, to recognize that these new opportunities do not benefit all scholars equally. Investments that advantage some scholars will disadvantage others. Technological investments may defer funds from field research, travel to libraries and archives where unique materials are held, and other forms of scholarship that are less dependent on a data-intensive infrastructure. Comparing the practices of multiple research communities will reveal how requirements vary for the tools and services of digital scholarship.

What's New about E-Research?

Among the strongest claims for digital scholarship is that it will enable fundamentally new kinds of research that heretofore were not possible. What is "new" is rarely made explicit, though. A simple indicator of the claims for new research is to count the occurrences of the word "new" in foundational e-Research documents (Borgman 2006b). It is a popular term in those documents, occurring 133 times in 84 pages (Atkins et al. 2003), 36 times in 8 pages (Atkinson et al. 2004), 24 times in 5 pages (Hey and Trefethen 2005), 92 times in 50 pages (Berman and Brady 2005), and 89 times in 64 pages (Unsworth et al. 2005).

New is never explicitly defined in these documents; rather, claims are made for the dawning of a "new age . . . in scientific and engineering research," pushed by advances in technology and pulled by the increasing complexity of research problems. Technical capacity has now "crossed thresholds" that "make possible a comprehensive 'cyberinfrastructure'" (Atkins et al. 2003, 31). That report goes on to describe in detail new technologies to be developed, and new kinds of research that are made possible by combining data and expertise via computing networks. A later document depicts "data-intensive science" as "a new paradigm." What is "new" are the volume of data being generated, the requirements for new analytic methods, and the quality of the data (Gray et al. 2005). The UK documents use new in referring to tools, data, methods, and infrastructure (Atkinson et al. 2004; Hey 2005; Hey and Trefethen 2003, 2005). Francine Berman and Henry Brady (2005) make comparable statements about what's new for the social, behavioral, and economic sciences. Tony Hey and Anne Trefethen (2005, 818), writing in *Science*, are explicit in stating that "it is important to emphasize that e-Science is not a new scientific discipline; rather, the e-Science infrastructure developed by the program should allow scientists to do faster, better, or different research."

Social scientists provide some historical context, claiming that access to usable data is a "a driving force in social science progress" dating to the "18th and 19th century invention of national statistics" (Brady 2004). Humanists and social scientists expect new communities to arise around new forms of data and tools, offering examples of "new fields of study, such as archaeometrics, archaeogenetics, music informatics, new facets of bioethics, and the anthropology of the Internet" (Unsworth et al. 2005, 18).

The proof of the e-Research vision will lie in whether new forms of data-intensive, information-intensive, distributed, collaborative, multi-, inter-, or cross-disciplinary scholarship result from these investments. More problematic is setting and applying criteria for what is new. In practice, individual scholars will have to make their own claims. Whether those claims are accepted will depend on norms for peer reviewing, hiring, tenure, and promotion, and the rate at which those norms change.

Conclusions

Information technologies have matured sufficiently to enable rich new forms of data- and information-intensive, distributed, collaborative scholarship. The production of more digital content is pushing the development of scholarly information infrastructure technologies to manage it, and the availability of more digital content, tools, and services is pulling more scholars toward using them. The push and pull of these technologies for scholarship are not occurring in a vacuum. Rather, they exist in a complex environment of social, technical, economic, and political trends. Along with the opportunities are many constraints.

While the grand visions of e-Science and cyberinfrastructure are presented as boldly new and revolutionary, they follow the pattern of several centuries of visions to unite the world's information infrastructure. The national and international visions of today are embodied in funding programs to produce an Internet-based scholarly infrastructure to facilitate distributed, collaborative, multidisciplinary research and learning that relies on large volumes of digital resources. To gain public acceptance, grand visions claim to be radical departures from the past. However, to borrow the title of Bruno Latour's (1993) well-known book, "we have never been modern." Rarely is anything a complete break with the past. Old ideas and new, old cultures and new, old artifacts and new, all coexist. It is necessary to recognize the relationships and artifacts around us, while at the same time being able to critique them.

3

Embedded Everywhere

Scholarly information infrastructure is an amorphous concept. Notions of scholarship, information, and infrastructure are deeply embedded in technology, policy, and social arrangements. Twenty-first century initiatives in e-Research and cyberinfrastructure build implicitly, and sometimes explicitly, on twentieth-century advances in computer networks, telecommunications, knowledge organization, information retrieval, digital libraries, and tools for collaborative work. In turn, those advances build on earlier work in publishing, printing, distribution, and communication technologies. Underlying the technical and policy developments are theories and philosophies about what is socially acceptable and appropriate. An important step in examining directions for digital scholarship is to make the invisible assumptions visible.

Theory and Policy Frameworks

Several theoretical and political frameworks are relevant to studying scholarship in the digital age. Some are implicit in proposals for e-Research, while others are explicit approaches to studying e-Research. The sciences have received much more attention than other fields, but many research and policy issues that arise in the sciences have parallels in the social sciences and the humanities.

Basic, Applied, and Use-Inspired Research

An initial question in constructing a scholarly information infrastructure is what to build when we know so little about how it will be used. Fundamental inquiry, applied research, and practical technical expertise all are required.

The idea of pure inquiry without use in mind has a long history in Western philosophy. Researchers pride themselves on exploring fundamental concepts and properties; few wish to be characterized as doing "applied research." Technologists build things for practical ends, but even they may be asking fundamental questions relative to their own fields. The notion that a firm dichotomy exists between basic and applied research can be traced to Vannevar Bush's report to U.S. president Franklin D. Roosevelt. His report laid out a framework for postwar science policy; a cornerstone was the establishment of the National Science Foundation. Bush argued against mixing basic and applied research on the grounds that applied research would drive out pure research. Also present in that report is the aphorism that "basic research is the pacemaker of technological progress" (Bush 1945b, 19).

The dichotomy of basic and applied research has become embedded deeply in Western science policy, including the statistical categories in which countries report their research funding activities. The dichotomous model was not without dissenters, even at the time it was first promulgated. Traditions of using an understanding of the natural world to achieve purposive ends is evident in Francis Bacon's work, and was incorporated in the charter of the Royal Society when founded in the seventeenth century. By the late twentieth century, the inadequacy of the basic versus applied categorization of research had become increasingly apparent.

Donald Stokes's (1997) thoughtful historical analysis of scientific and technological innovation, titled *Pasteur's Quadrant*, often is oversimplified to the quadrant model itself. One dimension is whether or not the purpose of the research is a quest for fundamental understanding. The other is whether or not the research considers uses to which the results might be put. Research with only fundamental understanding in mind is exemplified by the work of Niels Bohr in physics; research with only use in mind is typified by Thomas Edison's work on electricity. Louis Pasteur's work on fermentation represents the quadrant where both fundamental understanding (the fermentation process) and use (controlling fermentation to limit spoilage) drove the research. Pasteur's ability to combine understanding and use led to the process that bears his name: pasteurization.

While "Pasteur's quadrant" is extremely valuable as a simple explanation of the kind of research required for information infrastructure,

Stokes's analysis is more nuanced, reflecting an interplay between factors. One factor is whether research is classified as basic, applied, or mixed before or after it is done. Research that is initiated with only fundamental understanding in mind may result in specific applications. Conversely, research that is undertaken for a specific purpose may end up exploring a more fundamental understanding than originally anticipated. Another important factor is who does the classifying. Funding agencies may lay out a programmatic research agenda to accomplish specific goals (for example, building the middleware components of an information infrastructure). Those conducting the research may view their work as contributing to basic understanding within their fields (for example, understanding semantic aspects of interoperability between middleware components).

Technology and research are intertwined and mutually influencing in many respects. Creating an advanced information infrastructure requires designing and deploying technology with specific uses in mind. Identifying those uses requires an understanding of the social and political contexts in which information infrastructure exists. To reach that understanding, research is needed in many fields, from many perspectives. Much of it may be "use-inspired basic research," whether from the viewpoint of the researcher, the funder, or the user.

Open Science

Scholarship is a cumulative process, and its success depends on wide and rapid dissemination of new knowledge so that findings can be discarded if they are unreliable or built on if they are confirmed. Society overall benefits from the open exchange of ideas within the scholarly community. This notion of "open science" arises early in Western thought, dating back to Saint Augustine in the fourth and fifth centuries (Dalrymple 2003; David 2003, 2004). Open science has been subjected to rigorous economic analysis and found to meet the needs of modern, market-based societies. As an economic framework, open science is based on the premise that scholarly information is a "public good." Public goods have two defining elements. One is that they can be shared without lessening their value; the economic term is "non-rival." Paul David (2003, 20) quotes Thomas Jefferson's eloquent statement in 1813 on this point: "He who receives an idea from me, receives instruction himself without lessening mine; as he who lights his taper at mine receives light without darkening me." The second characteristic of public goods is that they are difficult and costly to hold exclusively while putting them to use; the economic term is "non-excludable" (Arrow 1962, 1971, 1974; Arrow and Capron 1959; Dasgupta and David 1994; Nelson 1959).

The emphasis in e-Research on enhancing scholarship by improving access to information is an implicit endorsement of open science. While the foundational policy documents of e-Science and cyberinfrastructure may not mention open science per se (the policy documents tend to be ahistorical and provide only a modicum of references), other writers make explicit links between open science and digital scholarship (David 2003, 2004; David and Spence 2003; Huysman and Wulf 2005; Reichman and Uhlir 2003; Uhlir 2006). Earlier policy documents identify open science as the motivation to promote the sharing of research data (Fienberg, Martin, and Straf 1985), an issue that is central to e-Research.

Open science has come under threat in recent years due to changes in intellectual property regimes, an increasing emphasis on data as scientific capital, and new models of electronic publishing. Emerging models of scholarship such as open access publishing and knowledge commons reflect efforts to reinstate the fundamental principles of open science.

Mertonian Norms

Robert K. Merton remains the most famous sociologist of science—his illustrious career ending in 2003 when he died at the age of ninety-two. He articulated norms that govern scientific practices, such as the competition for priority of claims, the communality of scientific knowledge, "disinterestedness," universalism, and how the peer-review process governs scholarly publication. He explained, for example, how cooperation and competition could coexist in science. Merton's theoretical work drew on a long history of Western thought about the nature of science and scholarship. In a memorable essay commemorating the four hundredth anniversary of Bacon's work, Merton (1961) explains how Bacon set down "what amounts to a charter for the human sciences." Merton's work was extremely influential in guiding theory, empirical research, and policy in science. His ideas were also influential in developing normative theories of citation, and exploring networks of relationships among scholars via the references they make to each other's work (Cole 2004; Cronin 2004; Merton 1963a, 1963b, 1968, 1969, 1970, 1972, 1973a, 1973b, 1984, 1988, 1994, 1995, 2000; Merton and Lewis 1971; Small 2004; Stephan 2004; Zuckerman and Merton 1971a, 1971b).

Merton's norms provide a neat and concise way to explain how science operates. Taken at face value, they can be used as templates to construct the tools and services of e-Research. Still, their very neatness makes them problematic, as they tend to oversimplify the mechanisms of scholarship. Much of the subsequent social studies of science literature takes a more constructionist perspective, finding that scientists may state norms as a convenient shorthand to explain themselves, but in fact, their practices are local and vary widely. Close study of scientific and other scholarly practices should guide the design of tools and services for e-Research (Knorr-Cetina 1999; Latour and Woolgar 1979, 1986; Lynch and Woolgar 1988; Woolgar 1976).

Sociotechnical Systems

While Merton studied the behavior of scientists and social scientists, information technology was not among his central concerns. Much of today's analysis of scholarship addresses the intersection of behavior and technology. The social studies of knowledge, science, and technology are referred to collectively as "STS." The initialism is interpreted (if spelled out at all) as science, technology, and society; science and technology studies; social studies of science and technology (Van House 2004); or sociotechnical systems. STS has its origins in sociology, anthropology, communication, philosophy, feminist theory, and the history of science. Only a few academic departments are wholly concerned with STS topics; scholars are scattered across departments in many social science disciplines, and some are located in schools of business or the departments of the scientific topics under study. Scholars in these areas convene around a few journals (e.g., *Social Studies of Science* and *Social Epistemology*) and conferences (e.g., the Society for Social Studies of Science, the European Association for the Study of Science and Technology, and the Association of Internet Researchers), although their work appears in many other forums. Some of the fundamental papers in STS exist in the form of edited books, a genre that is not well indexed in bibliographic databases, making such works particularly difficult to locate.

Among the theoretical and methodological approaches of STS relevant to digital scholarship are the social shaping of technology (MacKenzie and Wajcman 1999; Schwartz Cowan 1985), actor-network theory (acknowledged by its proponents to be a method rather than a theory) (Callon 1986; Callon, Law, and Rip 1986; Kaghan and Bowker 2001; Latour 1987), laboratory studies (Latour and Woolgar 1986), the social construction of technology (Bijker, Hughes, and Pinch 1987; Kline and Pinch 1999), epistemic cultures (Knorr-Cetina 1999), work practices (Lave and Wenger 1991; Suchman 1987), and the diffusion of innovations (Rogers 1995). These are explored further in chapters 7 and 8.

The e-Research discourse, as discussed in chapter 2, is about enabling new forms of research and producing new forms of knowledge never before possible. Implicit in much of this discourse is the sense of "technological determinism," or the belief that "technical forces determine social and cultural changes" (Hughes 1994,102). Social studies of technology arose partly as a response to extreme forms of technological determinism. Much of the early STS discourse tended to the other extreme, which is the belief that "social and cultural forces determine technical change" (Hughes 1994, 102). Both extremes of technological determinism and social construction have drawn considerable criticism. "Sociotechnical systems" is the more moderate middle ground, which starts from the premise that technology and society are deeply intertwined and mutually influencing (Iacono and Kling 1996; Lievrouw and Livingstone 2002; Van House 2004).

Research on the information aspects of scholarly information infrastructure is at the core of the field of information studies. This field grew out of library and information science and archives, with influences from the social sciences, humanities, and computer science. Research and practice on automated information retrieval systems has a fifty-year history, which builds on several hundred years of work on the organization of information. Many of these programs call themselves "I-Schools," and are attracting scholars and students from a wide array of social, technical, and policy fields (i-Conference 2006).

At the intersection of STS and information studies is "social informatics," a term coined by Rob Kling. While research on sociotechnical systems incorporates institutional, economic, policy, design, and use factors, social informatics focuses on information aspects of technology use. The confluence of information studies and social studies of knowledge, science, and technology is a fertile plain on which to explore long-standing questions about behavior, technology, and policy. Practical concerns for building a digital scholarship workforce also lie at this intersection. More people with expertise in information systems and services are needed to support the research enterprise. Scholars in all subject domains could use more expertise in managing their data and documents. Academic programs that combine information, technology, and subject expertise will help build the human capacity necessary for digital scholarship (Borgman et al. 1996; Kling 1999; Kling, McKim, and King 2003; Lamb and Johnson 2004; Social Informatics Web Site 2006; Social Informatics Workshop 2006; Van House 2004).

Taking an Information Perspective

To date, scholarly information infrastructure, whether as a technical, political, or social framework, is much more about infrastructure than about information. Programs in e-Research are concerned largely with building the networks, tools, and services that will enable people to use information. Relatively little attention is being paid to what information will flow through these networks, other than that it will consist of data, documents, and complex objects, and that large amounts of it will flow. Information can be expensive to produce and maintain, and much of it will outlive the technologies used to create it. Thus, the nature of the information in the scholarly information infrastructure deserves a close analysis.

Information

Philosophers since Aristotle and Plato have wrestled with the concepts of information, data, knowledge, and meaning. A. J. Meadows (2001), in a book on information, notes that several hundred definitions of the term exist. Yet few discussions of information infrastructure define information; even fewer explore the history and philosophy of the term. Conversely, Ronald E. Day (2001) devotes a book to the history of information, including the technology of reproduction, but does not address information infrastructure per se.

Donald Case (2002, 40–79) devotes a chapter of his book on information-seeking behavior to explicating the concept of information. In reviewing many of the best-known definitions, Case identifies "five problematic issues in defining information." These are *uncertainty*, or whether something has to reduce uncertainty to qualify as information; *physicality*, or whether something has to take on a physical form such as a book, an object, or the sound waves of speech to qualify as information; *structure/process*, or whether some set of order or relationships is required; *intentionality*, or whether someone must intend that something be communicated to qualify as information; and *truth*, or whether something must be true to qualify as information (50). Definitions of information can be distinguished by the assumptions they make on each of these issues.

Case also notes that three of the mostly widely cited definitions are tripartite in structure. Brenda Dervin (1976, 1977) draws on Karl Popper's work (1972) to distinguish between information that is objective and external, subjective and internal, and for the purposes of sense making. Her theory of sense making explains how people move between objective and subjective forms of information to understand the world. Brent Ruben (1992) distinguishes between three "orders" of information. The first order is environmental, the second is internalized and individualized, and the third is socially constructed. Michael Buckland's (1991) model of information as process, knowledge, or thing is particularly appropriate in the context of information systems, as discussed below.

As others have concluded, a single definition of information is unnecessary. Definitions can coexist, as they serve different purposes in different contexts (Artandi 1973; Belkin 1978, 2002; Day 2001; Ingwersen and Jarvelin 2005; Meadows 2001). Several definitions of information are relevant to scholarly information infrastructure.

Information Systems   When viewed as a technical framework, the information in a scholarly information infrastructure usually refers to the bits that flow through computing and communication networks. The bits could be any form of data, information, or transaction. This approach is consonant with the mathematical definition (known as "information theory") that was formulated by Claude Shannon and Warren Weaver (1949) for telecommunication networks.

Michael Buckland (1991, 351) clusters information concepts into three categories:

• information-as-process, or becoming informed
• information-as-knowledge, or that which is perceived in information as process
• information-as-thing, or an object such as a document that is informative or may impart knowledge

Buckland's information-as-thing fits well in the technical models of information infrastructure, for it describes the objects that may be created, shared, distributed, stored, and managed via computer networks. *Things* are the contents of digital libraries and other forms of information systems. Because the term *document* is inadequate for the range of digital objects (e.g., voice, video, e-mail, images, and data sets), the phrase "document-like objects" is sometimes used (Buckland 1997; *Dublin Core Metadata Initiative* 2006; Weibel 1995).

Data versus Information   Meadows's (2001) treatise on information examines related concepts such as data, classification, storage, retrieval, communication, knowledge, intelligence, and wisdom. He distinguishes between data, facts ("inferences from data" [8]), and information, and yet does not offer firm definitions of any of them. Rather, he acknowledges the "hazy border" (14) between data and information. What are raw and unprocessed data to one person may be meaningful information to another. Similarly, data that are background context to one researcher, such as micrometeorologic measurements, may be the focus of research to another.

Discussions of digital scholarship tend to distinguish (implicitly or explicitly) between data and documents. Some view data and documents as a continuum rather than a dichotomy (Hey and Trefethen 2003). In this sense, data such as numbers, images, and observations are the initial products of research, and publications are the final products that set research findings in context.

Infrastructure of or for Information

Taking an information perspective requires a close inspection of the relationship of information to infrastructure. In comparing the discourses of digital scholarship to those of sociotechnical systems, the distinction between an infrastructure *of* information and one *for* information becomes apparent.

Infrastructure of Information   e-Research is infrastructure writ large: a global framework to facilitate information exchange. Much of the effort is devoted to building a technical infrastructure over which any kind of bits can flow. The tools and services are the means by which information will be gathered, shared, analyzed, visualized, and stored. Information will consist of quantitative or qualitative data, documents, and other document-like objects.

Similarly, in the earlier national and global information infrastructure frameworks, information could be any kind of content, personal or professional, public or private, free or fee, data or documents. In all of these cases, the emphasis is on building a framework to support any kind of content; the meaning is in the eyes of the sender and the receiver. Thus, it can be viewed as an infrastructure *of* information.

Infrastructure for Information   In contrast, most sociotechnical studies focus on infrastructure writ small. The work of Geoffrey Bowker and Susan Leigh Star provides salient examples of this approach (Bowker 2000a, 2000b, 2005; Bowker and Star 1999). They are studying the processes by which mechanisms for information organization—such as thesauri, ontologies, and classification systems—are created and how they are used in a social context. Bowker and Star have shown that these mechanisms are by no means rational, objective, uncontested representations of "the real world." Rather, the meaning often is negotiated and political, and determines actions (and actors) in the real world. In their study of nursing classifications, for example, they found that how a procedure is classified determines the level of expertise authorized to perform it (e.g., a nurse, a nursing assistant, or a physician). The authorization and performance of a procedure, in turn, influences whether, and how much, insurance agencies will pay. This body of work is concerned with infrastructure *for* information.

The Bowker and Star approach arises from a long tradition in sociotechnical systems research that views knowledge as *social* and *material*—two themes that guide information studies (Van House 2004). Knowledge—or information—is social in that it is situated in a context, understood within a community, and arises from the day-to-day practices of scholarship or learning. Knowledge is material in that it is represented in the real world (Bowker and Star 1999).

Information systems are representations of information. Ideas, people, places, and objects have labels, and those labels are organized within lists, hierarchies, facets, or other structures. Documents are described according to established sets of rules (e.g., the *Anglo-American Cataloging Rules*), and ordered by other sets of rules (e.g., *Library of Congress Classification* or *Universal Decimal Classification*). Librarianship tends to focus on methods of constructing organizational tools that reflect the world in the most authoritative manner, while recognizing that no organizational tool is static. Rather, it must be updated continuously, via a consensus process, to maintain its currency and relevance (Svenonius 2000). Sociotechnical studies, in contrast, tend to focus on how these representational tools construct the world, and how they both facilitate and constrain behavior (Bowker 2005; Knorr Cetina 1999; Star 1995).

Setting a Research Agenda

The technology of e-Research is not an end in itself. Rather, it must serve the purposes of its users, which are to conduct research, share that research with others, and learn. The best technologies often are those that are the least visible. Whether e-Research is deemed a success will depend on the degree to which it enhances scholarship and learning. People want to spend less time wrestling with technology, and more time doing science or social science, studying the humanities, or learning in those disciplines. Thus to build an effective infrastructure, we need to understand more about the practices, behaviors, policies, and institutional frameworks of the fields it will serve.

Agendas for the technical framework to support e-Research already exist, as outlined in chapter 2. Individual fields have agendas for developing their own tools, services, and repositories of information. At least two agendas for research on the sociotechnical aspects of digital scholarship have been proposed. Steve Woolgar (2003) conducted an international survey of selected members of the STS community on behalf of the UK Economic and Social Research Council, as background for developing a funding program. He clustered topics arising from the survey into four themes:

1. The genesis of new grid technologies
2. The social organisational features of design, uptake, and use
3. The changing nature of science and social science
4. International comparisons

The first topic includes historical comparisons with other information and communication technologies, and the institutional and political contexts from which they arise. The second topic considers the present and future uses of e-Science and e-Social Science technologies along with associated concerns such as sharing, privacy, trust, collaboration, and intellectual property rights. Information issues are at the core of the third area, which would explore the changing nature of knowledge in individual fields and associated information practices, including teaching and publishing. The last area addresses topics of national science policy within and between countries.

About a year later, Paul Wouters (2004) took a complementary approach, identifying four ways to study e-Research as infrastructure. These are paraphrased as follows:

1. Analysis of e-Science as a political movement
2. Technology assessment studies
3. Case studies of hands-on scientific practice
4. Studies of networks and connections

Although Wouters provides little explanation for the first approach, Christine Hine (2006) already is studying e-Science as a "computerization movement." Wouters argues that the second kind of study is important to produce "encyclopedic descriptions" of relevant developments. Work is under way here also (Nentwich 2003). The third approach, he claims, can look beyond the promises of technology to set the "supposedly global stuff" in a local context. Wouters, however, views the fourth approach as most promising because it could balance the "inherent myopia" of case studies with the "totalising perspective" of a unified e-science. Network studies of digital scholarship are taking both qualitative approaches, such as "virtual ethnography" (Hine 2000), and quantitative, bibliometric approaches (Caldas 2004; Thelwall 2006; Thelwall, Vaughan, and Bjorneborn 2005).

All of the research areas identified by Woolgar and Wouters, and even more, should be explored in the pursuit of building a usable and useful scholarly information infrastructure. Basic, applied, and use-inspired research will provide insights into social, technical, and political considerations for design. Research that is basic to one field or team may be applied research to another. Conversely, funding agencies may support applied research on infrastructure, especially in technology areas, that requires basic inquiry to accomplish. The Woolgar and Wouters agendas are best categorized as use-inspired ones, the uses being distributed, collaborative, multidisciplinary, data-intensive, information-intensive research and learning. No shortage of research questions exist on the push and pull of information technologies for e-Research, the adoption and adaptation of tools and services across scholarly fields, assessments of technologies, and scholarly practices in the use of these tools, services, and information resources. Merton's norms also can be revisited in the context of today's technology-driven research environments.

e-Research did not emerge from a political vacuum. In many respects, it is a return to centuries-old principles of open science in response to challenges wrought by changes in technology and social policy, especially with regard to intellectual property. Also implicit in e-Research policy is that some fields and types of research will be advantaged, while others will be disadvantaged. Incentives and disincentives to participate in the development of e-Research programs will vary accordingly. Only with more sociotechnical study of e-Research will we make visible the invisible assumptions and perceptions of the many stakeholders in scholarly information infrastructure.

4
The Continuity of Scholarly Communication

Communication is the essence of scholarship, as many observers have said in many ways (Garvey 1979; Meadows 1974, 1998; Paisley 1984). Scholarship is an inherently social activity, involving a wide range of public and private interactions within a research community. Publication, as the public report of research, is part of a continuous cycle of reading, writing, discussing, searching, investigating, presenting, submitting, and reviewing. No scholarly publication stands alone. Each new work in a field is positioned relative to others through the process of citing relevant literature.

Between the most public and private forms of communication lies a wide range of channels and activities. Scholars communicate with each other not only through books and journals but also through manuscripts, preprints, articles, abstracts, reprints, seminars, and conference presentations. Over the course of the twentieth century, they interacted intensively in person, by telephone, and through the postal mail. Scholars in the twenty-first century continue to use those channels, while also communicating via e-mail, blogs, and chat. New dissemination channels for written work include personal Web sites, preprint archives, and institutional repositories.

An information infrastructure to support scholarship must facilitate these myriad means of communication. Scholars use the Internet to communicate with more people, and more frequently, than was feasible in the days of paper and post. They also can share much larger volumes of data and documents. The Internet has led to more, faster, and cheaper communication among scholars. Because anyone can "publish" online, the balance between authors, publishers, and librarians has shifted radically. Digital documents are malleable, mutable, and mobile, which leads to many new forms of use and distribution (Agre 2003; Bishop and Star 1996; Latour 1987, 1988). Digital distribution can be wide and rapid, but it also can be controlled through legal contracts and digital rights management technology. Preserving the scholarly record is more difficult in a digital world than a print one, due to the rapid evolution of technology, changes in intellectual property regulations, and new business models for publishing.

Scholarly communication is a rich and complex sociotechnical system formed over a period of centuries. Despite new technologies and economic models, the purposes of scholarly communication have remained remarkably stable. This chapter examines the ends of scholarly communication, laying a foundation to explore the restructuring of means wrought by electronic publishing (chapter 5) and by treating data as a publishable product of research (chapter 6).

The Many Forms of Scholarly Communication

Scholarly communication and scholarly publishing are sometimes conflated, especially in research library contexts (Hawkins and Battin 1998). In the larger sphere of activities among scholars, "publication" occurs when a document is "made public" with the intention that it be read by others. The term scholarly communication is used here in the broader sense to include the formal and informal activities associated with the use and dissemination of information through public and private channels. Research on scholarly communication includes the growth of scholarly information, relationships among research areas and disciplines, comparisons of communication activities between fields or specialties, the information needs and uses of individual user groups, and the relationships among formal and informal aspects of communication.

Public and Private, Formal and Informal

Although it may appear that the Internet is blurring the boundaries between public and private, and between formal and informal communication, these lines were never distinct. *Formal* scholarly communication is that which is "available over long periods of time to an extended audience," while *informal* communication is "often ephemeral and [is] made available to a restricted audience only" (Meadows 1998, 7). The same people are both authors and readers; thus, scholarly communication can function as a relatively closed system within individual fields and specialties. Scholars shape and reshape the same content for different audiences as oral presentations, technical reports, conference presentations, or papers, and later as journal articles or books. William Garvey and Belver Griffith mapped the interplay of public and private communication for the field of psychology, as it existed in the early 1960s. Their famous chart (Garvey and Griffith 1964, 1657) is reproduced as figure 4.1.

Their chart aggregates data from several studies and attempts to show the dissemination of a "typical research report published in a core psychological journal." Any given research report may be disseminated in only a subset of the many manifestations shown. The order in which these communications occur may vary, as may the elapsed time between stages. Especially notable in their chart is that the majority of communication is to a restricted audience (private or informal), such as talks, manuscripts, preprints, and reports to funding agencies. Only a small portion of the communication of a research report takes place in public, through formal publication.

What has changed most since the days of print and post is the balance between public and private communication. Conversations that previously were oral are now conducted by e-mail or online discussion lists, sometimes leaving a public record for a long period of time. Presentations that would have been heard by a few people at a seminar are now widely available online via the posting of slides, speaking notes, and Webcasts. Manuscripts, preprints, technical reports, and other written works that were circulated privately are now posted publicly. Online communication has accelerated the amount of informal communication among scholars and simplified the dissemination of formal products of scholarship.

The Role of Preprints

The most significant weakness of the scholarly communication system, when studied in the 1960s, was the long time lag from the submission

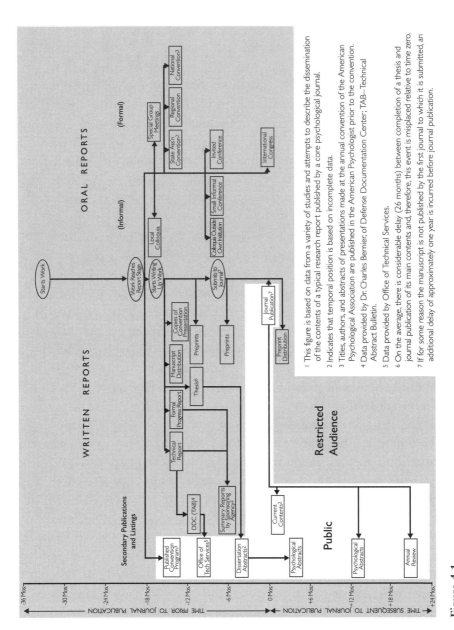

Figure 4.1

The Dissemination of Scientific Information in Psychology

Reprinted with permission from W. D. Garvey and B. C. Griffith (1964), Scientific information exchange in psychology, *Science*, 146(3652): 1657. Copyright 1964, AAAS. Figure redrawn by Jillian C. Wallis.

to the publication of journal articles, and from journal publication to listings in indexing and abstracting services. Note the thirty-six-month lag from the start of a project to its journal publication in the Garvey and Griffith chart above, for example. Preprints served an important role in filling the gap between a manuscript and its formal publication. In a print world, mimeographs were used to make multiple copies of type-scripts, which then were distributed to colleagues at conferences or sent by.post. Preprints have a long history as a "guild publishing model" within specialties (Kling 2004; Kling, Spector, and Fortuna 2004). If the distribution of preprints within a community was sufficiently intensive to function as a journal, a new journal might be established, thus crossing the invisible boundary from informal to formal scholarly communication.

The term "preprint" is often used ambiguously to refer to any document circulated among scholars. More precisely, *manuscripts* are documents not yet accepted for publication, and *preprints* are documents that have been accepted for publication in a specific conference, journal, edited book, or other forum. Once published, scholarly papers in journals are referred to as *articles*, while those in conference proceedings usually are referred to as *papers*, regardless of whether the form is digital or print. Kling (2004, 600) makes a further distinction between electronic versions of manuscripts and preprints as "e-scripts" and "e-prints," respectively. In some fields, technical reports or working papers are the equivalent of manuscripts. Sometimes publication status is specified by terms such as "unrefereed preprints" (Harnad 1998), but more often no distinction is made. Despite the risk of confusion, preprint is used here to include manuscripts and preprints, in both their print and electronic forms, following common usage. When the distinction is significant to the discussion, manuscript, preprint, article, and paper are used as above.

In the Internet age, preprints continue to fill the temporal gap between a manuscript and its formal publication. Preprints in digital form, though, also fill a gap between private and public communication. In the days of paper documents, preprint exchanges were organized by "an elite few" in a "single specialty" (Garvey and Griffith 1967, 1012). Those within an "invisible college" (Crane 1972) of peers known to each other would share reports of research well in advance of publication and listings in indexing and abstracting services.

Scholarly fields vary in their dependence on preprint distribution, but all fields appear to use them to some degree (Crane 1972; Garvey 1979; Kling 2004; Meadows 1974, 1998; Nentwich 2003). The most detailed data from the print era are available for psychology, due to the intensive study commissioned by the American Psychological Association (Garvey and Griffith 1964, 1966, 1967, 1971). About 40 percent of the authors distributed preprints, with an average of ten copies, ranging up to two hundred. The average time lag from submission to publication in psychology then was nine months, and authors might distribute preprints before or after journal submission. Abstracts of articles did not appear in *Psychological Abstracts* until another fifteen months after journal publication. Hence, those receiving preprints might have the results in hand one to two years before the general readership of the field was alerted to their publication.

These figures are striking in comparison to the immediate and broad distribution provided by online preprint services such as arXiv for physics, mathematics, and computer science (arXiv.org e-Print Archive 2006). Preprints in arXiv may be downloaded hundreds or thousands of times, starting within hours of deposit. Such repositories serve an international audience far beyond the "elite few" of guild models (Kling 2004). Many of the innovations proposed in the 1960s' reformation of the scholarly communication system were aimed at shortening the time lag from research to dissemination, but the present speed is far beyond what was then imagined.

The Role of Conferences

The interplay between formal and informal aspects of scholarly communication is particularly evident at conferences. Networked information technologies are being used in innovative ways to enhance scholarly conferences, but also to reinforce social norms.

Informal and Formal Purposes of Conferences   The role of conferences varies considerably by field, ranging from "the epitome of informal interaction" (Meadows 1998, 137) to the most formal publication outlet.

At the informal end of the spectrum, social interaction and reports of research in progress are the main purpose of the gathering. Submissions are in the form of abstracts for talks, and no proceedings are published. Contributors may bring preprints to distribute at the session in which they speak, just as in the 1960s, except that these are photocopies rather than mimeographs. Poster presentations are popular because they encourage discussion. Organizers may provide complimentary food and drink at poster sessions to promote attendance.

When scholarly conferences do not publish formal proceedings, it is expected that the papers will be published later in journals or books. Such conference papers are viewed as an intermediate and semipublic means of dissemination. Conferences of this sort may offer yet another intermediate form of publication, which is to maintain a Web site on which presenters can post their papers before, during, or after the meeting. An example is the Web site of the Society for Social Studies of Science and the European Association for the Study of Science and Technology 2004 meeting (Public Proofs 2004). Such Web sites may be useful for some months or years to come, but their hosts rarely promise that these will be permanent archives of papers.

At the other end of the spectrum are scholarly conferences where full papers are submitted, rigorously reviewed, and published as the formal record of the meeting. In fields such as computer science, the rejection rate for conference papers may be higher than it is for journal articles. These conference papers may be the final form of publication for a research project, and are considered to be valuable scholarly contributions for the purposes of promotion and tenure. Such proceedings usually are sold by the sponsoring societies, and may be a significant source of revenue. Most conferences sponsored by the Association for Computing Machinery fall into this category, including the Joint Conference on Digital Libraries (which is cosponsored by the Institute of Electrical and Electronics Engineers).

Conference papers, whether informal manuscripts or formal publications, often are posted on authors' personal Web sites or contributed to institutional repositories. Once posted, conference papers are easily found via search engines. They are a crucial source of information on research in progress and recently completed research.

Conflicts between Informal and Formal Purposes When the public record of a conference becomes sufficiently valuable to substitute for journal publication, the informal aspects of the conference can suffer. If a paper is submitted to a conference and is accepted, good scholarly citizenship requires that at least one author of the paper attend the conference and present the paper. Some conferences with prestigious proceedings have had such a sufficiently high no-show rate that organizers have had to enforce attendance. At least one author is required to register and pay fees prior to the date that the proceedings go to press. If no author registers, the paper is removed from the schedule and the proceedings. These are unstated norms that had to be stated only when they were violated. As conferences become more international and interdisciplinary, it is likely that more implicit norms will be violated. Some will be reinforced, and others will change with time and experience.

Some scholarly practices have changed little over the last several decades. In commenting on the importance of understanding the relationship between formal and informal communication, Garvey and Griffith (1967) cited the example of making a presentation at a scientific conference as a means of obtaining travel funds to attend the meeting. Conference organizers today remain conscious of the need to provide sufficient opportunities for presentation to assure adequate participation, while not diluting the prestige of the conference. Program committees set the rejection rate at an appropriate level for their fields. If the rejection rate is too low, the conference will not serve a gatekeeping role, and people may not attend if they think the conference consists of an unfocused array of mediocre work. If the rejection rate is too high, then too few people can obtain funding to participate. If too few people attend, the conference may not recapture its break-even costs, and might even be canceled. Conferences are an essential source of revenue for many scholarly societies; thus, much is at stake in these decisions.

Organizers have various strategies to achieve a balance of gatekeeping and attendance, such as inviting long papers, short papers, posters, and demonstrations, with decreasingly stringent criteria for acceptance. Another strategy is to add tutorials or workshops on hot topics before or after the main conference, providing additional opportunities for participants to acquire travel funding (and additional income for the conference).

Uses of Technology in Scholarly Conferences   Information technology pervades scholarly conferences. Speakers illustrate their presentations with computer-based slides, images, movies, and live connections to remote resources. A remote audience can be engaged in real time by Web casting conference presentations or by individuals posting their observations on blogs. Conversely, remote speakers can make presentations to conference audiences by videoconferencing technology.

Some of the most effective uses of networked information technologies occur behind the scenes, in the organization and management of scholarly conferences. Authors submit papers, posters, and panel proposals by uploading them to the conference Web site. Program committee members obtain the submissions from the site and submit their reviews online. When the reviewing process closes, an algorithm is run to summarize rankings and compile textual comments.

While the technology accelerates and simplifies the conference management process, decisions remain firmly under the control of the program chair and committee. The results of the review process often are input to face-to-face discussions by the committee. Twenty to thirty people may spend a weekend together to discuss the reviews, make final decisions, and organize the accepted papers into a coherent program representing the public record of the field at that point in time. In most cases, proceedings are printed in time for conference registration, so participants have the paper physically in hand when hearing presentations.

Scholarly Communication as a Sociotechnical System

Scholarly communication consists of many interconnected activities. These take place within an institutional, political, social, and economic infrastructure. As the means for knowledge sharing and publication have changed, so have relationships among the many stakeholders in scholarly communication. Individual actors see their part of the larger infrastructure, and often are unaware of how their parts interact with others until an important component of the infrastructure breaks down or a change elsewhere substantially affects their own concerns. Many of the processes, structures, and relationships of scholarly communication are invisible most of the time.

Academic scholarship has operated in what anthropologists refer to as a "gift exchange culture" (Lyman 1996). Universities pay faculty salaries. Government agencies and foundations pay research expenses, including student wages. The copyright in publications resulting from research usually is assigned to publishers without a fee (except for books), and authors may pay "page charges" or open access fees for having their work published, especially in the sciences. Publishers add value through editorial, production, and distribution processes. Market forces and gift exchange are complementary in this system: libraries buy publications and then make them available to their patrons at no direct cost. While research and development in the private sector operates under different principles, private research benefits from the open flow of ideas produced by universities and other parts of the public sector. Public and private research are complementary, if they remain in balance (David 2003).

Open science and the open flow of information are essential to the exchange of ideas. Sharing knowledge is the social glue that holds academic communities together, and publication is the coin of the realm. As the processes and structures of scholarly communication evolve, basic tenets of peer review and intellectual property that underlie the open science model are being questioned.

Process versus Structure

The process and structure of scholarly communication can be difficult to compare because studies draw on different variables and levels of analysis, and apply different theories and methods. Research on *processes* is concentrated in social studies of science, with some work in information studies. Much of this literature consists of case studies and ethnographies, which look closely at individuals and small groups (e.g., Collins and Evans 2002; Dirk 1999; Forsythe 1993; Hine 2002; Latour 1987; Latour and Woolgar 1986; Morrison 1988; Vaughan 1999). Other work considers motivations that drive the scholarly communication system (e.g., Cronin 2005; Hermanowicz 2003; Kling and McKim 1999; Lievrouw 1988, 2002, 2004; Nentwich 2003). Research on scholarly communication *structures* is scattered across information studies, bibliometrics, scientometrics, and "webmetrics" or "webometrics," with some coverage in social studies of science (e.g., Borgman 1990b;

Borgman and Furner 2002; Caldas 2004; Ingwersen 1998; Ingwersen and Jarvelin 2005; Kling 2004; Kling and Callahan 2003; Thelwall 2006; Thelwall, Vaughan, and Bjorneborn 2005). Structure is studied via the characteristics, distributions, and relationships among products of scholarly communication. Structures can be examined on a large scale and over time.

Leah Lievrouw (1990) attempted to reconcile structure and process approaches by studying "invisible colleges." Her study reveals how the meaning of a construct that is central to a field can change over time, and how widely its measurement can vary. The concept of invisible colleges dates back to the Royal Society in the seventeenth century, at which time it described a group of scholars who were in geographic proximity and had common interests, but lacked a formal institution or college. Derek de Solla Price (1963) resurrected the concept to mean the informal affiliation of scholars from many institutions, often in distant geographic locations. Although Diana Crane's (1972) book remains the most widely known empirical work on invisible colleges, she was criticized for not distinguishing adequately between the structure of relationships between scholars and the nature of those relationships (Chubin 1976). Lievrouw also builds on Nicholas C. Mullins's (1968) work to ask whether invisible colleges are structures that are discernible and measurable by others, or whether they are processes that can be perceived only by the scholars involved.

A structure-process dichotomy underlies the distinction that Rob Kling and Ewa Callahan (2003) make between a "standard model" that focuses on the "information processing properties" of paper and digital media and a "socio-technical network model" that focuses on the interaction between "information processing features of artifacts" and social behavior. The professional literature on libraries and publishing exemplifies the first model, and the literature on sociotechnical systems the second. In assessing relationships between scholarly communication, electronic publishing, and the Internet, Kling and his colleagues conclude that most of the future scenarios for electronic publishing did not play out as predicted due to a focus on structural factors (the standard model) without adequate account of the social factors (Kling and McKim 2000; Kling and Callahan 2003; Kling, McKim, and King 2003).

Quality Control

Quality-control processes affect the structure of scholarly communication in ways that are sometimes subtle and sometimes significant. Such processes can be divided into two general categories that often are conflated: quality of the scholarly content, and quality of the scholars. Scholarly content in the form of publications (e.g., journal articles, conference papers, and books) is assessed for correctness and whether the content is significant enough to warrant publication. Peer review, also known as "refereeing," is the usual mechanism for assessing quality in these senses. Fields vary greatly in their criteria for correctness and significance, and in the means by which they conduct peer review.

Scholars are evaluated for the purposes of hiring, promotion, and rewards such as research funding. Evaluation can be holistic, taking into account the quality of individual publications along with other contributions such as grants, mentoring students and colleagues, teaching, lecturing, and editorial and administrative service. Evaluation also can be mechanistic, using publication indicators as proxies for quality of scholarship. In these cases, quality-control processes for scholarly content can easily become distorted.

Quality Control of Scholarly Content   Quality control of scholarly content can occur before or after publication, or independent of publication. Prepublication methods are "ex ante" forms of quality control (Nentwich 2003, 2004a, 2004b). Individual documents submitted for most forms of publication, such as conferences, journals, or books, are reviewed by peers before being accepted. Grant proposals undergo a similar evaluation process. Quality criteria vary widely by field, but all have to do with whether the work meets acceptable norms for method, validity, reliability (in the case of empirical research), evidence, documentation of sources, adequacy of claims, quality of writing and presentation, and degree of contribution to the field. Reviewers advise whether a paper should be accepted, rejected, or revised and resubmitted, and explain their reasons to the authors and the editors. The rigor of the review may depend on the degree of formality of the publication. Journal articles are more rigorously reviewed than conference papers, except in fields where conferences and journals have equal status.

Journals and conferences become more prestigious by setting higher standards, which usually means a higher rejection rate of submitted papers. A paper rejected by a more prestigious journal may be revised and submitted to a less prestigious one.

Criteria for peer review are independent of the format of publication. Standards for quality of content can be equally rigorous for peer-reviewed journals in print and electronic forms. Similarly, open access journals differ from traditional scholarly ones only in who pays for the publication (the authors or the authors' institutions versus the readers and libraries). Some open access journals, such as those published by the Public Library of Science, already are among the most competitive and are ranked in the top tier of impact factors (Public Library of Science 2006). Models and implications of open access publishing are discussed at length in chapter 5.

Scholarly books often are peer reviewed twice by publishers. Authors submit book proposals, which usually consist of tables of contents, sample chapters, and explanations of the target audience. Publishers may accept or reject book projects based on proposals, and may negotiate changes in the scope or audience. Authors sometimes skip the proposal process and submit full book manuscripts to publishers. Whether or not the book project is already under contract, the full draft manuscript usually is sent out for peer review before being accepted for publication.

Prepublication review, whether of articles, conference papers, or books, is intended to improve the published product. Reviewers can request minor or major revisions, including new data analyses, a reframing of the theoretical or evidential basis of the claims, or a radical reorganization. Additional improvements may be made through the publisher's copyediting and design processes. Thus, publications should be more than the sum of the manuscript plus reviewer comments, although even this outcome is debated (McCook 2006).

Postpublication quality control, or "ex post" review, occurs after a work is published. Some journals publish extensive commentary and rejoinders to articles, which are a form of postpublication review. Another method is online commenting or annotation after publication, creating a "living document" of the original plus all the comments. A similar model is to rate posted documents, with scores computed and posted, as is done by online bookstores and auction sites. Counts of how frequently a document is cited, downloaded, linked to, or otherwise used are postpublication indicators particularly suited to online environments. None of the postpublication methods are as widely accepted as prepublication review, however.

Book reviews appear to be a unique form of postpublication review. Each journal that reviews books usually sends a book only to one reviewer. Those reviews typically are published with minimal editorial review; they serve more as invited commentary. Authors rarely are contacted by the journals reviewing books, and even more rarely are they invited to respond.

Problems with Peer Review   Peer review is itself a subject of study and periodic conferences. It is a social process, with all the attendant flaws. Despite well-documented problems, peer review remains the most widely accepted means to assess the quality of scholarly content (Cronin 2005; King et al. 2006; Weller 2001). Calls for reform have accelerated for two reasons: the availability of new means to evaluate digital documents, and the use of peer-review mechanisms for unintended purposes.

Calls for change in peer review arose at the dawn of electronic publishing (Harnad 1998; Kling and Covi 1995; Kling and McKim 1999). Among the earliest, most radical, and best known is Steve Harnad's (1991, 1995) "subversive proposal" for a decentralized model where scholars self-publish their work, and may or may not submit it to peer reviewed channels later. His proposal would restructure scholarly communication by altering relationships between authors and publishers.

The use of a publication forum as a proxy measure for the quality of research productivity has distorted the peer-review system so severely that some consider it "broken." Peer reviewing is an expensive process, requiring considerable time and attention of editors, editorial board members, and other reviewers. Top journals in the sciences and medicine may put fewer than half of the submitted papers through a full peer-review process, rejecting the remainder on an initial editorial review, and ultimately publish 6 to 10 percent of the total submissions. Particularly in the sciences, researchers are under so much pressure to place papers in top-tier journals that they submit to these same journals, whether or not the content is appropriate. Five top scientific and medical journals reported a doubling of manuscript submissions over the previous six months to six years (McCook 2006).

Among the many aspects of peer review being debated are the value of confidentiality, the degree of fairness and objectivity, and the ability of the process to detect inaccuracies and fraud. Confidentiality is a core tenet of most peer-review processes, whether single- or double-blind. The value of confidentiality rests on several premises. One is that reviewers are acting on behalf of the scholarly community, rather than as individuals. Another is that reviewers will be more honest in their assessments if their identities are unknown to the authors. In single-blind reviewing, the authors do not know the identity of the reviewers. In double-blind reviewing, neither the authors nor the reviewers know the others' identities. Double-blind reviewing is difficult to maintain, especially in online environments, as authors often can be identified by searching for similar work on the topic of the paper.

Models of peer review with lesser degrees of confidentiality are now in place. Several major science journals are requiring reviewers to sign their reviews and make their names known to the submitting authors on the grounds that the reviewers will be more thorough and constructive. Among the counterarguments are that fewer reviewers will participate if they must sign their reviews and that animosity may result from signed critical reviews (McCook 2006; *Nature* 2006).

A more extreme departure from single- and double-blind reviewing is completely open peer review. In this model, manuscripts are posted and anyone may comment. Open review has the advantage of speeding and democratizing reviewing, and could result in better manuscripts being submitted (Shatz 2004). It has disadvantages such as self-selected reviewers, and perhaps no reviewers. If papers do receive reviews, the authors may still benefit from criticism (Harnad 1991, 1995, 1998; Nentwich 2003). Open posting and ranking, whether conducted pre- or postpublication, raises questions of "who is a peer?" Scholarly communication has operated as a relatively closed system in which the same people are the authors and the reviewers. Those who contribute to the system are assumed to be the best judges of the quality of new work.

Self-selected reviewers can skew reviews in highly positive or negative directions.

Another concern about completely open peer review is whether readers will trust the results or be willing to read through all the reviews to make their own assessments. Prepublication mechanisms serve as expert filters on what becomes part of the scholarly record, winnowing out the researchers' reading list (King et al. 2006).

The fairness, objectivity, and qualifications of peer reviewers are continuing concerns. Reviewers may not be sufficiently familiar with the literature to recognize duplication of work; they also may fail to detect errors and be biased in favor of authors from prestigious institutions. Reviewers of a paper often disagree with each other, sometimes sharply. Reviewing can be a conservative process that is more likely to reinforce the norms of a field than to identify significant breakthroughs. Articles that ultimately are highly cited often have had difficulty getting published (McCook 2006; Meadows 1998; *Nature* 2006; Shatz 2004; Weller 2000, 2001).

Recent cases of fraud that went undetected by the peer-review process have attracted the attention of the mainstream press. In several highly public cases, papers published by *Science* and *Nature* were later withdrawn due to fraudulent data. The most public case is that of Woo-Suk Hwang, who became a national hero in South Korea for his pathbreaking research on human embryonic stem cells. His claims began to unravel due to alleged bioethical lapses in how tissue was collected and problems with his supporting data. After an extensive investigation, it was determined that the cloned stem cell lines did not exist. Professor Hwang and five of his collaborators were indicted on varying counts of fraud, violation of ethics laws, destroying evidence, and misappropriation of funds. Among the many issues raised in the ensuing public and scientific debates are the degree to which peer review can or should detect fraud, the responsibilities of reviewers to verify or recompute results, and the criteria for labeling withdrawn or questioned papers in the scholarly record (Bhattacharjee 2005; Brumfiel 2002; Check 2005; Couzin and Unger 2006; Cyranoski, 2005, 2006; Dobbs 2006; Normile, Vogel, and Couzin 2006; Stephenson 2006; Wohn and Normile 2006).

The sciences are not alone in publishing questionable data or unsupported conclusions. Several notable cases of problems with data and plagiarism have arisen in the social sciences and humanities in recent years. In one case, allegations of inadequate, inaccurate, and unverifiable data to support much-publicized conclusions about the historical rates of gun ownership led to the revocation of a major book prize and the loss of the author's university position (Gross 2002; Kennedy 2003; Olsen 2002). A prominent history journal sponsored a public debate with a response from Michael A. Bellesiles, the author of the book in question, *Arming America*. Had the book not been on such a controversial topic, drawing the attention of the National Rifle Association, the data might not have attracted such close scrutiny. As Jon Wiener (2002), another well-known historian, commented on the case, "Historians whose work challenges powerful political interests like the NRA better make sure all their footnotes are correct before they go to press."

Publication Indicators as Proxies for Quality   Despite the many problems with peer review, publication indicators are used to evaluate scholars for hiring, promotion, funding, and other rewards. Whether appropriate or not, outputs of the system in the form of data, documents, and publications are easier to measure than are inputs such as scholars' time, education, reading of scholarly literature, and research activities in their laboratories and libraries. More time in the laboratory or the library does not necessarily translate into more or better research, for example. While it is understandable that the recognition of scholars should be based heavily on quality assessments of their scholarly contributions to their fields, it is essential to distinguish clearly between quality of scholarship and the use of indicators such as the publication forum and citation counts as proxies for quality.

The rapid growth in submissions to top-tier journals is attributed largely to incentive systems in which scholars are rewarded directly (e.g., in the amount of research funding they receive) for publishing in certain journals (McCook 2006). The publication forum is an imperfect indicator of quality, however. Citations to highly cited journals are not evenly distributed among the articles it publishes. Placing a paper in a highly cited journal does not guarantee that the paper will be cited frequently nor that it is a scholar's best work (Cronin 2005).

Citations to publications also are used to evaluate scholarly productivity. Popular indicators include the rates of citation to individual articles and aggregates such as the work of an individual, a research team, a department, a university, or even a country. Universities consider these indicators in hiring and promotion decisions and libraries consider them in selecting journals. The most common source of data for citation rates are the three journal indexes (*Science Citation Index*, *Social Sciences Citation Index*, and *Arts and Humanities Citation Index*) published by Thomson Scientific, long known as the Institute for Scientific Information (ISI). Webmetric or webometric analyses of links between documents publicly available online provide a complementary approach to citation analyses (Caldas 2004; Ingwersen 1998; Ingwersen and Jarvelin 2005; Thelwall 2006; Thelwall et al. 2005; Vaughn and Shaw 2005).

The limitations of bibliometric and webometric indicators for quality control are well-known. Weaknesses include the ability to game the system by heavily citing one's own work or that of colleagues, and methodological difficulties in interpreting meanings of references, assigning weights to multiauthored papers, aggregating work distributed over multiple papers, and determining the time period to cover. On the latter point, the value of a publication declines in a matter of a few months in some fields (e.g., high-energy physics), while the value of publications in other fields may not become apparent for many years (e.g., history).

Neither bibliometrics nor webometrics provides a comprehensive measure of the citations or links received from the body of scholarly literature. The impact factors published by Thomson Scientific are based on a known set of journals (although the set changes from year to year) and a fixed time period, while webometric studies are based on a broader universe of documents (which varies by study) and variable time periods (tailored to each study). Complicating matters further, the *Science*, *Social Sciences*, and *Arts and Humanities Citations Indexes* are a closed system consisting of references made by established journals on a list selected by the editors at Thomson Scientific. Not all journals are included, and books and conference proceedings rarely are indexed. Webometric studies can include links to and from any type of document publicly available online. However, they rarely include references from formal publications that exist only inside proprietary publisher databases. A comprehensive source for assessing the quality, influence, impact, and use of scholarly literature has long been sought (Borgman 1990a; Borgman and Furner 2002; Cronin 1984, 2003; Davenport and Cronin 1990, 2000; Paisley 1990; van Raan 2000).

The influence of book reviews in the assessment of scholars is particularly problematic given how disconnected they are from the peer-review process. Hiring and promotion committees consider the prestige of the publisher, but often wait for reviews in journals to determine the value of the book. Published reviews also are highly influential in determining book sales. Publishers make a practice of scanning the literature for reviews of the books they publish, both as alerts to book authors and as advertising copy.

The Functions of Scholarly Communication

The scholarly communication system has been much studied since the mid-twentieth century, resulting in many models of its processes, structures, and functions. Process and structure are mutually influencing in peer review, as discussed above. Scholars' heavy reliance on peer-review processes influences their choices of publication forum and what to read. The set of publications forms a network between authors, journals, and publishers that reveals a structure of relationships. Implicit in these processes and structures is open science—the principle that a free flow of scholarly communication benefits both scholars and the society at large. By making research results and interpretations available quickly and widely, others can examine them, and then decide whether to build on, replicate, or reject that work. The public benefits both by economic efficiencies in the system and by having access to the products of scholarship. These are complex relationships that have evolved over decades and centuries. New technologies did not result in shifting the balance among stakeholders as radically or rapidly as some had hoped, largely because social practices are much more enduring than are technologies.

Scholarly communication also serves a number of distinct functions in validating the products of research, reaching present and future audiences, and establishing and maintaining the scholarly record. These functions, which go by many names, provide the continuity of communication that endures through changes in technology. They also reflect the choices that scholars make in what to study, with whom, what and where to publish, and how to position their work. The functions of scholarly communication can be grouped into three categories: legitimization; dissemination; and access, preservation, and curation.

Legitimization

Legitimizing scholarly work is an essential function of the scholarly communication system. Guedon (1994) uses the category "legitimacy and authority" to describe the expectations of the research community for quality control. Similarly, Meadows (1998, ix) comments that publications appear only after having been "scrutinized and accepted by colleagues." Nentwich (2003), building on other European perspectives (Kircz and Roosendaal 1996; Roosendaal and Geurts 1997), distinguishes between "certification" as the "quality stamp" given by the community and "registration," or the process of recording the results on behalf of authors. Establishing priority also is part of the legitimization function. Journal articles are marked with the dates that a manuscript was received and accepted; interim dates for revised drafts also may be identified. If disputes arise over who can claim priority for a finding, discovery, or interpretation, these registration and publication dates can have legal significance.

Trustworthiness subsumes the above aspects of legitimization in Kling's framework. Trustworthiness is viewed as part of a social process to assure readers that the contents meet community norms, whether achieved through peer review or by surrogate measures such as the reputation of the authors or their institutional affiliation (Kling 2004; Kling and McKim 1999).

While scholarly communication is a continuum from informal to formal, legitimization may be deemed to occur only at the "fixed point" established by the final published article after peer review. That fixed point, which constitutes "definitive publication" (Frankel et al. 2000), is the fulcrum on which scholarly publishing structures are delicately balanced. Debates over where that fixed point lies, whether it is a point or a region in the continuum, and over the community norms and social processes associated with determining that point or region underlie the competing models for scholarly publishing structures in a networked world.

Dissemination

The dissemination function of the scholarly communication system incorporates "communication and diffusion" (Guedon 1994), "awareness," "platform for communication" (Kircz and Roosendaal 1996), "transparency," and "discourse" (Nentwich 2003, 36). More simply, the function can be viewed as "publicity" (Kling 2004; Kling and McKim 1999). Some view dissemination as the essential purpose of scholarly communication: research only exists, in a functional sense, if it is communicated to others (Meadows 1974, 1998).

Diffusion and *publicity* capture the idea of awareness by others in the community. *Transparency* reflects scholars' responsibilities to register their work in the public sphere, both to legitimize it and to enable others to assess it. *Discourse* emphasizes the role that publications (formal communication) play in the scholarly community. Publishers play a central role in dissemination by producing, selling, and distributing publications. Scholars assist in the dissemination of their published works by sharing them with colleagues, posting lists of their publications, and posting their publications or earlier drafts on their Web sites or in repositories. Scholars also disseminate unpublished works, such as technical reports and conference presentations, by posting them online or sending them to colleagues.

The actions of scholars can increase others' awareness of particular works. Scholars respond to publications in public (e.g., reviews, critiques, commentaries, and replications and reanalyses of data), private (e.g., e-mail, telephone, and in person), and intermediate forums (e.g., symposia, talks, and conference panels).

Access, Preservation, and Curation

The record of scholarship is intended to serve present and future scholars, students, and other readers. Methods for accessing, preserving, and curating the scholarly record are fluctuating, resulting in disputed definitions. This set of functions encompasses and extends archiving, memory, preservation (Guedon 1994; Kircz and Roosendaal 1996; Meadows 1998; Nentwich 2003), and accessibility (Kling 2004; Kling and McKim 1999).

Access has multiple definitions in social, legal, and technical contexts. It can imply permission, rights (as in the "universal service" principles of telecommunications), physical connections to a computer network, and the requisite skills to make use of something once it is acquired. In the sense of "access to information," which is implicit in scholarly communication, access also requires that the content is in a useful and usable form (Borgman 2000a).

Archiving and preservation are terms used much differently in the library, archives, and computing fields. Their usage also varies between data and documents, between physical and digital records, and between disciplines (e.g., the sciences versus the arts and humanities). Across these contexts, both terms imply an institutional responsibility for maintaining the continuity of the record (Beagrie 2006; Fox, Wilkerson, and Warren 1998; Gilliland-Swetland 2000; *Reference Model* 2002).

Curation encompasses many of the preservation and archiving activities, especially in digital environments. It is the preferred term due to its active connotation and emphasis on a life-cycle approach to maintaining digital research (Beagrie 2006). After much community debate, a useful working definition of digital curation emerged: "broadly interpreted, [it] is about maintaining and adding value to a trusted body of digital information for current and future use" (Giaretta 2005). The same elements of curation are relevant to content in nondigital formats: maintenance, value added, trust, and temporality.

Access, preservation, and curation can be viewed as one composite function of scholarly communication, reflecting the continuous availability of the scholarly record. Terms such as "permanent access" (Hodge and Frangakis 2005) also reflect the life-cycle aspects of this function. Libraries and archives historically have borne the primary responsibility for access, preservation, and curation. Individual scholars, research teams, journals, and disciplinary groups are taking on some of this responsibility for digital objects (Digital Curation Centre 2006; Lord and Macdonald 2003; Network of Expertise 2006).

Author Roles and Functions

Scholars are researchers, authors, peer reviewers, mentors, advisors, editors, teachers, and often administrators. Of all these roles, it is as authors that they leave the most lasting mark on the scholarly record. Authors make many judgments in their capacities "(a) as *writers* (i.e., choosers of occasions for writing; of genres to write in; of subjects, themes, and arguments to write about; and of sentences and words to write); (b) as [*citers* or] *linkers* (choosers of documents to cite, acknowledge, or otherwise point, link, or refer to); (c) as *submitters* (choosers of journals or other sources to submit papers to); and (d) as *collaborators* (choosers of co-authors to work with, or institutions to affiliate with)" (Borgman and Furner 2002, 6). Their authorial activities interact with the functions of scholarly communication in complex ways. An examination of these interactions sheds light on the evolving sociotechnical system of scholarly communication.

Authors as Writers
Authors' activities as writers cut across the three functions of scholarly communication. By writing for publication, authors register a claim to their ideas and establish priority for their results, thus legitimizing their research or other scholarly contribution. Priority plays a role in determining what to write about and when. While the ability to replicate findings is essential to open science, more recognition comes to those who establish a finding or new interpretation.

Writing serves the dissemination function by publicizing results. The author's work becomes part of the discourse of the community, and others will respond to it, publicly and privately. Writing for publication also serves the transparency aspect of dissemination, informing a wide audience as to how public research funds were spent, for example.

Historically, access, preservation, and curation have not been the responsibility of authors but rather of librarians and archivists. Authors have begun to assume some of these responsibilities by posting their own work on personal Web pages. However, personal Web pages are much more effective for dissemination than for preservation functions. Personal Web sites lack the longevity and scalability of institutional approaches.

Authors as Citers and Linkers

Documents in a scholarly communication system are nodes in a network. Each scholarly document builds, implicitly or explicitly, on those that came before. When Isaac Newton spoke of "standing on the shoulders of giants" he was referring to the incremental growth of knowledge. The formal documents that constitute the public record of scholarship make those increments explicit by establishing relationships with other documents on which they build. In a print world, most relationships are bibliographic references to other documents or to data sources. In a digital world, these references can be automated links that will take the reader directly to the source document or even the cited passage within that document. "Linking," in this sense, captures the act of making relationships between documents, whether in print or digital form (Borgman and Furner 2002). In bibliometric parlance, references are made and citations are received.

The legitimization function is served by references that establish the basis for the present work. References to prior documents help to explain how and why the author's research is important, and to identify gaps that the research fills in the literature of the field. References can legitimize the choice of research method or source of evidence by showing how these methods or sources compare to those used before. References and links position a document in the network of literature. The structure of this network can be studied to identify relationships among producers of the communication (e.g., authors, or aggregates such as teams, institutions, fields, or countries), artifacts of communication (e.g., articles, journals, or books; these may be viewed either as content or channels of communication), and communication concepts (e.g., words used by the authors or the meaning of citations) (Borgman 1990a). The receipt of citations or links from documents subsequently added to the network also legitimizes an author's work. Thus, linking adds a temporal component to the legitimization function.

Automated links between digital documents can strengthen the legitimization function by making it easier to follow the trail on which the scholarship is constructed. In a print world, considerable effort may be required to obtain referenced works. With active links, readers can follow a trail directly to sources and data, and may be more likely to verify claims.

Referencing and linking serve access functions forward and backward in time. Each new document with links to prior works (necessarily earlier in time) serves as an entry point to the network of literature. Readers can find the prior work by following the path. Subsequent documents that link to a given document also can be found by searching forward in time. The ability to identify later documents that cite a given scholarly document was established on a large scale in the late 1960s by the *Science Citation Index*, which initially was a printed index to print literature. In the early 1970s, the *Science Citation Index* became one of the first bibliographic databases available online. Since then, the *Social Sciences Citation Index* and the *Arts and Humanities Index* have been established, and earlier literature was added to these indexes. Citation indexing originated in the field of law in the late nineteenth century with *Shepard's Citators*, now available online and in print (*Shepard's Citations Service* 2006). This old idea has become much more powerful with the ability to follow a digital path through the scholarly literature.

Authors as Submitters

Authors decide when, where, and if to submit a particular piece of work to a publication channel such as a conference, a journal, or a book publisher. They may post or distribute manuscripts for comment before deciding whether to revise them for publication. Some documents may be "scholarly skywriting" (Harnad 1991) to float an idea for discussion, while others are clearly intended for mainstream publication. Many documents exist indefinitely in the netherworld between manuscript and article, especially on the Internet. Print documents also can exist indefinitely as "to be revised" drafts, but are much less public when the master copy remains in the author's file cabinet.

When authors do decide to submit their work, their decisions on where to submit involve all three functions of the scholarly communication system: the legitimization and dissemination of their work, and its present and future accessibility. Sometimes these functions are nicely aligned with one journal or publisher. At other times, these functions may be in conflict, and authors must make trade-offs based on what is most appropriate for the specific document at issue.

The most assured means for authors to gain legitimacy is to place their work in a prestigious publication forum. Prestige is a subjective measure that varies greatly by the individual, their field, and the work in question. Generally speaking, journals gain prestige by being competitive (high rejection rates), being cited (as determined by citation indexes), being indexed (coverage in multiple indexing and abstracting sources), circulation (available via more libraries or to more individual subscribers), age (continuity of record), and intangible aspects such as reputation. These measures are highly interdependent. Older journals have had more time to build up a reputation, gain circulation, and become indexed, and as a result, become more competitive. Journals come and go, however. Some survive and thrive, while others cease publication, merge with other journals, or change their title and coverage. Even fewer objective measures are available for book publishers, as books have little presence in citation indexes or other indexing and abstracting services.

Among authors' considerations for dissemination are the prestige of the publication forum, the format, the timeliness, and the distribution. Some journals publish long articles, while others publish only short ones. Some publishers produce text-only versions; others will include high-quality color plates. A few will publish and curate data sources associated with a book or an article. Some encourage community discourse by publishing extensive critical responses and letters to the editor (forms of postpublication review). The time lag to publication can vary from weeks to a year or more.

The trade-offs between these criteria are highly individualized. When positioning one's major writing contributions, or when facing tenure and promotion decisions, prestige is likely to supersede all other considerations. This is among "the perverse incentives in scholarly publishing" (Odlyzko 1997a) that have limited the success of new journals and publishing models, whether in digital or print form.

Authors as Collaborators

For the most part, the choices that authors make as collaborators are related only indirectly to the functions of scholarly communication. Authors may choose to work with colleagues who are well-known because this association with prestigious figures may enhance their own reputation, or increase the likelihood of grants being awarded or papers being accepted. If these expectations are realized, legitimization may be enhanced. Collaborators will decide as a group how and where to disseminate their work. They may choose to submit work on different aspects of a project to different conferences and journals, with each collaborator taking the lead on one or more papers. Individual participants have obligations to their own communities, which may lead to a more diverse array of dissemination channels than any one author would achieve alone.

The transparency aspect of dissemination also may play a role in collaboration. Larger projects usually have external funding, and funding agencies expect the results of a project to be published in the scholarly record. Formal publications are the main product that funding agencies receive in return for money being granted. Publications legitimize the work of the funding agency as well as that of the authors who conduct the research. Funding agencies want their work to be accessible to the public, and thus access, preservation, and curation are of concern to them also.

Summary

Scholarly communication encompasses many forms of public and private interactions among scholars. Although individual acts of communication can be placed along a continuum from informal to formal, the boundary between those categories is blurred and disputed. Differences between fields in the roles of preprints and scholarly conferences highlight conflicts between the formal and informal, and identify the locations of boundaries between fields.

Scholarly communication is best understood as a sociotechnical system, with a complex set of interactions among processes, structures, functions, and technologies. The system is difficult to comprehend as a whole, due to the many methods, theories, variables, and levels of analysis applied. Yet efforts to restructure scholarly communication must be based on an understanding of the structures and processes involved. The system builds on long traditions in Western thought about open science and the social and economic benefits of the free flow of ideas. Quality control is accomplished through various forms of review, both before and after documents are contributed to the scholarly record.

The functions of the scholarly communication system can be grouped into the three categories discussed above: legitimizing scholarly work; its dissemination to an audience; and access, preservation, and curation of the scholarly record. Scholarly authors are actors in this system, taking on roles as writers, citers or linkers, submitters, and collaborators. These roles and functions influence day-to-day decisions that drive scholars' careers. While information technology has radically altered the means by which scholars communicate publicly and privately, the underlying processes and functions of communication have changed little over the last few decades. New innovations in scholarly communication are more likely to be successful if they work with, rather than against, the social aspects of the system.

5

The Discontinuity of Scholarly Publishing

The principles of open science have sustained the scholarly communication system for several centuries. For the latter half of the twentieth century, the legitimization, dissemination, and access, preservation, and curation functions of scholarly communication remained remarkably stable. It is the means by which these functions are accomplished that have metamorphosed through the use of networked information technologies. Scholarly practices vary greatly within and between fields, disciplines, and countries, yet as a whole the system seems to function fairly well. Economists and science policymakers generally agree that the open science model is effective and efficient, and thus they are reluctant to make dramatic changes, lest the system break down (Esanu and Uhlir 2003; Levien et al. 2005).

Scholars, libraries, publishers, and universities all have deployed networked information technologies to advantage. Many of their enhancements are intended to accomplish the same functions more efficiently and effectively. Other changes are due to external pressures on the scholarly communication system. Shifts in intellectual property policy, the economics of scholarly publishing, and relationships between stakeholders have contributed to systemic restructuring.

Proposals for reform range from a comprehensive reorganization of the scholarly communication system to better ways of accomplishing the current functions. Some proposals would expand participation in the quality-control system, others would register documents earlier in their life cycle, some would shift the cost of publishing from the reader (or the reader's institution) to the author, and some would locate copyright with the author rather than the publisher. The challenge lies in using information technology to enhance essential aspects of scholarship while balancing the interests of the many stakeholders in the scholarly communication system.

Transformative social change rarely is apparent while in progress. Yet most, if not all, of the stakeholders in scholarly publishing agree that major changes are under way. They may disagree on whether the origins are in the 1960s' restructuring of higher education, the 1980s' and 1990s' consolidation of the publishing industry, or the 1990s' and 2000s' penetration of the Internet into scholarship and daily life. They have different opinions on how long the transformation will take, when it will be over, and how profound it will be. Little consensus exists on the benefits and damage resulting from this transformation.

No single chapter, or single book for that matter, can do justice to the full array of debates raging over scholarly publishing. Nor can any book stay current with the rapid pace of developments. Books are a better medium for analyzing long-term trends, and distinguishing between means and ends. This chapter explores both the opportunities and the threats to scholarship wrought by the evolution of scholarly publishing in the digital age.

New Technologies, New Tensions

Information technologies now enable anyone to be a publisher, in the generic sense that anything "made public" is published. Nevertheless, the supposedly low barriers to entry in a computer-based publishing system ignore the complex relationships between stakeholders. "Self-publishing" is an oxymoron in the scholarly world. Authors need peer reviewers; publishers need authors, editors, and reviewers; and libraries need content to collect, organize, make accessible, and preserve.

New technologies for access to information appear to be revolutionizing scholarly publishing. But how much is revolution and how much is evolution? How much is hyperbole and how much is a deep restructuring of functions and relationships? Changes in scholarly publishing can be attributed partly to the "pull" of new technologies and partly to the "push" of institutional restructuring.

The Pull of New Technologies

Technologies for the digital production (e.g., word processing, image processing, or visualization tools) and digital dissemination (e.g., electronic journals, Web sites, or digital libraries) of scholarly works facilitate distribution and access. Electronic publishing is much more than posting page images of printed documents. Publishers have added services to search, link, and analyze electronic journals and books. Electronic publications can include interactive and dynamic media not possible with print publications. Libraries also offer new services to discover, retrieve, and use scholarly content, and to integrate digital libraries with other electronic resources such as learning management systems. Search engines scour Web sites and repositories, providing ready access to current materials that may or may not be in the realm of formal scholarly publishing.

On the Internet, more people can discover, retrieve, and read more scholarly content than was ever before possible. Greater options for access, in turn, reinforce the traditions of open science. The research community needs access to verify and replicate results, which establishes trust in the scholarly process. Funding agencies are using the opportunities afforded by online access to reaffirm their responsibility to taxpayers, citizens, and the world community to make publicly funded research publicly available. New models of data- and information-intensive scholarship envisioned by e-Research presume that scholars can obtain access to the information they need. In principle, a scholarly information infrastructure could make data and documents permanently accessible throughout the life cycle of research and learning.

The Push of Institutional Restructuring

The delicate balance between the roles of scholars, publishers, and librarians that existed in the print world is now askew. By the latter 1990s, the traditional library model of journal subscriptions and book purchasing was deemed economically unsustainable (Hawkins 1998). As the head of collections for a major university library said at the time, "Faculty, librarians, and publishers are now one big dysfunctional family" (Schottlaender 1998).

Part of the institutional restructuring process is due to differences in the ways that print and digital objects are produced, managed, used, and perceived. Each format has advantages and disadvantages. For example, print publications exist in many copies, each of which can be read by only one person at a time. Reproductions are imperfect, whether transferred by hand or photocopied. Copies tend to be distributed widely, often internationally. It is nearly impossible to locate and destroy all extant copies of a printed publication once it is disseminated, which assists its long-term preservation. Because multiple copies exist in multiple places, it is not possible to alter the work, once it is published. Errata and retractions can be connected in the bibliographic record, but the original documents remain in static form. Most documents printed on paper can survive through benign neglect if they are stored with adequate temperature and moisture controls.

Digital documents differ in all of these respects, contributing to fundamental shifts in the sociotechnical system of scholarly communication. Digital documents are not fixed; they are malleable, mutable, and mobile (Bishop and Star 1996; Latour 1988). Only one master version exists, and it can be altered, destroyed, or become unreadable, either deliberately or through benign neglect. Perfect reproductions can be made and distributed widely, however. Documents can be revised without any indication that alterations have occurred. Other material (e.g., empirical data, supplements, appendixes, updates, comments, reviews, errata, and retractions) can be attached to a document, even after it is published.

Despite the fact that digital publications can be held to the same standards of peer review and authentication as print publications, many scholars remain suspicious. While they appreciate the ease of access to digital content, those at elite universities continue to value print over digital publication, both in choosing where to publish and in criteria for hiring and promotion. Digital products, whether journal articles, books, conference papers, or other objects, are subjected to a higher level of scrutiny than are print publications (King et al. 2006).

Universities see their future in the digital delivery of information services, although print is not expected to disappear entirely. Instructional materials for courses have moved online, as have many other university services. Students register for courses, pay fees, and obtain grades online.

Faculty members retrieve their class lists and submit their grades online. Official records, from memorandums to salary statements, are distributed by e-mail and access to secure Web sites. Most access to library digital collections takes place off-site, from offices, dorms, and homes. Faculty and students alike expect 24/7 access to library resources. The use of physical campus libraries continues to be high, however. Libraries provide print collections, audio and video collections, reference and assistance, space for private and group study, and wireless access (Duderstadt, Atkins, and Van Houweling 2002; Duderstadt, Atkins, Brown et al. 2002).

Many other external pressures are contributing to the institutional restructuring that affects the scholarly communication system. Changes in intellectual property laws, such as the Bayh-Dole Act of 1980 in the United States, enabled universities to commercialize products that resulted from government research funding. Patents and university-industry partnerships became new sources of revenue. As a result, many faculty and students became more cautious about what they published, where, and when, especially in the biosciences and engineering. Extensions and expansions of copyright, in the United States and internationally, led to changes in author-publisher copyright agreements along with much narrower definitions of "fair use" for scholarly and educational purposes. The narrowing of information access by these laws is partly countered by legislation in the United States, the United Kingdom and elsewhere to require open access to scholarly publications that result from public funding. These are but a few of the many external influences on the scholarly communication system (Cohen 2005b; Covey 2005; Lessig 2004; Bayh-Dole Act: A Guide 1999).

Stakeholder Roles in Print Publishing

The set of relationships between scholars, publishers, and librarians did not spring forth fully formed in the mid-twentieth century. Rather, it was part of the centuries-long transition from oral to print culture. In the early transitional period, people read their compositions aloud to an audience as a means of "publishing" them (Eisenstein 1979). The interaction between oral and written communication continues to be a topic of study (Boyarin 1993; Lyman 1996). Publishing was once a "gentlemen's profession" with little expectation of profit (Cave 1971, 2001; Feather 1998, 2003; Warburg 1959). Libraries were major publishers—a role to which they are returning.

Indexing services also have a long history. As the scholarly journal literature began to grow in the seventeenth century, indexes emerged as a means to provide access. Price (1975, 166) found that indexes began only a few decades after the first journals, and grew in parallel on a log curve over the next three centuries. Yet some ideas that seem old are fairly new. For example, the term *scientist*, to signify someone whose profession is to study science and disseminate that knowledge, was not coined until the nineteenth century (Dalrymple 2003).

The balance among stakeholders continues to shift, and their relationships in the latter half of the twentieth century are merely a snapshot in time. That snapshot is a useful point of departure, for most analyses of online publishing are compared to the immediately preceding models. Stakeholder roles in the three functions of scholarly communication are examined here first in contemporary print publishing, and then in emerging models of digital publishing.

Legitimization in Print

In the print world, multiple aspects of the legitimization function are accomplished by publication. The process varies between publication in journals, conference proceedings, and books, but all involve quality control, registration, and dissemination. Journal editors conduct the peer-review process by assigning reviewers and making decisions about required revisions. Book publishers tend to do more copyediting to improve the final product for publication than do publishers of journals. Conference papers receive widely varying degrees of review, as discussed in chapter 4.

In each of these cases, being published by a recognized source registers the printed document in the scholarly communication system so that it can become part of the community discourse. Once registered, publications can be referenced by subsequent works and serve as the formal embodiment of a set of ideas.

Libraries select individual printed journals, books, and conference proceedings for purchase based on local criteria. These criteria include not only quality of the content but relevance to the teaching and research mission of the university. Much deeper collections are required to support doctoral programs than undergraduate ones, for instance. Similarly, the selection policies of technical universities are much different than those of liberal arts colleges. Selection by libraries also confers status and legitimization on publications (Buckland 1988, 1992).

University hiring, tenure, and promotion processes have depended heavily on the quality control provided by publishers of printed scholarly works. Review committees consider not only what a scholar has published but also where. Older, established journals and book publishers are easier to assess, which is part of the reason why elite universities continue to place a higher value on print than electronic publications (King et al. 2006).

Dissemination in Print

Publishers play the primary role in disseminating print publications. They manage the production of the printed journals, books, and proceedings, distribute them to libraries and other buyers, and advertise them. Libraries raise awareness of new print publications via shelves of new book arrivals and reading areas for new journal issues, and by distributing tables of contents of new issues. Authors assist in disseminating their printed journal articles and papers by sharing offprints with colleagues. They may also publicize their books by distributing advertising flyers at talks and conferences. Access to current journal articles often takes place electronically, however, as most major journals published in printed form also are available online.

Access, Preservation, and Curation of Print

Libraries historically have taken responsibility for access to and preservation of all types of printed scholarly materials. They acquire and organize materials to make them available. They typically catalog printed books and monographs, but rely on indexing and abstracting services for descriptions of journal articles. Some construct indexes to local and archival materials for which no other access mechanisms are available.

Libraries have had the primary, if not sole, responsibility for the preservation of physical materials. (Data have a much different history, as discussed in chapter 6). They hold copies of publications long after authors are dead and publishers have merged or gone out of business. They have taken advantage of characteristics of print that make them amenable to preservation, such as survival under adequate storage conditions. Libraries work together as a community to ensure that at least one copy of most printed works survives. Rather than every institution trying to preserve everything it owns, libraries form consortia and international clearinghouses to share responsibility for maintaining the historical record. Indeed, they have a long history of cooperation for loaning documents and preservation, especially in the West (Higginbotham and Bowdoin 1993; Pafford 1935).

Printed materials require less active maintenance to survive, and hence the term curation is less often used in this context. Libraries do add value in the form of catalogs, indexes, and finding aids, although these are more for access than for curatorial purposes. Trust and temporality are less problematic than with digital documents, as printed journals and books remain in a stable physical format.

Stakeholder Roles in Internet Access to Scholarly Documents

The volume and variety of scholarly resources available on the Internet continues to expand. Much, but by no means all, of the scholarly journal literature is available online. Comparatively little of the monographic scholarly literature is online, but the volume is expected to grow rapidly. Preprints and manuscripts may be available online publicly through Web sites and repositories, or privately by collegial exchange. Research data also are online publicly via repositories or Web sites (e.g., census, survey, and geographic data, or economic indicators), and are exchanged privately. In this flood of online material, publication status often is unclear. The same or similar content can exist concurrently in multiple forms. Traditional models of scholarly publishing coexist with a parallel universe of digital distribution outside the control of publishers. Publishers are here to stay, but so is that parallel universe.

Tensions between ease of access and the desire to control that access are leading to complex interactions between the functions of the scholarly communication system. Progress and protests are strong at each end of the continuum. Technologies to facilitate discovery and retrieval (e.g., institutional repositories, search engines, and harvesting methods) are maturing. Digital rights management systems also are maturing, but have been deployed with stricter access controls in consumer markets (e.g., music, movies, and video games) than in the scholarly market. Similarly, technologies that facilitate the ability of individuals to distribute their creative work while reserving certain rights coexist with laws and policies that increase the control of publishers and the entertainment industry (Boyle and Jenkins 2003; Cohen 2005a, 2005b, 2006; Copyright Term Extension Act 1998; Creative Commons 2006; Digital Millennium Copyright Act 1998).

These tensions are best understood in the larger context of changes in higher education and the research enterprise. Public funding for universities and for research have declined, resulting in universities seeking a broader financial base (Clark 1998, 2004). The boundaries between basic and applied research are harder to identify, as discussed in chapter 3. Scientific problems often have both basic and applied components, the latter of which may have great economic value. Bio- and nanotechnologies are high-profile examples of this trend, and university-industry partnerships abound in these areas. Multidisciplinary scholarship is increasing in response to complex problems that are not easily categorized within a single field. Research in general and science in particular are less isolated from society.

As research crosses more organizational and disciplinary boundaries, it is more difficult to apply singular standards for evidence, quality, value, or "truth." Multidisciplinary projects and university-industry partnerships can lead to contentious discussions about criteria for peer review, grant funding, hiring decisions, authorship of publications, and the ownership and control of data. The criteria employed in the Research Assessment Exercise (2006) in the United Kingdom, which is a periodic review of academic departments, are highly influential in scholars' decisions about what and where to publish. Quality-control mechanisms are shifting from a strong focus on the product of research (i.e., publications) toward monitoring the quality of the research process, especially in Europe (Hemlin and Rasmussen 2006). The proliferation of accountability requirements for the protection of animals, human subjects, and hazardous materials are examples of the growing emphasis on continuous monitoring in many parts of the world.

Legitimization in Digital Form

The legitimization function of scholarly communication encompasses authority, quality control, certification, registration in the scholarly record, priority, and trustworthiness. Print publication in a prestigious journal, conference proceedings, or book series can accomplish all of these elements at once. In the online world, they may be accomplished separately or in combination. The existing means of legitimization remain in force, but new technologies are enabling these functions to be accomplished in new ways. Most of the quality criteria applied in the peer-review process still require human judgment, such as the significance of the work, while some criteria such as statistical accuracy and originality can be augmented by technical methods of verification. As a result, scholars, publishers, and librarians are reconsidering the notions of legitimacy in the online world.

Whom Do You Trust?   The question posed in chapter 4 with respect to new forms of pre- and postpublication peer review was "who is a peer?" When considering the legitimization of digital documents online, the ·question becomes "legitimate to whom?" Scholarly documents achieve trustworthiness through a social process to assure readers that the document satisfies the quality norms of the field. Readers who are scholarly peers and have extensive access to the literature of their fields may make fine distinctions between publication channels in assessing the quality of a document. Students, practitioners, scholars with minimal access to the published literature, and the general public usually are happy to read and cite any free version of a document they can find online.

The simplest approach to clarifying the legitimacy of digital documents is to rely on traditional quality indicators such as the imprimatur of well-regarded publishers. This approach, however, cedes much of the control for legitimization to publishers and discourages experimental forms of publication. For example, if the only publications valued for promotion, tenure, and institutional reviews are those that appear in journals with a high-impact factor as measured by ISI citation statistics (discussed in chapter 4), journals indexed by the ISI have an inordinate power over the quality-control system. Relying on publishers to certify scholarly products emulates the print publication system (Frankel et al. 2000; Harnad 1998, 2001; Monastersky 2005).

Quality monitoring, which focuses on the process, may lead to more socially relevant knowledge, as Sven Hemlin and Søren Rasmussen (2006) suggest, but it also is difficult to measure. They advocate the use of a "multitude of quality criteria" as a means to encourage organizations to adapt to internal and external change (193). Similarly, the usual counterargument to a reliance on publication indicators as proxies for quality of scholarship is to encourage review committees to read publications closely enough to make their own judgments.

While the ultimate responsibility always has fallen to the reader for determining the quality of a document and whether it was worth citing, more institutional mechanisms existed for guidance. Those indicators included publication channels, selection by libraries, and citation rates. With fewer external quality clues available, individuals must make more sophisticated judgments about whether to trust a document or a source. "Information literacy" can be taught as part of critical thinking skills, which are a core component of undergraduate education. Libraries are expanding their role in instruction about online information sources, especially at the undergraduate level (Rockman 2004). Graduate degree programs are adding or extending modules on information sources in their fields. While learning to think critically about information sources is an essential part of becoming educated, these are not skills that are easily taught. The criteria for selection and authority often are subjective, context sensitive, and tacit. Moreover, criteria also vary widely by field and specialty area. Scholars learn to judge the value of the sources in their fields through experience.

Registration and Certification   In a print world, publication in a journal registers the document in the scholarly communication system, establishes the dates for priority of claims, and certifies that the article passed through a peer-review process. In a digital world, it is possible to accomplish these aspects of the legitimacy function independently. The difficulty lies in establishing mechanisms that fit comfortably into the scholarly communication systems of individual fields.

Registration and certification have marked the point where a document crosses the boundary from informal to formal communication. Manuscripts disseminated by e-mail and personal Web sites are not registered and remain informal. If and when the manuscript, or more likely a later version of it, is published, it may not be linked to its prior variations. The lack of links between versions of documents can be the source of much chaos in scholarly communication. Multiple people may read and cite nearly identical versions of a document that appear in a publisher's database, an institutional repository, a preprint server, on an author's home page, or that were received as e-mail attachments. Differences between versions may be subtle or significant (NISO/ALPSP Working Group 2006).

Herbert Van de Sompel and his colleagues (2004) use arXiv to show how legitimization functions can be separated in digital environments. arXiv is an e-print service for the fields of physics, mathematics, non-linear science, computer science, and quantitative biology (arXiv.org e-Print Archive 2006). When scholars deposit manuscripts or preprints, their document is registered in the database with a date that can serve priority claims. arXiv provides a basic form of certification by requiring that potential submitters be endorsed by peers (arXiv Endorsement System 2004). Manuscripts and preprints in arXiv are certified implicitly by the journals in which the articles are published. In addition, "overlay journals" select manuscripts from arXiv. By registering manuscripts when they first enter the scholarly communication network, links can be made to subsequent variants as they appear.

The arXiv model appears to work well for the participating disciplines, but is not necessarily a universal model that will find equal success in other fields. It also emulates the print model to a certain degree. However, it reflects a thoughtful analysis of how scholarly communication functions can be separated and recombined in a scholarly information infrastructure.

Legitimacy via Selection   When research libraries were almost the sole means of access to scholarly publications, inclusion in collections was a quality indicator of journals, books, proceedings, reports, and other documents. Even this indicator has become less reliable with online access to publications. Rather than selecting individual journals for their collections, current business models dictate that libraries acquire access to bundled packages of journals. After paying for the bundles, libraries have fewer remaining funds to acquire other journals and books. While many libraries use standing orders and approval plans to select books, they still have more discretion on the choice of individual titles than they do with electronic journals. As more books become available in electronic form, similar issues about the selection of book bundles are arising.

Even more complex is the selection process for the vast universe of resources online that are not formally published. By assuming that most of the unpublished manuscripts, technical reports, and conference presentations eventually found their way into the formal publication system, research libraries acquired a substantial portion of the scholarly record by capturing works at the time of publication. Now that so many resources remain outside the formal publication system for their entire life cycle, this assumption is less viable. Libraries are collecting manuscripts, data sets, digitized images and texts, and other artifacts of scholarly communication into institutional repositories. They also are cataloging some public online items, thereby making them a virtual part of their collections. By these activities, libraries are legitimizing some forms of scholarly content that are outside the scope of traditional publishing.

Dissemination in Digital Form

The dissemination function of scholarly communication incorporates communication, diffusion, awareness, and publicity of scholarly products, and making those products part of the discourse of a community. In digital environments, dissemination can be difficult to distinguish from access.

Rather than selling physical artifacts to libraries, which then provide access, most published digital content remains in publishers' databases. Journals and conference proceedings may be included in multiple databases. Various representations of a document (e.g., the bibliographic record, abstract, or full text) may appear in each database. While duplication increases the likelihood that a publication will be discovered, it also causes confusion.

What and when scholars themselves choose to disseminate online depends on a wide variety of factors, few of which are well understood. Some err in the direction of posting everything they write or compile (e.g., talks or data sets), as quickly as possible, to reach the widest possible audience. Others do not post any of their own documents, leaving that to the publishers. In between are all combinations of posting documents before, after, and concurrent with their availability via formal publication channels.

Authors have more options to disseminate their journal publications now that most publishers allow digital distribution. Variations in publisher policies include posting preprints only, postprints only, both pre- and postprints, on personal Web sites but not in institutional repositories, after an embargo period, or none of the above. Some allow the reposting of the published version, and others allow the posting of author versions only. Some authors who post their publications adhere closely to publishing contracts and guidelines. Others ignore dissemination restrictions in the contract, assuming they are unlikely to be enforced (Cox and Cox 2003; Gadd, Oppenheim, and Probets 2003; Harnad and Brody 2004; King et al. 2006; Poynder 2006; SHERPA/RoMEO 2006).

Access, Preservation, and Curation in Digital Form
Access depends on the ability to discover and retrieve documents of interest, and then follow a trail through the scholarly record. Preservation can be a passive process, while curation is an active one. Digital objects, unlike printed publications, cannot be preserved through benign neglect. Curation adds value through migration to new formats, adding metadata, and ensuring trust in the integrity of the objects through technical and institutional mechanisms (Beagrie 2006; Giaretta 2005). The technology and economics of digital access, preservation, and curation are a particularly problematic aspect of scholarly information infrastructure.

A Bit of Digital History   The ability to search, find, and retrieve scholarly publications has improved radically through the use of information technologies. These technologies have a much longer history than does the Internet, however. They build on an infrastructure for information access that dates back centuries, in the case of standards and practices for bibliographic control, and decades, in the case of automated information retrieval.

Access to publications long has relied on bibliographic records (e.g., author, title, publisher, place, journal name, volume, issue, date, and page numbers). Bibliographic records are a form of metadata or data about data (Baca 1998; Weibel 1995). Many other forms of metadata exist to describe documents or data within specific disciplines, or by the type of media (e.g., images, numeric data, or text). Consistent use of metadata improves searching by bringing together records under common forms of names, titles, descriptors, subject headings, places, and so forth. Descriptive metadata are used to verify whether the object retrieved is indeed the one sought. While the undergraduate student may be satisfied with any version of Hamlet, for example, the Shakespearean scholar usually wants a specific edition or copy.

Libraries maintained catalogs of their manuscripts long before Gutenberg, and thus bibliographic control predates printing. Despite variances in local practices, libraries jointly developed bibliographic control principles, first for print materials, and later for digital records and content. By the latter 1960s, the "Paris Principles" for cataloging rules and the MARC (MAchine Readable Cataloging) record for exchanging bibliographic data were accepted standards (Avram 1976; Svenonius 2000). These principles and structures, which are updated continually by international working groups, establish the choice and format of data elements for bibliographic records. Overlaid on bibliographic record formats are an array of technical standards that enable the interoperability of information systems between libraries, publishers, universities, governments, and other entities.

Automated information retrieval originated in the 1950s as batch-processing systems (Perry, Kent, and Berry 1956). Online interactive retrieval became commercially viable in the early 1970s over private telecommunications networks. The first services offered a few databases of indexes and abstracts of scholarly literature. These databases contained bibliographic descriptions of journal articles that were searchable by keywords in author and title, and sometimes by journal name or subject heading. The user interfaces were crude, the access was expensive, and searching was done by librarians on behalf of "end users" (Borgman, Moghdam, and Corbett 1984).

Online catalogs became available in the late 1970s within physical libraries. Catalogs gradually became available on the Internet beginning in the latter 1980s, but until the early 1990s, the Internet was available only to the research and education communities. Many libraries offered direct dial-up access for those without Internet connections. Online access to catalogs and to indexing and abstracting databases began to converge in the mid-1980s. In some of the experimental ventures, library users were given access to publishers' computers. In a few other cases, universities mounted publisher databases on their own computers. The University of California offered selected databases to its nine campuses over its statewide telecommunications network, for instance. The business model that prevailed was for publishers to host in-house databases, which offered various advantages. Then they began to offer direct access to individual users through contracts with libraries. Full text and numeric databases gradually were added to these services throughout the 1980s and 1990s. Libraries also focused on integrating their online services into coherent views of their collections (Borgman 1997; Ekman and Quandt 1999; Lynch 1994, 2001c).

Searching, Discovering, and Retrieving   Access to scholarly resources on the Internet depends on many technical, economic, and business considerations outside the realm of scholarly communication. Until recently, most metadata were ignored by search engines, despite the massive investments of libraries and publishers in describing the contents and subject matter of scholarly books and journals. Metadata were ignored because they are so easily and commonly misrepresented on the World Wide Web. Web sites manipulate their metadata in hopes of increasing their rankings, while search engines adjust their algorithms to maintain some objective standards of relevance. Search engines and Web site owners are in constant competition for rank ordering of retrievals. Database owners, including publishers and libraries, rarely allow access by search engines due to security concerns. A substantial portion of scholarly content lies inside proprietary databases, behind firewalls, or is otherwise hidden from search engines. The unindexed component of the Internet is known as "the deep, dark, or invisible web" (Levien et al. 2005).

Changes in technology and policy have greatly increased the degree of online access to library catalogs, publisher databases, and institutional repositories provided by search engines such as Google, Yahoo, and MSN Search. Technologies such as the Open Archives Initiative Protocol for Metadata Harvesting (OAI-PMH) enable libraries, publishers, and other institutions to expose metadata (such as bibliographic descriptions of books and journal articles) without providing full access to their databases (Lagoze 2001; Van de Sompel, Nelson et al. 2004). Libraries developed these technologies to provide access to their own resources and to improve interoperability between systems. As search engines became the dominant means of online searching and discovery, publishers saw economic incentives to make their metadata discoverable.

Search engines can retrieve links to scholarly content without regard to business model. References to books and journal articles may be interspersed with references to preprints, manuscripts, technical reports, discussion lists, and blogs. Only when a link is selected do searchers learn whether the content is available with or without a fee. The fee basis for commercial services may vary depending on whether the searcher is affiliated with an institution that has paid for access to that resource. Context-sensitive links, such as OpenURL, will transfer an authorized user directly to the resource. Searchers without authorized access (or who have authorized access, but have not set their authentication correctly) may be asked for payment to see more than a journal abstract or a few pages of a book. Other forms of context-sensitive linking may identify the nearest library that owns a book of interest (Bekaert and Van de Sompel 2006a; Chudnov et al. 2005; OpenURL and CrossRef 2006; Van de Sompel, Hochstenbach, and Beit-Arie 2000).

The uses of metadata are evolving rapidly in this environment. Documents are easier to discover, retrieve, and verify if they are described with appropriate metadata. Cataloging and indexing, however, are expensive endeavors. Some metadata can be generated automatically, at less expense than with human indexing. Metadata are often a higher priority for images, video, numeric data, and other formats that are less "self-describing" than text. Libraries continue to invest in cataloging and indexing to improve access in the short and long term. Publishers assign persistent identifiers to their products (to each book and journal article, and sometimes to parts of articles such as tables), which also facilitate discovery, verification, and linking. Advertising descriptions and tables of contents in publisher and bookseller databases make current books easier to find. With the growing amount of full text available, searching relies less on metadata than it did in the past.

Scholarly content on the open Web, such as preprints posted on personal Web pages, rarely has metadata or persistent identifiers. Discovery depends heavily on full text searching. Verifying the source or publication status of documents, once retrieved, can be difficult.

Following the Scholarly Trail   Scholars follow trails through the literature to trace the origins of an idea and relationships among prior works. In print environments, these were laborious manual tasks, tracking citations and retrieving documents. In digital environments, each relationship can be represented by a link to another object. If intellectual relationships can be represented by links, scholarly discourse will be enhanced.

Still, establishing and maintaining valid links is a nontrivial challenge. In a print world, two conditions are required to establish a reliable trail from one document to the next. The first condition is that an accurate bibliographic description exists of the target (cited) work. The second is that the target document exists in many copies, any of which is acceptable. Readers use the bibliographic description (metadata) to locate a copy of the work in a library or through some other source. Bibliographic access thus rests on a decentralized system.

The print model does not transfer well to the digital world. For reliable retrieval, links must originate from, and point to, the unique original rather than a copy. Direct links between objects do not require bibliographic descriptions, although descriptions may be necessary to determine whether the object retrieved is the one intended. Maintaining a digital trail, then, depends on the ability to identify individual documents, data sets, and other forms of digital objects. The identifier must be unique, so that the links to and from the object are unambiguous. It must be persistent, so that the link can be followed over long periods of time, during which the object might be moved to a different computer or even a different format (e.g., migrating to later versions of software). URLs are not sufficiently stable to serve this purpose in their present form, but methods such as "robust hyperlinks" could solve this problem in the Web environment (Phelps and Wilensky 2004).

A more general approach to the problems of uniqueness and persistence is to base identifiers on some agreed-on name space or naming system. A name space is a set of names, determined by a set of rules, that can be used as labels or pointers to a set of objects (*Dictionary of Computing* 2006; *Dictionary of the Internet* 2006). Name spaces are most effective when they are part of an institutional framework that other organizations will use and trust. Multiple name spaces can be used to point to an object. For example, the elements of a bibliographic description of a book are taken from the name spaces of authors, titles, publishers, subjects, and the International Standard Book Number (ISBN), as shown in figure 5.1.

Institutional frameworks exist for name spaces such as the ISBN, the International Standard Serial Number (ISSN), subjects (e.g., Library of Congress Subject Headings), and records for author names (e.g., Name Authority Cooperative Program 2006), assuring continuous maintenance and wide deployment. The ISBN applies not only to books but to "software, mixed media etc. in publishing, distribution and library practices" (International ISBN Agency 2006). To accommodate the growing demand for ISBNs, the standard was revised from 10- to 13-digit numbers beginning in 2007 (ISBN Standard Revision 2006). The ISSN is an 8-digit number assigned to serial publications; more than one million ISSNs have been assigned (International Standard Serial Number 2006). The assignment of these identifiers is managed by international agencies, with ISBN based in Berlin and the ISSN based in Paris.

At present, multiple competing name spaces exist for digital objects, some of which are extensions of name spaces for print publications and others of which are new for digital objects. ISSNs are used for electronic and print journals. ISBNs are deployed widely for books, but do not yet

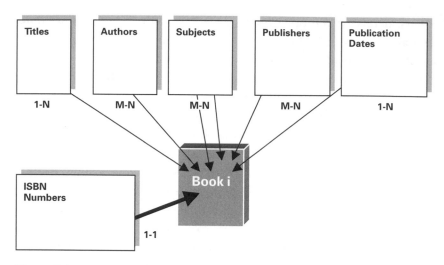

Figure 5.1
Elements of Book Description Drawn from Multiple Name Spaces (1–N = one from the name space; M–N = many from the name space; 1–1 = unique identifier) Reprinted with permission of Roger Levien.

have the associated technology to support linking (Vitiello 2004). Digital Object Identifiers (DOI) have been adopted by major publishers to identify individual journal articles and other publications in digital form (Paskin 2003; Digital Object Identifier System 2006). Although anyone can use them, DOIs are not widely deployed outside the universe controlled by publishers. The DOI name space supports other technologies to link references within and between databases. Other standards build on top of these name spaces. OpenURL supports context-sensitive links between objects in multiple name spaces and the Info URI scheme maps ISBNs, ISSNs, DOIs, and other name spaces to uniform resource locators (Chudnov et al. 2005; CrossRef 2006; Hellman 2003; OpenURL and CrossRef 2006; Van de Sompel, Hochstenbach, and Beit-Arie 2000; Van de Sompel et al. 2006).

DOIs, in turn, are an implementation of the Corporation for National Research Initiatives's Handle System (2006). Handles are designed to be stable identifiers, and are less likely to break than are URLs. A different implementation of the Handle System to identify documents uniquely is employed by DSpace, which is a popular open source software package for institutional repositories (DSpace 2006; Smith et al. 2004; Tansley, Bass, and Smith 2003). These are but a few of the schemes proposed for a universal system of persistent identifiers—none of which have achieved wide success on the Internet (Levien et al. 2005).

While the progress toward standards that bridge name spaces is promising, consistency and persistence are continuing challenges. Control over formal, published materials is easier to achieve because institutional frameworks exist. Few mechanisms and incentives exist to guarantee the identification and persistence of informal communications. The degree of stability required for these types of materials may depend on whether they are intended for short-term access or long-term preservation.

What Will Be Saved, and by Whom?   Preservation is an expensive, long-term commitment. Files must be mounted, computers must be maintained, software must be updated, data must be backed up and migrated, and people must be paid—even if no new data are added to the database. The two parts of the digital curation problem, as identified by Nentwich (2003)—what will be archived, and who will take responsibility?—are deeply intertwined. Content for which an institution chooses to take responsibility is the most likely to be preserved. The library and archives communities recognized the impending crisis in digital preservation from the early days of electronic publishing and the digitization of print. Starting in 1990, the Council on Library Resources began issuing a series of reports on the technology and policy aspects of creating, managing, and preserving digital resources (Lesk 1990). Similar reports were issued in Europe and elsewhere about the risks of losing cultural heritage.

The preservation, curation, and "stewardship" of the digital record is an amorphous problem due to the many types of content and formats, the number of stakeholders, the complex contractual and policy arrangements, and the varying technical and economic requirements. Digital content has become the authoritative record of scholarship, making libraries the obvious institution to take responsibility for continuity. Scoping the problem is itself an issue. Libraries tend to be more concerned about content that is "born digital" than with content that is digitized from other formats. Once digitized, however, that content also needs to be maintained. It can be difficult to set boundaries for preservation, as documents often are interlinked. A related concern is maintaining the software (and sometimes the hardware) used to produce and manage digital objects. Without the appropriate software, digital content frequently cannot be read or interpreted.

Among the aspects on which libraries agree are that institutions should work cooperatively to avoid a duplication of effort, that standards and practices are improving, and that much more research is needed on preservation technology and economic models. Few are satisfied with "dark archives" that ensure preservation but provide no access.

Strategies for preservation and access differ between scholarly books and journals. Libraries typically license access to journals in digital form, with content remaining in publisher databases. These licenses prevent or limit libraries' abilities to preserve this content, even if they were willing to absorb the cost of doing so (Farb 2006). Publishers and libraries are partnering on projects to preserve e-journals, but most of these projects are in the experimental or evaluative stages (Kenney 2006). The digitization of books has accelerated rapidly since Google announced its partnership with five major research libraries in late 2004. Subsequently, Microsoft and Yahoo established the Open Content Alliance with other major institutions. Both consortia continue to add partners. Several libraries, including the University of California, now participate in both the Open Content Alliance and Google Print projects. France has announced a comparable project for French books, and other countries are likely to follow. Mass digitization raises technology and information policy issues such as copyright, the quality of digital representation and authentication, long-term preservation responsibility, standards and interoperability, and business models for libraries, publishers, and booksellers (Courant 2006; Kenney et al. 2003; Lavoie and Dempsey 2004; Lavoie, Silipigni-Connaway, and Dempsey 2005; Lynch 2004; Markoff and Wyatt 2004; *Mass Digitization* 2006; Powell 2004; Rusbridge 2006).

Preserving access to the scholarly record is a growing public policy concern. Many in the academic community are reluctant to assign responsibility for the scholarly record to commercial entities, whether publishers or search engines. Publishers may cease business without a clear legal successor to maintain the archive. Unprofitable back files may not be maintained, may not be migrated to new hardware and software, or could be destroyed. Book preservation and access are even greater concerns than for journals, due to the vital role that books play in cultural heritage. Libraries and archives have served an essential, and relatively objective and apolitical, role in assuring permanent access to scholarship over the course of centuries (Lynch 2001a; Nentwich 2003; Waters 2006).

The preservation of the scholarly record that falls outside the scope of publishing and libraries is yet more problematic. Preserving the data on which scholarly publications are based is a key concern of e-Research, as discussed in chapter 6. Governments are responsible for maintaining access to records on behalf of their citizenry, although policies and practices vary by government and political era. Private entities have legal responsibilities to maintain certain records, but few requirements to maintain public access to online publications or Web sites, for example. Libraries often capture ephemeral materials, both physical and digital, for which ownership is unclear. Whether or not they preserve these resources depends on factors such as cost, long-term value, and the ability to determine ownership. Private ownership and control must be balanced with the public interest in preserving the cultural record. It is even less obvious who, if anyone, will maintain access to informal content such as discussion lists, home pages, blogs, and collections of bookmarks and links. The origins and ownership of these types of content are diffuse. The Internet Archive (2006) is capturing Web content on a periodic basis, and is partnering with national libraries and archives to preserve selected portions of these resources.

Convergence and Collision

In the present disarray, it is difficult to distinguish the long-term restructuring of scholarly publishing from short-term developments. Several factors will influence how, how much, when, to whom, and under what conditions access to the scholarly record will be available in the present and the future. Issues of what constitutes a "publication," the open access movement, intellectual property, and economics each have deep roots and long-term implications for scholarly publishing.

What Constitutes a "Publication"?

Many of the debates over legitimization, dissemination, and access and curation rest on differences of opinion about what it means to publish something. For the purposes of copyright, publication is defined as follows: " 'Publication' is the distribution of copies or phonorecords of a work to the public by sale or other transfer of ownership, or by rental, lease, or lending. The offering to distribute copies or phonorecords to a group of persons for purposes of further distribution, public perform-ance, or public display constitutes publication. A public performance or display of a work does not of itself constitute publication" (U.S. Copy-right Act 1976).

This legal definition, however, does not necessarily reflect scholarly practices, especially in digital publication. The act of publishing a phys-ical artifact has three important characteristics, none of which may be true for a digital publication: "It is public, it is irrevocable, and it pro-vides a fixed copy of the work" (*Digital Dilemma* 2000, 42). Works can be removed from databases, suppressed, and altered after publication. Under these circumstances, the notion of publication has become fluid and contentious.

In the transition from print to electronic publishing, some unstated or obscure norms became apparent. For example, when scholars first started to post manuscripts and preprints online, some publishers embraced a broad interpretation of "the Ingelfinger rule." In 1969, Franz Ingelfinger, editor of the *New England Journal of Medicine*, formalized the norms about the release of scientific findings. One aspect of the rule is that the *Journal* would only consider papers not previously published elsewhere, to protect its reputation for registering findings and estab-lishing priority. Second, the contents of manuscripts were not to be released to the press before publication, due to the public health risks of circulating information not verified by the peer-review process (Toy 2002).

In the view of a number of prestigious journals and societies, online posting constituted prior publication, and they refused to consider any manuscript that previously had been posted online in any form. Harnad (2000) tackled the Ingelfinger rule head-on, claiming that electronic dis-tribution allowed most of Ingelfinger's concerns to be addressed in other ways. Public health hazards involve a small minority of journal publication, and the rules should not be generalized. Harnad concluded that the real reason for the stringent enforcement of the Ingelfinger rule was to protect the revenue stream of the *Journal*.

At first, these strong stances on what constitutes prior publication were effective in discouraging online posting. Then the trend shifted. When a sufficient number of scholars contributed their papers to repositories such as arXiv and posted them on Web sites, publishers were forced to back down, lest they lose access to a sufficient flow of manuscripts to publish. Posting a document online was no longer considered prior publication, and such practice returned to the status of informal communication. Concerns shifted to posting or depositing articles after publication, lest the publishers lose subscription income. Publishers lost ground here also, and now most copyright agreements for journal articles allow authors to post or archive some form of their articles.

The most visible part of the discussion of what constitutes publication has focused on journal articles. Yet a much broader set of issues is bubbling upward as new genres emerge that are not easily categorized. Rich scholarly Web sites in the humanities, for instance, contain data in many media, consolidating the results of years of research. They have few analogs in print publication. Electronic books and theses also have features not replicable in print form (e.g., moving images or links to external sources), but are otherwise analogous to traditional books and theses. Simulations, data repositories, and other complex content with interactive links may be considered publications, especially in data-intensive fields, despite few print analogs (Shortliffe et al. 2004; Suleman et al. 2001; Unsworth et al. 2006).

Even more complex is the array of informal scholarly communication genres. These include discussion lists, blogs, chats, RSS feeds, and others soon to be invented. Collections of links are somewhat analogous to bibliographies, but "social bookmarking tools" (Hammond et al. 2005a, 2005b) are specific to online environments. While most of these new genres are too informal to have been considered publications in a print realm, they do contain important discussions, facts, and reports that are part of the scholarly discourse of a field. Furthermore, they can be captured because digital communications leave a trace.

Open Repositories, Open Archives, Open Access

The open access movement emerged in the mid-1990s and was flourishing by the mid-2000s. A categorized, scholarly bibliography on the topic lists more than thirteen hundred sources (Bailey 2005). Yet the word "open" appears so frequently in discussions of publishing and technology that it has lost a clear sense of meaning: open archives, open repositories, open access, open source, and so on. Generally speaking, these uses of the term refer to minimal restrictions on use; frequently they mean that something is available without direct monetary payment. Complicating matters further, the word free is often used in defining open, without making Richard Stallman's (2002) famous distinction between "free speech" and "free beer."

Definitions of Open Access   Among the most succinct explanations of open access is set in the context of repositories: "The Open Access research literature is composed of free, online copies of peer-reviewed journal articles and conference papers as well as technical reports, theses and working papers. In most cases there are no licensing restrictions on their use by readers. They can therefore be used freely for research, teaching, and other purposes" (Leaflet on Open Access 2005).

This explanation is extended further to say what open access is not: "It is not self-publishing, nor a way to bypass peer-review and publication, nor is it a kind of second-class, cut-price publishing route. It is simply a means to make research results freely available online to the whole research community" (Leaflet on Open Access 2005).

Some definitions are narrow and explicit, while others are broad and vague. Willinsky (2006, 211–216), in a book-length analysis of "open access to research and scholarship," identifies "ten flavors of open access." These are:

1. *Home pages*, where faculty post papers and make them available without charge

2. *E-print archives*, either supported by disciplines (e.g., arXiv in physics and RePEc in economics) or institutions (e.g., universities)

3. *Author fee*, whether paid by the authors, the authors' institutions, or by membership

4. *Subsidized*, where universities, scholarly societies, foundations, or other entities cover the publishing costs

5. *Dual-mode*, in which the print version is sold for a fee and the online version is free

6. *Delayed*, where articles are available only by a fee or subscription during an embargo period, and are free thereafter (typically six months or more)

7. *Partial*, such as offering some articles in each issue for free, or free initial access under fair use provisions and subscription access thereafter

8. *Per capita*, usually free access in countries with per capita incomes below a certain level

9. *Indexing*, where the bibliographic descriptions of journals are freely available (e.g., PubMed for life sciences and ERIC for education), but access to the full content may require a subscription or fee

10. *Cooperative*, or centralized support for multiple forms of open access publishing

Motivations for Open Access   The open access movement has its roots in the principles of open science that have sustained scholarship for several centuries. Scholarship progresses by discussion, transparency, and accountability, all of which require that scholarly works are widely and readily available. Tensions between the greater access facilitated by the Internet and the greater controls (and higher prices) imposed by publishers were an important impetus for open access. To frame the open access movement as simply a tug-of-war between authors and publishers would oversimplify significant debates about the future of access to scholarly information.

One of the primary motivations for open access is to make scholarly publications immediately and widely available, thereby enhancing authors' visibility. The claim that papers in open access repositories would be more highly cited than those in publisher databases alone has been confirmed by several studies (Harnad and Brody 2004; Kurtz, Eichhorn, Accomazzi, Grant, Demleitner, Henneken et al. 2005; Kurtz, Eichhorn, Accomazzi, Grant, Demleitner, Murray et al. 2005; Lawrence n.d.). Proponents of open access to published, peer-reviewed articles distinguish between the "Green Road" of self-archiving by depositing articles in repositories and the "Gold Road" of publishing in open access journals (Harnad 2005a, 2005b). Definitions of self-archiving and open access journal for the Green and Gold roads are drawn from the Budapest Open Access Initiative (2005).

Despite the potential for increased visibility of one's published work, self-archiving has been vastly less successful than predicted by open access advocates. While the institutional commitment is strong, especially in Europe (Berlin Declaration 2003; Harnad 2005c), success depends on the efforts of individual authors. Outside of physics and computer science, the voluntary deposit rates average about 15 percent (Poynder 2006). The implications for scholarly information infrastructure of these low participation rates are discussed further in chapter 7.

The library community makes a strong case for institutional repositories as a means to provide open access, but with different arguments. As presented in a seminal position paper (Crow 2002), institutional repositories arose in response to two strategic issues facing universities: to reform scholarly communication by disaggregating the functions of publishing, and to provide "tangible indicators of an institution's quality." Each university can showcase the work of its faculty in institutional repositories, and those repositories can be interoperable, thus expanding access. Universities can assert more control over the scholarly communication system and save money. The registration, certification, dissemination, and preservation functions of publishing can be separated. Repositories also can provide additional services such as managing reports of publications to personnel review committees and funding agencies (J. Hey 2004).

Although incentives differ, the interests of authors, libraries, and universities in the use of institutional repositories to self-archive publications are aligned. Still, approaches to such use began to diverge as the low participation rates of authors became apparent. Libraries, having begun to build the technology, saw additional uses for it. They could capture other valuable content in digital form, including manuscripts, reports, instructional materials, data sets, digitized materials, and university documentation, all of which they are under pressure to preserve. Repositories could therefore legitimize a wider array of scholarly communication than just peer-reviewed publications. The broader array of content serves the stated library goals, but from the perspective of self-archiving advocates, dilutes the goal of immediate access to peer-reviewed publications. Larger and more diverse repositories also are a more expensive undertaking with greater requirements for preservation. As repositories expand in scope to become digital libraries, the definition of institutional repository becomes ever more vague (Jacobs 2006; Lynch 2003a; Poynder 2006).

Research funding agencies, both public and private, have yet another set of incentives for open access to publications. Repositories offer a mechanism to ensure that the research they fund is disseminated and accessible. Proposed legislation in the United States, the United Kingdom, and elsewhere would require recipients of public funding to deposit such underwritten publications within a specified time period. Publishers are vigorously opposed to most of these proposals. Some of this legislation has passed, but in diluted forms. Most visible in the United States are the debates over access to biomedical literature. The National Institutes of Health (NIH) proposals to require the deposit of articles in PubMed Central were substantially weakened under pressure from publishers. The resulting voluntary program had an initial participation rate of less than 4 percent. Subsequent proposed legislation attempts to strengthen the deposit requirements for the NIH, and extend the program to the NSF and other federal agencies (Drott 2006; Fazackerley 2004; Kaiser 2004b, 2006b; Kling, Spector, and Fortuna 2004; RCUK Position Statement 2005; Waltham 2005; Zerhouni 2004, 2006).

Publishers initially viewed most forms of open access as a substantial threat. As open access gained momentum, publishers began to experiment with forms that offered new revenue streams such as author fees, dual mode, delayed, partial, and per capita (Willinsky 2006). Author-pays models, such as the Public Library of Science, are successful in the sciences, but few expect this model to be viable in the social sciences or humanities. Publishers are finding that self-archiving increases the visibility of journals and does not necessarily diminish subscription revenue. Open access to the full content of books, such as that provided by the National Academy Press, can increase book sales (Lynch 2001a, 2004). Publishers vary in whether they allow authors to post the final published form of an article. The argument in favor is to preserve the integrity of the record by assuring that the definitive form of publication is read and cited. The argument that favors the posting of author but not publisher versions is that readers still will go to the published source. Many people read author-posted versions and cite the published versions, however, whether or not they have obtained the final product.

Technology and Services for Open Access   Technology and services vary greatly by the type of open access. Open access journals differ from other forms of journals only in their economic model, and thus the same technologies can be used for each. Self-archiving on personal home pages relies on World Wide Web technology. Most institutional repositories are based on one of several open source software packages, such as DSpace (Division of Shared Cyberinfrastructure 2004; DSpace 2006; Smith 2004; Tansley, Bass, and Smith 2003), Fedora (Staples, Wayland, and Payette 2003), Greenstone (Witten and Bainbridge 2003), or e-Prints (Liu et al. 2002). Each of these systems supports the Open Archives Initiative Protocol for Metadata Harvesting (OAI-PMH) that enables searching across compliant repositories anywhere in the world. In theory, a document deposited in any compliant repository can be found by these tools (Arms 2003; OAIster 2006; Van de Sompel, Young, and Hickey 2003; Van de Sompel, Nelson et al. 2004)

At their core, repositories consist of digital library software with publishing capabilities. These technologies, in combination with open access to large collections of scholarly content, make possible an array of new services. Universities and members of their communities can become less dependent on the collections of their campus libraries. For example, people can search for digitized books to read or to mine as data sets. Humanists can analyze the use of language and the origin of ideas in these digital libraries. Scientists can assemble findings on molecules, spectra, or models of interest. Social scientists can follow policy trends over time. New reference sources such as ontologies, indexes, vocabulary maps between disciplines, and gazetteers can be generated automatically. What is at stake in open access to scholarly content, according to Clifford Lynch (2006), is a "fundamental reconceptualization" of the use of scholarly literature and scholarly evidence.

Intellectual Property

At the core of most debates about open access and other new models of scholarly publishing are competing ideas regarding intellectual property. Stakeholders differ in their opinions concerning who should hold what rights in what content, over what period of time, and at what price. The mass digitization of books raises unforeseen issues such as "opt-in" or "opt-out" models for participation by copyright owners (Lynch 2006; *Mass Digitization* 2006).

Misconceptions about the definitions and scope of intellectual property abound, therefore a brief review of the basic premises here will inform the discussions for the remainder of this book. Intellectual property is an umbrella term that incorporates copyright, patents, and trademarks. In the context of scholarly publishing, the most contentious issues are copyright, digital rights management, fair use, orphan works, the public domain, and the "information commons."

Copyright and Rights Management   The original purpose of the copyright was to promote human progress by making ideas more widely available. All too often in current discourse, though, its purpose appears to be control and protection rather than dissemination and access. Confronted by confusing copyright agreements, even experienced authors are unsure of what rights they can retain in their publications. The requirements for obtaining copyright, the range of legal protections in copyright, and the length of term have changed substantially over the course of the last century.

Most of the basic principles have been unified in recent years, although specific copyright laws are in force in each country (World International Property Organization 2006). Copyright protection no longer requires publication, as it did in the U.S. Copyright Act of 1909. Until 1978, it was necessary to place a copyright notice on a document to obtain copyright protection. Thereafter in the United States, "copyright in the work of authorship *immediately* becomes the property of the author who created the work . . . from the time the work is created in fixed form." Copyright protection covers "original works of authorship," which include "literary, dramatic, musical, artistic, and certain other intellectual works" (*Copyright Circular* 2000). The owners of the copyright have the exclusive right to do and to authorize others to do the following: *To repro-duce* the work in copies or phonorecords; To prepare *derivative works* based on the work; *To distribute copies or phonorecords* of the work to the public by sale or other transfer of ownership, or by rental, lease, or lending; *To perform the work publicly,* in the case of literary, musical, dramatic, and choreographic works, pantomimes, and motion pictures and other audiovisual works; *To display the copyrighted work publicly,* in the case of literary, musical, dramatic, and choreographic works, pantomimes, and pictorial, graphic, or sculptural works, including the individual images of a motion picture or other audiovisual work; and In the case of *sound recordings, to perform the work publicly* by means of a *digital audio transmission.* (*Copyright Circular* 2000; emphasis in original)

Thus, copyright is available for most published and unpublished works, and carries extensive rights.

Recent changes in U.S. copyright law have restricted the access to, and use of, content in digital form, and have lengthened the term of copyright. Digital rights management technologies can be used to enforce contractual agreements or place arbitrary limitations on use. Technical controls often are more restrictive than copyright laws (Cohen 2003a, 2003b; *Digital Dilemma* 2000; Elkin-Koren 2004; Felten 2003; Fox and LaMacchia 2003; Litman 2001; Samuelson 2003).

Copyright and the Public Domain   Intellectual property regimes have broad economic and policy effects on scholarly publishing and access to the scholarly record. Changes in the scope of the public domain are implicit in many discussions of copyright and open access.

The public domain, in legal terms, can be defined as "sources and types of data and information whose uses are not restricted by statutory intellectual property laws or by other legal regimes, and that are accordingly available to the public for use without authorization" (Esanu and Uhlir 2003, v). Data and information in the public domain thus are those not covered by copyright, usually because they are old enough that the copyright has expired or they are types of materials that cannot be copyrighted.

The public domain has become much smaller due to the expansion in the scope of material that can be copyrighted and the extension of the copyright term's length. The initial length of a copyright in the U.S. Constitution was fourteen years. Until 1978, the initial term was twenty-eight years, and had to be renewed to maintain protection beyond that point. The pre-1978 requirement to affix a copyright notice resulted in about 95 percent of everything written becoming part of the public domain immediately (Boyle and Jenkins 2003; Litman 2001). Under current law, documents automatically are copyrighted when set in a fixed form, whether print or digital. In the United States, a copyright now extends seventy years after the author's death, and even longer for some materials (Copyright Term Extension Act 1998).

Categories of information that previously were not copyrightable, such as business processes or sequences of data like the human genome, now fall under the copyright law. Europe adopted the Database Directive in 1996, giving extensive copyright protection to compilations in databases. Similar laws were proposed in the United States, but failed in legislation and the courts. James Boyle (2004) compared the European and U.S. database industries from the time their copyright laws began to diverge as a "natural experiment" to determine whether the European laws resulted in the promised economic benefits. Quite the opposite of predictions, the European market for databases stagnated after the directive, while the U.S. market thrived under open conditions. Based on several comparisons, Boyle concludes that the monopoly effect of the European laws created more harm than good. Of general concern is the fact that intellectual property policy, both nationally and internationally, is being determined without adequate economic analyses of its effects.

Fair Use and Orphan Works   Fair use is another complex and misunderstood aspect of copyright law. Notions of fair use, which had been interpreted by the courts, were codified in the U.S. Copyright Act of 1976 so that use "for purposes such as criticism, comment, news reporting, teaching (including multiple copies for classroom use), scholarship or research, is not an infringement of copyright" (Copyright Act 2000, sec. 107). Four conditions are considered in determining whether a use is infringing or fair: "(1) the purpose and character of the use, including whether such use is of a commercial nature or is for nonprofit educational purposes; (2) the nature of the copyrighted work; (3) amount and substantiality of the portion used in relation to the copyrighted work as a whole; and (4) the effect of the use on the potential market for or value of the copyrighted work" (Copyright Act 2000, sec. 107). Each of these four factors is a judgment call, and the final arbiter may be a judge in an infringement case. The Digital Millennium Copyright Act places additional limitations on fair use, especially for digital content. The U.S. Copyright Office offers this advice: "The safest course is always to get permission from the copyright owner before using copyrighted material" (*Copyright Circular* 2000).

As the public domain has narrowed, the need to obtain permission has expanded. For scholars in most fields, much of the scholarly evidence on which they rely is now under copyright. Some publications that previously were in the public domain were brought back under copyright with the most recent term extension. Locating the copyright owner to ask permission can be extremely difficult. Current copyright law in most countries does not require works to be registered, so no clearinghouse exists to determine who may own what.

The vagaries of fair use contribute to the "orphan works" problem. Orphan works are those for which copyright owners cannot be identified or contacted to obtain permission for use. The Library Copyright Alliance, a consortium of library associations, compiled dozens of examples in which important older works are not being quoted or reproduced because rights cannot be cleared. These include library collections of hundreds of thousands of photographs, few of which indicate the photographer, and large collections of folk music recordings, historical images, photographs from scientific expeditions, obscure novels or other literature, and articles from journals. These works are orphaned because the owner either cannot be identified (e.g., there is no name on the document, the author is deceased and the heirs are unknown, or the business has ceased and the current rights are unknown), or if identified, cannot be contacted (no details other than the name can be found), or if contacted, has never responded (Library Copyright Alliance 2005; Selected Resources on Orphan Works 2005).

In most cases, it is assumed that if the rights holders could be found, they would welcome the visibility provided by using their work in scholarly publications, textbooks, or course packs. Often the desired reuse is sufficiently obscure that it is unlikely the owner would even be aware that it occurred. Many authors, publishers, and libraries choose not to reuse works without explicit clearance, even with due diligence to locate the owners, for fear of a "land mine"—that the owner will file suit for substantial damages. Others consider these to be cowardly interpretations of fair use, arguing that the public interest is better served by actively asserting fair use rights (Courant 2006; Covey 2005; Fox and LaMacchia 2003; Unsworth et al. 2006).

Commons-Based Approaches   Digital technologies facilitate the dissemination and access of scholarly content, while current intellectual property regimes and economic policies constrain access to those same resources. Open access is one set of solutions to this paradox. Commons-based frameworks are another. Legal and policy experts have made specific proposals for reconstructing the commons for scholarly information and data through contracts.

These proposals rest on legal, political, and economic notions such as public goods and common-pool resources. As discussed earlier in the context of open science, information has the "public goods" characteristics of being nonrival and nonexcludable. Information goods and physical property such as land can be managed under common use rights. Public lands often are used as "common-pool resources" for purposes such as grazing animals or public parks (Benkler 2004; Boyle and Jenkins 2003; David 2003, 2005; Lessig 2001, 2004; Libecap 2003; Reichman and Uhlir 2003; Tragedy of the Commons? 2003; Uhlir 2006).

An information commons is not the same as the public domain, although the terms sometimes are used synonymously. The public domain is usually viewed as "unowned" content available for exploitation, while the commons may have many owners. Owners of "common use materials" can protect their collective use rights. Creative Commons (2006) licenses, for example, are a "some rights reserved" model, in contrast to a copyright, which is an "all-or-nothing" model. Copyright owners have a broad set of rights, and if the ownership is transferred, as happens when authors assign the copyright to publishers, those rights go to the new owner. Creative Commons licenses give owners ways to make their creative works available while controlling how those works are used. Among the choices available for Creative Commons licenses are whether commercial use or derivative works are allowed, and what type of licensing is associated with each. The licenses also vary in the type of authorship attribution required. Creative Commons licenses have been adapted to the legal regimes of many countries. They are being used in place of a copyright for many open access applications, including institutional repositories. Nevertheless, these licenses do not yet address the looming issue of ownership in new information products that result from mining publicly accessible content (Lynch 2006).

A number of groups, ranging from the United Nations Educational, Scientific, and Cultural Organization (UNESCO) and the Organization for Economic Cooperation and Development (OECD) to the American Library Association, are promoting the development of an "information commons" as a means to expand access to information. This approach would reconstruct the public domain through contracts and information policy (David 2005; Kranich 2004; Uhlir 2006).

Economics and Business Models
Implicit in the debates about open access and other new forms of scholarly publishing are competing assumptions about information economics and business models.

Economics of Scholarly Publishing   Although often commodified and treated as property, information has different characteristics than hard goods such as furniture or real property like land (Lessig 2004). These characteristics of information make it difficult to price. Most of the costs involved in producing information are intellectual. The first copy is expensive; subsequent reproduction and distribution are relatively inexpensive. For these reasons, most business models for information are based on demand rather than production costs (Kahin and Varian 2000; Quandt 2003; Shapiro and Varian 1999; Varian 2000).

Despite the difficulty of determining the costs to produce information, many have tried, with wildly varying results. The basic problem is determining what elements to include. Many types of services can be incorporated under the umbrella of electronic publishing. Expenses incurred for both print and electronic formats of a journal (e.g., peer review and editing) can be allocated in different ways. Accounting practices vary in where costs are charged. Continuing development costs sometimes are included and sometimes not. Costs are obscured due to cross-subsidies, especially in scholarly societies with large publishing programs. Electronic journals also vary in form and function. Some are simple replications of printed pages, while others include searching capabilities along with additional content and features not available in the print edition. Other cost elements specific to electronic publishing include digital archiving, the conversion of back files, new technologies, and customer service (Costs of Publication 2004; Esposito 2003; Odlyzko 2001, 2002; Publication Business Models 2004; Willinsky 2006).

At the dawn of electronic publishing, many predicted it would be so inexpensive that publishers would disappear, leaving their roles to authors and universities (Harnad 1991, 1995; Odlyzko 1995, 1997a, 1997b). Those proposals made many assumptions about scholarly practices, including the amount of volunteer labor that would be contributed to the publishing process (Borgman 2000a). Meanwhile, publishers continued to invest in information technology to improve their products and services.

The cost models for repositories are even less clear. They will add new costs to university budgets, with the possibility of some savings from reducing subscription costs, the duplication of resources across university libraries, and the consolidation of various information management services. These costs will vary depending on the scope and function, such as whether repositories are primarily for current access or long-term preservation. Repositories, in some form, are expected to become an essential part of the infrastructure of research universities (Duderstadt, Atkins, and Van Houweling 2002; Duderstadt, Atkins, Brown et al. 2002; Lynch 2003a; Uhlir 2006).

Business Models for Scholarly Publishing   University administrators often complain that they are paying twice to acquire publications: once for the salary of their faculty members who did the research, and a second time to buy their scholarly products back from the publishers. As long as the price for the added value was deemed reasonable, libraries and universities were willing to pay publishers their asking price for the products and services. Libraries and publishers now negotiate not only over price but also the contract terms for access, accountability, and preservation.

Because information goods typically are priced by demand rather than the production cost, publishers are leasing "bundles" to libraries. Bundle pricing is based on the number of users rather than the prices for content. As a result, different libraries may pay different prices for any given journal, reference source (e.g., online dictionaries and encyclopedias), or indexing and abstracting service. Access to electronic resources usually is leased for the time period of the contract, rather than selling subscriptions to resources that libraries continue to own. Major university libraries acquire multiple bundles to meet their collection requirements. Because the same journals may be included in multiple contracts, these libraries often are paying for duplicates. Small college libraries are more likely to expand the scope of their collections through bundled contracts than are large libraries.

The many flavors of open access have their own implicit business models. In some cases, costs are shifting from readers or readers' institutions to authors and funding agencies. In other cases, those willing to pay for immediate or full access to content or print subscriptions are subsidizing partial or delayed access for others.

The economics of open access publishing are similar to those of the open source software movement. Economists initially viewed the movement as an anomaly, questioning why so many people would contribute voluntarily to creating goods with a market value. As quality products emerged from this voluntary process, and other nonmonetary forms of recognition became more valued, the economic motivations became more apparent. The framework for sustainable economic models was not at all obvious at the beginning of the open source movement, but over time, viable models emerged. Economists are now studying the parallels between the open source and open access movements (Dalle et al. 2005; Ghosh 2005; Harhoff, Henkel, and Hippel 2003; Open Source Definition 2006; Stallman 2002; Willinsky 2005).

Business models for the publishing of digital books is far from settled. Books serve many different purposes for many different audiences. Reference books (e.g., dictionaries, thesauri, technical handbooks, and encyclopedias) made the most successful transition to digital form. These materials are most useful as databases—they are searchable, easily and frequently updated, and most users only need to view small segments at a time. Monographs intended to be read linearly are a much different matter. Despite the ease of searching for journal articles, most people still print them out if they intend to read more than a few paragraphs. Even fewer people will read a 200- to 800-page monograph on a computer screen. Printing full volumes is expensive, and printouts are more cumbersome than bound books. Even if people wish to print a book, publishers often use digital rights management technology to limit the amount that can be viewed or printed at any one time. Models that replicate library circulation by allowing only one user at a time to "check out" an electronic book also have hampered adoption. Printing on demand is a promising solution made possible by digital publishing, but is still a niche market. Publishing printed books will remain a viable market, perhaps forever, for certain kinds of content.

New business models for publishing scholarly books in digital form are emerging. As older materials are digitized, scholars are beginning to learn how they can search, mine, and recombine content. The use of older materials will provide insights into products, services, and economic models for new content. Dissertations and theses were among the first forms of monographs to adapt to digital publishing on a large scale. Authors can add images, animations, videos, and links to external sources not possible or affordable with print publication, and they reach wider audiences (Networked Digital Library 2006). The adoption of digital book publishing is slow, but some authors and publishers are starting to take advantage of the capabilities in these ways.

Business models for book publishing may follow the leased bundles models of journals. Libraries and individuals could subscribe to digital books, much as they subscribe to movies with Netflix. Rather than borrow or purchase individual titles, they may have access to a fixed number of titles at a time, or "check books out" for a fixed period of time. These models raise a host of questions about relationships among publishers, libraries, and readers with regard to the privacy of reading habits, the continuity of access, preservation, and censorship. As Lynch

(2001a) noted, losing a single book is unfortunate, but losing access to one's entire personal library would be tragic. Much is at stake in the business models and policies for access to digital books. Books carry many of the "big ideas" of a culture. We hand books down to subsequent generations. Receiving a subscription to a digital library is much different than inheriting physical artifacts that have been read, annotated, and contemplated by generations before. The conversation about the future of the book is just beginning.

6
Data: Input and Output of Scholarship

The predicted data deluge is already a reality in many fields. Scientific instruments are generating data at greater speeds, densities, and detail than heretofore possible. Older data are being digitized from print and analog forms at a prodigious rate. As data storage capacity increases and storage cost decreases, preserving these vast amounts of data is becoming feasible. Improvements in searching, analysis, and visualization tools are enabling scholars to interpret ever-larger amounts of data.

This wealth of data and tools offers an array of research opportunities for the sciences, social sciences, and humanities. Data sets are becoming an end product of research, supplementing the traditional role of scholarly publications. Open science and open scholarship depend on access to publications, and often to the data on which they are based. If related data and documents can be linked together in a scholarly information infrastructure, creative new forms of data- and information-intensive, distributed, collaborative, multidisciplinary research and learning become possible. Data are outputs of research, inputs to scholarly publications, and inputs to subsequent research and learning. Thus they are the foundation of scholarship.

The infrastructure of scholarly publishing bridges disciplines: every field produces journal articles, conference papers, and books, albeit in differing ratios. Libraries select, collect, organize, and make accessible publications of all types, from all fields. No comparable infrastructure exists for data. A few fields have mature mechanisms for publishing data in repositories. Some fields are in the stage of developing standards and practices to aggregate their data resources and make them more widely accessible. In most fields, especially outside the sciences, data practices remain local, idiosyncratic, and oriented to current usage rather than preservation, curation, and access. Most data collections—where they exist—are managed by individual agencies within disciplines, rather than by libraries or archives. Data managers usually are trained within the disciplines they serve. Only a few degree programs in information studies include courses on data management.

The lack of infrastructure for data amplifies the discontinuities in scholarly publishing. Despite common concerns, independent debates continue about access to publications and data. This chapter juxtaposes those debates, drawing attention to the importance of assessing the common issues and their implications for scholarly information infrastructure. Chapter 7 explores how information is embedded in scholarly practices, and chapter 8 compares social practices in the use of information between disciplines. Together, these three chapters appraise the complex challenges of building a comprehensive and coherent scholarly information infrastructure.

The Value Chain of Scholarship

"Value chain" is a business term originated by Michael Porter (1985) to describe the value-adding activities of an organization along the path from inbound logistics, production, outbound logistics, and on to sales, marketing, and maintenance. The concept has been extended to include entire supply chains, with particular emphasis on information flows. The term is now found in general discussions of strategy without reference to Porter. An information infrastructure that can maintain links between the associated data, publications, and interim forms of communication will enhance the value chain of scholarship. Scholarly documents and the data on which they are based are much more valuable in combination than alone.

Enhancing the value chain of scholarship is implicit in the e-Research proposals for data- and information-intensive scholarship, as discussed in chapters 2 and 3. The data deluge is an explicit driver of e-Science initiatives (Hey and Trefethen 2003, 2005), and "data-intensive science" is being promoted as a "new paradigm" for cyberinfrastructure (Gray et al. 2005). Improving access to data will benefit scholars in all fields, to varying degrees. Scientists will be able to construct better models of physical phenomena, and social and behavioral scientists will be able to develop more realistic models of complex social phenomena. Humanists can gain insights into literature and historic texts with new tools to study, analyze, explore, and compare data in digital form. Many kinds of tools are available to aggregate, integrate, and analyze data from multiple sources. Geographic information systems are used to layer spatial data for weather forecasting, demographic trends, and activities in ancient cities. Data visualization and data-mining tools are used to identify and interpret patterns, from the environmental sciences to art history. Modeling and simulation tools are used with or without empirical data, depending on the application. Databases of biological models are now freely available. Data "mashups," analogous to mashups of music and images, are used to weave together data from multiple sources or to plot many types of data on to a common map (Berman and Brady 2005; Butler 2006; *E-Resources for Research* 2005; Krieger 2006; Westrienen and Lynch 2005).

While a Research proposals include linking data and documents among the great benefits of a distributed infrastructure for scholarship, only a few exemplar projects exist. Experiments with crystallography information, for example, illustrate the difficulty of establishing standards for metadata and identifiers within one research area (Duke et al. 2005). The lack of a direct relationship between documents and data sets also hampers linking. Depending on the field and the project, one publication can draw on multiple data sets, or one data set can be used in multiple publications. Rarely can a one-to-one mapping be assumed. Some journals in the sciences store data sets and supplemental materials with published articles. These methods, however, tend to be journal specific and often proprietary, rather than generalizable models to facilitate linking between multiple sources and sites.

The most comprehensive value chain proposal is for the field of biology, linking articles in open-access journals and data repositories. Philip Bourne (2005), who is both editor in chief of the Public Library of Science journal *Computational Biology* and codirector of the Protein Data Bank, uses these two resources to illustrate the added value of linking. In this field, data are deposited, reviewed, certified, and assigned a persistent identifier. Journal articles are peer-reviewed and published with persistent identifiers. By linking these entities, the article becomes the description and documentation of the associated data set. Both the journal and the data repository can be viewed as databases. One can read an article and go directly to the data, in the context of the article, and perhaps use tools provided by the journal to analyze the data further. Conversely, one can search for a data set on a molecule or chromosome location of interest, and go directly to the papers that resulted from these data sets. The ease of moving between publications and data in this model depends on both being openly accessible. Bourne proposes several scenarios and experiments to test the generalizability of the model and to encourage community discussion.

Value of Data

Once captured in computer-readable form and documented, data can be distributed around the world—or more likely, stored in repositories that are accessible from anywhere. These data can be shared and combined in many ways. Yet generating, capturing, and managing these data in the short and long term is a nontrivial challenge. Activities that were local and tacit become global and explicit. Finding ways to scale data management practices to the growth in data volume is essential if the value in the chain is to be realized.

When publications were viewed as the sole end product of scholarship, few incentives existed to curate data for use by other researchers. Data might be destroyed or left to deteriorate once the publications on which they were based appeared. If preserved, they were likely to remain in nonstandard, local formats. As opportunities for data reuse increased, more scholars began to recognize inherent value in their data. Data from multiple research projects can be combined or compared, and results can be replicated or validated. Data- and text-mining methods enable new research to be done with old data. Research data also can be used for teaching purposes, from primary through graduate school. Another reason for the growing value of data is the recognition that many types of observations and records never can be re-created, and may become more valuable over time. Environmental and anthropological observations fall into this category, as do data from costly scientific projects such as space missions. Other types of data are important to preserve because the research site (e.g., an archaeological dig) is destroyed in the process of data production (Ananiadou et al. 2005; Borgman et al. 2005; Lord and Macdonald 2003).

In fields such as astronomy, the creation of large data sets for open access has supplanted many individual data collection projects. More than thirteen hundred scholarly papers already have resulted from analyzing data in the Sloan Digital Sky Survey, for example. Papers are listed on the Web site in a format that includes descriptions of the portion of the Sloan Digital Sky Survey (2006) data set on which they are based, publication status, links to the full text, and links to related repositories and sources. In physics, data sets are so large that they are treated as databases. Rather than transferring data to an investigator's site for analysis, investigators can conduct their analyses at the site of the data set (Gray et al. 2005; Szalay 2006).

Data collected for one purpose can prove useful many years later in distant disciplines and applications. To solve a murder in a remote mountain area of California, a small-town police department "mined obscure scientific databases," and drew on the expertise of academics in anthropology, stable isotope geochemistry, and DNA analysis. Using samples of bones, teeth, and hair, they identified the victim's ethnic origin, where she spent her childhood (near a small Zapotec Indian village in Oaxaca, Mexico), and what she ate in her childhood and adulthood. Tooth samples were used to identify the origin of the water she drank. University researchers cooperated because they saw an interesting new use of their data and methods, despite a lack of expertise in forensics. Both science and detective work were advanced in this case (Quinones 2006).

Definitions of Data

Information is a complex concept with hundreds of definitions, as discussed in chapter 3. Data is a narrower concept with fewer definitions, but also subject to many different interpretations. Definitions associated with archival information systems are useful for distinguishing notions of information and data. The following definition of data is widely accepted in this context: "A reinterpretable representation of information in a formalized manner suitable for communication, interpretation, or processing. Examples of data include a sequence of bits, a table of numbers, the characters on a page, the recording of sounds made by a person speaking, or a moon rock specimen" (*Reference Model 2002*, 1–9).

Definitions of data often arise from individual disciplines, but can apply to data used in science, technology, the social sciences, and the humanities: "*Data* are facts, numbers, letters, and symbols that describe an object, idea, condition, situation, or other factors. . . . [T]he terms *data* and *facts* are treated interchangeably, as is the case in legal contexts" (*A Question of Balance* 1999, 15).

Sources of data include observations, computations, experiments, and record keeping. *Observational* data include weather measurements, which are associated with specific places and times, and attitude surveys, which also might be associated with specific places and times (e.g., elections or natural disasters), or involve multiple places and times (e.g., cross-sectional, longitudinal studies). *Computational* data result from executing a computer model or simulation, whether for physics or cultural virtual reality. Replicating the model or simulation in the future may require extensive documentation of the hardware, software, and input data. In some cases, only the output of the model might be preserved. *Experimental* data include results from laboratory studies such as measurements of chemical reactions or from field experiments such as controlled behavioral studies. Whether sufficient data and documentation to reproduce the experiment are kept varies by the cost and reproducibility of the experiment. *Records* of government, business, and public and private life also yield useful data for scientific, social scientific, and humanistic research (Hodge and Frangakis 2005; *Long-Lived Digital Data Collections* 2005).

As is evident from the above definitions and examples, data can be many things to many people, depending on the context. A sequence of bits from seismic sensors are data to seismologists, rock samples are data to geomorphologists, recorded conversations are data to sociologists, and inscriptions in cuneiform are data to those who study Near Eastern languages. The cuneiform also could be data to archaeologists or to environmentalists tracking historical weather patterns. Similarly, the seismic data could be useful to biologists studying animal behavior. More problematic, as discussed in chapters 7 and 8, is that data carry little information in and of themselves. Data are subject to interpretation; their status as facts or evidence is determined by the people who produce, manage, and use those data.

Levels of Data

Some users want the outputs of data analysis, such as models, charts, and graphic visualizations. Others want to replicate the original experiment or research project, which usually can be done only from the less-processed forms of data. Information is lost at each stage of processing, hence careful distinctions are made between stages or levels of data.

The levels usually are based on the degree of analysis, although the terminology varies by field. For example, the "data products" of the U.S. National Aeronautics and Space Administration's Earth Observing System Data Information System are divided into six data levels. These range from level 0, which is "reconstructed, unprocessed instrument and payload data at full resolution," to "model output or results from analyses of lower level data (e.g., variables derived from multiple measurements)" at level 4. In between (levels 1A, 1B, 2, and 3) are data with increasing degrees of processing and analysis (*NASA's Earth Science Data Resources* 2004, 3–1). Quantitative social sciences and humanities data (e.g., surveys, sensing data, or archaeological data) also identify the levels of processing, but the levels often are specific to the type of data and project.

Data levels are more ambiguous in the qualitative areas of the humanities and social sciences, especially when generalizing across disciplines and research methods. Data, sources, and resources are sometimes used interchangeably, confusing matters further. Although the terms "source" and "resource" tend to be used interchangeably, they do have different meanings in the context of data and information. According to the *Oxford English Dictionary* (noun, 4.e), a source is a "work, etc., supplying information or evidence (esp. of an original or primary character) as to some fact, event, or series of these. Also, a person supplying information, an informant, a spokesman." A resource (noun, 1.a), in contrast, is "a means of supplying some want or deficiency; a stock or reserve on which one can draw when necessary." Thus, a source is the origin of some data or information, while a resource could be data, documents, collections, or services that meet some data or information need.

Humanists and social scientists frequently distinguish between primary and secondary information based on the degree of analysis. Yet this ordering sometimes conflates data, sources, and resources, as exemplified by a report that distinguishes "primary resources, e.g., books" from "secondary resources, e.g., catalogues" (*E-Resources for Research* 2005, 9). Resources also categorized as primary were sensor data, numerical data, and field notebooks, all of which would be considered data in the sciences. But rarely would books, conference proceedings, and theses that the report categorizes as primary resources be considered data, except when used for text- or data-mining purposes. Catalogs, subject indexes, citation indexes, search engines, and Web portals were classified as secondary resources. These are typically viewed as tertiary resources in the library community because they describe primary and secondary resources.

The distinctions between data, sources, and resources vary by discipline and circumstance. For the purposes of this book, primary resources are data, secondary resources are reports of research, whether publications or interim forms, and tertiary resources are catalogs, indexes, and directories that provide access to primary and secondary resources. Sources are the origins of these resources.

Sources of Data

Many sources of data exist for research, some of which are intended for reuse, and others not. Data resulting from government funding are a major source for many fields, as these include the products of research, social and economic indicators, and records of environmental monitoring. Policies for access to government-generated data vary by country, such as whether data are available with or without fees, to whom, and when. The United States is unusual in using intellectual property law to prohibit the U.S. government from claiming copyright on its publications, thereby releasing most of the data and documents produced by the government into the public domain. A significant proportion of the U.S. federal research budget (which was $55.2 billion for fiscal year 2006) is invested in data at various levels of analysis along with scientific and technical information such as reports, technical papers, and research articles (Copyright Act 2000).

Jerome Reichman and Paul Uhlir (2003) include private-sector data, along with government-generated and government-funded data, as a traditional part of the "research commons." Data that are generated privately, especially through government contracts, may be available for reuse through licensing or other agreements. Some data in the research commons are available through repositories, while others remain with the researchers who generated them. Scholars often acquire data from each other privately, whether through contracts, research collaborations, or on an exchange basis.

Policies to Encourage Data Sharing   The need to leverage investments in research data is not a new issue in science policy. Policy studies on strategies to promote the sharing of research data have appeared with increasing frequency since the mid-1980s (Fienberg, Martin, and Straf 1985). E-science and cyberinfrastructure programs have renewed the concerns of funding agencies, and intensified their efforts to encourage data sharing by their grantees. The United Kingdom established a digital curation center to explore tools and policies for permanent access to research data (Digital Curation Centre 2006). The United States issued a policy document that addresses national and international requirements to maintain data for research and education purposes (*Long-Lived Digital Data Collections* 2005). Other countries, funding agencies, and multinational agencies are establishing policies to require or encourage the digital deposit of data and documents. Several of the policies and studies recognize the need for international coordination, as data that originate in different countries are often compared and combined (Arzberger et al. 2004a, 2004b; *Bits of Power* 1997; Esanu and Uhlir 2003, 2004; Lord and Macdonald 2003; Wouters 2002; Wouters and Schroder 2003).

Investigators sometimes are required by clauses in contracts for their research grants to share data. For example, the standard clause in contracts from the U.S. National Science Foundation states the responsibility of investigators to share their data:

Investigators are expected to share with other researchers, at no more than incremental cost and within a reasonable time, the primary data, samples, physical collections and other supporting materials created or gathered in the course of work under NSF grants. Grantees are expected to encourage and facilitate such sharing. Privileged or confidential information should be released only in a form that protects the privacy of individuals and subjects involved (*Grant Policy Manual* 2001, sec. 734b).

Policies on data ownership, retention, and sharing vary within and between agencies of the U.S. government. Some divisions and programs of the NSF have more specific policies about their data-sharing requirements than those in the *Grant Policy Manual*. The National Institutes of Health has multiple policies that apply to data, model organisms, and publications. The definitions of data to which these rules apply also vary (*Access to and Retention of Research Data* 2006). Not only is international coordination an issue; the coordination of policies within countries is problematic.

Data resulting from grants made by nongovernmental agencies such as universities and philanthropic foundations do not automatically fall into the public domain. Often these data are made available through contracts similar to those of the NSF. Wellcome Trust and Mellon Foundations, for example, have promulgated policies to promote the sharing of data and publications (Explanatory Statement 2001; Wellcome Trust Policy 2001; Wellcome Trust Position Statement 2005).

Policies and strategies to share research data have been promulgated for several decades, but the same issues persist. One explanation for this is the lack of enforcement of current policies. Publication requirements are enforced more stringently than are data-sharing requirements. Reviewers of subsequent grant proposals assess the published products of previous research, yet they rarely put much weight on whether data from prior grants were made available. Some agencies are starting to require data management plans in proposals for large grants, which raises awareness of these issues. A few are considering withholding funds until data are deposited. The investigators, though, may lack both the expertise to write plans that guarantee data curation and the institutional infrastructure to implement those plans. Government funding agencies in the United States, for instance, hold universities responsible for maintaining data and other records of research for at least three years, but provide few specific guidelines for what is to be maintained and in what form (*Access to and Retention of Research Data* 2006).

Another explanation is the lack of incentives on the part of researchers. In only a few fields do researchers consistently deposit their data in a form intended for reuse by other individuals and communities. In most fields, scholars have few incentives to invest the necessary effort to make data useful to others; indeed, many disincentives exist. Data are tangible products of research, but they also are intangible commodities that represent evidence and trust in social relationships, issues that are explored in chapters 7 and 8.

Generation of New Forms of Data The documentary record of research, communications, and public and private life is an expanding source of data. While record keeping always has been essential to research, new technologies make it possible to generate and capture far more data than was previously possible. In areas such as biodiversity, efforts are under way to document all known species of flora and fauna, in multiple competing repositories (All Species Foundation 2004; Web of Life 2006). Data collection projects in biodiversity, the human genome, and digital sky surveys for astronomy are examples of a new kind of science where the database is an end in itself. The information collection effort in these and other areas of science and technology worldwide is "heroic" (Bowker 2005).

Social science and humanities researchers are mining the documentation that results from interpersonal conversations and other informal interactions taking place online. Social scientists also are generating and assembling large amounts of empirical data, some of which they collect online in the form of surveys, observations, and indicators. Other data sources include technologies such as digital photography and global positioning systems that generate massive amounts of data, and the digitization of censuses and records of business, government, and culture (e.g., genealogy and local history). Once in digital form, these data can be analyzed for scientific, social scientific, and humanistic research and learning. New audiences will find new and unanticipated uses.

Data Collections   The array of data collections available for research purposes also is expanding. The three functional categories identified in a report on scientific data apply to most disciplines. *Research data collections* are those that result from one or more research projects, have had minimal processing or curation, and may or may not conform to community standards. These may be novel types of data for which no applicable standards exist. In most such cases, the investigators did not intend to maintain the data beyond the end of the project, either due to their small audience or a lack of funding. *Resource or community data collections* serve a single disciplinary community or research specialty. These digital collections usually do meet community-level standards, and may have played a significant role in the selection or establishment of those standards. Funding agencies support the maintenance of these collections, but often for unknown periods due to changing agency priorities. The third category is *reference data collections*. These typically are intended to serve a large and diverse user community that includes scholars, students, and educators from multiple disciplines and institutions. Long-term funding, adherence to community standards and practices, and professional management are essential for reference data collections. They may have multiple sources of funding, both national and international (*Long-Lived Digital Data Collections* 2005).

Any of these three types of collections can exist in one physical location or be distributed. An entity that began as a research data collection might later become a community data collection, and ultimately a reference data collection as it grows in size, use, and sophistication. The Protein Data Bank (2006) is a notable example of a data collection that started small and over the course of three decades became an essential international resource.

Other examples of reference data collections in the sciences include the British Atmospheric Data Centre (2006), which operates over the UK National Grid as part of the e-Science efforts, and the Earth Science Data Centers (2006) of NASA, with collections such as land processes, snow and ice, ocean processes, and geospatial data. Fields such as seismology and earthquake engineering each have their own data collections (Incorporated Research Institutions for Seismology 2006; National Earthquake Engineering Simulation Cyberinfrastructure Center 2006).

Ecology and biodiversity have multiple data collections and networks (Bain and Michener 2002; Conservation Commons 2006; Higgins, Berkley, and Jones 2002; Knowledge Network for Biocomplexity 2006). Data centers can be one function of a distributed research network (Biomedical Informatics Research Network 2006; Geosciences Network 2006; Global Earth Observation System of Systems 2006; National Ecological Observatory Network 2006). The Virtual Observatory, which has partners from the United States, Canada, the United Kingdom, Europe, Australia, Japan, and elsewhere, is a distributed network. Common data standards facilitate searching within and across partner collections (International Virtual Observatory Alliance 2006). While deposit and access are highly distributed, many of the U.S.-funded data repositories reside on computers operated by the San Diego Supercomputer Center, located in Southern California (Data Central 2006).

Examples of reference data collections in the social sciences include the UK Data Archive (2006) and longitudinal survey data based at the University of Michigan (Survey Research Center 2006), the University of California, Berkeley (Survey Research Center 2005), and the University of California, Los Angeles (Higher Education Research Institute 2006). Similar repositories exist in the humanities (Arts and Humanities Data Service 2006).

Growth of Data

Measuring the growth of data or information is notoriously difficult because of the many ways in which these terms can be defined. Peter Lyman and Hal Varian (2003) documented information growth, both digital and analog (e.g., telephone conversations), using rigorous methods to ensure consistency across sources and over time. They estimated that "the amount of new information stored on paper, film, magnetic, and optical media" roughly doubled between 1999 and 2002, at a growth rate of about 30 percent per year. The Lyman and Varian data are frequently cited as estimates for the scale and growth rate of digital data and documents. Hey and Trefethen (2003), in the same year, offered examples of databases in the sciences, social sciences, and medicine that were predicted to grow at rates of many terabytes per year. In the time since these statistics were last updated, digital cameras, cell phones (many with cameras), personal digital assistants, portable media players, sensor networks, and other technologies that generate and store large amounts of data have proliferated. Thus, the volume of new information (data and documents) being stored presumably is growing at a rate greater than 30 percent annually.

Scientific data definitely are growing in volume at a prodigious rate. The Sloan Digital Sky Survey, for example, has increased in density by about four orders of magnitude from the first survey in 1990 to the fifth survey, which will run to 2008. Today's instruments can capture as much data in four nights as the original instruments were able to capture in ten years. The storage cost for each of the five data releases is comparable, however, due to technical advances. These data are heavily used, with about 160 million Web page hits in five years. While about two-thirds of these page hits are by indexing robots, one-third of the traffic is for scientific purposes (Szalay 2006). Embedded networked sensing may achieve comparable increases in the volume of data for applications in the environmental sciences, seismology, and other areas. In one study in progress at the Center for Embedded Networked Sensing (2006), investigators spent about eighteen months hand coding 60,000 digital images of root growth that were captured while monitoring soil conditions. If computer vision algorithms can be made accurate enough to identify changes in these roots, the researchers plan to capture 60,000 images per *day*. This is but one instance of how sensor network technology is being used to increase the frequency, spatial density, and accuracy of in situ data collection.

Interpreting Data

Gathering or generating data is often the simplest part of the research process. Designing the study, determining what to collect and how, calibrating instruments (whether sensors or surveys), cleaning and verifying the data, and analyzing and interpreting the results usually are far more labor intensive, and require much more expertise. Those who collected the data are in the best position to interpret them, as they understand the context for the questions asked and the decisions made in the collection and analysis processes. Documenting data for one's own immediate use is a straightforward process compared to documenting them for use by others not involved in the study.

Without associated documentation, data are just strings of numbers, variables, images, text passages, audio or video clips, or other discrete elements. In the case of digital data, they may be uninterpretable without the associated software. Data are much less "self-describing" than are journal articles and other text-based communication. Documenting data accurately for curatorial and sharing purposes depends more heavily on metadata and standards for data structures. Getting individuals, teams, and communities to agree on standards for data description cuts to the very core of the theory, method, instruments, and paradigms of a field, all of which change continuously. Due to the degree of consensus required for use and documentation, data collections tend to be associated with research specialties rather than broad disciplinary communities. Often these are internally consistent "data silos" that do not interoperate with collections in related fields (Bishop, Van House, and Buttenfield 2003; Bowker 2005; Bowker and Star 1999; Ribes and Bowker forthcoming; Van House 2003, 2004).

Most problematic in interpreting data collected by others is the degree of tacit knowledge required—issues that are pursued in more depth in chapters 7 and 8. Fundamental information such as instrument settings or field conditions may not be documented because it is part of the day-to-day knowledge or practices of the investigators. To interpret the data of others, scholars often rely on their own knowledge of field practices and their familiarity with the practices of the investigators who collected them. Similarly, the process of sharing knowledge among local teams is so embedded in practice that many essential aspects of gathering, processing, and interpreting data remain unspoken and undocumented. Professional data managers and data scientists add value to data collections by working with the producers and users of data to improve documentation, and thereby facilitate reuse.

The Role of Data in Scholarly Communication

Data are integral to the publication of scholarly work, and can be communicated separately from the publication process, yet little attention has been paid specifically to the role of data in scholarly communication. Drawing direct comparisons between documents and data in scholarly communication is not easily done, however. One reason is the lack of direct mapping between the two. Data are inputs and outputs of scholarly publishing, but also can be used for other purposes such as teaching and policymaking. The management of data can be independent of the scholarly publishing process, as data can be used and reused for multiple publications over long periods of time. Not all scholarly publications include data, and those that do may draw them from multiple sources.

A second difficulty in making comparisons is the lack of a common literature. The literature about documents addresses social, behavioral, professional (e.g., libraries and publishing), and policy issues (e.g., intellectual property). That literature spans several centuries of research and practice. The study of data is much more recent, and addresses the behavior of individuals (e.g., ethnographic studies of the generation of data in scientific laboratories), technical matters (e.g., metadata and interoperability), or policy issues (e.g., intellectual property, preservation and curation, and international exchanges). Third, the use of data varies so much across disciplines that only general commonalities can be identified. Each field has its empiricists who collect data and its theoreticians who rely on data gathered by others. Each field also has its own practices for determining acceptable choices of data, and ways in which those data are analyzed or interpreted.

Comparisons between disciplines in the use of documents and data are the subject of chapter 8. Here, the focus is on commonalities across disciplines that underlie the value chain of data and documents. These commonalities are analyzed in terms of the tripartite model of scholarly communication functions introduced in chapter 4: legitimization, dissemination, and access, preservation, and curation.

Legitimization of Data

The legitimization function of scholarly communication incorporates authority, quality control, certification, registration (in the scholarly record), priority, and trustworthiness. In the days when publishing was done exclusively in print, peer-reviewed publications accomplished all aspects of legitimization. Electronic publishing already has begun to separate them. Registration and certification, for example, might occur independently as a research report moves from a less formal to a more formal status in the scholarly record of a field.

The value chain of scholarship rests on the quality of the data from which conclusions are drawn. Arguments for access to data include the needs to verify and replicate findings and to combine data from multiple sources. If the data are available, then a more rigorous review of the scholarship becomes possible. If data are accepted as an end product of scholarly work, as is the case in some fields, then data must be legitimized by means similar to the peer review of publications. Yet the peer review of publications has few analogs for data. Questions loom about how data should be legitimized in the value chain and at what point in their life cycle that review should occur. The chain of trust, like other chains, is only as strong as its weakest link (Atkins et al. 2003; Berman and Brady 2005; Bowker 2005; Lyon 2003).

Trust in Data   In the peer review of scholarly publications, questions arise such as "who is a peer?" and "whom do you trust to evaluate the quality of scholarly documents?" Similar questions arise in the peer review of data. These concerns are addressed differently when assessed in the context of a publication reporting data and in the submission of a data set to a repository. Prepublication review includes assessments of whether the choice of data, method of collection, analysis, and reporting of the results meet community standards. This form of peer review assesses the value of the data in the context of the manuscript, considering whether the data are adequate and appropriate for the narrative. When readers are judging which publications to trust, they also are judging whether to trust the data reported in those publications.

Trust in other scholars' data is partly a function of whether those data can be interpreted. Personal knowledge of the authors' research methods is one source of trust. Others include indicators such as the peer-review processes of the journal or repository. The criteria may vary depending on whether the data are central to their research questions or will be used for context, as is often the case with micrometeorologic measurements or census records. Potential users of data often contact authors by e-mail or telephone to learn more about the origins of data, methods, and associated analysis processes. Metadata that identifies the data origins and subsequent transformations can increase trust in these data. Not only could such provenance metadata be used as selection criteria, their existence may encourage scholars to contribute data to the community, as credit could be assigned more accurately and publicly. Provenance metadata also could enable processed data to be "rolled back" through transformations for the purposes of correcting errors at interim stages or computing different transformations (Buneman, Khanna, and Tan 2000, 2001; Lynch 2001c; Rajasekar and Moore 2001; Zimmerman forthcoming).

Trust can be placed in the data repository, whether a research, resource, or reference data collection. Some of these acquire content through submission by investigators, and others by harvesting. Harvesting can be done automatically through Web crawling or manually through hand selection. In either case, the quality criteria for selection are determined by the managers of data collections, usually in consultation with their community. The peer review of data submitted to repositories can be as rigorous as the peer review of publications. The quality of the selection and curation of a collection should engender trust in the community, which is an argument for investing in reference data collections (*CODATA-CENDI Forum* 2005; Hodge and Frangakis 2005).

Registration of Data   The registration of scholarly documents occurs when the item is made publicly available through some mechanism recognized by others in the field. It can occur with data, but the mechanisms are not as well established or consistent.

Registration is most consistent for data that are contributed to, or originate in, public data collections. Government-generated data (e.g., census or econometric indicators) are, in effect, registered at the time they appear in publicly available government databases. Investigator-generated data are registered when a data set is added to a public repository such as the Biomedical Informatics Research Network (2006), Geosciences Network (2006), Protein Data Bank (2006), Arts and Humanities Data Service (2006), or one of the social survey research centers (Survey Research Center, Institute for Social Research 2006; Survey Research Center, UC-Berkeley, 2005). Each repository has its own procedures and requirements, but all include some form of registration and acknowledgment of receipt. Once accepted for deposit and archived, the data become available to the public or participating partners. Deposited data sets usually receive a persistent identifier, which assists in citing and linking publications and data.

The registration of data occurs, in a sense, when they are presented in a journal article or other publication. Nevertheless, it is difficult to trace this form of registration because the data and data collections from which they are drawn are not consistently cited in publications. Indexing and cataloging practices do not cover these aspects of documents well, either. Searching for the existence of data, types of data, data from a specific collection, or data gathered by a specific research method in publications is difficult because of the lack of consistent bibliographic control. Part of the problem is the lack of a common name space for data and data sets. Some progress is being made in this area—for example, the creation of Digital Object Identifiers for data (Paskin 2005). Better description methods, if widely adopted, would improve the registration of data through the publication process. Standard referencing practices would also enhance the value chain by improving the ability to link documents and data sources.

Certification of Data   The certification of research reports occurs when a manuscript has passed a quality-control check such as peer review. As with registration, the certification processes for data are less well established and less consistent across fields than for scholarly publications.

For publications that report data, the data are implicitly certified as part of the peer-review process. Reviewing data in the context of a publication, however, is much different than assessing their accuracy and veracity for reuse. Reviewers are expected to assess the face validity of the data, but only in certain fields are they expected to recompute analyses, verify mathematical proofs, or inspect original sources. Only a few scientific journals require authors to provide the full data set. Some fields, such as crystallography, involve data structures and methods amenable to computational verification. Crystallography reviewers can verify data with software that determines whether the molecules or protein structures are consistent with prior results in the field, flagging outliers or other suspicious data points for authors to investigate for accuracy. In most disciplines, data are not sufficiently consistent that computational verification is possible. Even manual verification is infeasible for most forms of qualitative data, as they tend to be highly contextualized observations. In the social sciences and humanities, full verification of data might require travel to distant libraries and archives.

While the ethical responsibility of peer reviewing is taken seriously, few scholars are able or willing to spend hours, days, or weeks verifying the data in an article they have been asked to review. Reviewing is typically an unpaid contribution to the scholarly community. When cases of fraudulent data in publications occur, as discussed in chapter 4, questions are raised about whether the peer reviewers should have caught them, and whether journals should change their review processes to look more closely at the data. These issues figured prominently in the Woo-Suk Hwang case. Referee responsibilities for assessing data also were central to an earlier case in physics in which research "findings adorned the covers of *Nature* and *Science*" (Brumfiel 2002). The editor at *Nature* who was responsible for accepting several of the papers later deemed fraudulent acknowledged that some referees had questioned how the data were interpreted (*Report of the Investigation Committee* 2002).

Cases such as these undermine the public trust in science. They are expensive for the scholarly community in many respects. Researchers may devote weeks, months, or years trying to replicate major findings that turn out to have been falsified. Indeed, it is often these attempts to replicate that lead to the identification of falsified data.

Certifying the quality of data, in any sense comparable to certifying the quality of scholarly articles, is among the most problematic aspects of the value chain. Individual repositories have standards and best practices for the description of data, the use of specific metadata formats, documentation, and other characteristics. Even with these standards and practices in place, it is difficult to judge how "good" deposited data are in any objective sense. Data centers vary widely in their evaluation practices, from a cursory review of structural characteristics to intensive reviews by panels of scientific peers. Some data centers ask other scientists to "test drive the data" before accepting it.

In 2000, the United States passed the Data Quality Act, which applies to data issued by the U.S. government, but the act is controversial and already subject to lawsuits (Kaiser 2006a). Public concern over the incomplete release of safety data by pharmaceutical companies for anti-depressants and COX-2 inhibitors such as Vioxx resulted in proposed U.S. federal and state legislation to create clinical trials databases that are openly available. These proposals also are controversial as they risk substituting data release for rigorous scientific review (Fisher 2006). The lack of agreed-on metrics or criteria for assessing data quality, or determining what data deserve to be long-lived, has become an urgent policy issue (Audit Checklist 2005; *CODATA-CENDI Forum* 2005; Higgins, Berkley, and Jones 2002; Hodge and Frangakis 2005; Wiser, Bellingham, and Burrows 2001).

Informal, community-based quality-control mechanisms continue to play important roles in data assessment. A common saying in the data community is "data that get used, improve." Subsequent users of data sets provide feedback to the original investigators about likely errors or inconsistencies that can be corrected in the data set and in future data collection efforts. External concerns such as public trust in science are putting internal pressures on communities to formalize data certification mechanisms. As data reuse becomes more common, the pressure on reviewers to assess and certify data will only increase.

Dissemination of Data

In scholarly publishing, dissemination is the process of making the community aware of the existence of the products of research and writing. Just as with digital documents, chaos reigns in the dissemination of data, and the line between dissemination and access is blurred.

Scholars in all fields are eager to make their publications widely known. In only a handful of fields are they eager to publish their data, however. Fields in which data dissemination is the norm, such as human genome, protein data structures, and seismology, are still exceptions in scholarship. Data deposit in these fields arose largely through bottom-up efforts by scientists who saw great value in shared community access. They have established norms whereby data deposit is mandatory or strongly encouraged as a condition of journal publication.

Other fields are promoting data dissemination by establishing common instrumentation for data collection and the associated metadata structures. The National Ecological Observatory Network (2006), Global

Earth Observation System of Systems (2006), Collaborative Large-Scale Engineering Analysis Network for Environmental Research (2006), and Geosciences Network (2006)—all nascent networks of observatories— are notable examples of this trend. Whether they will be successful in data dissemination on a large scale remains to be seen. A study of one of the longest-running observatory networks reveals some of the many challenges in the consistent capture and maintenance of these forms of data (Karasti, Baker, and Halkola 2006). Little is known about why data sharing varies so much by field and specialty. Today's data-sharing communities may be the leading edge of a broad trend, indicative of areas where data sharing has the greatest value, or coincidental occurrences of where funding was available for large coordinated projects.

National and international policies to encourage data sharing will increase awareness of sharing mechanisms such as data repositories, metadata standards, and commons-based licenses. Reference data collections staff offer tutorials and workshops, and make presentations at conferences as means of disseminating their data resources. Dissemination is more challenging for collections of diverse data such as cultural resources, whose communities are less readily bounded. National libraries and archives, for example, have international audiences that cut across disciplines, applications, and age groups. They promote awareness of their collections by various outreach mechanisms, including talks, brochures, and articles in general-interest publications. These institutions also take advantage of distributed technologies for dissemination by maintaining rich Web sites describing their collections, which can be indexed by search engines.

Access, Preservation, and Curation of Data

Data differ from scholarly publications in many aspects of access, preservation, and curation. "Permanent access," which has become a term of art in library and archival practices, applies both to data and documents. Preservation can simply imply storage. Content must be kept in forms that are continually usable. Active curation is required for permanent access to digital records, which typically requires migrating data, documents, and the links between them through changes in hardware and software (Hodge and Frangakis 2005).

Some History   Data preservation and curation are not new problems. Record keeping by governments began long before the scholarly equivalent. Government records of taxes, economic activity, and demographics are among the oldest documents still in existence. Extremely old public records, such as those of the Roman Empire and early Chinese dynasties, continue to be useful to historians, economists, demographers, political scientists, sociologists, and many others. Early climate data, whether from observations, experiments, or records of taxes on crop yields, provide important benchmarks for the study of climate change.

Each new generation of technology offers new ways to manage data. Herman Hollerith invented the 80-column punched card for the 1890 U.S. census. His card technology was the basis for the company that became IBM (Hollerith Census Machine 2006). Data that are recorded by one generation of technology must be transferred to the next if those data are to remain accessible. The fields known as "systematics" or "taxonomy," for example, have kept detailed data of flora and fauna for at least two centuries, adapting their practices to the technologies of the time (Hine 1995; Knapp et al. 2002).

Data survive, or fail to survive, for a number of reasons. Government records often exist because legislation requires their capture and maintenance, but they are subject to changes in priorities. Over the centuries, new regimes sometimes destroyed the records of previous ones. Observational, experimental, and computational data endure because generations of scholars, archivists, and librarians have invested the effort, time, and money to curate them. It is impossible to know what has been lost due to changes in priorities and discontinuities in curation. Once lost, few of these data ever can be recovered. Examples of tragic data loss include data on magnetic tapes from early NASA missions, records of where hazardous waste is stored, and the destruction of the national library in Sarajevo (Sanders 1998). While not yet officially declared lost, NASA has been unable to locate the original video recording of the first moon landing in 1969, despite eighteen months of searching. Backups exist of these and many other missing records from the Apollo lunar missions, but they are of lower quality than the originals (Reuters 2006; Update: Apollo 11 Tapes 2006).

Searching and Finding   Searching for publications can require navigating through many digital libraries, search engines, catalogs, and indexes. Searching for data sets is similar when the quest is for current digital data in public collections. These processes can be tightly coupled, especially in cases where publications and data sets are linked, and both are publicly accessible. As Bourne (2005) illustrates, journals can be treated as databases, enabling one to search for a publication and retrieve the data on which it is based, or to search for data and retrieve the publications in which the data are described and analyzed. That ideal implementation of the value chain of e-Research remains rare, however.

Searching for publications also is a means to discover data of interest. If an article reporting data does not include the data or links to them, readers may contact the authors to request the data. In the absence of data repositories, this is the most common method by which data are shared. Authors may or may not provide the requested data, though.

Several factors complicate the search for data. Researchers within a field may know what repositories exist and where, but locating the existence of repositories in adjacent or distant disciplines is hampered by the lack of a common registry or descriptive practices. Inconsistent referencing practices, as noted earlier in the section on registration, apply both to repositories and data sets. One paper may reference a collection and another may reference a subset of the same collection. Reconciling citation units within and between collections is a fundamental problem in data provenance. To use a common example, the Bible can be cited in many ways, such as the aggregate of "the Bible" (any version), a specific edition ("King James"), specific books of the Bible, a particular book and chapter, or a specific book, chapter, and verse. These combinations can be structured in many ways, making it difficult for information retrieval algorithms to reconcile them automatically (Buneman 2005; Buneman, Khanna, and Tan 2000).

One of the primary barriers to discovering data of interest is the level of description. Many data sets and collections are described only as aggregates. A collection of ten thousand photographs may be described as "photographs of the Southwest United States," and have some temporal descriptors such as "late nineteenth century" or "1920s." Such a collection might be a rich source of information on the culture and landscape of the period, and might contain images of people, plants, or other objects of interest. Describing each object individually is prohibitively expensive, which is why archival practice focuses on finding aids that describe the collections sufficiently to match users and content. Many of the finding aids to important collections around the world have yet to be digitized. Making these tertiary resources available online will aid in their discovery, enabling scholars to spend their time on using, rather than locating, collections of interest.

Permanent Access   As with scholarly documents, the urgent questions are what will be saved, and by whom? Difficult as these questions are to address for documents, they are even harder with data, as the volume of data has grown much faster than have the practices, policies, or business models to preserve them. As with documents, those data for which someone takes responsibility are most likely to be preserved.

Far more data exist than can possibly be collected into repositories or curated. While data protection policy focuses on data that are long-lived—that is, a period of time long enough "for there to be concern about the impacts of changing technologies" (*Reference Model* 2002, 1–11)—little agreement exists on what data deserve to be long-lived. Just because data have managed to survive for a while does not necessarily mean that they are worth perpetuating. Conversely, new data that appear at first to be ephemeral may have significant value over the longer term.

The extremes of the spectrum are easiest to identify. Cultural heritage data and the products of large international science projects remain permanently valuable to many scholars, and to society as a whole. Data from small exploratory studies that failed to confirm hypotheses rarely are preserved. The majority of data fall somewhere in between. The choice of what to save is often a matter of who perceives the long-term value, and is in a position to ensure access and curation. Some data have been preserved, only to have minimal use, while other data with great potential usefulness were lost. Anticipating the future value of data is frequently as much art as science. The consensus of individual communities is the most promising means to set preservation criteria.

Determining who will save the data is equally problematic. The number of data repositories is growing, but not fast enough to capture all the potentially useful data being generated. Many of the repositories that do exist are focused more on increasing their assets to achieve a critical mass, whether through harvesting or deposit programs, than they are on permanent access to those data (Hodge and Frangakis 2005).

University libraries and archives often are mentioned as potential managers for data collections, given their expertise in selection, collection, organization, and preservation. These institutions have a long history of maintaining access to paper documents and records. Yet few university libraries or archives have the resources or expertise to curate digital data. As the demand for data curators grows, education for data management will need to scale up from a craft learned on the job. Expanding the human capacity to provide permanent access to research data is another urgent challenge in maintaining the value chain of scholarship (Carlson 2006; King et al. 2006).

The literature on data management is rife with calls for business models to sustain permanent access to data. While studies of cost-benefit trade-offs and sustainable sources of funding are needed, the economic issues are too complex to be solved by good management alone. The economics of scholarly data and information is a complex topic that is well beyond the scope of this book. Issues of who pays, for what, and at what stage in the life cycle of data have deep roots in the infrastructure for research funding and in university and governmental policies and practices. Many of these factors differ by country and discipline.

Weak Links in the Value Chain

The value chain of scholarly communication rests on permanent access not only to scholarly documents and the data on which they are based but the ability to maintain links between data and documents. Assuring permanent access to either type of resource involves difficult policy, funding, and management issues. Data and documents that are related intellectually in the value chain may be owned or controlled by different entities, each of which has different policies, practices, and schedules for access and preservation. Links might be permanent bindings between objects or relationships that must be reconstructed at the time of retrieval. Policies and practices for data ownership, control, and access are shifting, and often are in conflict.

Reuse of Data

Among the most obvious criteria for determining what data deserve to be long-lived is the likelihood of reuse. Future uses are difficult to anticipate, however, because reuse is often for purposes other than those for which the data were created. The next question may be, reuse by whom? If the investigators are the only ones likely to reuse the data, then local management may be sufficient. If a large audience for the data can be identified, then investment in documentation and dissemination is justified. Most data fall in between, and potential uses of the data may not be apparent to those who collected them.

The cost per use is one metric to determine whether and how long to curate the data. This metric is problematic because it favors popular collections and may not weight temporal factors adequately. Collections or items may remain dormant for years, and suddenly become popular due to current events, new discoveries, or changes in technology. Medical literature found a broad general audience when Medline became available to the public. Interest in the U.S. census of 1900 surged when the National Archives made it available online. Nineteenth-century novels that were considered "trashy" at the time of publication are among the most popular books in old library collections.

Business models based on usage, whether for profit or other forms of value, depend on valid and reliable usage metrics. The ability to measure the use of information is a challenge that plagues libraries and archives. Should use be measured in terms of days, weeks, months, years, decades, or centuries? Is a hit on the Web site of a library, archive, or data collection a "use"? Is downloading a data set or an article? Is citing a data set or an article? Is replicating a study based on publicly available data and documents? Is a profitable company or product resulting from data analysis, even if years later, a use? If so, how should the value be allocated between multiple data and documents used, and over what period of time? Replicating a study is a much more extensive use than is viewing a Web page, but how can the difference in value be measured? Similarly, downloading or photocopying an article is a different use than citing a document. No satisfactory means has been found to reconcile these types of uses in assessing the value of library collections. Measuring the use of data will be no easier than measuring the use of documents.

Technology and Services

The preservation of and access to documents has a long enough history that people disagree about the means rather than the ends. With data, the long-term value is less clearly established. One of the findings of a U.S. policy review on data and documents is that "key social, political, and economic issues remain, including the need to develop a 'will to preserve and provide permanent access' within the scientific and technical community and society in general" (Hodge and Frangakis 2005, 7). Data repositories must justify their existence continually, while setting priorities for services that address both short- and long-term requirements. Repositories are components of the scholarly infrastructure. Investments in infrastructure always compete for funds against spending on new projects, whether for research grants, roads, or energy plants.

Progress in standards for data, metadata, and especially the preservation of metadata is improving discovery, use, and curation (e.g., PREMIS 2006). It remains much easier, though, to search for specific types of objects than for compound objects, as suites of standards exist for each of text, images, audio, video, and numerical data. Searching across document and data types is an old problem in information retrieval (Croft 1995). Progress also is being made in searching across data repositories and data types, which will aid in data discovery (Bekaert and Van de Sompel 2006b; Biozon 2006; Conservation Commons 2006).

Intellectual Property and Economics

As the value of data increases, so does the frequency of clashes over their ownership and control. Digital research data are being viewed as "a third stream of scientific capital," with "human capital and the instrumental capital goods" being the first two streams (Schroder 2003). The intellectual property concerns for data are similar to those for publications, although the discussions have remained largely separate until recently. Current efforts to create an "information commons for science" address documents and data together (David 2005; Uhlir 2006). The obstacles to the use of copyrighted materials for educational purposes apply not only to scholarly publications and data but to popular culture such as television, movies, music, newspapers and other mass media (Fisher and McGeveran 2006). These are not issues that will be resolved soon; rather, they are ongoing policy discussions. As noted in chapter 5, economists are studying the parallels between the open-source software movement and open access to publications and data to identify viable economic and policy frameworks (Dalle et al. 2005; Willinsky 2005).

Science Commons (2006), a project of Creative Commons, has identified three areas of concern with regard to data as intellectual property. First are the expansions of intellectual property law that can create additional obstacles to sharing data among scientists or with the public. Second is the potential for forced choices between "all rights reserved" and "no rights reserved." Science Commons is promoting a commons-based license as a middle ground of "some rights reserved." The third area of concern is "a wasteful data economy" in which data are not made available, either through policies or practices.

Examples of these three problems abound. In Europe, scientific data collections fall within the scope of the Database Directive (discussed in chapter 5), which hinders their use in research. While the data per se cannot be copyrighted, the database is copyrighted and the data cannot be extracted without the permission of the rights holder. Thus, it is the database creator/owner who has the rights to release the data and not the creator of the data (Elliott 2005). Other problems arise from patents and copyrights on scientific data. In the United States, for example, two broad patents on human embryonic stem cells that were granted in the early years of this research area (1998 and 2001) have constrained domestic research, leading to lawsuits challenging the patents, and great differences between countries in the conditions and prices for access to cell lines (Loring and Campbell 2006).

Profit versus Value   Simply putting data online will create new audiences for it, if the success of online book and music stores is an appropriate predictor. Chris Anderson's (2004, 2006) argument—that all information has its audience, and use depends primarily on availability—

has attracted a following in business and academic circles. Services such as Amazon.com, BarnesandNoble.com, Netflix, and eBay have introduced old and obscure materials to new audiences, and revived interest in many scholarly books. Entertainment content has a "long-tailed" distribution curve, to use Anderson's metaphor. A small number of books, movies, and music are popular "hits," in his terminology. These are frequently purchased or rented, while the majority of products are requested rarely, if at all. In these for-profit environments, income from the occasional purchase of items in the tail may cover the costs of offering them for sale or rent. Making obscure books, music, and movies available requires putting extant metadata online (e.g., the catalog records of authors, artists, actors, musicians, and titles of works) and having a business network to deliver items when requested.

This business model does not necessarily transfer to research data, despite the likelihood of a similarly long-tailed distribution. A small portion of research data will receive heavy usage, while the majority of data would be used infrequently, if at all. Data have great value, but rarely can they be priced in ways comparable to books, movies, and music. Data resulting from publicly funded research projects usually are public goods, yet many forms of research data are subject to intellectual property constraints. Patented information or specimens, as in the human embryonic stem cell cases noted above, are particularly problematic. Patent owners, whether public or private, can charge universities tens of thousands of dollars for access to the research data they control.

Research data also differ from popular entertainment commodities in that their scope is not readily defined. Almost anything is research data to someone, as discussed in chapter 8. A general catalog of research data is unlikely to emerge, given the vast diversity of data sources, types, and audiences. Multiple, federated digital libraries of research data are a more feasible model. Initial investments in identifying and describing research data are best directed at the "hits" that will receive wide use. Some sought-after content such as the Sloan Digital Sky Survey already is online. The lessons learned about how popular resources are used can guide choices of subsequent data to make available online.

Undoubtedly, many forms of research data would receive an audience if they were made available. Finding the appropriate economic models is a key challenge for e-Research. Government agencies and publicly supported data collections may not necessarily show a profit but they must show value and justify their investments.

Public Domain for Data Historically, U.S. information policy has been among the most open in the world, encouraging the broadest possible dissemination of data produced by the government or government-funded sources. Government-funded or sponsored research in the United States is by far the largest source of public domain data for scientific research and education, and hence the value and influence of these data is hard to overstate. These policies were implemented by prohibiting intellectual property protection of these types of data, reinforcing the "sharing ethos of science" through research funding contracts, and by other "immunities and exceptions that favor science and education" (Reichman and Uhlir 2003, 318–319).

Much of the credit for the success of the U.S. scholarly enterprise is attributed to the open access regime that fuels scholarly progress (David 2003; Esanu and Uhlir 2003, 2004; Reichman and Uhlir 2003; Stokes 1997). Studies conducted in Europe and elsewhere also have documented the social and economic benefits of open access to public data (Arzberger et al. 2004b; Boyle 2004; Boyle and Jenkins 2003).

Concerns about constricting the public domain for research data and the resulting scholarly, economic, and policy implications have been the focus of policy studies in the United States (*A Question of Balance* 1999; *Bits of Power* 1997; Esanu and Uhlir 2003, 2004; *Digital Dilemma* 2000), the United Kingdom (*E-Resources for Research* 2005; Lord and Macdonald 2003; *Specification for the Second Phase Nodes* 2004; Woolgar 2003), Canada (Strong and Leach 2005), and by international bodies such as the Organization for Economic Cooperation and Development (Arzberger et al. 2004b; Normile 2004). While these discussions began with scientific, technical, and medical information, they have since expanded into the social sciences and humanities arenas (Berman and Brady 2005; Besek 2003; *E-Resources for Research* 2005; Smith et al. 2004; Unsworth et al. 2006).

Commons-based mechanisms are among the most promising avenues to expand access to research data. The commons approach to licensing places greater emphasis on attribution and control than on monetary compensation. For example, the rights to reuse and embargo periods for release can be specified. Generalized licenses may reduce the effort required to negotiate individual intellectual property agreements for each collaborative relationship. While scholars recognize the need for agreements about data access, many are concerned about the potential for a large bureaucracy resulting from an excessive number of individual contracts. Pressure for standard contracts may come from research administrators outside the purview of scholars conducting the research (David 2003, 2004; David and Spence 2003; Reichman and Uhlir 2003).

Open Access, Open Data   The arguments for open access to data are comparable to those for open access to publications. Open access promotes the principles of open science and scholarship, removes barriers to participation in research and education, and serves the public good. "Open" connotes minimal restrictions on use, but not necessarily without a fee. Content may be freely available, but not for "free."

Technology and policy considerations differ for access to publications and to data, however. When publications are sought for reading and printing, then access to documents as whole units is sufficient. When data are required for research purposes, or when publications or other texts are treated as data, more discrete access is needed. Unstructured text, especially if fixed in file formats such as PDF, cannot easily be extracted, mined, or recombined. Interest in text and data mining has amplified the tensions between using institutional repositories to provide access to current publications and creating new models of publishing, as discussed in chapter 5.

The availability of large bodies of text offers "stunning opportunities" for new forms of scholarship (Lynch 2006). In the sciences, papers can be mined in search of specific chemicals, molecules, chromosome locations, or other discrete elements. Chemistry is in the forefront of this trend. Chemical nomenclature was standardized a century ago, making the literature amenable to automatic searching. Charts and tables in publications are necessary for interpreting data, but insufficient to search for data or to reanalyze them. Peter Murray-Rust coined the term "open data" to distinguish machine-understandable data from other forms of open access. His team also coined the term "datument" to emphasize the computational use of documents, and initiated CML, the chemical markup language (based in XML, or extensible markup language) to facilitate access to chemical data (Murray-Rust 2005; Murray-Rust and Rzepa 2004; Murray-Rust, Mitchell, and Rzepa 2005; Murray-Rust et al. 2004). These technical advances met with political opposition, as chemistry data can have great economic value. Those who control chemical data in proprietary databases have resisted open access initiatives by governments and funding agencies (Marris 2005).

Text and data mining offer similar grand challenges in the humanities and social sciences. Gregory Crane (2006) provides some answers to the question "What do you do with a million books?" Two obvious answers include the extraction of information about people, places, and events, and machine translation between languages. As digital libraries of books grow through scanning efforts such as Google Print, the Open Content Alliance, the Million Books Project, and comparable projects in Europe and China, and as more books are published in digital form, technical advances in data description, analysis, and verification are essential. These large collections differ from earlier, smaller efforts on several dimensions. They are much larger in scale, the content is more heterogeneous in topic and language, the granularity increases when individual words can be tagged, they will be "noisier" than their well-curated predecessors, and their audience is more diverse, reaching the general public in addition to the scholarly community. Computer scientists are working jointly with humanists, linguists, and other domain specialists to parse texts, extract named entities and places, augment optical character recognition techniques, and advance the state of the art of information retrieval. Still, clearing the rights for access to these texts is often a harder problem than the technical requirements, which is why open access for digital books is such a great concern. Kevin Kelly (2006, 71) proposes that copyrights should be balanced with "copyduties" to allow works to be searched: "no search, no copyright" would radically alter the nature of access to information in the digital age.

7

Building an Infrastructure for Information

Scholarly publishing is in the midst of restructuring, and data are becoming a valued end product of scholarship. New technologies, economics, and policies enable scholars to disseminate their publications more widely and to explore new research questions by mining publicly accessible data. Yet scholars' participation in self-archiving and institutional repositories is low, and data sharing is the norm in only a few fields.

The risks in constructing grand technological infrastructures lie in assuming that "if we build it, they will come." Scholars make large investments of time and money in creating their work environments. They become accustomed to their own tools to conduct research, analyze and manage their data, and publish their papers. They teach their students to use these same tools and resources, and hand down practices from one academic generation to the next. Scholars do adopt new technologies when they see sufficient advantage in doing so, but they adapt them to their needs. Thus, to determine what infrastructure tools and services will be most useful, it is necessary to understand who the users are and how they conduct their research.

Construction of an advanced scholarly information infrastructure is well under way, but it is far from complete, making this an optimal time to assess design directions. The later in the systems design process that problems are identified, the more difficult they are to correct. Early decisions create "path dependency," in economic terms, predetermining the trajectory of subsequent technologies (Arthur 1989; Callon 1994; David 1985).

The development of scholarly information infrastructure has focused much more on building a framework to support any kind of information without regard to its meaning—an infrastructure *of* information, as discussed in chapter 3—than on building a framework to provide context for the interpretation, use, and reuse of content—an infrastructure *for* information. This chapter explores scholarly practices associated with the uses of information and data. The intent is to integrate the earlier discussions of scholarly communication and to lay the groundwork for comparisons between disciplines in chapter 8.

Scholarly Disciplines

Scholarship is organized by discipline and topic of study, so an examination of the nature of disciplinarity is a good place to begin an exploration of scholarly practices. Today's notions of disciplines are fairly recent, however, and no simple or widely accepted typology of disciplines exists. Until the late nineteenth century, all scholarly fields were considered sciences, regardless of their research methods. Universities now organize academic units by discipline and field, but the boundaries vary greatly within and between countries, and local considerations often determine the scope of a department. Common interests create departments, and divisive interests often separate them (Becher 1989; Klein 1996). For the purposes of discussion here, a dictionary definition of discipline will suffice: "(a) branch of instruction or education; a department of learning or knowledge; a science or art in its educational aspect" (*Oxford English Dictionary*, noun, 2). The word "field" is sometimes used synonymously with discipline. Discipline is employed here in the broader sense, such as the sciences, social sciences, and humanities, and field is used in the narrower sense, such as chemistry, sociology, and classics. Even narrower are specialties such as crystallography, art history, or the social studies of science.

From an information perspective, the interesting differences between disciplines include research methods, such as empirical, analytic, or interpretative (Meadows 1998), and "knowledge territories" such as basic characteristics (method, or pure or applied orientation), shared theories or ideologies, common techniques, and sociocultural characteristics (e.g., the people-to-problem ratio, frequency and form of publication, or incidence of collaborative work) (Becher 1989).

Disciplinarity and Interdisciplinarity

Although disciplines in their present form are only about a century old, they are powerful forces in the academy. Individual scholars self-identify with their fields more than with their universities, seeing their departments as local chapters of national and international enterprises. A strong affiliation does not preclude crossing boundaries to other fields, however. Interest in interdisciplinary work has been growing since the 1920s, long predating e-Research. Terms such as inter-, multi-, and cross-disciplinary often are used interchangeably. In other cases, these terms are used either to distinguish between knowledge brought *to* a collaboration and knowledge resulting *from* a collaboration, or between research that integrates knowledge from multiple disciplines and that which borrows tools, methods, or theories (Clark 1983; Cummings and Kiesler 2004; Klein 1993, 1996; Machlup and Mansfield 1983; Sonnenwald 2006, 2007).

Disciplines, Communities, and Cultures

Disciplines and fields are often too large an aggregate on which to draw inferences about behavior. Communities of practice and epistemic cultures are groupings commonly used in the social studies of science. Communities of practice is a concept originated by Jean Lave and Etienne Wenger (1991; Wenger 1998) to describe how knowledge is learned and shared within groups. The concept has been much studied and extended. Carsten Osterlund and Paul Carlile (2005) compare "relational forces" found in seminal works on communities of practice: difference (e.g., identity, and variance in practice based on experience or knowledge), dependencies (e.g., how newcomers become integrated into a community), change (e.g., shifts in knowledge or a person's role), power (e.g., ability to control role in community), blurring categorical boundaries (e.g., learning, identity, and innovation), empirical practices (e.g., unit of activity and temporal factors), and structures, whether emergent or historically constituted. Communities of practice, as construed in this body of research, are much smaller than disciplines, fields, or even research specialties. They are more likely to be working groups or perhaps small invisible colleges.

Epistemic cultures, in contrast, are neither disciplines nor communities. They are more a set of "arrangements and mechanisms" associated with the processes of constructing knowledge, and include individuals, groups, artifacts, and technologies (Knorr-Cetina 1999; Van House 2004). Common to both communities of practice and epistemic cultures is the idea that knowledge is situated and local. Nancy Van House (2004, 40) summarizes this perspective succinctly: "There is no 'view from nowhere'—knowledge is always situated in a place, time, conditions, practices, and understandings. There is no single knowledge, but multiple knowledges."

Boundaries, Barriers, and Bridges

The existence of boundaries and borders between groups is among the classical concepts of social science, and one that has received renewed attention since the mid-1990s (Lamont and Molnar 2002). Most of this body of work considers social boundaries as manifestations of social differences. Boundaries keep people in professional, ethnic, or other social groups, and keep others out. Examinations and board certifications, such as those required in law and medicine, mark the formal dividing line between those authorized to practice in a field and those not. Other fields mark territory by requiring certain degrees (e.g., a Master of Business Administration, Master of Library and Information Science, or Master of Fine Arts), but lack the legal enforcement status of law or medicine, where practicing without a license is a punishable offense.

Although the doctorate (usually a Ph.D. or D.Phil.) has become a requirement for scholarly and research positions, disciplines rarely certify membership in a formal way. Lacking other certifications, disciplinary affiliation is an important marker for professional identity as groups compete for legitimacy of expertise and authority. Being a member of the faculty of a history or computer science department enables one to self-identify as a historian or computer scientist, respectively. When faculty members have terminal degrees in fields other than those in which they teach, they may self-identify with the field of their degree or department, depending on the situation. History departments may employ faculty with degrees in anthropology, philosophy, or cultural studies, and computer science departments often hire faculty with degrees in mathematics or engineering, for example (Abbott 1988; Gieryn 1999).

In contrast to the usual view of social boundaries as "markers of difference" (Lamont and Molnar 2002, 180), Susan Leigh Star and her collaborators conceptualize "boundary objects" as entities straddling the borders between groups. These are objects that can facilitate communication, but that also highlight differences between groups. The categories of boundary objects include material artifacts, organizational forms, procedures, or conceptual spaces. Organizational forms such as standards for data structures, metadata, and tools that rely on these standards are boundary objects that enable groups to exchange data and documents (Bowker and Star 1999; Star and Griesemer 1989; Star, Bowker, and Neumann 2003).

Digital libraries are a canonical form of boundary object, because their contents can be useful to multiple communities, allowing them to carry meaning across the borders of multiple groups. For example, data collected by one team for a specific purpose (e.g., biologists studying birdsongs as behavioral indicators) may be useful not only to biologists studying the relationships between the locations of bird and plant species but also to anthropologists studying the relationships between the music patterns of humans and indigenous bird species. Each of these groups will interpret these data differently, despite drawing them from a common repository (Bishop and Star 1996; Bishop, Van House, and Buttenfield 2003; Borgman et al. 2005).

Professional Identity

Changes in scholarly practices such as mining data sets can have significant influences on scholars' professional identity. Shifts in technology and funding that favor computational methods may disadvantage those whose research is based on fieldwork, for instance. These transitions can create a double bind for these research areas. More funding for computational modeling may mean less funding for field research to collect new data. Not only does less data get collected but fewer students are trained in field methods. Substantial expertise in data collection and the ability to interpret older data may be lost. Conversely, those who rely on computational methods must have sufficient knowledge of how the data were collected to be able to interpret them. They too require adequate training in data collection methods. As noted in chapter 6, trust in data often is based on trust in the scholars who collected the data. Research specialties that use more computational methods are seeking a balance between a steady supply of new data, avoiding duplicate or redundant data collection where possible, and training students in field research and computational methods. Thus, new technologies for producing and analyzing data may have subtle but important influences on scholars' career paths (Lamb and Davidson 2005; Lievrouw 1995; Zimmerman forthcoming).

Scholarly Practices

Scholars engage in many professional practices, not all of which will inform the design of infrastructure. The practices related to information creation and use offer the most promise for design. Leah Lievrouw's (1988) typology of "four programs" of scholarly communication remains useful in this respect, as she identified a continuum of assumptions about information ranging from the inherent value in artifacts to the social construction of information, independent of objective measures of value. Her four programs are artifact, user, network, and laboratory studies. None of these programs of research provides a comprehensive view of the social practices associated with information. Taken together, they offer an array of perspectives on systems design.

The analysis presented in this section draws on Lievrouw's typology, but builds an argument in a different sequence. First is a review of studies of individual behavior in the use of information. Second is an assessment of studies of the artifacts of scholarly communication, such as publications, data, and interim products like research notes. The third perspective on scholarly practices is that of laboratory studies. These take a contrasting approach in which information is socially constructed, rather than grounded in objective reality. Last is collaboration, which is a subset of Lievrouw's category of network studies. Information is the fabric of collaboration. By understanding more about how scholars collaborate and compete, we can design better tools, services, and policies for information access and sharing.

Seeking and Using Information

How individuals seek and use information is among the most researched topics of scholarly practices, with thousands of studies since the 1940s. The findings from this body of work can be used to improve retrieval mechanisms and automatic methods for information organization, and to set priorities for resources to be digitized.

Information-Seeking Behavior The earliest behavioral research addressed the use of printed indexes, abstracts, and scholarly publications. Later work studied the use of online databases and library catalogs. Research topics include behavior, the use of specific sources, and how this use varies over time. The largest body of information-seeking research focuses on scholars, especially on scientists and engineers. Progress on information-seeking research is assessed regularly in the *Annual Review of Information Science and Technology* chapters on "information needs and uses" (e.g., Allen 1969; Crane 1971; Dervin and Nilan 1986; Kling and Callahan 2003; Menzel 1966; Paisley 1968; Pettigrew, Fidel, and Bruce 2001; Solomon 2002). Donald Case (2002) provides the most comprehensive synthesis of this massive literature, which ranges across library and information science, information studies, communication, sociology, and other disciplines.

Information seeking tends to have several stages, which may occur in sequence, overlap, or be repeated. Among the common elements of models of information-seeking behavior are the choice of systems or sources, the satisfaction or nonsatisfaction of "need," the success or failure of the search process, and individual characteristics (demographics, cognitive aspects, and motivations). Other variables include interpersonal relationships, the degree of active or passive searching, time pressure (the immediacy of need for information), and the relevance or utility of the results. One of the findings worth revisiting is that prior to the 1990s, accessibility was the most important consideration in source selection. As information access improved, relevance and quality became the most important selection factors, which has implications for the design of searching tools (Case 2002, chapter 6).

Several theoretical approaches can be taken to information-seeking behavior, including the principle of least effort, uses and gratifications, sense making, media use as social action, play theory, and entertainment theory. People often choose the path of least resistance, settling for the information nearest at hand rather than the best or most authoritative sources. Uses and gratifications has a long history in communication research, considering the choices that people make among information channels and what they expect to get from those channels (Blumler and Katz 1974). Sense making draws on a variety of philosophical traditions to identify "gaps" people perceive in their knowledge that lead to seeking information that might fill those gaps (Dervin 1992). The implications for design are that searching is not just about keywords. Searching has multiple motivations, each of which influence people's choices among results (Case 2002, chapter 7).

Scholars seem to be even more dependent on library services for access to scholarly publications than in the past. Personal subscriptions to journals have declined substantially. Faculty and students have been known to panic when unable to access online library services, whether due to system failures or incorrect authentication settings. Students' dependence on these services becomes especially apparent when they graduate and no longer have access. Librarians learned early in the days of online catalogs that people rely on online sources, even if those sources are incomplete. Older material accessible only via the card catalog was quickly "widowed," which was a primary motivation for libraries to complete the retrospective conversion of card catalogs to digital form. The same phenomenon occurred with online access to journals. The more access that libraries provide, the greater the depth of coverage that users expect. The use of printed indexes in libraries has dropped to near zero, although printed finding aids remain popular in archives (I. Anderson 2004; Bishop 1999; Borgman 2000a; Lynch 2003b; Tenopir and King 2002; Tibbo 2003).

Reading habits also are changing. Scholars are reading more articles now than they were a decade or two earlier, as evidenced by longitudinal studies of reading behavior. They are not spending more time reading; they appear to be spending less time per article. High-achieving scholars, based on several measures (awards, high-level committees, etc.), read more articles than do lower-achieving scholars (Tenopir 2003; Tenopir and King 2000, 2002).

Humans remain important sources of information, whether for direct answers (i.e., the person is the information resource) or pointers to other sources (e.g., people, data sets, documents, libraries, government agencies, and research groups). E-mail, videoconferencing, online chats, telephones, text messaging, and other communication technologies extend the opportunities for interpersonal information seeking.

Temporal Factors   Information seeking and use exhibit several temporal characteristics that have implications for the design of information infrastructure. Reading patterns, the distribution of citations, and the availability of resources online all vary over time. Availability influences use in ways that suggest priorities for digitization and access.

While reading patterns are assumed to vary by the age of the material, little empirical research exists on this topic. Carol Tenopir and Donald W. King (1998, 2000, 2002, 2004) have conducted the most recent and extensive behavioral research on the temporal characteristics of scholarly reading. They found that most of the time scholars spend reading is devoted to articles less than two years old. New articles often receive only a quick read. Older works receive more attention, and frequently are being read for a second or third time. As much as 60 percent of the reading of the scientists, social scientists, and engineers studied was devoted to articles less than nine months old, but 7 percent of the time was devoted to works more than twelve years old (Tenopir and King 1998). They found that the time spent to browse, search for, and then locate an article roughly doubled from 1984 to 2000 (2002, 263). The time difference lies in locating, displaying, and downloading or printing digital articles versus locating and photocopying printed articles. Their measures do not appear to include the time spent going to libraries, however. Once found, the time spent reading or using the article was about the same.

A larger body of research on the temporal characteristics of scholars' use of publications relies on bibliometric indicators instead of direct observation or interviews. The age distribution of the references in articles is an indicator of what scholars are reading, but it is not a direct measurement. The temporal distributions of citations, however, may reflect the rate at which ideas are adopted and absorbed by a community (Barnett, Fink, and Debus 1989). Despite the methodological limitations, temporal metrics such as "half-life" often are used to select which journals to acquire, cancel, and curate (Line 1993). The concept of half-life, borrowed from physics, has been used since the 1950s to estimate the decay rate of citations to individual articles or journals (Száva-Kováts 2002). J. D. Bernal (1959, 86) defined "the true half-life of a particular piece of information" as "the time after publication up to which half the uses (references) or enquiries" about it are made. Because this statistic is hard to determine, he offered the more practical measure of the "back half-life" of a group of similar pieces of information (e.g., papers in a given journal) as the time in which half the requests for, or references to, the information have occurred (quoted in Száva-Kováts 2002, 1100).

Half-life studies are used to identify temporal variations in the use of literature by discipline. Most such studies indicate that the humanities have the longest citation half-life and the sciences the shortest, with the social sciences in between (Meadows 1998). In other words, scientific articles reference the most recent publications and humanities articles the least recent ones.

George Barnett, Edward Fink, and Mary Beth Debus (1989) constructed a "mathematical model of citation age" to test this ordering, using large data sets from each of the *Science Citation Index, Social Sciences Citation Index*, and *Arts and Humanities Citation Index* published by the ISI. In each of these three sets, the citation age of an average article reaches its peak in less than two years, with the arts and humanities peaking soonest (1.164 years), and the social sciences peaking latest (1.752 years), contrary to expectations. The maximum proportion of citations did have the predicted ordering, with science the highest, and the arts and humanities the lowest. While the models presumed that citation rates were stable over time, a close examination of the data revealed that citations per article increased substantially over the time period of the study (in science, from 12.14 per article in 1961 to 16 in 1986; in the social sciences, from 7.07 in 1970 to 15.6 in 1986; no citation per article data were given for the arts and humanities). Indicators in the ISI citators are the least valid for the arts and humanities because they only include references made by journal articles. Much of the core humanities literature consists of books, and references made by books are not included in the ISI data.

Content that is online gets more use than that which is not, and use varies by age of content. Thus, the next question to ask is how the temporal distribution of online content varies by field. The depth of coverage in the *ISI Web of Knowledge*, which is among the most comprehensive online bibliographic databases, is deepest in the sciences, shallower in the social sciences, and most shallow in the humanities. The *Science Citation Index* has articles online back to 1900 (although the earlier material is highly selective), the *Social Sciences Citation Index* back to 1956, and the *Arts and Humanities Citation Index* back to 1975 (as of September 2006). *Scopus*, which claims to be "the largest abstract and citation database" (*Scopus* in Detail 2006), indexes science, technology, medicine, and social sciences literature from publishers, OAI-compliant repositories, and the World Wide Web only for the prior ten years. Its coverage is based on market research indicating that a decade of literature satisfies 86 percent of the need (*Scopus* FAQ 2006). The *Web of Knowledge*, then, embraces the long tail business model, providing access to older and less-used content, while *Scopus* embraces the hits model of offering only the most used content. The proportion also follows Chris Anderson's (2004a, 2006) model, which claims that about 15 percent of the total use is from the tail of the distribution.

The sciences have the longest runs of journals online. Scientists read and publish in journals more than in books, and they rely on more recent literature than do other disciplines. Therefore, scientists are the most advantaged in accessing the relevant publications for their research. Humanists and social scientists are relatively disadvantaged, having shorter runs of their journals online, and relying on books in addition to journals, and drawing on older literature. As the access to monographic literature online improves through mass digitization projects and digital publishing, the balance between disciplines will improve. Until the retrospective conversion of journals in the social sciences and humanities is accomplished, these fields will continue to have less of the literature they require for their research online. Some older journals provide only the most recent few years online, while others offer all their back issues (e.g, the entire 125-plus years of *Science*, stretching back to 1880, is online). In other cases, especially outside the sciences and medicine, only the back issues are online. JSTOR, a name derived from "journal storage," has improved the online access to important scholarly journals. It began in 1995 and already contains articles from more than 400 journals issued by some 230 publishers (Guthrie 2001; JSTOR 2006). To obtain the rights to digitize older materials, JSTOR avoids jeopardizing the current revenue stream of publishers. Digitization continues up to a "moving wall," which is usually three to five years prior to the present.

Scholarly Artifacts

Scholarly artifacts such as publications often are treated as objective commodities that can be counted as indicators of productivity. Publications also can embody the relationships between cited and citing authors. Features such as page length, section headings, choice of bibliographic referencing styles, and use of footnotes can be used to identify scholarly practices in a field. The highly stylized nature of academic writing reflects the ways in which knowledge is constructed. Academic writing both shapes and is shaped by disciplinary norms (Bazerman 1981, 1988; Cronin 2005; Edge 1979; Kircz 1998).

Forms and Genres Printed books and journals are constrained in form by the limitations of the physical page and the economics of printing and distribution. Electronic publications have far fewer constraints. Multimedia and interactive content can be included or linked, length limits are constrained by editorial policy rather than the cost of printing and mailing each journal issue, and the content can be revised or supplemented after publication. Despite these new capabilities, books and journal articles as literary genres have been remarkably stable for several centuries. Books and journals take somewhat different forms within each field, and these too are relatively stable.

The stability of these forms reflects scholarly practices rather than a rejection of technological capabilities per se. Particularly counterintuitive is the fact that existing forms do not necessarily serve scholars well, yet new genres that take advantage of the malleable, mutable, and mobile nature of digital objects have been slow to emerge. Most of today's online journals are "nauseatingly identical" (Lynch 2004, 610) to print journals. They replicate the printed page, complete with page numbers, footnotes, and often dual columns. These formats are difficult to read on-screen, and not surprisingly, most people print articles on to paper if they plan to read more than a few paragraphs. The difficulty of reading monographs on-screen also has limited the popularity of digital books and e-book readers.

Print formats and their emulations hinder scholarly reading practices. Behavioral studies reveal that people skim titles, abstracts, and sometimes conclusions to determine whether to read the full article. Sometimes they then will read the full article closely from beginning to end, but more often they skip around through methods, results, tables, or other sections that are of immediate interest. Rarely are journal articles read in a linear fashion. Scholarly readers disaggregate the contents of articles, and later may reaggregate them in new ways to mobilize the information for use in their own writing (Bishop 1999; Dillon 1991, 1994). The same practices appear to occur with scholarly monographs, but even less is known here. Book readers also skim and skip around, only rarely reading entire monographs from beginning to end (Thompson 2005).

These practices were recognized in the early days of electronic publishing, resulting in proposals to decompose and index articles in modular forms, and use hypertext features to enable readers to follow their own paths (Davenport and Cronin 1990; Kircz 1998; Nelson 2004; Shneiderman 2003; Shneiderman and Kearsley 1989). Yet scholars are not making extensive use of the sophisticated tools for search refinement or reading that do exist, mostly because of apparent mismatches between the tools and their interests (Bishop 1999; Foster and Gibbons 2005; King et al. 2006). The failures of early technologies may have discouraged subsequent designers of electronic publishing tools, but clearly it is time to revisit the implications of these practices for the design of scholarly information infrastructure.

Reading between the Lines   Authors use these forms and genres to tell the narrative story of their research, analysis, or interpretation. Research in scholarly communication can study these forms to determine the cultural practices of a field or specialty. Research in computer and information science can study these forms to identify features that can be described automatically such as names and places, and to extract units that can be disaggregated such as tables and figures. Large bodies of text already are available for mining. Algorithms can be devised and tested on known literatures and adapted to other literatures as they become digitized, and as forms and genres evolve in the future.

Journal literature is an obvious starting point to improve the tools for information seeking, reading, use, and reuse. Not only are these essential scholarly resources, but explicit guides exist that describe these forms and genres. They are known as "style" or "publication" manuals. Most publication manuals are issued by publishers or professional associations (e.g., *Chicago Manual of Style* 2003; Gibaldi 1988; *Publication Manual of the American Psychological Association* 2001; *Style Manuals and Citation Guides* 2006). Some of these are used by journals in many other fields. For example, those of the American Psychological Association (APA) and Modern Language Association are influential well beyond the societies that publish them. *The Bluebook* (2005) for law is specific to that field, however. Individual journals may require authors to use a standard style manual for the basic editorial structure, but maintain a specific format for bibliographic references. Software to manage references in scholarly writing such as Endnote, ProCite, and RefWorks may include several hundred templates for bibliographic references for individual journals.

Because the guidance in style manuals reflects the practices of a field, they identify specific features and explain their purposes. The genre features described include the sequence of headings for introduction, literature review, research methods, discussion, and results, and specific instructions and examples for how to reference other works. One of the main differences between styles is whether the bibliographic references are identified by author name or number in the text. Journals using the American Psychological Association (APA) style, popular in the social sciences, reference documents in the text by the name of authors and date of publication; these are shown in parentheses at the appropriate point in the text. The MIT Press house style differs from the APA style largely in punctuation. Science and technology journals tend to reference documents in the text by number, or a code consisting of letters of the author name and publication date (e.g., [BORG99] for Borgman 1999). This approach saves space in the text, but requires the reader to flip back and forth between the text and reference lists. Some numerical formats list references by the sequence of referencing in the text and others number the references in alphabetic order. Humanities journals typically use footnotes for references. Each footnote may include one or more bibliographic reference. The footnotes are presented in the order of referencing and may be shown only at the bottom of the page of text. This model facilitates reading references in the context of the narrative, but does not give the reader a summary listing of the literature on which the article is based.

Styles also differ in the granularity of referencing. The APA and other formats that list author names in the text usually reference the full publication. Specific page numbers in the referenced work are necessary only for direct quotations. Conversely, humanities articles not only refer to specific pages of a cited work, they may include extensive glosses about it in the footnotes. Footnotes in humanities journals also are used for side commentary that can run a page or more. In law review articles, it is not unusual to have more lines on a page devoted to footnotes than to the narrative. Legal footnotes include references to publications, statutes, legal cases, and commentary. The APA style contrasts strongly with the practices of the humanities and legal fields, explicitly discouraging the use of footnotes for substantive material because "they are distracting to the reader and expensive to include in printed material" (*Publication Manual of the American Psychological Association* 2001, 163).

Despite these many differences in referencing practices, the data elements in bibliographic references are fairly consistent. Most include author names, dates, and the name of the article or book. For journal articles, the volume, issue, and page numbers are included. The publisher and place are included for books. Conference proceedings, edited books, and other formats have similar data elements. The journal *Science* is unusual in omitting the titles of journal articles from citations, but otherwise uses standard elements. Law also differs from other fields by citing laws and legal cases, which have their own citation structure (e.g., "In re Drexel Burnham Lambert Group, Inc., 120 B.R. 724 (Bankr. S.D.N.Y. 1990)") (*The Bluebook* 2005).

Journal articles differ in a few other ways that can be useful in information organization and retrieval. Scientific articles tend to be shorter,
although this varies by field within the sciences. Law review articles can
run up to one hundred pages or more, with hundreds of footnotes. Some
are nearly the length of books in the social sciences and humanities.

The styles of artifacts are sufficiently consistent within and distinct
between fields that automatic methods can be used to extract specific elements. Within style categories, features such as tables, charts, and bibliographic references can be identified. For instance in chemistry, which is
highly structured, entities such as molecules can be extracted. By contrast, in more amorphous textual styles, such as those of humanities
monographs, the techniques used to extract entities may vary by the language and the period of work. Once disaggregated, tools to discover
these sections and entities will facilitate scholarly use. Readers can move
more easily between problem statements and methods, compare tables
of findings from related articles, and skim relevant headings. Behaviors
such as these that are not well supported in print environments, or in
digital emulations of them, can be supported with new infrastructure
tools and services.

Constructing Knowledge
Artifacts of scholarly communication, such as publications and e-mail
messages, are objects that can be used as whole units, or disaggregated
and reaggregated. They can be counted, mined, stored, retrieved, and
preserved. Artifacts are not knowledge, however. Knowledge is socially
constructed. It cannot be recorded directly into data sets, publications,
or digital libraries. Only representations of knowledge can be disseminated, preserved, curated, and accessed. Reducing knowledge to artifacts
that can be exchanged over a distributed computer network inhibits communication, sometimes severely.

Representing Knowledge   Research on "representational practice," as
this construct is known in the social studies of science, offers insights
into how scholars use devices such as "graphs, diagrams, equations,
models, photographs, instrumental inscriptions, written reports, computer programs, laboratory conversations, and hybrid forms of these"

(Lynch and Woolgar 1988, 1). Artifacts such as data and documents are not "natural objects"; rather, they are products of culture that have evolved over long periods of time within specialties, fields, and disciplines. The documents of scientific research, in particular, are referred to as "inscriptions" (Latour 1988; Latour and Woolgar 1979, 1986; Lynch and Woolgar 1988). These are the canonical "lab studies" in Lievrouw's (1988) typology.

Among the relevant findings of this body of work is that scholars draw on a rich array of expertise, methods, and tools to conduct research. As experts, they rarely follow "cookbooks" with explicit instructions. Methods texts offer guidance, but scholarship advances by identifying innovative new sources of data and clever research designs. Scholars usually begin with a set of tools and methods, which they adjust as contingencies arise. Decisions are based on multiple types of evidence. It is the ability to think like detectives, combining observations, data, and logical relationships, that marks good scholarship in any field. This is not to say that research methods are ad hoc. A biologist goes out in the field with hypotheses to test, but may be unable to specify the exact placement of instruments in advance of their deployment. Once in the field, local conditions such as soil moisture, temperature, and water chemistry determine the optimal positions from which to take samples and observations. Similarly, the historian travels to an archive known to contain papers and manuscripts on events of interest, and then refines his or her searching and note taking based on the specific material found. In both cases, data collection is guided by standards of evidence for their fields (Hilborn and Mangel 1997; Lewis-Beck, Bryman, and Liao 2003; Lynch and Woolgar 1988; Scheiner 2004).

Tacit Knowledge   The greatest barrier—and challenge—in designing tools and services to facilitate knowledge representation is tacit knowledge. It is inherent in the nature of expertise that much knowledge is abstract, deeply embedded, and not readily represented in documentary forms. While scholars do record details of methods, sources, and decisions in research notebooks or their digital equivalents, tacit knowledge that may be essential to interpreting data often remains undocumented. Knowledge that would be familiar to others on a project—such as field conditions or instrument settings—or to other scholars in a specialty—such as the rules for gaining access to historical archives—are the least likely to be recorded. Specialties, by definition, have their own sets of practices to facilitate communication, including methods and terminology. Tacit knowledge that eases communication within a specialty often marks the boundary between specialties. To conduct research in an adjacent field or to use their data, one may need to identify unmentioned methods and reconcile variances in terminology.

Tacit knowledge is most easily explained by the epistemological distinction between knowing *how* and knowing *that* (Duguid 2005). Gilbert Ryle (1949) and Michael Polanyi (1966) both argue that knowledge of *how* and *that* are complementary. We can learn *that* from codified information such as reading articles and books. To learn *how* requires applying knowledge of *that* in practice. For example, students can learn from a textbook that two chemicals interact in a certain way; until they have tried the experiment in a laboratory, they will not understand how the interaction works. Simple science experiments with vinegar and baking soda are much more effective for learning how acids and bases react than is any lecture or text.

Communities of practice are as much about practice as about community. Individuals learn *how* from practice in their communities; the codified knowledge of *that* is necessarily incomplete (Davenport and Hall 2002; Knorr-Cetina 1999). Tacit knowledge is "displayed or exemplified" rather than "transmitted," and thus usually is learned in local, face-to-face interactions (Duguid 2005, 113). Practice can be distributed in networks, such as the international networks of physicists in which the concept of epistemic cultures originated. In these cases, participants can exchange knowledge of *that* and utilize it locally, provided they have common understandings and tools.

Data repositories, digital libraries, and other infrastructure tools and services transfer knowledge only to the extent that tacit knowledge can be captured and represented. Efforts to make tacit knowledge "mobile" so that it can be shared indicate how difficult this process is. Representing research data in standardized formats can involve considerable information loss. Data may be forced into categories that are inappropriate or inadequate. Insufficient context may be recorded for others to interpret the data. Most scholars record sufficient explanations of their data for personal reuse in the short term. Sole investigators rarely need to record tacit knowledge beyond "notes to self" about what decisions were made, when, and why. The effort required to explain one's research records adequately increases as a function of the distance between data originators and users. Documenting research data for use by team members is more difficult than documenting them for personal use. Documenting them for off-site collaborators is still more difficult. The most difficult of all is documenting them for unknown future users. For example, describing an experiment sufficiently so that others can replicate it may require many pages of procedures, equipment specifications, instrument settings, and associated diagrams. How scholars resolve the tension between embedded and mobile knowledge influences their collaborations with others, both inside and outside their specialties (Bowker 2005; Callon 1994; Duguid 2005; Kanfer et al. 2000; Olson and Olson 2000; Sonnenwald 2006, 2007).

Sociologists and economists often disagree about the degree to which tacit knowledge can be made explicit or mobile. The economic argument for open science relies on the notion of scientific knowledge as a public good. Goods can be assigned an economic value. The sociological counterargument claims that scientific knowledge is so deeply embedded in other structures and practices that it cannot be extricated, and thus cannot be treated as a good. The sociological contention still places a high economic value on science, but for reasons of variety and flexibility in social networks rather than as goods (Callon 1994; Cohendet and Meyer-Krahmer 2001; David 2003; Huysman and Wulf 2005; Maskus and Reichman 2004; Stephan 1996, 2004).

Making Knowledge Mobile   Methods for describing and organizing information artifacts help to make knowledge mobile. For scholars to reach their audiences, their products must be discoverable, whether as publications, data, or other forms of communication. Once written and disseminated, "documents . . . quickly have to fend for themselves," because authors cannot retain control over how their writings are interpreted (Brown and Duguid 1996). The same can be said for data, once they are contributed to repositories.

   Published information is described and organized by library practices. Because people use the same words to mean different things and different words to mean the same things, catalogers and indexers build thesauri that establish the meaning of individual terms. The choice of terms is determined by consensus, drawing on authoritative sources in a field of study. The description of documents and data also are controlled through the use of standard formats for structural elements, whether for journal articles (e.g., author, title, journal date, volume, issue, or pages) or data (e.g., instrument, time, date, reading, or calibration). Cataloging and indexing methods attempt to be objective, taking information artifacts out of context and describing them in ways that anyone seeking them might be able to find them. Librarians' and archivists' goals are to make documents and data mobile, in the sociological sense, so that information seekers might later discover these resources for purposes related or unrelated to their origins.

   Unpublished documents, data, research records, and other forms of scholarly information also need to be represented, described, and organized. As the volume and variety of scholarly products has grown, scholars have become more familiar with metadata, ontologies, and other forms of information description and organization. Individual fields are developing their own standards and structures.

   Ontologies are similar to thesauri in that they establish terminology by consensus and map relationships between concepts, but more extensive in that they attempt to reflect the epistemology of a knowledge domain. They are complex and expensive to build because of the investments necessary to identify terminology, establish consensus, and maintain usefulness through changes in terminology, topics, and methods. Ontologies depend on a tacit knowledge of concepts and the relationships among them, and thus senior members of fields must participate actively in their development. The success of ontologies in reconciling terminology differences has been mixed (Bowker 2005; Goble and Wroe 2005; Hovy 2003; Ribes and Bowker 2006).

Collaboration and Social Networks
Information is the glue that holds social networks together (Lievrouw 1988). Much of that glue is tacit knowledge, a form of information that

is not easily exchanged over computer networks for the purposes of collaboration. Another impediment to collaboration is that open science is not absolute. Scholars do not share all of their information, all of the time. Even in effective collaborations, scholars are unlikely to take the Three Musketeers' pledge of "all for one, and one for all." More often, they are "flying in formation, for as long as the relationship is fruitful," as one senior scientist put it.

The cohesiveness of social networks is easier to maintain through face-to-face relationships than over distances, especially when computer networks are the primary communication channel. Information technologies can aid or hinder collaboration. Facilitating distributed collaborations is among the primary goals of e-Research, and hence it is essential to understand the relationships between information technologies and scholarly practices.

Characteristics of Collaboration   Collaboration is among the most studied and least understood aspects of information infrastructure. Scholars compete for funding, jobs, students, publication venues, awards, priority of findings, and authority. The scholarly incentive structure rewards those who are the most competitive. But scholars also collaborate to gather the expertise necessary to study complex problems, share scarce or expensive equipment, and to share data and other information resources (Axelrod 1984; Merton 1973a, 1984, 1994; Traweek 1992).

Collaboration is more difficult over distances than if done locally, and more problematic between than within disciplines. Joint projects do not always achieve their intended goals. Research partnerships are not necessarily voluntary, nor do they serve the interests of investigators equally. Some partnerships are encouraged or required by funding agencies, either to promote interdisciplinary research or to include partners who would have difficulty conducting research on their own. Scholars in less developed parts of Europe are incorporated into some European projects, and scholars in less research-intensive universities are incorporated into some U.S. federal funding projects (Cummings and Kiesler 2004; Finholt 2002; Olson and Olson 2000; Sonnenwald 2006, 2007).

Distributed collaborations can serve a number of different purposes. The most comprehensive structure, and the one for which the term "collaboratory" was coined (Wulf 1989, 1993), is a distributed research center with the full range of functions of a local center. Collaboratory can be defined as "an organizational entity that *spans distance*, supports rich and recurring *human interaction* oriented to a *common research area*, and provides *access* to data sources, artifacts and tools required to accomplish research tasks" (Olson 2005, 3; emphasis in original). The term "virtual organization" also is found in e-Research contexts.

Research collaborations that take place over the Internet can have a narrower focus, such as shared instrumentation or a community data system. Paul A. David and Michael Spence (2003) offer a taxonomy of collaborative research activities on the Internet of community-, data-, computation-, or interaction-centric virtual labs. Data sharing can thus be either the primary purpose of a distributed collaboration or a core component of a broader collaboration.

One way to study research partnerships is through the resulting artifacts. Coauthorship of publications is an important indicator of collaboration. Not surprisingly, the frequency of coauthorship and other forms of collaboration such as joint grants are related. Coauthorship, collaboration, and the use of information technologies are sometimes correlated, with the most active collaborators being more adept in using computer-based tools (Nentwich 2003).

Coauthorship and collaboration are not coextensive, however. The notion of authorship varies widely between fields and can be a source of friction in collaboration. In some fields, everyone associated with a project may be listed as an author, whether or not they participated in the writing. In others, only those with a substantial writing role are listed as authors. Fields and individual projects also vary in whether they give authorship credit for technical support such as designing and deploying equipment. The acknowledgments section of publications often lists people who assisted in ways not reflected by the authorship. Collaborations also may yield papers from individuals or subgroups of large projects who report on specific aspects, or who frame the results for specialized audiences (Cronin 2005; Nentwich 2003).

Distributed Collaboration   Distributed collaborations rely heavily on information and communication technologies. These technologies are most effective when they complement existing work practices. Explanations that are easily conveyed in a face-to-face discussion between people who know each other well are much more difficult to communicate over distances. Even with tools that facilitate sketching and oral discussion, extra care is needed to make sure that everyone has the same "inscription" (whether a table, diagram, model, or other representation) in hand and is looking at the same part of it. The feedback obtained by eye contact across a table while pointing to a shared document is difficult to replicate in teleconferencing, videoconferencing, or other technologies for distributed communication (Bowker 2005; Kanfer et al. 2000; Latour 1988; Livingstone 2003; Olson 2005; Olson and Olson 2000; Sonnenwald 2007).

Since the sixteenth century, the universality of science has depended on the ability to codify data and information in standardized ways. In distributed environments, common communication technologies and the infrastructure support to use them are additional requirements for collaboration and knowledge sharing. As Gary Olson and Judith Olson (2000) put it, "distance matters."

Information in Collaboration   Information may be the glue of social relationships, but it also can be the cement that forms a barrier between partners. The means by which tacit or embedded knowledge is made mobile for sharing is a much-studied topic in research collaborations. Alaina G. Kanfer and her colleagues (2000) identify three elements of the tension between embedded and mobile knowledge: characteristics of the knowledge that is shared, the group context, and communications technology. These factors overlap with the four core concepts for collaboration success identified by Olson and Olson (2000). Their factors include a *common ground* between the players, which includes a common vocabulary and prior experience working together; *coupling in work*, which includes the degree to which the work can be partitioned between the players; *collaboration readiness*, or the motivation of the players; and *technology readiness*, which includes both infrastructure and local support.

In both models, a common vocabulary and codification of common knowledge are predictors of success. Knowledge within a team is not something that can be shared directly; it is interpreted and reinterpreted in context, and may or may not become information that can be shared. Collaborators rarely become truly bilingual in all of the partner disciplines. Rather, they learn a pidgin or creole form of their partners' languages, and work within a "trading zone" (Galison 1997). Researchers who borrow tools, methods, theories, or data need to learn the language of the borrowed discipline sufficiently to understand its content and articulate their ideas to multiple audiences.

The process of negotiating shared meanings can be a positive, constructive one. By exchanging ideas openly, partners can learn that what one group dismisses as something that "everybody knows already" is someone else's core research problem. They may also learn that each of the groups began with an "everybody knows that" assumption about the other's work. Discussion may reveal that neither of the supposedly solved problems has been subjected to empirical assessment, and both (or neither) are worthy of investigation. Similarly, "what is a 'misunderstanding' from one standpoint, may be a 'new twist' from another standpoint" (Kanfer et al. 2000, 321).

Differences in knowledge about methods, such as the time required to analyze certain kinds of data or to build models in a partner field, are a common problem. What one group may assume is a trivial request may actually require months of effort for their partners to accomplish (Sonnenwald forthcoming). Partners also can be unaware that each is imputing different meanings to shared terms. Differences in language and terminology can be substantial barriers to communication. Basic terms such as reference, file, dictionary, and library have different meanings in computer science and information studies, for example. Thesauri and ontologies can be constructed to establish shared meanings of terms, but only after the confusions in terminology are identified. Even then, collaborations must be large enough in scope and long enough in duration to justify investments in formal vocabulary structures.

Sharing Information Artifacts   Of all the aspects of distributed collaboration, scholarly information infrastructure is most suited for sharing publications, reports, data, models, and other information artifacts. Digital libraries and data repositories can store, preserve, and provide access to digital objects anywhere in the world. Nevertheless, providing distributed access to digital content is not merely a technical matter to be resolved. The sharing of artifacts is mired in social practices and policy debates.

Sharing scholarly publications would seem to be the easiest problem to solve, as scholars want their published projects to be disseminated and read widely. Tangible recognition—including hiring, promotion, prizes, and obtaining new grants and students—all depend on others having access to one's publications. Yet as discussed in chapter 5, self-archiving occurs for only 15 percent or so of publications, and institutions are having difficulty acquiring their faculty members' scholarly products for their repositories. The low participation rate has received surprisingly little study. Studies in the United States (Foster and Gibbons 2005) and the United Kingdom (J. Hey 2004) found that faculty are more interested in simple ways to manage their own publications than in open access as a public service to the community. Functions that facilitate the personal use of publications such as generating reports for departmental and personnel reviews are greater incentives to contribute than are benefits such as improved metadata. Faculty members are willing to invest only a little time in document deposit; tools that are simple to learn and use are essential. Thus, tools to input scholarly content will be an important component of information infrastructure. If authors can easily transfer their files from word-processing software into digital libraries, participation is likely to increase, especially if other attractive features for managing personal collections are offered.

Scholars' incentives to provide access to their data are much more complex than for access to publications. As discussed in chapter 6, data take many forms and may exist concurrently at multiple levels of processing. Determining what data to preserve, in what form, and for what purposes are unresolved problems for many investigators and for many fields. Data are enshrouded in tacit knowledge. Representing them in ways that can be interpreted by others is among the greatest challenges in building data repositories.

Access mechanisms vary considerably by the type of data. In some cases data are transferable as artifacts (e.g., samples or numerical data), and in other cases access requires training someone in a novel technique. Another critical dimension is the "factual status" of data. Some elements are uncertain and unverified (or unverifiable), and others are considered reliable and valid. Data are continually interpreted and reinterpreted in the research process. Temporal factors arise, as data may be ready for access only after certain amounts of processing and interpretation are completed to the satisfaction of the investigators (Hilgartner and Brandt-Rauf 1994). Access to data therefore encompasses the problems of "making order out of chaos" to write a scholarly paper (Star 1983) and making tacit knowledge explicit so that it can be shared.

Intellectual property concerns strongly influence how and whether research data are shared. The ownership of data often is ambiguous or unknown, and people may control data without legally owning them. Ownership is most clear when data are produced by private research entities such as pharmaceutical companies. It is much less clear when data are produced using public funds. In the United States, data resulting from federal research grants usually falls into the public domain. Some exceptions apply—for example, when investigators and universities can apply for patents resulting from grant projects. In Europe, research data may fall under the Database Directive, giving rights to the database creator rather than the producer. In some countries, the government owns data that were produced with public funds. Determining data ownership is especially problematic for research collaborations that cross legal jurisdictions.

Consequently, scholars rarely own the data they produce, at least in the legal sense. They typically feel a sense of ownership, whether or not they have proprietary rights. Given the complexity of intellectual property laws, researchers may not know what rights, if any, they have in their data. Researchers in the sciences, technology, and medicine usually are the most aware of the nuances of data ownership. These are the fields that rely most heavily on grant funding and corporate partnerships. They also are those most likely to obtain patents. Researchers in the social sciences and humanities rely less on grants, and often are less familiar with issues of data ownership. Yet all of these relationships are changing with the advent of data and text mining. Ownership in the products of mining is a relatively unexplored legal area, as Lynch (2006) notes.

Regardless of whether scholars legally own their data, they do control them. They also control the point at which ideas, observations, or instrument readings become data, and when data become facts. When embedded knowledge is made mobile, information is released to a wider audience. Sometimes the release is desirable, and sometimes not. Once data are contributed to a repository or a database shared with collaborators, scholars may no longer control these data. Release may be mandatory as a condition of acquiring grant funds, however. In some cases, investigators find that deposit is beneficial as it relieves them from responding to individual requests for and about their data. In other instances, deposit or other forms of data release is costly, in that those data may no longer be used as barter in exchange for others' data or for funds, equipment, and other resources (David and Spence 2003; Hilgartner and Brandt-Rauf 1994).

Even when investigators are willing to share their data, it may be unclear who has the authority to convey access, to what, and under what conditions. These issues are especially complex in large, collaborative projects. Scholars understandably wish to avoid codifying rules for administrative management, including rules on data, in order to maintain maximum flexibility in their research directions. Excessive codification also can undermine trust in collaborations. Pressure for the codification of rules on data access and ownership is more often driven by university officers than by scientists, as it is these officers who are responsible for legal contracts, patents, and licensing (David and Spence 2003; Lievrouw 2004).

Some data are more amenable to sharing than others. Market value is a particularly contentious factor. Chemical data, for example, are important digital assets in the pharmaceutical industry. Academic chemists have encountered many political and technical obstacles to accessing data and to sharing their own data with others, as discussed further in chapter 8. Libraries are making their book collections available for digitization in the interest of sharing the content and obtaining the resulting digital assets. Publishers have imposed legal obstacles in return.

Wrapped up in these debates is a complex set of legal, cultural, and technical issues that will not be resolved anytime soon.

Sharing data with minimal resale value, such as cultural ethnographies or backyard bird counts, is less politically contentious. Astronomy data often are cited as an example of resources with broad interest but minimal economic value, and without the sensitivity of data on human subjects, animals, or rare species. Still, astronomy data became widely available only with the creation of large sky surveys for general use, such as the Sloan data sets (Sloan Digital Sky Survey 2006). In earlier days, astronomy data were laboriously collected by investigators who had privileged access to observatory telescopes. These data were not so readily shared, and parts of today's sky surveys duplicate data that are held by earlier investigators. Access to data, then, is much more than an economic issue.

Temporal factors also influence the market for data. Current weather data have high monetary value to government and industry because they can be used to protect people and crops. Early warnings enable airplanes to be moved out of the path of hailstorms, for instance. Similarly, satellite data on the location of schools of fish can be sold to fishing fleets at high prices, and made available to scientists at a lower cost a few days or weeks later. Stock market data are especially time sensitive. These data are sold at top prices in the first few seconds, when they can be used to move markets; a lesser price for about twenty minutes, when they are still of value to speculators; and usually offered free to the public after a twenty-minute embargo. Perceptions of ownership and economic value also differ between fields, and can be a source of friction in collaborations.

Individual fields and projects address these issues in a variety of ways. Data may be released after an embargo period that is long enough to allow investigators to publish their findings, but short enough for the data to remain useful to others. Finding this middle ground requires difficult compromises, as some data increase in value and utility as they cumulate over longitudinal studies.

Finally, stakeholders may have competing interests that influence how, when, and whether information is shared. Scholars share information in the interests of collaboration and open science. Public policy that encourages sharing may serve different purposes. Wouters (2004), studying science policy, identified three categories of scientists' motivations to share information resources: what scientists wish to share (tools and data sets), why they wish to share them (to verify or refine findings, to ask new questions, to reduce the duplication of effort, and to reduce costs), and who would benefit most (multidisciplinary teams or new researchers). He found that public policy motivations, especially in the United States, are based on open science principles: data that are collected with public funds should be in the public domain, the receipt of public funds for research increases the obligation for scientific openness and accountability, and data access improves national competitiveness. The motivations of scholars and those who make public policy are related, but far from identical. A scholarly information infrastructure will be most effective in facilitating access to the artifacts of research if it takes into account the motivations of those who produce and control those artifacts.

8
Disciplines, Documents, and Data

The scholarly information infrastructure will be of little value without a rich and robust content layer on top. Information from all parts of the life cycle—raw data through final publications—is even more useful when linked into a value chain. Libraries and publishers assure access to publications, but no comparable infrastructure exists for access to data and unpublished resources. Because the academic reward system relies heavily on publication, scholars have strong incentives to publish their scholarly work and to ensure that it is widely disseminated and accessible. They have far fewer incentives, and many disincentives, to share their data or to make them publicly accessible.

Despite many common activities, both the artifacts and practices of scholarship vary by discipline. The artifacts vary as scholars make choices about sources of data, along with what, when, where, and in what form to disseminate the products of their work. Scholarly practices vary in the ways that scholars create, use, and share documents, data, and other forms of information.

A discipline-based examination of artifacts and practices reveals both common and competing requirements for information infrastructure. The nature of artifacts, the associated practices, and the incentives for scholars to contribute their work to the content layer are assessed first for the sciences, then the social sciences, and lastly the humanities. The sciences are addressed first and in the most depth because they are the most widely studied, and because analyses of practice and policy in the social sciences and humanities often are based on comparisons to the sciences. Issues that cross disciplines are introduced in the context of the sciences and then compared in subsequent sections.

A discussion at this level of generalization necessarily overlooks some important differences within disciplines. Nonetheless, the differences between disciplines are striking. The comparisons presented here reflect priorities for development, policies that encourage or inhibit cooperation, and practices that do and do not transfer well to distributed environments. Some problems have obvious solutions and others may be intractable. Taken together, they provide an agenda for research on a unified scholarly infrastructure for information.

Sciences

Science, technology, and medicine (often referred to as STM) are significant economic drivers. These fields receive large amounts of public and private research funds. Although collectively referred to as the sciences, the discipline can be divided into the physical sciences (e.g., atmosphere and oceans, chemistry, biochemistry, earth and space, and physics and astronomy), the life sciences (e.g., biology, physiology, and psychology), and mathematics and statistics; technology, which includes computer science and engineering; and medicine, which includes allied fields such as nursing and public health. Within universities, these fields are aggregated and disaggregated in various ways. At UCLA, for example, biology is studied in the academic departments of ecology and evolutionary biology; microbiology, immunology, and molecular genetics; and molecular, cell, and developmental biology. Conversely, mathematics and statistics are departments within the physical sciences division.

Thus, neither the boundaries between scientific fields nor between the sciences and other disciplines are firm. The sciences intersect with the social sciences in areas such as the environment, epidemiology, and geography, and with the humanities in areas such as bioethics and forensic metallurgy (e.g., the study of archaeological relics that contain metals).

The sciences, generally speaking, are more cumulative than are other disciplines. New ways of understanding the world eventually replace older theories and views. These processes are gradual, and not without contention. The theory of plate tectonics was proposed early in the twentieth century, for instance, but not widely accepted until the 1960s. Instrumentation developed in the 1940s and 1950s enabled the mapping of the seabed, yielding evidence that supported this theory and disconfirmed aspects of prior theories. At other times, scientists may reframe problems, rather than reject prior theories outright. Scientific criteria for adjudicating disputes and accepting new theories are applied within a complex social framework that varies by field. The ability of a community to validate new explanations has a profound influence on the artifacts, practices, and temporal characteristics of the sciences (Bowker 2005; Kuhn 1962; Polsby 1998).

Information Artifacts in the Sciences

The sciences create and use an array of documents, data, models, and other information artifacts. They were pioneers in the use of information technology and have the greatest online presence of any of the disciplines. Yet the digitization of scientific information resources is far from complete, and far from consistent across the scientific fields.

Scientific Documents   Scientific publication practices, which are oriented toward journal articles and conference papers rather than books, have reflected a steady shift from paper to electronic forms. Indexing and abstracting databases of scientific journals came online in the early 1970s, followed by the full text of articles starting in the early 1980s. The large, international, commercial publishers and scholarly societies that dominate scientific publishing made major investments in technology to expand their content and services.

By 2003, 83 percent of science, technology, and medicine journals were reported to be available online (Cox and Cox 2003; Garson 2004), although the number of online issues varies by journal. Bibliographic coverage in the *Science Citation Index* dates back to 1900; coverage for the first half of the twentieth century is highly selective, however. As discussed in chapter 7, the half-life of literature in the sciences is the shortest of the disciplines, which means that the sciences rely on more recent publications than do other disciplines. *Scopus*, the competing Elsevier product, indexes science, technology, medicine, and social sciences literature only for the prior ten years (*Scopus* in Detail 2006). Thus, the *Science Citation Index* provides deep historical coverage of journal literature, while *Scopus* offers shallow coverage of recent literature and

Web resources. The sciences also led in establishing preprint repositories for open access to publications and working papers. Taking these factors together, it is apparent that most of the scholarly literature used by scientists is now available online, although the indexing coverage varies widely.

The sciences create a variety of other objects that fall in the gray area between documents and data. Examples include laboratory and field notebooks, slides from talks, and composite objects such as graphic visualizations of data. Laboratory notebooks often are classified as data because they are records of research. Slides from talks, which once were ephemeral forms of communication, now are commonly posted on conference or personal Web sites or distributed with conference proceedings. Graphic visualizations of data can be linked to scholarly documents that report the research or to the underlying data.

Scientific Data   Scientific data are the fastest-growing portion of the content layer. The data deluge has arrived, but the means to capture and curate it are in their infancy. We have only begun to understand how to emulate the legitimization, dissemination, and access and curation functions of the scholarly publishing system for data, as discussed in chapter 6.

Among the first steps in deciding what data should be in the content layer is deciding what *are* data. Following are a few examples of scientific data:

- Medicine: X-rays
- Chemistry: protein structures
- Astronomy: spectral surveys
- Biology: specimens
- Physics: events and objects

Most data in the sciences are created by and for research purposes. The vast majority of scientific data in documentary form (e.g., text, numbers, and images) now are "born digital," including many types that previously were created in media such as film (e.g., X-ray images). While laboratory and field notebooks still exist on paper, a growing proportion of research notes are taken on handheld devices or laptop computers.

Data are difficult to separate from the software, equipment, documentation, and knowledge required to use them. For example, if data are produced by an instrument such as a sensor network, interpreting those data requires an understanding of the instrument—for example, what do the sensors detect, under what conditions, at what frequency of observation, and with what type of calibration? Similarly, a data set may be uninterpretable without the software used to create or analyze it (and perhaps the same version or release of that software). Representations of protein structures and physical specimens (e.g., cells, animals, or water and plant samples) can be stored digitally, but the data per se may remain stored on a shelf or in a freezer. As discussed in chapter 7, not all scientific knowledge can be made mobile. Some essential knowledge will remain "excludable" from representations that can be documented and exchanged in digital forms. Specialized laboratory mice and cell lines may not be transferable between laboratories unless accompanied by graduate students or postdoctoral fellows with the appropriate expertise, for example (Bowker 2005; Callon 1994).

Complicating matters further is the question "*when is data?*" An instrument reading carries some form of information, but that information may not be considered data until it is cleaned and verified. Determining how much cleaning, analyzing, and verification is required before observations or experimental results become data with any scientific factual value is a matter of judgment. Those judgments vary from person to person and field to field. The judgments also may vary between collaborators. For example, to the engineer building a sensor network, a reliable stream of bits may be data. Until the sensor network can detect biological phenomena in a reliable way, those bits may not be scientific data to a biologist. Scientists often are not willing to release data to others until those data meet their personal criteria as valid scientific indicators.

Efforts "to database the world" of science are creating large repositories in some fields (Bowker 2005). Fields that rely heavily on technical instruments, such as physics, chemistry, astronomy, medicine, and the environmental sciences, are generating a deluge of digital data. Substantial repositories are being constructed in these data-intensive fields. Most experimental data can be re-created, whereas most observational data cannot, as they are associated with a time and place. In some fast-moving research areas, data can be superseded quickly by new results or better instrumentation. In many areas, data remain useful indefinitely. Chemical data and biological specimens are among those that have long-term value. For instance, twenty-first-century scientists studying the avian flu were able to resurrect the early twentieth-century pandemic virus by using preserved tissue from a 1918 victim (Kaiser 2005).

Scientific data will not be "all digital" anytime soon, however. Substantial amounts of important "legacy data" remain in paper form, in both public and private hands. An estimated 750 million specimens in U.S. natural history museums, for example, lack digital descriptions (Schnase et al. 1997). An effort is under way to digitize these descriptions on a large scale, using bar-coding techniques (Barcoding of Life 2005; Marshall 2005). Digitizing historical documents such as newspapers, handbooks, directories, and land-use records will benefit the sciences in addition to the humanities and social sciences. These records are used to establish historical patterns of weather, crop yields, animal husbandry, and so forth. An untold wealth of scientific data lies in private hands. Individual scientists often keep the records of their research career in their offices and laboratories, limited only by storage space on the shelves and in refrigerators, freezers, and digital devices.

Description and Organization in the Sciences   Describing and organizing information can aid the discovery of resources, whether for reading or use as data. Information organization mechanisms also can ease communication within and between communities. The sciences have pioneered tools and services for many of these purposes.

Scientific literature is well organized, and the terminology is more controlled than in other disciplines. Chemistry and medicine, for example, are notable for their sophisticated and consistent vocabulary and naming structures. Chemists agreed on how to describe molecules in the nineteenth century, providing remarkably consistent retrieval mechanisms for today's databases (Wiswesser 1985). Fields within medicine and health have individual thesauri that are bridged by the Unified Medical Language System (McCray 1993). The sciences also are leaders in taxonomy, with a variety of resources that serve an international audience and are revised continually. Not all scientific fields have their own thesauri or ontologies, however, and differences in terminology continue to create barriers to interdisciplinary collaboration (Bisby et al. 2002; Godfray 2002a, 2002b; Godfray and Knapp 2004; Integrated Taxonomic Information System 2006; International Union of Biological Sciences 2006; Knapp et al. 2002; *Marine Organisms Database* 2005; Web of Life 2006).

Thesauri and taxonomic structures long predate automated information retrieval. Their purpose is to standardize the use of terms and establish relationships between concepts. They are extremely useful in discovering and retrieving documents, and following paths through literature. These features also can assist in text and data mining, which holds great promise for the sciences. Text mining in the biosciences, for example, is expected to facilitate drug discovery, the identification of protein interactions, and to inform public health policy (Ananiadou et al. 2005; Murray-Rust, Mitchell, and Rzepa 2005; National Centre for Text Mining 2006).

Data description is more advanced in the sciences than in other disciplines, but still is in its infancy compared to the description of scholarly literature. This is not surprising, given how recently data have become a scientific end product to be curated and reused. The number and variety of data forms are vast. Fields and specialties may have their own standards and metadata formats, or no consensus-based standards. Large volumes of scientific data exist in digital form, but may be in local formats that are difficult to identify or interpret. Most data repositories use consensus standards specific to their research fields for data description and structure. Data mining is much easier within than between research fields, and even that is rarely easy.

In fields where data standards exist, scientists do not necessarily use them, though. Many prefer to maintain their data in familiar local tools such as spreadsheets. People become experts at the use of their tools, and do not adopt new ones until they see sufficient advantage in doing so.

The greatest investments in ontologies and metadata standards are in fields with large, distributed, and collaborative research. When many scholars are sharing data, they have incentives to invest in consistent methods for documenting that data. Even here, efforts to establish ontologies reveal how much variance exists in the use of terminology within and between fields (Bowker 2000a, 2000b, 2000c, 2005; Bowker and Star 1999). David Ribes and Geoffrey Bowker (2006), studying geosciences, and Carol Goble and Chris Wroe (2005), studying bioinformatics, found that domain scientists had great difficulty articulating the definitions of concepts and the relationships between them. Goble and Wroe cleverly frame the challenges of ontology building as a conflict between computer scientists in the role of the House of Montague, whose interests are in logic and languages, and life scientists in the role of the House of the Capulets (the feuding families in Shakespeare's *Romeo and Juliet*), whose interests lie in the more pragmatic aspects of scientific application. Computer scientists in their project wanted to build a perfect ontology as an end in itself, whereas the life scientists wanted simple solutions that worked immediately, even if they were imperfect.

Information Practices in the Sciences

To be useful, the content layer must include the right resources, tools, services, and policies for the communities it serves. The information practices identified in chapter 7 suggest a number of lessons and questions for how to design the content layer for the sciences.

Practices Associated with Scientific Documents   Journal articles are the only type of scientific scholarly document that is consistently available online. Even so, only recent articles in mainstream journals may be readily available, and these only by institutional subscription. As the universe of scientific content grows, mainstream journals become a relatively smaller portion of the information useful to scholars, students, and the public. Digital repositories are filling some of the gap, collecting both published and unpublished documents. The success of arXiv led many to assume that the implementation of repositories by the rest of science, and eventually all of academe, was just a matter of time (Ginsparg 2001; Kling and McKim 2000). Other scientific fields have established open access repositories and promoted self-archiving initiatives, but adoption is far from uniform.

Open access is highly inconsistent across the sciences. The sciences are leaders in establishing open access journals, with the Public Library of Science as the most ambitious effort to date. Several of its journals already have achieved high impact factors, establishing themselves as premier scientific publications. PubMed Central is a blend of repository and open access publishing, providing free access to bibliographic records along with the full text of biomedical and life sciences literature. Some articles are available immediately on publication, others are available after a time delay, and still others are considered open access. Conversely, in biotechnology the motto of some researchers is "patent first, publish later" (Lievrouw 2004, 167). Access to chemical information is subject to contentious intellectual property debates, resulting in a mix of open and closed models of access to chemistry publications and data (Braman 2004; Duke et al. 2005; Garson 2004; Marris 2005; Murray-Rust, Mitchell, and Rzepa 2005; Public Library of Science 2006; PubMed Central 2006).

Research collaboration requires the sharing of information. Fields with higher rates of collaboration may be more likely to share their work, whether via repositories or other means. The sciences have the highest rates of coauthorship of any discipline, although coauthorship is increasing in most fields. "Hyperauthorship" is an indicator of "collective cognition" in which the specific contributions of individuals no longer can be identified (Cronin 2005). Physics has among the highest rates of coauthorship in the sciences and the highest rates of self-archiving documents via a repository. Whether the relationship between research collaboration (as indicated by the rates of coauthorship) and sharing publications (as reflected in self-archiving) holds in other fields is a question worth exploring empirically.

Ideally, the content layer should contain all manner of scholarly products, from informal to formal, from data to publications, and links between them. Mechanisms to establish direct links between data and documents in the value chain still are new and few, as discussed in chapter 6, but are a promising development. Bourne's (2005) model of database relationships between journals and data repositories exemplifies the rich array of possibilities for the discovery, access, and use of these resources (Duke et al. 2005; Lyon 2003; Van de Sompel and Beit-Arie, 2001a, 2001b).

Data and documents do not always map easily, as scientific publications tell a carefully crafted story of the research, deleting many details. Star (1983, 205), for instance, describes how neuroscientists "represent chaos in an orderly fashion." Her examples include simplifying terminology to interact with specialists in other fields or to report to outside agencies, collecting less data than desired due to technical constraints, reporting data sooner than desirable due to pressures from the reporting agencies, and limits on presentation based on the format requirements of journals or other venues. Thus, when an investigator or another scientist asks for access to the data on which a paper is based, the boundaries of that data set may be fuzzy. In the "disarticulation" between publication and data, the story of the data can easily be lost (Bowker 2005; Latour 1988; Lievrouw 1995).

Practices Associated with Scientific Data   Data-intensive research is a primary driver for building an advanced information infrastructure, although not all scientific fields or specialties are data intensive or highly instrumented. Among the most interesting questions to explore are ones concerning the sharing or contributing of data. As this is an underexamined topic, the analysis draws on knowledge gleaned from an array of sources and from observation.

One explanation for the diversity of sharing practices in the sciences is cultural differences between fields. If so, we would expect fields that share documents also to share data, and vice versa. This pairing does not appear to hold, however. High-energy physics, which makes its publications more widely available than any other scholarly field, shares data among collaborators but rarely makes those data publicly available (Wouters and Reddy 2003). Biotechnology, which is among the most competitive in terms of publication and patent rights, is among the most open in depositing genome and protein structure data. Even in these areas, sharing is not uniform. Several studies of geneticists' practices indicate that data often are withheld from other investigators (Campbell and Bendavid 2003; Campbell et al. 2002; *Long-Lived Digital Data Collections* 2005; Protein Data Bank 2006).

Factors other than culture may explain the relationship between collaboration and data sharing. Funding agencies often require collaborations in research areas having costly equipment, such as astronomical observatories and linear particle accelerators. Agencies wish to leverage their funds, avoid the duplication of equipment and effort, and encourage communities to work together. Hence, collaborations may be driven by agency requirements rather than arising from within those communities. Whether by nature or design, work in the sciences has a greater division of labor than in the social sciences and humanities, and thus is better suited to collaboration, especially over distances. To establish collaborations, investigators must reach agreements about sharing the data that result from a project. Data sharing, then, may be a necessary consequence of scientific collaborations (Burk 2000; David and Spence 2003; Kuhn 1962; Olson 2005; Olson and Olson 2000; Polsby 1998).

The willingness to use the data of others also may predict sharing behavior. Scholars in fields that replicate experiments or draw heavily on observational data (e.g., meteorologic or astronomical records) may be more likely to contribute data for mutual benefit within their fields. Many scholars work only with data they have produced, rarely or never acquiring data from others, and thus are not in a position to reciprocate. If they do not expect to share their data beyond their research group, they have little incentive to standardize their data management practices. Local description methods are common in fields such as environmental studies where variables and data types often are project specific. Heads of small labs frequently have difficulty reconstructing data sets or analyses done by prior lab members, as each person used their own methods of data capture and analysis (Estrin, Michener, and Bonito 2003; Taper and Lele 2004; Zimmerman 2003, forthcoming).

In fields where sharing expensive equipment is a driver for collaboration, then collaboration, instrumentation, and data sharing are likely to be correlated. The relationship between instrumentation and data sharing appears to be more general, however. A small but detailed study conducted at one research university found that scholars whose data collection and analysis were the most automated were the most likely to share raw data and analyses; these also tended to be the larger research groups. If data production was automated but other preparation was labor intensive, scholars were less likely to share data. Those whose data collection and analysis were the least automated and most labor intensive were most likely to guard their data. These behaviors held across disciplines; they were not specific to science (Pritchard, Carver, and Anand 2004).

Current research in the environmental sciences is yielding similar findings about instrumentation. Scholars whose work is most handcrafted and labor intensive are reluctant to share data until their results are published. As their work with instrumented data collection intensifies, they are seeking ways to automate their data management and analysis functions, and are more willing to capture their data in standardized forms that facilitate the use of available software tools. In turn, they appear more willing (and able) to share data with other scientists using similar methods. Therefore, scaling up to more instrumented data collection appears to promote data sharing. Many of the scientists still express considerable concern for how their data might be used by others, and set specific conditions for release (Borgman, Wallis, and Enyedy forthcoming).

Although instrumentation can change rapidly based on technological advances, research methods are handed down through academic generations and change slowly. Only a few fields appear to train graduate students in data management practices that will lead to sharing data using standard structures and tools. A clue to these differences may lie in Lisa M. Covi's (2000) finding that graduate students in high-paradigm fields such as molecular biology and classics were more likely to use the same tools and information resources as their advisors, while students in low-paradigm fields such as computer science, sociology, and literary theory were more likely to seek new information tools and techniques.

The willingness to release data can vary based on characteristics of the data themselves. Investigators may be disinclined to share scarce or novel data such as a new cell line, because they may yield subsequent data and publications (Hilgartner and Brandt-Rauf 1994). Scarce or novel data usually are labor intensive to create, and so are more likely to be guarded, consistent with other findings. Scientists express greater ownership of data that were difficult to gather, such as water samples from a dangerous swamp, than of data produced by instruments such as sensor networks (Borgman, Wallis, and Enyedy 2006).

Two other data characteristics that can influence release are market value, as discussed in chapter 7, and sensitivity. Data from biotechnology studies that could lead to patents or inventions are less likely to be shared than are data from seismic monitoring, which have more scientific than monetary value, for example. Several types of sensitivity can influence release. One is the privacy and confidentiality of human subjects records, which is a major concern in medicine and the health sciences. Rigid practices for data management and conditions for data release are enforced in these areas. Similar issues arise in the biological sciences with data on rare or endangered species. The locations of such species are obfuscated in publications, following ethical practices. Reviewers may be given sufficient details to verify the methods and results.

The questions of "when is data?" discussed above also influence what is released and when. Collaborators may release data only when all parties agree that data have been verified sufficiently to be trustworthy. Notions of trust and verification vary widely, and can reveal different assumptions by research partners and third parties about who may subsequently use the data. Water-quality assessments that are appropriate for publication in an environmental sciences journal, for instance, may use different metrics than those of government water-quality boards. Communities sometimes make fine distinctions between verified and certified data.

Record-keeping practices that are transparent within one field may be opaque to another, hampering the exchange of data between research collaborators. These differences can have far-reaching effects on scientific careers, as in the very public case charging Thereza Imanishi-Kari with research fraud. It is widely known as the "Baltimore case," because Imanishi-Kari's coauthor David Baltimore, winner of a Nobel Prize, defended her throughout the process. Over a period of ten years, the investigation involved the U.S. Congress, U.S. Secret Service, and NIH's Office of Research Integrity. The Secret Service was asked to compare the lab notebooks in question to other sample notebooks as a means to determine whether errors in several publications were fraudulent or simply due to sloppy record keeping that was within the range of accepted scientific practices. Relying on forensic methods, the Secret Service was unable to establish a norm for record keeping. Partly as a result of these findings, all charges ultimately were dismissed, closing an unpleasant chapter in science (Baltimore 1991, 1996; Corrections and Clarifications 1996; Friedly 1996; Kennedy 2004; Shankar 2002).

Another public saga involving differences in research methods, record keeping, and charges of fraud is that of cold fusion. If nuclear fusion can be achieved above subfreezing temperatures, it offers great promise as an inexpensive form of power. The first team to accomplish cold fusion in the laboratory heralded its results with a press conference rather than a peer-reviewed paper, thereby raising suspicions. Several hundred laboratories tried to replicate and extend the results, with minimal success. Meanwhile, money and reputations were at stake. Public agencies and private energy companies were prepared to invest substantial sums in research, provided the initial findings could be substantiated. Hope gradually faded after many months of intense activity and argument, but the search for the holy grail of cold fusion continues. Subsequent researchers were eager to distance themselves from the field's early proponents (Pool 1989, 1990; Seife 2005; Taubes 1990).

The diversity of records practices is likely to decline through the increased use of automated tools and standardized compliance procedures for the handling of hazardous materials, animals, and human subjects. Record keeping never will be rigorously consistent across fields due to ever-changing research questions, variables, and instruments. The lack of consistency may work against data sharing, but is often necessary in order to ask new questions in new ways.

Incentives and Disincentives to Build the Content Layer for the Sciences
The policy pressure to enhance the scientific content layer is building rapidly. Individual countries and international agencies are promulgating proposals to improve permanent access to scholarly publications and research data, as discussed in chapter 6. Scientific information is a central concern in these policy proposals and background studies.

The arguments for improving access to scientific information are diverse. Those associated with e-Science and cyberinfrastructure tend to reiterate the principles of open science, such as verifying and refining research findings, building on historical observations, avoiding the duplication of research, leveraging research investments by addressing new questions from extant data, and addressing questions that require data from multiple disciplines or countries. Another justification is obligations to the citizenry to preserve information produced with public funds.

On close inspection, it is apparent that most claims for access to scientific information are made from the viewpoint of the prospective information *user*: if these resources were available, the larger scientific community and the public would benefit in many ways. Comparatively little attention has been paid to the perspective of the information *creator* who would contribute documents, data, and other objects to the content layer. Many incentives, but also many disincentives, exist to share one's intellectual products with the larger scientific community and the world. Scientists sometimes find themselves in conflicting positions depending on whether they are potential data providers or data users.

Incentives for Scientists to Share Information   Scholarly information is inherently shareable as a public good because others can have information without lessening its value, as discussed in chapter 2. Scholars want to make their publications widely available to legitimate, disseminate, and make their work accessible to readers. Usually scholars presume that once published, libraries and publishers will ensure that their work is permanently accessible.

Incentives to make documents available that are less formal than full peer-reviewed publications vary widely between fields. Some scholars share manuscripts privately with a few trusted colleagues prior to journal submission. Others submit drafts, working papers, and technical reports to repositories, and also post them on their personal Web sites.

Scientists more often contribute to repositories in their disciplines, when those repositories exist, than to institutional repositories based at their universities. The canonical example is arXiv, which began in 1991 for physics, and now receives more than 4,000 submissions per month in physics, mathematics, the nonlinear sciences, computer science, and quantitative biology, with a total of more than 380,000 documents by late 2006. According to arXiv's statistics, as many as 15,000 to 38,000 connections per hour are made to the main server, not counting access to mirror sites around the world. It has become an essential resource for the participating fields.

Success in computer science appears uneven by comparison. Computer scientists first established a disciplinary repository as a research project known as NCSTRL (pronounced "ancestral"). NCSTRL is now a static repository of about 30,000 records. In 1998, the Association for Computing Machinery established the Computing Research Repository, combining NCSTRL with the computer science papers in arXiv. The Computing Research Repository continues to grow, receiving more than 500 submissions per year by 2001, and over 900 in 2005. Although computer science is a much smaller field than physics, these are not large numbers. Nevertheless, computer scientists already had the practice of depositing technical reports in departmental repositories, so a shared repository may not have offered enough additional advantages (Computing Research Repository 2003; Networked Computer Science 2006).

Institutional repositories based at universities have the potential to become an important component of the content layer in all fields, as discussed in chapter 5. These systems are driven more by concerns for providing access to the university's scholarly and educational products rather than the self-archiving of publications. Institutional evaluation, accountability, and improved information services are key incentives (Lynch 2003a; Poynder 2006; Uhlir 2006). The number of repositories varies from about 5 to 100 percent of universities per country (of the thirteen countries studied), and the content is a mix of articles, books, theses, research data, video, music, and course material (Lynch and Lippincott 2005; Westrienen and Lynch 2005). These data are early and incomplete but suggest a growth trend.

In principle, anything available on the Internet—whether on a Web site, or in a repository or digital library—can be considered part of the content layer of the scholarly information infrastructure. Search engines are increasing in sophistication, and specialized scholarly search mechanisms such as Google Scholar and *Scopus* are making objects on academic and research Web sites easier to find. Objects in repositories are more easily found both because they have more metadata, and because they can be retrieved with cross-repository search tools such as ARC and OAIster. The more significant differences between access to objects on Web sites and in repositories involve preservation and curation. Repositories maintain access to resources throughout changes in technology, whereas Web site maintenance is much less consistent (ARC: A Cross Archive Search Service 2006; OAIster 2006).

Are better access and curation sufficient incentives for scholars to contribute to repositories? Librarians make this argument to faculty as incentives to contribute documents to institutional repositories. Proponents of open access contend that documents in repositories are more highly cited than those appearing only in scholarly journals. So far, neither of these incentives has resulted in the massive growth of university-based institutional repositories. Early studies suggest that faculty are more interested in repositories as a means to manage their own collections of publications (Foster and Gibbons 2005). Simpler tools, more human assistance for contributing documents, and better services to manage personal collections may be greater incentives than is the potential for increased citation.

Lastly is the question of "carrots versus sticks." These issues vary for publications and data. The low response to the self-archiving of publications resulted in calls for mandatory contributions to repositories of universities, research fields, and funding agencies. Mandatory deposit has had a more receptive response in countries with centralized funding for higher education and research, as in the United Kingdom, much of Europe, and elsewhere. Centralized evaluation and accountability systems, such as the Research Assessment Exercise in the United Kingdom, have considered whether to compel deposit. None of the proposals for the mandatory deposit of publications has met with much success, due to resistance from publishers, a lack of enthusiasm on authors' parts, the lack of infrastructure to enforce deposit (including staff to identify, gather, document, and input publications), and because alternative mechanisms exist to obtain publications (Berlin Declaration 2003; *Government Response* 2005; Harnad 2005c; Kaiser 2004b; Poynder 2006; Research Assessment Exercise 2006; *Scientific Publications* 2004; Zerhouni 2004, 2006).

The mandatory deposit of data has met with more success, especially when the deposit requirements are established as a condition of receiving funding or being published in a specific journal. Even so, the success of a compliance approach is limited by scholars' willingness to participate. Investigators may contribute only the minimal amount necessary to satisfy the requirements, limiting the value of the resulting repositories.

Disincentives for Scientists to Share Information   Despite the growth of repositories in the sciences and the policy pressure to increase sharing, many reasons exist for individual scholars not to share their scholarly products through channels other than formal publication. The disincentives to share data receive more attention than for documents, but the issues appear to be similar. Much more study is needed to identify the motivations for sharing.

The disincentives to share scholarly information can be divided into four categories: (1) rewards for publication rather than for data management; (2) the amount of effort required in documenting data for use by others; (3) concerns for priority, including the rights to control the results or sources until the publication of research; and (4) intellectual property issues, both the control and ownership of one's own data as well as access to data controlled or owned by others. These four obstacles are discussed in the context of the sciences, and compared in subsequent sections on the social sciences and humanities.

The first, and often greatest, barrier to sharing is that scholars are rewarded for publication rather than for document and data management. Hiring, tenure, promotions, grants, and other aspects of the academic reward structure are based on producing peer-reviewed publications. An institutional infrastructure exists to make publications available; these enter the content layer without further effort by the author. The self-archiving of publications is a duplication of scholars' efforts, but reaches a broader audience. In fields without a strong open access culture, scholars may feel little personal obligation to self-archive publications or data. Studies by the library community suggest that relatively few faculty are following the changes in publishing, intellectual property, and technology closely enough to recognize the barriers that others encounter in gaining access to their publications.

Few universities include incentives in their tenure and promotion criteria for scholars to contribute data or unpublished documents to the research enterprise. The rewards are at best indirect, such as receiving more citations by posting their work, or the respect of their colleagues and collaborators who write reference letters for them. Many scholars view the time spent marking up documents for repositories or documenting their data for use by others as time not spent on their own research. Only a few fields such as computational biology recognize database building as a scholarly contribution. Even if peers acknowledge the value of these contributions within fields, scholars will not be rewarded unless tenure and promotion committees can be convinced. If external accountability measures such as the Research Assessment Exercise in the United Kingdom offer credit for data contributions, these would become important inducements also.

The second obstacle to providing access to scholarly information products is the amount of effort required in documentation. Providing access to publications, reports, and working papers is easier than it is for data. Preparing these materials for repository submission takes a few minutes to a few hours, depending on the state of the document, experience with the process and the system, and the tools available. Even this much effort is an excuse for not contributing; indeed, librarians are providing most of the labor in markup and adding metadata. In contrast, posting an article on one's Web site may require only the few seconds to drag a file from one folder to another.

Providing access to data is much more complex. Knowledge about data is deeply embedded in social practices. Data make little sense to others without detailed descriptions of the conditions under which the data were collected, what instruments were used, how they were calibrated, explanations of the variables, the names of the data elements, and various other project-specific information. Producing this level of documentation is labor intensive and requires high levels of expertise. Scholars often hold documentation for shared data to higher standards than for data held locally and privately. They are understandably concerned about the risks of their data being misinterpreted or others finding errors in their data (Arzberger et al. 2004a, 2004b; Hilgartner and Brandt-Rauf 1994).

Data-sharing studies in genetics, medicine, and the life sciences have compared the perspectives of users and providers. Despite the requirements to share data made by funding agencies and journals in these areas, surveys reveal that researchers' requests for access to data frequently were declined. The most common reason that geneticists gave for denying access was the effort required to produce the requested materials or information (Campbell et al. 2002).

Insights into the anomaly in physics, whose researchers share publications on a massive scale but rarely share data, can be found in both the artifacts and the practices of the field. In assessing the characteristics of high-energy physics data, Paul Wouters and Colin Reddy (2003) conclude that only the results of experiments are useful; the data themselves rarely are reused. High-energy physics is among the most close-knit of all scientific fields. Physicists read preprints, and if they wish to know the details, they often contact one of the authors to talk about the paper. The international language of physics is English, "spoken with an American accent" (Traweek 2004). If physics data are not useful for reanalysis, and if scientists can learn what they need to know by talking to the authors of a paper, there may be little demand to create repositories for these data. Efforts are under way, however, to build an archive of older physics data for historical and teaching purposes (Traweek and Nakayama 2005).

The third category of obstacles in providing access to research data involves scientific priority. Priority, in the sense of scholarly communication (see chapter 4), is the notion that the first one to register a claim for a new discovery or finding receives the scholarly credit for it. Scholars will jealously guard their data until publication, as everything from patents to Nobel Prizes can rest on who registers a claim first. The factors noted earlier about the interaction between sharing practices and data characteristics (e.g., the degree to which data collection and analysis are automated) influence whether data are shared after publication. Regardless of the type of data, scientists often are unwilling to release data until they have exhausted them for their own research purposes. Public policy pressure may not be enough to get scientists to release data prior to publication. International agencies have been unsuccessful in obtaining agreement among investigators to share data on the avian flu virus (H5N1), despite the risks of an international pandemic (Enserink, 2006a, 2006b).

The high stakes on making data available prior to establishing a scientific claim are illustrated by the dispute over the discovery of a "10th planet." The incident illuminates how differing perceptions of priority may clash in the public world of the Internet, and some of the ethical issues involved in access to data. A team at Caltech headed by Michael Brown (2005) had been tracking an astronomical object for some time before determining its path was sufficiently regular to qualify as a planet. They submitted a journal article for publication, but did not release the data or make a public announcement, pending the outcome of peer review. The Caltech team also submitted an abstract about this research to an astronomy conference using their code name for the planet, not realizing that their data were on an unsecured site. A team in Spain quickly did a Google search on the code name in the abstract, found the data, and matched it to some earlier observations of their own. They submitted a paper claiming that they had discovered the planet, without making reference to Brown's data. Computer logs confirmed the identity and time of access to the Caltech data by the Spanish team. The dispute was resolved by the Minor Planet Center, which is the arbiter for this field (Kerr 2005). Brown's team ultimately received credit for the discovery of Kuiper Belt object UB313, nicknamed Xena, which is larger than Pluto. It was a Pyrrhic victory for Brown and his team, however, as the discovery reignited long-standing debates about the definition of a planet. Under the new definition established by the International Astronomical Union, both Pluto and Xena were demoted to "dwarf planet" status.

Priority and access to data sometimes are balanced through embargoes. Even when funding agencies or journals require data deposit, investigators usually have exclusive rights to the data for a period of months or years (e.g., one year for the NIH and two years for the Incorporated Research Institutions for Seismology). Yet genomes are posted within twenty-four hours of their sequencing. The NSF rules say "within a reasonable period of time," although divisions of the NSF may have more specific requirements. In fields without clear rules or consistent practices on embargoes, individual researchers are left to interpret the meaning of "a reasonable period." Scientists are expected to publish their data before releasing them, and the embargo period encourages faster publication. Enforcement is often minimal, as discussed in chapter 6 (Genome Canada 2005; *Grant Policy Manual* 2001, sec. 734b; Hilgartner 1998; Wellcome Trust Statement 1997).

Related to priority issues are concerns for "free riders" in the economic sense. Those who have devoted the effort to obtaining the research funding and gathering the data may be reluctant to release their data to others who may benefit without having made those investments. Scholars often are more willing to share data privately with known colleagues than to contribute those same data to a repository. They may feel that such access is more likely to be reciprocated and that they are more likely to receive credit as the originators of the data. The release may also depend on the intended use of the data, which can only be ascertained by personal contact. Some are more willing to release data for research questions that do not compete with their own, for example (Arzberger et al. 2004a, 2004b; Borgman, Wallis, and Enyedy forthcoming; David and Spence 2003; Lamb and Davidson 2005).

The fourth category of disincentives involves the loss of control over intellectual property. Several aspects of behavior, policy, and law intermingle to create substantial barriers to sharing information. Scientists control the data they generate, and often feel a sense of ownership, whether or not they actually own them legally. They have considerable autonomy in determining what data to release, to whom, in what form, and when. Even when clear rules apply for contributing data to repositories, for example, it is the scientists who determine which data have sufficient factual status to be released. Data often are closely held by investigators even in private research organizations, despite the clear ownership by the parent company. Data can be bartered for other data, for access to laboratories, patents, or training in novel techniques, or can be "prereleased" to corporate sponsors. Once released to a repository, scientists may no longer be able to use those data as barter. They will have relinquished control over data they may have spent days, months, or years collecting. Scientists trade off a number of considerations in deciding when and how to release data. In some cases, they restrict access to the data stream; in other cases, they might target the release by using data access as a negotiating point; and in yet other cases, they may provide general access. Early access may be counterproductive if the data were not adequately verified, or if it allows free riders to get ahead. Late release may leave scientific claims inadequately supported or may be viewed as uncollegial (Hilgartner and Brandt-Rauf 1994).

In many cases, the ownership of data is not clear. Ownership and control may be spread among many collaborators, funding agencies, and jurisdictions. Data may not be released because no one can determine easily who has the authority to release them. In other instances, a university intellectual property office may determine whether data are to be released. The "ethos of sharing" is threatened by changes in intellectual property models which encourage the ownership of data that previously would have fallen into the public domain (*Access to and Retention of Research Data* 2006; Cohen 2006; David and Spence 2003; Reichman and Uhlir 2003; Bayh-Dole Act 1999).

Ownership and control of data are significant barriers to access in all fields. In science, where most data are produced for research purposes, ownership issues usually involve the division of rights among funders, investigators, and collaborators. If the research combines data from multiple sources, the rights of each party must be ascertained. Rights vary depending on whether the research is publicly or privately funded, on how the public-private partnerships are arranged, and the policies of individual countries. Research in big science, data-intensive fields often involves collaborators from multiple institutions and countries, leading to complex intellectual property agreements. The administrative overhead involved in these arrangements is more than many researchers wish to bear.

Social Sciences

Scientists want e-Research infrastructure in order to do science. Social scientists want e-Research in order to do social science, but they also want to apply the knowledge and methods of their discipline to assist in the design of that infrastructure. These dual research agendas are evident in two U.S. policy studies (Berman and Brady 2005; Unsworth et al. 2006) and the mission of a national center in the United Kingdom (ESRC National Center for e-Social Science 2006). This section is concerned with the former theme: how the practices and policies in the social sciences may influence the use of a distributed, collaborative, data- and information-intensive information infrastructure for scholarship.

Social, behavioral, and economic research attempts to understand, or at least to describe, human behavior. Such research may or may not have specific policy purposes. The discipline has a broad scope and tends to be defined only by listing the academic fields it incorporates. These usually include anthropology, economics, political science, sociology, and psychology. The social sciences border the sciences in fields such as biology and geography, where the scientific findings are set in social contexts. They also border the humanities in fields such as history that mix analytic and interpretative approaches. The social sciences can cluster with either the sciences or humanities, depending on the issues involved. One study of infrastructure for the social sciences addressed partnerships with computer sciences and engineering (Berman and Brady 2005), while another focused on the common needs of the social sciences and humanities (Unsworth et al. 2006). A third study considered the information resources needed by the social sciences and humanities (*E-Resources for Research in the Humanities and Social Sciences* 2005).

Data sources for the social sciences, like the sciences, include observations, computations, experiments, and records. They use a variety of quantitative and qualitative methods, including sophisticated computational models. Competing explanations of social phenomena coexist more comfortably than do competing explanations of physical phenomena, however. The social sciences are slower to reject prior theories than are the sciences; rather, old debates about social issues may be revisited repeatedly. Current publications may subsume prior knowledge only within a particular school of thought, and thus one must read widely to achieve a comprehensive view of the theory and evidence on social science topics (Cronin 2005; Polsby 1998).

Information Artifacts in the Social Sciences

Like the sciences, the social sciences create and use many forms of information. Yet they differ in the sources of the data. While almost all scientific data are created by and for scientific purposes, a significant portion of social scientific data consists of records created for other purposes, by other parties.

Social Scientific Documents   Journal articles dominate publication in the social sciences, but books also play an important role. The amount of scholarly literature online in the social sciences has grown continuously since the 1980s, although the depth and breadth of coverage are considerably less than in the sciences. One reason is that the university presses, scholarly societies, and small publishers that dominate scholarly publishing in the social sciences and humanities have invested less capital in electronic publishing than have the large commercial publishers that dominate the sciences (Unsworth et al. 2006).

The unevenness of the access to social science and humanities journals is reflected in a British Academy survey finding that just over half the scholars who responded agreed that most of the journal literature they needed was online or could be accessed easily (*E-Resources for Research in the Humanities and Social Sciences* 2005, 41–42). Bibliographic coverage also is shallower than in the sciences, based on the ISI statistics noted in chapter 7. The ISI science indexes date back to 1900, but its social science indexes only go back to 1956. JSTOR, which is an important source of full-text journal content in the social sciences, digitizes issues up to a "moving wall" of three to five years earlier. Older issues of social science journals may be online, but the most recent issues of some journals are available only in print, leaving interim gaps. JSTOR is complemented by Project MUSE, which like JSTOR, began as a Mellon-funded prototype. Project MUSE provides immediate access to three hundred journals in the humanities, social sciences, and arts from sixty publishers (JSTOR 2006; Project MUSE 2006). The social sciences also rely on monographic literature and will benefit from the various book digitization projects under way.

The half-life of journal literature in the social sciences is longer, on average, than in the sciences, meaning that articles remain useful for more years. An early study of JSTOR usage comparing the ISI citation statistics to article usage found that the articles most often retrieved were scattered across the chronological spectrum. Usage in fields with "classic articles," such as those in economics on the cost of capital or monetary policy, is clustered around those classics (Guthrie 2001). This finding might explain why Barnett, Fink, and Debus (1989) found that the citation age of an average article was longest in the social sciences, as discussed in chapter 7. Such results reinforce the notion that the social sciences are less cumulative than are the sciences. In sum, social scientists require more historical depth and breadth in the type of scholarly resources than do scientists, but less of their literature is available online.

Social Scientific Data   Data in the social sciences fall into two general categories. The first is data collected by researchers through experiments, interviews, surveys, observations, or similar means, analogous to scientific methods. Most new data are generated in digital form. Data originating in other forms may be converted to digital form for analysis, further increasing the available stock. The second category is data collected by other people or institutions, usually for purposes other than research. These sources include government and institutional data such as census figures, economic indicators, demographics, and other public records. Many of these data are online, especially government data. The availability of some government information is growing through e-government initiatives, but the outsourcing of data gathering and publication is limiting access to other types. Mass media content (e.g., radio, television, and newspapers) and records of corporations also can be valuable social science data sources. Private agencies are less likely to offer their data, but public agencies such as the British Broadcasting Corporation are making important sound and video archives available. Physical documentary sources such as maps, institutional records, and archives also can be research data. Some useful data are easily identified and of obvious significance, while others are transitory or ephemeral.

Deciding *what* are data is even more difficult in the social sciences than in the sciences due to the volume and diversity of data sources and the lack of control over sources created by third parties. Social science efforts "to database the world" (Bowker 2005) are unlikely to be as comprehensive as those of the sciences. One reason is that the amount of potentially valuable content residing in the world's libraries, museums, archives, government records systems, and personal collections is too massive to digitize. Another is the inability to enumerate or describe all potential sources of data. Social scientists always are looking for new data, and new methods to collect and analyze data.

Questions of "*when* is data?" are at least as complex in the social sciences as in the sciences. The data are both intrinsically and extrinsically complex. Data from interviews, for example, require interpreting a person's cognition or intent, which may be captured in text, audio, video, or in multiple media. These data are gathered in a social context (e.g., time, place, current events, relationships, or role) that must be considered in interpretation. It is difficult for the research team that generates the data to capture their meaning; coding these data for interpretation by others is even more difficult. Social science data are subjected to processes of cleaning, analyzing, and verifying before they have factual status. Judgments of when that status is reached vary from person to person and field to field. Here, the problems of making embedded knowledge mobile are similar to those of the sciences. Scholars must represent their knowledge in ways that can be transferred to others, whether as readers of publications or users of their data.

Data acquired from outside sources such as polls, census records, or economic indicators also are problematic, as scholars usually are dependent on the documentation provided by the originating agency. The tacit knowledge problem here is somewhat different than in the sciences. Social scientists often must interpret representations of knowledge that were produced by nonresearchers, for nonresearch purposes.

Social scientific data are further distinguished from scientific data by the problems of privacy, secrecy, confidentiality, and copyright that Brady (2004) labeled "intractable." Data about individuals must be collected and managed in ways that assure confidentiality. The rules for managing data vary by jurisdiction and by circumstance, such as current versus historical records. Data acquired from third parties may be subject to copyright and other constraints that limit their use and publication. These include contractual agreements regarding the purposes for which the data may be used, the time period of use, and conditions for further release.

Description and Organization in the Social Sciences   The language of description in the social sciences varies from field to field, as it does in the sciences and humanities. Many notable subject vocabularies exist for individual fields such as psychology, sociology, and education. Description and representation can be more difficult in the social sciences than in the sciences due to the multiple audiences involved. On the input side, social scientists often are taking data and documents produced for other communities and describing them for their own research purposes. On the output side, they make their data and documents understandable not only to other scholars in their own field but frequently to scholars in other fields, other audiences such as policymakers, and to the general public. Information standardization efforts in the social sciences are less focused on subject terminology than on structural characteristics and technical documentation, such as the Data Documentation Initiative (2006). Text and data mining to identify patterns and relationships also are useful in the social sciences (Ananiadou et al. 2005; Lynch 2006; National Centre for Text Mining 2006).

Social scientists are especially concerned about how to describe complex digital objects (e.g., economic studies that combine interviews, government records, news reports, and other records), given the multiple origins of their data and the need to make these combined objects usable by others. The replicability and extensibility of social models, such as political trends or regional, national, or international cultural migrations, are among the most valuable and challenging applications of e-Research in the social sciences (Berman and Brady 2005).

Information Practices in the Social Sciences

E-Research encompasses a disruptive set of technologies with the potential to revolutionize the social sciences. Social scientific practices differ from those in the sciences on a number of dimensions, reflecting the contrasting needs of this community.

Practices Associated with Social Scientific Documents   Like scientists, social scientists vary in how they seek, use, and share information (Ellis 1993; Ellis, Cox, and Hall 1993). Preprint practices are an interesting case to consider, given their historic role in scholarly communication. Michael Nentwich (2003, 139) tested Tony Becher's (1989) claim that preprints play a larger role in fields that are more competitive and "teamwork-oriented." He found the "preprint culture" to be highest in economics and lowest in history, anthropology, and parts of sociology (but higher in others), of the social science specialties he studied.

In this comparison, Nentwich equates preprint practices with open-access repositories. While similar in original intent, repositories and the self-archiving movement have diverged since the time of Nentwich's analysis. The comparison between preprint culture and sharing documents via self-archiving is worthy of further analysis. Both cognitive psychology and economics have notable repositories, for example, but they operate on different premises. Cogprints, in psychology, is one of the earliest self-archiving repositories and remains true to its roots. Individuals self-archive full texts of their papers, similar to the arXiv model. Cogprints is now a component of the e-Prints archive based at the University of Southampton, and contains papers in psychology and related areas of computer science, philosophy, and linguistics.

RePEc, in economics, does not accept personal contributions. Self-archiving only occurs through departmental and institutional repositories. Nor does it contain the full text of articles and papers. Entries are bibliographic references with links to the full text; access to the full text may require a subscription or contacting the authors. RePEc is therefore more a catalog than a repository. It reflects a community initiative, however, using volunteers in forty-eight countries to collect papers in economics. By late 2006, the RePEc database held more than four hundred thousand records, of which more than three hundred thousand were available online (arXiv.org e-Print Archive 2006; Cogprints 2006; Research Papers in Economics 2006).

Thus, practices for preprint circulation and self-archiving vary even within the social sciences. Few social science fields have sufficient resources to invest in large projects such as disciplinary repositories. Economics and psychology are known for their departmental collections of working papers, so it is not surprising that these were among the first fields to coordinate their efforts, albeit in different ways. Collaboration and coauthorship are lower in the social sciences than in the sciences, although interest in collaboration and interdisciplinary work continues to grow.

Practices Associated with Social Scientific Data   The social sciences are facing their own data deluge, as they capture observations of human interaction online, and mine large collections of demographic, economic, and other data sources. Those whose research depends on large, quantitative data sets are eager to have tools, computational resources, and archiving facilities comparable to those of the sciences (Berman and Brady 2005). The degree of automation of data collection and analysis appears to be associated with the willingness to share data, regardless of academic discipline (Pritchard, Carver, and Anand 2004).

While relatively little research exists on the "fact-making" activities of social scientists, the processes are similar, as evidenced by Brady's (2004) analysis of the characteristics of social science data noted earlier. As in the sciences, data are cleaned, verified, codified, interpreted, and rein-terpreted. The challenges of making tacit knowledge explicit enough to be shareable are at least as difficult, given the contextual complexity of human activity being studied. Bowker's (2005) concerns about the dis-articulation of data and the publications that describe them apply equally to the social sciences.

Information practices probably vary more widely within the social sciences by research method than by field. Quantitative data are more easily coded for analysis (although not "easy" to code) than are qualitative data. Compared to qualitative methods, quantitative methods are more amenable to the partition of labor and thus to collaboration. Coding qualitative data requires an intimate knowledge of the context in which they were collected. Nevertheless, efforts are under way to increase the sharing of qualitative social science data through consistent metadata and markup (Online Qualitative Data Resources 2005).

Social scientists often combine quantitative and qualitative data from multiple sources, especially when studying current events such as elections and natural disasters (e.g., polls, interviews, news media reports, campaign literature, and demographics). The products of social science research can be complex digital objects that incorporate a variety of data types.

Research methods, both quantitative and qualitative, are more formalized and embodied in social science textbooks than they are in other disciplines. Whereas graduate students in the sciences and humanities learn most of their research methods through practice and mentorship, graduate training in the social sciences normally includes multiple courses in methods of research design and data analysis. Students are encouraged and sometimes required to cross departmental boundaries to take the methods courses most appropriate to their research topics.

Quantitative methods courses in the departments of sociology and psychology, and qualitative courses in history and anthropology, for example, may draw students from a wide range of social science fields. Thus, research methods unify, as well as divide, the social sciences.

Incentives and Disincentives to Build the Content Layer for the Social Sciences

Access to the publications and data of scientists has been a greater public policy concern than access to the work of social scientists or humanists. The evaluation and accountability of scholarly work in all academic fields, though, is among the key drivers for institutional repositories. Open access to scholarly work is another concern that transcends disciplines. Pressure for improving information infrastructure in support of the social sciences also comes from within its constituent fields. The arguments are comparable to those of the sciences, focusing on how better data, tools, and computational services will enable a more comprehensive understanding of human and social behavior. Other benefits would accrue to the public by having better access to the cultural records of society (Berman and Brady 2005; Lynch and Lippincott 2005; Unsworth et al. 2006; Westrienen and Lynch 2005; Willinsky 2006).

Incentives for Social Scientists to Share Information   The incentives to make one's scholarly products available differ little between the sciences and the social sciences. Social scientists are as eager to have their work published and available as scholars in other disciplines. They self-archive papers on their Web sites, and contribute to disciplinary and institutional repositories. Comparative rates of contribution between disciplines are not readily available. Lacking evidence to the contrary, participation in self-archiving in the social sciences is presumed comparable to the low rate in other disciplines (see chapter 5). Social scientists have established important data repositories, especially for large survey data sets, as discussed in chapter 6.

Social scientists are under some pressure from funding agencies to make their data more available, but to a lesser degree than in the sciences. The many social scientists who rely on data produced by other researchers have reciprocity inducements to make their data available.

Those who rely on data from nonresearch sources such as governments and private agencies are in a different situation. These data flows are unilateral; scholars may have no data to offer in return. Sometimes investigators can offer expertise, early access to results, or other resources in exchange for data. While governments generally are obligated to release data, they may not necessarily release precisely the data desired, in useful formats, in a timely manner, or at a fee that researchers can afford. Private agencies may have few motivations other than goodwill to release data for research purposes. The inducements for nonresearch agencies to provide data for research purposes is a major issue in building the content layer for the social sciences.

Disincentives for Social Scientists to Share Information   The same four categories of disincentives to sharing in the sciences exist for the social sciences, although the balance is somewhat different. Complicating matters further is the use of content not generated by the social sciences research community.

First, scholars in all fields are rewarded for publication but rarely for managing their information. Social scientists are no more likely to receive credit in hiring, tenure, or promotion for contributing to repositories than are scholars in other fields. Data are even less a stream of capital in the social sciences than in the sciences, so awareness of the value of these activities may be lower. Nonetheless, because the social sciences have established their own data repositories and are accustomed to combining data from multiple sources, this community may soon place greater value on contributing to these resources.

The second obstacle is the effort required in documenting information artifacts to make them useful to others. When scientists deny others access to their data, the effort to describe, represent, and codify them is commonly cited as the reason. Social scientists have at least as much difficulty making tacit knowledge explicit as do other scientists. Social sciences data arguably are harder to interpret by others due to the "variety, complexity, incomprehensibility, and intractability of the entities that are studied" (Brady 2004).

Documenting research data in the social sciences is complicated further by rules on access to human subjects and the confidentiality of records. To provide access to data sets containing information on individuals, data must be made thoroughly anonymous and specific clearances may need to be obtained from human subjects protection committees (formally known as Institutional Review Boards or IRBs in the United States). The standard practice in the social sciences is to separate research data (e.g., answers to interview questions) from personal identification, but additional data cleaning may be required to ensure that others cannot determine identity by matching these data with another data set, for example. IRBs often prefer that data sets be destroyed at the end of research projects to guarantee that records with personal identification cannot be accessed. The destruction of data sets assures confidentiality, but it also means that these data cannot be combined or compared with other sources in the future.

These review boards are under pressure both to increase compliance with rules on the protection of human and animal subjects and to decrease the constraints they impose on investigators. Rules made with the best of intentions can severely limit researchers' abilities to collect, manage, and share data. Opinions on the appropriate balance of rights and responsibilities vary widely, and are the subject of contentious debates in universities, funding agencies, and national and international policy arenas (Gunsalus et al. 2006).

As in the sciences, the third barrier to providing access to data involves priority. The less cumulative nature of the social sciences makes priority not so great a barrier to sharing as in the sciences, however. A particle can be discovered only once, but a social survey can be interpreted many times, in many ways. Even so, social science investigators are similarly reluctant to release their data until they have published their results and perhaps exhausted further uses of the data.

The fourth obstacle, intellectual property rights, and related concerns about the ownership and control of data that social scientists produce, resemble those of the sciences. These include the vagaries of ownership, the authority to release data, and the use of data as barter. Collaborative efforts are smaller and less frequent, so the social sciences have somewhat less overhead in reaching agreements among multiple collaborators in different universities and political jurisdictions.

For data that social scientists acquire from public agencies, corporate entities, and other third parties, the issues differ from the sciences. Each data source may be available under different contractual terms with respect to how the data may be used, reused, or cited, and over what period of time. When data are combined from multiple sources, the property rights may become entangled, preventing others from reusing or building on the combined product. While scientists may encounter some of these issues in acquiring scientific data from other investigators, social scientists frequently obtain data from nonresearch sources. The requirements for use and release can be complex, and lacking reciprocity, social scientists may have minimal bargaining power in obtaining access to desired data.

Ownership and control issues are made more complex by the confidentiality requirements of social science data. For instance, to observe or interview individuals, social scientists usually must obtain their signatures on consent forms. Following IRB rules, the consent forms specify what data are being collected and the purposes for which they are to be used. Reusing the data for another study may require contacting the subjects to obtain new consents. The overhead of this effort may be prohibitive in time and expense. Indeed, it may be impossible if the links between the subjects' identities and their responses were destroyed, as is often required.

In an international, multidisciplinary study of policies on data sharing, the responding agencies ranked legal problems (including privacy) as the greatest barrier to promoting access to research data. Following closely behind were technical problems and standards, with institutional barriers and prohibitive cost much further down the ranking (Wouters 2002, 19). Many individuals and agencies have called for a concerted effort to address the intellectual property issues endemic to social scientific data so that they can be shared, used, and reused in ways similar to that of the sciences (Berman and Brady 2005; Brady 2004; ESRC National Center for e-Social Science 2006; Unsworth et al. 2006).

Humanities

Like social scientists, humanities scholars want e-Research tools and services for their work, and wish to participate in shaping the technology and policy for scholarly information infrastructure. Requirements for the humanities are receiving more attention since a U.S. policy study that conducted public hearings (Commission on Cyberinfrastructure 2006; Unsworth et al. 2006) and a U.K. study on information resource needs (*E-Resources for Research in the Humanities and Social Sciences* 2005). The use of information technologies in the humanities is now a topic of many books and the focus of several research centers (Cohen and Rosenzweig 2005a, 2006; Hayles 2005; Humanities Advanced Technology and Information Institute 2006; Institute for Advanced Technology in the Humanities 2006; Lanham 1993; Liu 2004).

Also like the social sciences, the humanities often are defined only by listing constituent fields such as philosophy, literature and languages, linguistics, and musicology, and sometimes also the arts and theater. History straddles the boundary between the social sciences and the humanities; academic history departments are found in both disciplines. The humanities border the sciences in fields such as bioethics and cultural geography. Some aspects of information-related behavior and technology use vary as much within the humanities as between the humanities and other disciplines (Nentwich 2003; Stone 1982). The discipline does have a unifying theme, however, as explained by Bernard Frischer (2004): "Since the ancient Greeks, the essential feature of the study of humanity is that it makes 'man the measure of all things; of the things that exist, how they exist; of the things that do not exist, how they do not exist.'"

Humanities scholarship is even more difficult to characterize than are the sciences and social sciences. Generally speaking, the humanities are more interpretative than data driven, but some humanists conduct qualitative studies using social sciences methods, and others employ quantitative methods. Digital humanities scholarship often reflects sophisticated computational expertise. Humanists value new interpretations, perspectives, and sources of data to examine age-old questions of art and culture.

Humanities research using digital technologies takes place both in universities and in the cultural heritage sector (libraries, archives, and museums), although the term cultural heritage is more widely used in Europe than elsewhere. Phrases such as "digital history," "digital humanities," and "computers in the humanities" usually refer to the use of computers in research, while "humanities computing" is more likely to mean technical support for teaching and research in humanities subjects

(Cohen and Rosenzweig 2005b, 2006; Geser and Pereira 2004a, 2004b; Jose 2004; Ross, Donnelly, and Dobreva 2004; Ross et al. 2005).

Information Artifacts in the Humanities

Artifacts in the humanities differ from those of the sciences and social sciences in several respects. Humanists use the largest array of information sources, and as a consequence, the distinction between documents and data is the least clear. They also have a greater number of audiences for their data and the products of their research. Whereas scientific findings usually must be translated for a general audience, humanities findings often are directly accessible and of immediate interest to the general public.

Humanistic and Cultural Documents For authors in the humanities, scholarly monographs remain the gold standard for publishing. Journals and conference papers play an important role, but to a much lesser extent than in the sciences or social sciences. The restructuring of scholarly book publishing has contributed to the restructuring of scholarly communication in the humanities. As it becomes more difficult to get books published, scholars in these fields have become more amenable to writing journal articles and presenting their work as digital products.

As readers, humanists have access to the smallest proportion of their literature online of any discipline. The bibliographic coverage of journal literature is shallow in the humanities, with the ISI *Arts and Humanities Citation Index* providing coverage only back to 1975 (compared to 1900 for the sciences and 1956 for the social sciences). *Scopus*, despite claiming to be the largest online literature database, does not include the humanities (*Scopus* in Detail 2006). The amount of scholarly journal literature online does continue to grow, and JSTOR (2006) and Project MUSE (2006) are essential resources for this community. ARTstor (2005), also developed by the Mellon Foundation, provides access to a diverse lineup of images and photographs.

Relatively few scholarly monographs have been digitized, but the situation is changing rapidly with mass digitization projects involving some of the world's major research libraries. Literature in the humanities goes out of print long before it goes out of date, so efforts to make older, out-of-copyright books available greatly benefit these fields. Project Gutenberg (2006), which came online in 1971, is arguably the first digital library of monographs (Hart 1992). It now contains the full text of more than sixteen thousand out-of-print books. The Internet has improved access to older and out-of-print materials in many ways. Online book-sellers and auction sites have become essential resources to obtain used books, for instance.

While the half-life of literature is considered to be the longest in the humanities (Meadows 1998), the large comparative study discussed earlier found the shortest citation age of an average article in the humanities (Barnett, Fink, and Debus 1989). Kevin M. Guthrie's (2001) JSTOR study also found that the usage of history articles was much more concentrated in recent publications than was the usage of articles in economics or mathematics (the three fields studied). A close inspection revealed that the use of history articles was widely scattered across time periods, without the clustering around classic articles found in the other two fields. Although history can be considered within either the humanities or the social sciences, comparisons between these findings do reinforce others' conclusions that humanists may read current journal articles to keep up with their fields, but rely more heavily for their research on sources not covered by journal indexes. The findings also amplify concerns about the validity of citation studies of journal literature in the humanities, given the reliance on monographic and archival sources.

In sum, the humanities draw on the longest literature time span of any of the disciplines, and yet have the least amount of their scholarly literature online. So far, they are the discipline most poorly served by the publications component of the content layer. Their situation soon may change radically, however. The mass digitization projects currently underway, such as the Open Content Alliance, Google Print, and other partnerships mentioned in chapter 5, promise to make scholarly books much more widely available online. As the heaviest users of the older monographic literature being digitized, humanities scholars are likely to reap the greatest benefits from these projects.

Humanistic and Cultural Data   What seems a clear line between publications and data in the sciences and social sciences is a decidedly fuzzy one in the humanities. Publications and other documents are essential sources of data to humanists. Newspapers, unpublished correspondence, diaries, manuscripts, and photographs are among the most heavily used sources by academic historians, for example (I. Anderson 2004; Tibbo 2003). They are analyzed for facts, evidence, themes, and interpretations. Text mining is especially fruitful in the humanities, as computers can generate concordances, extract text strings in which names and places are mentioned, and accomplish many other analyses that are tedious or impossible to accomplish manually. The humanities will be greatly advantaged by the availability of large bodies of digitized text, provided they can obtain access to them for computational purposes.

Data sources for the humanities are innumerable. Almost any document, physical artifact, or record of human activity can be used to study culture. Humanities scholars value new approaches, and recognizing something as a source of data (e.g., high school yearbooks, cookbooks, or wear patterns in the floors of public places) can be an act of scholarship. Discovering heretofore unknown treasures buried in the world's archives is particularly newsworthy. Musical scores by prominent composers and drawings by influential artists have lain undiscovered for hundreds of years, making famous the scholar who finds them. It is impossible to inventory, much less digitize, all the data that might be useful scholarship in the humanities.

Also distinctive about humanities data is their dispersion and separation from context. Cultural artifacts are bought and sold, looted in wars, and relocated to museums and private collections. International agreements on the repatriation of cultural objects now prevent many items from being exported, but items that were exported decades or centuries ago are unlikely to be returned to their original sites. Those who hold cultural artifacts create the records that describe them, and thus the records also are dispersed (Geser and Pereira 2004b; Paterson 2005).

Digitizing cultural records and artifacts makes them more malleable and mutable, which creates interesting possibilities for analyzing, decontextualizing, and recombining objects. Yet digitizing objects separates them from their origins, exacerbating humanists' problems in maintaining the context. Removing text from its physical embodiment in a fixed object may delete features that are important to researchers, such as line and page breaks, fonts, illustrations, choices of paper, bindings, and marginalia. Scholars frequently would like to compare such features in multiple editions or copies. Converting content to digital form sometimes is incomplete, leaving out portions of text, footnotes, appendixes, and other elements. Missing parts are much easier to notice in physical objects—pages are torn out or the numbering has gaps. If the pages are simply scanned, then omissions may be detected. When processed through optical character recognition software to become digital text, however, pages renumber dynamically, leaving no indication of missing pages. Page images are better for comparing features of the original artifact, and digital texts are better for keyword searching and text mining.

Physical objects and digital texts differ in other important ways. Printed books are better for linear reading, although readers do skip around in them. Books have owners, who annotate them, and libraries that catalog them. The physical artifact may contain other information that is difficult to replicate in digital environments, such as doodles, marginal notes, and borrowing history. While physical documents can indicate their relationships to other documents via references and pointers, only in digital texts can readers (or text miners) jump directly to those related objects.

Both the literature and the data of the humanities are long-lived. Exceptions certainly exist, such as studies of contemporary culture, but even these may draw historical comparisons. Determining which sources are worth digitizing and preserving may be the most difficult to accomplish in the humanities. The volume and variety of content are vast, the frequency and conditions of reuse are difficult to anticipate, and new documents and data do not necessarily replace the old. Valuable content for studying culture continues to accrete over centuries. The diversity of sources used to construct digital humanities projects, and the diversity of audiences they serve, present challenging problems in preservation and access.

Description and Organization in the Humanities   Methods for organizing information in the humanities follow from their research practices. Humanists do not rely on subject indexing to locate material to the extent that the social sciences or sciences do. They are more likely to be searching for new interpretations that are not easily described in advance; the journey through texts, libraries, and archives often is the research. Books, which constitute the core of the humanities literature, usually are cataloged with only two or three subject headings. Primary source materials are described by "archival finding aids," which may consist of detailed inventories, registers, indexes, and other types of guides to collections. Humanities scholars use these organizational tools to determine what resources exist, and where, enabling them to spend their research time and travel much more effectively (Ellis and Oldman 2005; Encoded Archival Description Finding Aids 2006; Stone 1982; Wiberley 1983, 1988; Wiberley and Jones 1989, 1994, 2000).

Humanists also rely on reference sources to identify the many variants in the names of people, places, and objects. Because so much of cultural research focuses on a time and place, geographic information systems have become valuable tools. Many essential reference tools are now available online (e.g., *Art and Architecture Thesaurus Online* 2000; Baca 2002; *Lexicon of Greek Personal Names* 2006; *Thesaurus Linguae Graecae* 1972; *Union List of Artists' Names Online* 2000).

Access to humanities literature in both libraries and archives has become much more automated since the mid-1990s. Major research libraries have completed the conversion of their catalogs to online forms, and most are available on the Internet. Catalogs and finding aids of many other types of important collections also are accessible online. Archives and libraries have joined forces to standardize their cataloging and organizing practices, extending library methods to reflect archival practice and jointly developing standards (*Encoded Archival Description* 2006; Tibbo 2003; Yakel 1992, 2005; Yakel and Kim 2005).

Humanists are leading many standards efforts for encoding text, images, and art objects. They are now extending this expertise to automated feature extraction. Algorithmic methods for locating features such as names, places, and historical events from large bodies of text are complex. Humanists have a particularly challenging task, as they mine texts in many languages and from many historical periods. Their expertise and algorithms are applicable to texts in many other fields (Crane 2006; Crane et al. 2001; Godby, Young, and Childress 2004; Metadata

Encoding and Transmission Standard 2006; Smith, Mahoney, and Crane 2002; Text Encoding Initiative 2006).

Information Practices in the Humanities

Humanities scholars integrate and aggregate data from many sources. They need tools and services to analyze digital data, as others do in the sciences and social sciences, but also tools that assist them in interpretation and contemplation.

Practices Associated with Humanistic and Cultural Documents   In the humanities, it is difficult to separate artifacts from practices or publications from data. The library is their laboratory, as the old aphorism goes. Although humanists make good use of online catalogs, indexes, and finding aids, they spend more time in libraries than do scholars from other disciplines. They browse bookshelves and trace chains of references. They also spend a lot of time in archives, where they work closely with archival staff. Only recently have digital resources in the humanities begun to achieve a critical mass, and therefore little is known about the use of these resources. Initial studies suggest that online searching in the humanities continues to be more complex than in other disciplines, as interpretative research does not lend itself to keyword retrieval. Searching on proper names, geographic places, and chronological periods is common. These types of queries require more sophisticated interfaces that can filter and match structured fields. Indeed, information retrieval for cultural materials has become a research specialty, as more attention is paid to their distinctive requirements (I. Anderson 2004; Bates, Wilde, and Siegfried 1993, 1995; Dalbello 2004; Duff, Craig, and Cherry 2004; Duff and Johnson 2002; Ross et al. 2005; Siegfried, Bates, and Wilde 1993; Stone 1982; Tibbo 2003; Toms and Duff 2002; Wiberley 1983, 1988; Wiberley and Jones 1989).

Humanistic scholarship tends to be more individualistic than in other disciplines. As Blaise Cronin (2005, 25) put it, publishing in the humanities "assumes *a* work written by *an* author." Reading a sole-authored book or article in these fields is a conversation with the author. The humanities are at the opposite extreme from the sciences, where "collective cognition" is valued. They have the lowest rates of coauthorship and collaboration of the disciplines, with the higher rates of collaboration occurring in digital projects. E-Research is expected to promote collaboration in the humanities, due to the size of projects and the range of expertise required.

Practices Associated with Humanistic and Cultural Data   Humanistic research takes place in a rich milieu that incorporates the cultural context of artifacts. As in other fields, the humanities use information technologies to search for patterns and to construct models. Electronic texts and models change the nature of scholarship in subtle and important ways, which have been discussed at great length since the humanities first began to contemplate the scholarly applications of computing (Frischer 2004; Hart 1992; Lanham 1993; Liu 2004; Lynch 2001a; Thompson 2005).

Digital humanities projects result in two general types of products. Digital libraries arise from scholarly collaborations and the initiatives of cultural heritage institutions to digitize their sources. These collections are popular for research and education. The Beazley Archive (2006), for example, had by the end of 2005 more than two hundred thousand records on ancient Greek pottery and related culture, and received more than two hundred thousand searches of its database per day. The Electronic Cultural Atlas Initiative (2006) brings together many collections across time and space. A digital library of cuneiforms enables scholars to assemble units of writing that are scattered around the world. Perseus (2006), which began as a digital library for the Greek classics, expanded into other historical periods and regions. National and international centers coordinate discovery and access for digital content in the humanities (Arts and Humanities Data Service 2006; Crane et al. 2001; Cuneiform Digital Library Initiative 2006; EDSITEment 2006; Marchionini and Crane 1994).

The other general category of digital humanities products consists of assemblages of digitized cultural objects with associated analyses and interpretations. These are the equivalent of digital books in that they present an integrated research story, but they are much more, as they often include interactive components and direct links to the original sources on which the scholarship is based. The Valley of the Shadow, for instance, takes a disparate array of letters, maps, photographs, and other records, and knits them together into a richly textured story about two communities at the time of the U.S. Civil War. The data are not new; the story is the scholarship. Annotations on individual items were created as part of the scholarship, making those items more useful to others. Rome Reborn draws on archaeological, architectural, anthropological, and literary scholarship to reconstruct the Roman Forum, Horace's Villa, and other sites in ancient Rome. Visitors can "walk" through three-dimensional models of buildings as each existed at multiple periods in history, with light and shadows accurate for the time of day and the day of year. Each reconstruction is linked to the scholarly sources on which it is based. Where scholars disagree, multiple variants and the reasons for the disputes are provided. Specialized tools such as avatars that demonstrate dances from the records of choreography suggest the vast opportunities for the use of digital data in the humanities. These are but a few examples from a rich and growing array of digital humanities projects. Scholars can reach far broader audiences for their ideas and interpretations with products such as those (Ayers 2004; Frischer and Stinson 2002; Ross, Donnelly, and Dobreva 2004).

Projects that integrate digital records for widely scattered objects are a mix of a digital library and an assemblage. Two projects by the Mellon Foundation, for example, are providing access to documents and images from the Caves of a Thousand Buddhas near Dunhuang, China, a remote outpost on the ancient Silk Road in the middle of the Gobi desert. Early in the twentieth century, a trove of nearly fifty thousand documents, some of which are considered to be the earliest printed books in the world, were found there. The majority of these documents now reside in Britain, France, and the United States; most of the remainder is in Beijing. The International Dunhuang Project (2006) is digitizing the documents, and the Mellon International Dunhuang Archive (2006) is creating a repository of images of the art in the caves. The photographs can be stitched together into three-dimensional virtual models of the caves. The caves became a UNESCO World Heritage site in 1987. Few individuals are privileged to visit in person, due to the remote location and limited access for preservation reasons, making the digital resources the only way that most people can experience these treasures.

Incentives and Disincentives to Build the Content Layer for the Humanities

Access to the publications and data of humanists has been a minor public policy issue compared to access to scientific information. Interest in scientific information is rooted in economic competitiveness, whereas the significance of humanities resources derives from their cultural value. Both concerns rest on principles of open access to scholarship. Cultural institutions such as libraries, museums, and archives have attracted attention to their rich collections by making digitized resources available online. The popularity of these online collections for education and general-interest purposes, in turn, attracts public and private funds. The Library of Congress receives far more visits per day to its online American Memory Project than it does in-person visitors to its impressive physical collections. Thus, the pressure to build the content layer for the humanities comes more from the public than from scholars, but scholarly interest is accelerating.

Incentives for Humanities Scholars to Share Information   Humanists have dual incentives for investing in information infrastructure: improving humanistic research, and making contributions to society by improving access to cultural heritage. As in the sciences and social sciences, humanities scholars view e-Research as an opportunity to ask new questions with new data. By digitizing more cultural content and making it available, the public also will have fuller access to the records of their cultures.

Sharing data in the humanities is a somewhat different issue than in other fields. The interim products of research, such as interview transcripts and research notes, are no more readily shareable than in other fields. The raw data of research often consists of documents in libraries and archives. Most of these materials are available to all scholars equally; rarely is access an issue of one scholar releasing these resources to another.

Disincentives for Humanities Scholars to Share Information   The first obstacle—that scholars are rewarded for publishing, not for managing data—is especially strong in the humanities. Here, the view still prevails that technology is not a necessary tool for research. Risk taking, particularly in the use of technology-based scholarship, rarely is rewarded in tenure and promotion. Although digital scholarship is viewed as "the inevitable future of the humanities and social sciences" (Unsworth et al. 2006, 47–48), it presently lacks adequate support in the academy.

The second barrier—the effort in documenting information to make it useful to others—also plays out differently in the humanities. When generating their own data such as interviews or observations, humanists' efforts to describe and represent data are comparable to that of scholars in other disciplines. Often humanists are working with materials already described by the originator or holder of records, such as libraries, archives, government agencies, or other entities (e.g., corporate records). Whether or not the desired content already is described as data, scholars need to explain its evidentiary value in their own words. That report often becomes part of the final product. While scholarly publications in all fields set data within a context, the context and interpretation are the scholarship in the humanities.

The third barrier to sharing—issues of priority—is more like the social sciences than the sciences. Cultural and historical events can be reinterpreted repeatedly. Prizes are based on the best interpretation rather than on the first claim to a finding. Humanists may claim priority over sources for their research, however. When a useful archive, manuscript, or other data source is identified, a scholar may mine the resource in private until ready to publish. Control over sources can go to extremes in the humanities, as in the case of the Dead Sea Scrolls. These were discovered in the Judean desert in the 1940s and held exclusively by Israeli scholars until 1991. Release of the scrolls occurred only when the Huntington Library (a private research institution in San Marino, California), in consultation with scholars, made available a microfilm copy it had long held for safekeeping (Schiffman 2002). It is not unusual for access to archaeological sites, records, and other cultural resources to be restricted to scholars of the country in which those resources are located. The situation is analogous to the sciences, where rare or unusual specimens, cell lines, or other data sources are guarded closely (Hilgartner and Brandt-Rauf 1994).

The fourth disincentive—control over intellectual property—is a double-edged sword in the humanities. One edge is the difficulty of obtaining access to content that can be used in digital humanities projects. Recent documents typically are under copyright, raising all the issues of fair use and orphan works discussed in chapter 5. Obtaining permission to quote from these in a printed journal article or book can be problematic; obtaining permission to post digitized versions on a public Web site is much more so. If the copyright owner can be found, permissions may be prohibitively expensive or simply denied. Humanities scholars often use older resources that are long out of copyright. Yet access to archival resources does not necessarily include the permission to reproduce the content in digital form. A scholar may publish excerpts and quotations from these resources, or collaborate with an archive to publish important works that have a substantial audience.

The other edge of the sword is that new rights inhere in compilations that result from digital humanities projects. These rights are not always clear, which is among the barriers to creating digital products by aggregating and integrating sources (Lynch 2006). Scholars may have to assign certain rights to the product in return for obtaining access to sources. Universities or other funders may want to commercialize the products resulting from digital humanities scholarship. Cultural heritage institutions frequently control content with digital rights management technologies such as "watermarking." Although most products of digital scholarship are published online without charge, the contents are not free for the taking. Most contain copyright notices, and many use software controls to prevent the text and images from being copied.

These intellectual property challenges in building the content layer are far beyond the control of the scholarly humanities community. The recommendations of the American Council of Learned Societies' Commission on Cyberinfrastructure for the Humanities and Social Sciences address multiple aspects of the problems of obtaining digital content and making the resulting products widely available. They view investments in cyberinfrastructure as a strategic priority for public policy. Policies that foster openness and access, cooperation between the public and private sectors, and open standards will contribute to the creation of more extensive and reusable digital collections (Unsworth et al. 2006).

Conclusions

The content layer of the scholarly information infrastructure will not be built by voluntary contributions of information artifacts from individuals. The incentives are too low and the barriers too high. Contributing publications through self-archiving has the greatest incentives and fewest barriers, but voluntary contributions remain low. Contributing data has even fewer incentives and even greater barriers.

Scholars continue to rely on the publishing system to guarantee that the products of their work are legitimized, disseminated, preserved, curated, and made accessible. Despite its unstable state, the system does exist, resting on relationships among libraries, publishers, universities, scholars, students, and other stakeholders. No comparable system exists for data. Only a few fields have succeeded in establishing infrastructures for their data, and most of these are still fledgling efforts. Little evidence exists that a common infrastructure for data will arise from the scholarly community. The requirements are diverse, the common ground is minimal, and individuals are not rewarded for tackling large institutional problems.

Building the content layer is the responsibility of institutions and policymakers rather than individuals. Individual behavior will change when policies change to offer more rewards, and when tools and services improve to decrease the effort required. Research funding is both field and country specific, while the needs for content are multidisciplinary and international. Coordinated international efforts are required. Policy documents for e-Research in the sciences, social sciences, and humanities all emphasize the need to lower the intellectual property barriers that have undermined the ethos of sharing in recent years. Universities and funding agencies would like to reward scholars for sharing publications and data. Sharing can be increased through changes in policy, subject to balancing the cooperation and competition that is endemic to scholarship.

Scholarly publications tell the story of data, regardless of whether those data are biological specimens, ecological sensor data, answers to interview questions, potshards found in an archaeological site, or themes in fourteenth-century manuscripts. The story may be lost when the data and the publications are separated. Making better links between data and the documents that describe them is a common need across disciplines.

Striking contrasts exist between disciplines in artifacts, practices, and incentives to build the content layer. Common approaches are nonetheless required to support interdisciplinary research, which is a central goal of e-Research. Scholarly products are useful to scholars in related fields and sometimes to scholars in distant fields. As the boundaries between disciplines become more porous, the interoperability of information systems and services becomes indispensable.

9

The View from Here

Work is well under way to build an advanced information infrastructure to support scholarship and learning within the rubrics of cyberinfrastructure, e-Science, e-Research, e-Infrastructure, and other terms soon to be invented. The details and deployments are changing too quickly to be captured here. Printed books such as this one are better forums to explore goals and principles in depth than to report current details, in any case. What is clear at this stage is that information is more crucial to scholarship than is the infrastructure per se. The content will outlive any technical architecture. Scholarly information is expensive to produce, requiring investments in expertise, instrumentation, fieldwork, laboratories, libraries, and archives. The economics of information are different from those of hard goods in that most of the expense and effort are involved in producing the first "copy." The subsequent copying and distribution costs for information in digital form are minimal. Yet the costs to make information permanently accessible are nontrivial. Digital documents, data sets, and composite objects must be maintained, migrated, and curated if they are to remain available and useful.

Thus, the real value in information infrastructure is in the information. Building the content layer of that infrastructure is both the greatest challenge and the greatest potential payoff of these programs. Only when the content layer is robust can data mining and other services succeed. Funding for e-Research has focused much more on technical infrastructure than on the content to support data- and information-intensive scholarship. Rich repositories have emerged from individual research areas, but they risk becoming independent silos unless they interoperate with each other. Institutional repositories are filling some of the gap, spanning disciplines and formats. Standards for content description and technologies to integrate disparate resources will help, to the extent that they are adopted across disciplines, institutions, and countries.

Of related concern is the lack of long-term funding for content construction and maintenance. The repositories associated with permanent social institutions such as national libraries will survive, but those established by volunteer consortia within disciplines may not. Many of these resources will cease being accessible after their funding ends, due to the lack of institutional frameworks to guarantee curation. Implicit in many efforts to construct the content layer is the assumption that those who produce information will share their products. Voluntary contributions will help, but cannot substitute for a robust institutional framework.

Content and Context

Information, whether documents, data, or composite objects, and whether in documentary form such as publications or physical artifacts such as plant specimens, is situated in a social context. When others wish to use the information later, they need to know the context in which it originated if they are to interpret it correctly.

The Sociotechnical Nature of Information

Information has a life cycle, and in the case of scholarly information, that life cycle can range from years to centuries in length. The diagram that resulted from a research workshop, the Social Aspects of Digital Libraries, more than a decade ago remains useful to illustrate context (figure 9.1). Three major stages of activity were identified, each with multiple steps of information handling and processing. The creation stage is the most active, in which authors may produce new information (e.g., generating data from instruments) or use other information to create something new (e.g., combining, extracting, or synthesizing). The organizing and indexing of data, documents, and objects are included in this stage. The searching stage is viewed as semiactive, because information may be used only intermittently. Storing, retrieving, distributing, and net-

Information Life Cycle

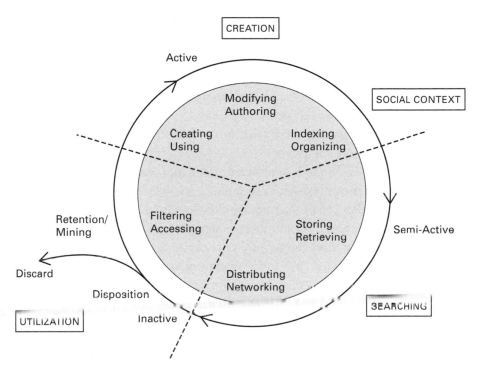

NOTE: The outer ring indicates the life cycle stages (active, semi-active, and inactive) for a given type of information artifact (such as business records, artworks, documents, or scientific data). The stages are superimposed on six types of information uses or processes (shaded circle). The cycle has three major phases: information creation, searching, and utilization. The alignment of the cycle stages with the steps of information handling and process phases may vary according to the particular social or institutional context.

Figure 9.1
Information Life Cycle
Reprinted from C. L. Borgman, M. J. Bates, M. V. Cloonan, E. N. Efthimiadis, A. J. Gilliland-Swetland, Y. Kafai, G. L. Leazer, and A. Maddox, (1996), *Social Aspects of Digital Libraries. Final Report to the National Science Foundation; Computer, Information Science, and Engineering Directorate; Division of Information, Robotics, and Intelligent Systems; Information Technology and Organizations Program* (http://is.gseis.ucla.edu/research/dl/index.html).

working are included here. The utilization stage is labeled inactive, as information may lie dormant for long periods of time. Decisions are made whether to retain the information, in which case curatorial processes would be applied, or to discard it as no longer useful. If kept, the information would remain accessible for mining and filtering. For any given set of documents or data, the steps and sequence will vary. Some information will be handled many times and indexed extensively (e.g., economic or census records that have many uses and users), and others will move swiftly from creation to disposal (e.g., extraneous or erroneous experimental data).

Each step in the cycle is influenced by the local context. The chemist designs an experiment based on an intimate knowledge of chemistry, the available data that can be incorporated, the literature that describes prior theory and results, and the journals, conferences, and repositories where the experimental results can be published or deposited. Little of this tacit knowledge is recorded in the documents or data associated with the experiment, yet other chemists can infer much of that knowledge through their own background and experience. They cannot infer all of the requisite contextual information, however, and crucial details about equipment, calibrations, and laboratory conditions sometimes fail to be recorded. Scientists in adjacent fields such as biochemistry will have even more difficulty inferring the context in which the information was created, due to differences in practices and instrumentation. The greater the distance from the origin, the more must scientists rely on documentary evidence in the record. Scholars in areas further afield from the branch of chemistry in which the experiment was conducted, students new to the field, teachers, and policymakers will be constrained in their interpretative ability by the available documentation of the context. The need for documented context increases over time as instruments, practices, and standards evolve.

Scholarly information never will be completely translatable between disciplines any more than languages ever will be perfectly translatable. Some ideas within fields cannot be fully expressed in the language of another field, just as some ideas in French or Chinese cannot be fully expressed in English. We can improve the transmission and translation of ideas through tools and practices, however. Each step in the information life cycle is associated with tools. Data are produced with instruments (e.g., surveys or sensor networks), and analyzed with statistical and visualization software. Documents are produced with word processors, and incorporate tables and images generated by data analysis tools. Documents and data may be combined with other content such as dynamic simulations or videos to form composite objects. These documents, data, and objects are stored in databases, digital libraries, and repositories. Collections may be local or distributed over networks. Search engines, data-mining software, and other information retrieval tools are used to search and combine results from these collections. Thus, these tools are cumulative, inheriting the strengths and weaknesses from the prior stage. Online searching is only as good as the digital collections available. The collections are only as good as the content available. The content is only as good as its origins and documentation.

A significant weakness of this information life cycle chart and others like it is that each unit of information is treated independently. Individual documents and data sets indeed have a life of their own, as represented here. Yet the real power in networked information is the ability to follow the value chain as each unit builds on others. Ideally, mechanisms in the information infrastructure should capture the provenance of data as they move through levels of analysis and chains of custody. Similarly, publications should link to prior versions (e.g., drafts or preprints) and the data on which they are based. Current research to establish the chain among versions and between documents and data is promising, but is far from a broad implementation. Much farther along are efforts to make explicit the implicit links between publications. The latter is an easier task because it builds on social practices already in place. Scholars cite other works to show where the new work fits in the literature of their fields. Turning those bibliographic relationships into actionable links is simply automating a social practice. Linking other parts of the chain requires that those relationships be made explicit, which requires changing social practices or finding ways to infer relationships reliably.

The lack of perfect translatability between academic fields is both a strength and a weakness of information infrastructure. It is a strength in that fields can express themselves in the full richness of their own languages. It is a weakness in that rich internal structures can create rigid boundaries between fields. Interdisciplinary work depends on the ability to span those boundaries. Data mining often depends on the ability to reconcile information from multiple sources. Forfeiting the richness of local language is too high a price to pay for interoperability. Better metadata, better mapping between metadata models, and better interoperability mechanisms will help. Strengthening the value chain between data, documents, and other objects also will help, as chains can be followed independent of language.

Malleable, Mutable, and Mobile

Another significant weakness of the information life cycle model presented above is the assumption that documents are fixed and bounded objects. Library and archival approaches to information management have been predicated on preserving fixed objects over time. Metadata are intended to provide the context necessary for these objects to be interpreted in the future, whether a month, a year, a decade, or a century later. Archivists are particularly concerned about provenance, or chains of custody, that assist in authenticating documents. Copyright also rests on notions of fixity; under the current U.S. copyright law, almost any creative work is protected by a copyright from the moment it is fixed in any medium. A key component of trust in documents is the ability to ascertain that the document has not been altered.

These notions of fixity are problematic in a digital, distributed world. Fixity will remain important for evidentiary purposes, such as the value chain in scholarship. It must remain possible to cite publications, data, and other sources in persistent ways, so that others can evaluate the evidence on which a scholarly work rests. Dynamic objects, however, will be increasingly common in scholarly work. Simulations of physical and social processes, visualizations of data, and aggregations of objects from multiple collections will exist in many states. The product of a simulation, visualization, or data-mining process may be created on demand, for a particular purpose, at a particular time. To the extent that the product is fixed, it can be described and preserved for future use. Fixity is most important in objects of long-term value. For some dynamic processes, a reasonable solution may be to preserve sufficient data, software, and documentation so that the objects and processes can be reconstructed. The latter approach cannot be a generic solution, because the data, software, and documentation may be under the control of different entities. Some may be preserved and some not. Sector and community approaches to managing dynamic content are more advantageous.

Complicating matters further is the difficulty of determining the boundaries of digital objects. People create and seek objects large and small. In some situations, a person may want to identify all the data repositories relevant to a project; in others, identifying one data point will do. A target resource may be a subunit of an extant object or an aggregation of many objects, including such items as specific documents, data elements, data sets, collections, Web pages, or Web sites. These units may or may not include links to related units, so one might retrieve a dataset independent of its documentation or the software used to create it, or a legal memorandum without the records supporting it. The appropriate units for description and retrieval and the amount of linking necessary will vary by discipline and application.

Building the Content Layer

The system of scholarly communication continues to provide the framework for the information life cycle. Scholars have incentives and mechanisms to legitimize their work, to disseminate it, and to make it accessible to the scholarly community and the larger public. Those incentives and mechanisms vary between disciplines, and all are evolving as new technologies are adopted and adapted. The institutions that are central to scholarly communication, such as universities, publishers, and funding agencies, change much more slowly than does the technology. The content layer is likely to be built more quickly and successfully if it works for the interests of the scholars and other stakeholders than if it works against those interests.

Information Institutions
Libraries, archives, and museums were not sitting idle during the period in which search engines emerged as a great technical and economic force. Rather, they have been adapting information structures, systems, and

services designed for physical artifacts to work more effectively in distributed environments. The distinction between content and surrogate, which is a basic tenet of knowledge organization in these fields, has gained renewed importance in distributed environments. Metadata can describe, or represent, content that exists only in physical forms such as printed books, journals, reports, botanical specimens, or sculptures. In these cases, the digital record is a surrogate for something that only exists off-line. If the content is in digital form, then the actual object may be searchable. Even here, metadata can act as a surrogate. Images are more easily searched by the textual metadata that describe them, for example.

Michael Buckland (1992) expected the distinction between content and surrogate to decline in importance with the transition from the paper library, to the automated library, to the electronic one. The paper library consists of paper records (e.g., catalog cards and printed indexes) as surrogates for paper documents (e.g., books and journals). The automated library, which predominated at the time of Buckland's manifesto, consists of digital records (e.g., online catalogs and indexes) as surrogates for paper documents. The emergent electronic library would consist of digital records for digital documents, blurring the distinction between the record and the document it describes. Although bibliographic descriptions still would be needed to identify the content uniquely, Buckland predicted that catalogs would become less necessary for describing local holdings.

The electronic library has not come to pass quite as he predicted. If a search is conducted completely within a database that contains the full content in digital form, such as electronic books or repositories such as arXiv, then the metadata and content are searched as one logical unit from the user's point of view. Technically, though, the system architecture may separate the index from the content for the purposes of computational efficiency, so one actually is searching metadata to identify the digital object desired. The content is duplicated and dispersed, especially for journal literature. Records on individual articles can be found in the databases of individual publishers and the databases of indexing and abstracting services such as the *Science Citation Index*, the *Sociological Abstracts*, and the *International Medieval Bibliography*. These services add value by controlling vocabulary (e.g., assigning terms from a thesaurus or ontology), standardizing author names, and other features such as citation linking. The record in these databases is a surrogate for the full digital content that usually resides in the publisher's database. Standards such as OpenURL and Info URI now enable direct links from the surrogate in one database to the content in another. The process is less seamless than Buckland imagined, but is becoming more transparent as the standards and technologies improve.

Publishers and booksellers are exposing their metadata for harvesting, which is why Google Scholar, *Scopus*, OAIster, and other search engines can retrieve surrogate records for journal articles and books. OpenURL provides context-sensitive services in coordination with OAI and OAIS (Reference Model for Open Archival Information Systems). OpenURL is used to determine the resources to which the user has access. If the article, document, data set, or other object is available without a fee, the search engine can take the user directly to the content. If the desired content is available only by a subscription or fee, the user is taken to the item if authorized, or if not, to a portal page for purchasing or for further information about how to acquire it. Again, metadata continues to serve a crucial role as surrogates in distributed architectures.

While the average user of search engines such as Google, Google Scholar, Yahoo, MSN Search, and specialty engines such as Dogpile and CITESEER may view the information world as seamless, the reality is far more complex. University research libraries subscribe to tens of thousands of digital resources. UCLA, for instance, holds licenses for access to about twenty thousand digital collections and provides access to an additional thirty thousand licensed resources via the University of California–wide California Digital Library (Strong 2006). While many of these are clusters of resources from publishers, overall they represent an enormous range of metadata structures, ontologies, and user interfaces.

Publishers and other database providers often are more concerned with branding their products, and thus distinguishing them from others, than they are with providing consistent user interfaces. Because each resource may supply its own metadata, libraries do not recatalog each individual item (which would be prohibitively expensive). They can only offer a description of the resource—a paragraph summary of the contents, keywords to categorize the subject area, a date range, the type of material, and so forth. Libraries devote considerable effort to disaggregating the resources that publishers aggregate in order to provide some coherency to the collections they offer. They are experimenting with "metasearch" mechanisms and other means to impart a coherent view of their collections and services. All of these efforts, and more, are needed to build a useful and usable content layer.

Organization and Business Models

Publishers, universities, and funding agencies are major stakeholders in building the content layer of the information infrastructure. They, in turn, have stakeholders, including boards of directors, stockholders, taxpayers, governments, and philanthropists. These entities are competing with others in their own sphere of influence and sometimes with those in other spheres. The business models that emerge from the current competition are likely to have profound influences on the shape of the information infrastructure.

Publishers   While the fundamental purposes of scholarly publishing—to legitimize, disseminate, access, and curate scholarly work—have remained relatively constant over several centuries, the means to accomplish these purposes have changed radically in less than two decades, as discussed in chapters 4 and 5. The business models of the publishing industry also have changed radically in this time period. What was a "gentlemen's profession" became a global industry marked by mergers, acquisitions, and market consolidation. Libraries and universities began to find the new pricing structures unsustainable for their own business models. Scholars and libraries found that changes in intellectual property regimes posed new barriers to fair use and the preservation of scholarly content.

Scholars, universities, and libraries collectively responded to changes in publishers' business models with new models of their own. These include open access publishing, disciplinary and institutional repositories, and the commons-based licensing of scholarly products. While publishers generally resisted these trends, sometimes aggressively, they also found ways to benefit. Many are allowing, if not necessarily encouraging, authors to make preprints and postprints available online in some form. Documents posted publicly are more easily found, and thus cited, bringing more recognition to the author, journal, and publisher. Publishers initially refused to make their metadata available out of fear of losing control over their products. As search engines became the first resort for information seeking, publishers realized the necessity of being visible. They began to expose their metadata to search engines as a marketing method, rather than hiding their content on the "dark Web."

The business models for scholarly publishing continue to evolve. Publishing is a mature market in the economic sense. Most of the big mergers already have happened. Profit margins will grow more slowly, if at all. The historical patterns of the business are shifting. For 200 years, from the eighteenth through the twentieth centuries, the number of indexing and abstracting services and the number of journals each grew exponentially, and in parallel—a pattern that held far longer than the much lauded 40-plus years of Moore's law for the computer storage capacity, stated in 1965. Indexing and abstracting services now struggle to survive as search engines encroach on their market. Such services add value in many ways, such as controlling the variants of names, places, and topics; offering tools to trace references and to analyze results sets; and selecting the most important journals in each subject area. Therefore, they provide context for searching within research specializations, fields, and disciplines. Much of the value they add is accomplished by manual methods, which are expensive and time-consuming. Indexes may lag days, weeks, or months behind the publication of the content being indexed. In contrast, the immediacy offered by search engines satisfies many people's needs, even at the price of consistency or authority. Indexing services are reevaluating their business models to determine where they can provide the most added value, to whom, at what price, and in what time frame.

Universities Universities are caught in a maelstrom of changing business models, public policies, scholarly practices, and technologies. As the price of scholarly publications spiraled upward, universities found themselves paying faculty salaries to produce publications and then paying publishers ever-higher prices to buy those products back. They responded by supporting open access publishing, building local repositories, and educating faculty about their intellectual property rights. Academic authors now weigh publishers' intellectual property policies when considering where to place their work.

The number of institutional repositories is growing, as is the number of signatories to open access initiatives such as the Berlin and Budapest Declarations, although the movement is stronger in Europe than in the United States. These developments indicate that universities are committed to maintaining access to the scholarly products of their faculty and research staff. How and why they will do so is not yet clear, however. Self-archiving and institutional repositories are no longer synonymous, as discussed in chapter 5. Universities recognize that both the documents and data of scholarship need to be captured and curated. Capturing documents is the easier part, and institutional repositories are accumulating current scholarly output such as faculty and student research and talks given at colloquiums. University-wide repositories of research data are more difficult to construct due to the specialized expertise required and the variance in data structures and practices across disciplines.

Universities also are considering various business models for maintaining access to online courses and the digital resources that supplement classroom courses. These resources are expensive to create, but they have value for subsequent courses. Some course modules are useful in multiple classes, such as undergraduate and graduate versions of a topic, or technical skills relevant to several fields. Cumulative data sets from scientific fieldwork and data from other student projects can have longer-term value. Students also may want to have their work products maintained online for their own use, and as evidence of their work for graduate school applications and future employers.

Issues in maintaining course management systems and student work products are deeply intertwined. The access and curation concerns are much different than for research work. Course content evolves fairly quickly, and the software on which courses are based may evolve even more rapidly. Rarely will the value of course content endure for as long as the research content. Such content must be appraised on a regular basis to determine whether to maintain access. Questions of what to keep available as living documents, what to keep as frozen records of courses, what to include in records, how long to keep records, and who has access to which records under what circumstances need to be considered (Lynch 2002).

Maintaining online access to student work raises intellectual property, privacy, and records retention issues. Students' data, papers, and online discussions often are integral to the course content. Student educational records, at least in the United States, fall under the strict privacy protection guidelines of the Family Educational Rights and Privacy Act (1974). Under this act, only a limited amount of information (such as directory records) can be released without explicit permission. Work done for classes can be kept confidential within the course and available only to the instructor, but this approach constrains teamwork, the reuse of student-produced course content, and the longitudinal use of data collected for coursework. Individual students can post their work on university-sponsored Web sites, but universities are unwilling to ensure that these resources will be maintained indefinitely. Sometimes students are proud to point to their course work of years past, and at other times they find that it haunts them. Universities are struggling with ways to balance privacy and publicity, current and archival access, and old and new models of instruction.

University efforts to stay on the cutting edge of technology and policy often seem at odds with the reward system for faculty. Academic practices for hiring and promotion—whether for tenure in the United States, the Research Assessment Exercise in the United Kingdom, or comparable systems elsewhere—change at a relatively slow pace. The conservatism of the reward system fosters continuity by making scholars less vulnerable to the whims of fashion or of individual administrators. The conservatism in the process, however, also reinforces the norms of earlier eras, making scholars reluctant to take risks on new venues for disseminating their work.

Many universities and national systems of higher education are still pursuing simple metrics for comparing faculty productivity across disciplines and institutions. Simple metrics tend to count what is easily counted, such as articles and citations in established journals, rather than what is most valuable or enduring. Contributions to new electronic journals, online discussion groups, data repositories, Web sites, and other new media receive minimal credit in most fields. Similarly, few promotion committees value poster presentations and other formats intended to stimulate discussion. Scholarship resulting in digital objects is especially risky in the humanities, where printed books remain the gold standard. Given the difficulties in getting credit for documentary publications in new forms and forums, it should not be surprising that few fields value the publication of data as scholarly products.

The quality of scholarly products varies widely, even in the best journals and most prestigious book series. Some excellent work appears only online, especially when that medium best serves the dynamic features of the content. In an information- and data-intensive, multidisciplinary, international, distributed world of scholarship, forms and genres will continue to proliferate. Publisher names and journal titles are less valid indicators in the digital environment. Hiring and promotion committees will have fewer external metrics on which to rely.

Universities have more carrots than sticks to use in altering faculty behavior. Change will occur most quickly when faculty are rewarded for experimenting with new forms of publishing such as open access and new scholarly products such as digital objects and data. Universities and higher education agencies risk undermining their efforts to reform scholarly communication if they merely reinforce the norms that serve print publication and that preserve the disciplinary boundaries of the past.

Funding Agencies   The changes in information infrastructure have led funding agencies to play an even larger role in public policy. They would like to foster the best possible research, in the shortest amount of time. One means to accomplish this goal is to disseminate the products of the research they fund—both publications and data—widely and rapidly. Dissemination leverages research investments by increasing the likelihood that others will read the work, be influenced by the results, and will reuse the data in subsequent research. Agencies are concerned that the traditional scholarly publishing system is serving this dissemination role less effectively than in the past. Price increases for publications and copyright controls over the reuse of content are limiting access to research reports. Funding agencies have promoted the open access movement by supporting the development of open access repositories, tools, and services, and promulgating policies that encourage their use.

Funding agencies have more leverage than most other players in the scholarly communication system. They can require document and data deposit as conditions of releasing grant funds or future funding, and they can require data management plans in grant proposals. Yet funding agencies are cautious in enforcing these requirements, for they know that their grantees must balance their responsibilities to multiple stakeholders. Even the largest and most prestigious funding agencies are having difficulty getting investigators to deposit the publications that result from their research grants. The U.S. National Institutes of Health proposed requiring its grantees to deposit final manuscript versions of journal articles that result from NIH funding. Under intense lobbying pressure from publishers, the NIH compromised with voluntary deposit and no penalties for failing to comply. The implemented policy "requests and strongly encourages all NIH-funded investigators to make their peer-reviewed author final manuscripts available to other researchers and the public at the National Library of Medicine's (NLM) PubMed Central (PMC) (http://www.pubmedcentral.nih.gov) immediately after the final date of journal publication" (NIH Public Access Policy 2005). Despite massive education efforts and extensive publicity, fewer than 4 percent of the eligible articles were deposited in PubMed Central in the first eight months of the policy (Zerhouni 2006). The NIH continues to experiment with embargo periods and incentive structures to improve compliance rates. The ability of funding agencies to ensure access to the products of the research it funds will be critical in establishing and maintaining the value chain of data and documents.

Although most major funding agencies appear to require or strongly encourage the deposit of data that originates in grant-based research, their enforcement of these policies varies widely due to the tradeoffs involved. If investigators are forced to release data prior to publishing their findings, they may be unable to claim priority. Not only would such a requirement run counter to scientific practice, it would deny credit to the funding agency for having supported successful research. Embargoes are the usual mechanism to address priority issues, although any fixed embargo period will advantage some types of research and disadvantage others. Shorter periods encourage faster publication; longer periods may discourage longitudinal and comparative research. Another concern of funding agencies is that investigators may comply with the letter of the law rather than its spirit, depositing poorly documented data that are of little value. In addition, legislative proposals to require open access to raw and summative evaluation data not only from successful clinical trials but also from failed, equivocal, and contradictory studies have provoked great concern for public health and safety. Ironically, these are the same issues that Franz Ingelfinger (1969) raised several decades earlier about the premature release of health science findings (Fisher 2006; Toy 2002).

Large national and international funding agencies also struggle to find the balance between funding infrastructure and funding new research projects. The Arpanet, Internet, supercomputer centers, data repositories, and programs on cyberinfrastructure, e-Science, e-Social Science, and e-Humanities are all investments in infrastructure to facilitate research. Infrastructure investments that enable new and different kinds of research do not benefit everyone equally. Many researchers view agency funding as a zero-sum game in which monies for infrastructure are monies not spent on grants to individual investigators. Some core infrastructure investments that appeared to benefit only a few, such as the original Arpanet, later proved to be fundamental resources for everyone. These tensions run high when the rate of funding is deemed low, as in the present situation. Funds for e-Infrastructure may pay for themselves many times in accelerating the time to discovery. Similarly, funds spent on data management may pay off manifold by enabling new research through data mining. Or they may just be funds not invested in new research projects. Funding agencies can address these difficult trade-offs only by taking a long view of societal benefit.

Information Commons

New relationships in the scholarly communication system are emerging. As the "gift-exchange" relationship between scholarly authors and publishers broke down, and the library-subscription and book-purchasing model ceased to be sustainable, open access was the first replacement model to appear. Calling open access "a model" is generous because it is presently a mixed array of methods and economic approaches. Open access is often characterized as the principle that scholarly work should be circulated as widely as possible (Willinsky 2006), although this is merely a restatement of the centuries-old principles of open science. While some advocates of open access would welcome the demise of scholarly publishers, publishers do add value, and a scholarly communication system without their participation is no more sustainable than is the subscription model. Others would gladly eliminate the copyright, given how today's intellectual property models complicate scholars' ability to disseminate their own work and to use the work of others. Intellectual property rights also serve useful purposes and will not disappear. Nevertheless, the relationships between authors, readers, publishers, and libraries must evolve toward a new equilibrium, as the present state of affairs does not serve any of the parties well.

The information commons is another ambiguous term, as examined in chapter 5. It is best understood as a set of new social and legal structures to facilitate e-Research on an international basis. As Paul David (2005, 1) explains, "This challenge should not be misconstrued and confused with the pursuit of a utopian dream of returning to some imagined golden age when property rights did not exist." The information commons subsumes the open access and open science principles within a larger framework. Open repositories are expected to become a fundamental component of the public research infrastructure. While many of these discussions are framed in terms of scientific content, the social and legal frameworks proposed will serve the full scholarly community. A growing cadre of legal, economic, and policy scholars is working out the details of commons-based approaches for scholarly and creative content. These efforts have backing from funding agencies, private foundations, universities, and international bodies such as UNESCO and the Organization for Economic Cooperation and Development. Given the broad coalition that is developing the information commons, workable solutions should emerge in the near future.

Some Solutions and Some Questions

Among the many sayings attributed to Yogi Berra (distinguished U.S. baseball player and manager) are "If you don't know where you're going, you might wind up somewhere else" and "It's tough to make predictions, especially about the future." The latter quote is properly attributed to Niels Bohr, the atomic scientist, however. Alan Kay (1971) offers constructive advice to those in a quandary about what the future will bring: "The best way to predict the future is to invent it." Understanding where we are and where we may want to go are essential for predicting or inventing the future. Technologies are adopted and adapted in unpredictable ways; few people have been successful in identifying future products or services with much specificity. Gordon Moore, the founder of Intel, famously (and accurately) predicted in 1965 that the number of transistors on a chip would double roughly every two years. Moore did not attempt to predict what could be done with faster and cheaper computer chips, instead leaving to others the responsibility to invent technologies, tools, and services that could take advantage of greater computing capacity.

Inventing the future can be a slow process, though. Vannevar Bush's (1945a) *Atlantic Monthly* article, "As We May Think," has become the canonical vision for digital libraries, hypertext, and distributed access to knowledge. An analysis of references to that article in the *Science, Social Sciences*, and *Arts and Humanities Citations Indexes* (conducted on the ISI Web of Knowledge, March 21, 2006) reveals the long gestation period of his proposal for a personal information system he called "Memex." For the first twenty years after its publication, the article received 4 or fewer cites per year. The vast majority of cites received in the first forty years were from the fields of library and information science, documentation, and information retrieval, plus a few from the history of science or technology. Only in the latter 1980s, with the growth of modern hypertext, were the origins of the ideas widely recognized. By early 2006, articles in more than ninety different subject areas had cited Bush's article a total of 717 times.

Bush tried to invent the future by proposing a radical new way of thinking about documents, links, tools, and user interfaces, long before the technology existed to accomplish it. Only those who were concerned about document management paid much attention at first. As the technology necessary to accomplish the vision matured, computer scientists began to recognize the research opportunities in information systems. Eventually Bush's vision caught the imagination of scholars in art, architecture, communication, education, ergonomics, management, music, psychology, and many other fields.

We are currently in the early stages of inventing an e-Research infrastructure for scholarship in the digital age. It may take twenty, forty, or sixty years to realize the vision, by which time the technology and tools will be quite different from today. Here, Fritz Dressler's (2005) observation is apt: "Predicting the future is easy. It's trying to figure out what's going on now that's hard." This book attempts to characterize what is going on today, and to set those developments in social, historical, and technological contexts. From an information perspective, four areas of research and development in scholarly infrastructure appear especially fruitful: (1) taking a long-term view on content, (2) balancing local and global requirements, (3) separating content from tools and services, and (4) identifying tools, technologies, and institutional mechanisms that balance the coherence and control of the content layer. This is not a comprehensive research agenda for e-Research infrastructure. Instead, it is a starting point from which to build an infrastructure *for* information.

Legacy Content: Past, Present, and Future

Most new scholarly information is being generated in digital form, and large portions of older data and documents are being digitized. It is tempting to assume that all of the important scholarly content soon will be digital, enabling future systems to manage consistent formats. Such an assumption is both risky and wrong. Librarians and archivists have seen formats come and go for centuries. They have no reason to believe that the present formats and structures will last more than a few years or decades. Floppy disks and tape backup systems have joined vacuum tubes and transistors as legacy technologies. The CD-ROMs, DVDs, and HTML of today eventually will become the legacy formats of tomorrow. Similarly, the URLs, ISBNs, and DOIs of today may eventually become the legacy name spaces of tomorrow. The Domain Name System has been a remarkably robust name space for about two decades, and even it is being stretched to its limits by the pressures to accommodate non-Roman character sets and other features unanticipated in the original design. While twenty years of stability is a long period in "Internet time," it is short in terms of scholarly information.

The New Becomes the Old   The world's legacy content and name spaces cannot be rebuilt with each new wave of technology. We must find ways to bridge formats and structures, just as we must find ways to bridge disciplines. Name spaces such as ISBNs, DOIs, and Library of Congress Card Numbers serve individual communities and types of resources. They are internally consistent frameworks that add value to the content that they identify. Replacing these name spaces with URLs might improve the interoperability in the short term, but would forfeit essential value in the long term. New approaches such as the Info URI scheme, sponsored by the National Information Standards Organization and approved by the Internet Engineering Task Force as a Request for Comments, map legacy name spaces into a URI format. The original structure is preserved, while enabling Web services to incorporate extant name spaces and content (Van de Sompel et al. 2006).

Investing in Digital Content   Content in digital form must be migrated to new media and formats as they are invented. Most digital data stored on the media of the 1980s and 1990s is now unreadable: 1,200-foot reels of tape in eight-bit format, floppy disks in 8, 5.25, and 3.5 inch formats, removable cartridges from tape backup systems, zip disks, and so on. Either the media have decayed, the equipment to read the media is no longer available, current computers lack the drivers to operate the equipment, data are stored in proprietary formats for which the software is no longer available, or all of the above. In other cases, the content has disappeared because the effort to migrate it to new computers or formats was not deemed worthwhile at the time. The ability to migrate data also depends on the quality of the metadata associated with it. If the content is adequately described, and the metadata formats and associated name spaces are supported in the new environment, then making it permanently accessible is easier. Incremental metadata may be added as the content moves from one format to the next, indicating format changes, provenance changes, ownership and rights changes, and other context necessary for use and interpretation.

Data migration is a necessary expense for maintaining digital content. Metadata provide consistent access mechanisms as content moves from computer to computer and format to format. Libraries understood the need to invest in metadata for long-term access back in the days of book and card catalogs. These lessons were relearned in the 1960s when libraries were offered "free" computers to automate their catalogs. It became painfully clear that the computers were the least of the cost; investing in the conversion and maintenance of digital catalog data was the overwhelming burden (Mason 1971).

Migration planning should be part of the initial design of any project to create or convert digital content. If the project originators take a long view, they can invest in metadata, name spaces, and format standards that will outlive the initial media in which the content is created. They will save time, effort, and money in the long run, and reduce the risk of data loss substantially. Unfortunately, few projects seem to take a long view. All too often, data migration and preservation are afterthoughts, addressed at the time that the project funding ends. Librarians are trying to intervene by educating faculty about preservation, after many unhappy experiences with last-minute, unfunded requests to take over the maintenance. Funders, including the National Science Foundation, are asking investigators to include data management plans in their grant proposals. Few university faculty or other researchers, however, have the data management knowledge to develop or execute adequate plans. Declaring that the university library will manage the data at the end of a project is not a plan. Libraries and archives are in no better position than other institutions to accept unfunded mandates. Conversely, they are in excellent positions to partner with faculty to address their common interests in the stewardship of scholarly information.

While better planning and infrastructure are optimal solutions to information preservation, other approaches also are needed. Projects frequently result in digital products that have more long-term value or wider audiences than was anticipated. Such content cannot be abandoned only because the initiators failed to plan for long-term curation.

The e-Research infrastructure will need to have repositories that can accept—and invite—contributions of digital resources at the end of projects. Arrangements for metadata, intellectual property, and access requirements will vary.

Digital Surrogates as Insurance   Legacy content in the form of artifacts such as biological specimens, archaeological objects, cultural materials in anthropological museums, and art objects such as statuary and paintings never can be digitized adequately, if at all. These resources have enduring value for scholarship. Although physical artifacts exist only in one place, the metadata describing them can be digitized and distributed. For some kinds of scholarship, knowing what exists and where is sufficient. For other kinds, a digital image or surrogate may be acceptable. For those who need to view or examine the original, the metadata are essential in identifying what exists and where, so that permission to study can be requested and trips planned.

Metadata on cultural and scientific objects, whether in digital libraries or museum curatorial databases, are proving to be exceptionally valuable in those unfortunate cases where the originals are lost or destroyed. Catalogs of books and curatorial files of cultural artifacts in Sarajevo and Baghdad, for example, are essential records to inventory items that were destroyed or to identify looted items that make their way to the black market. These records also can help in identifying duplicates or similar copies held elsewhere around the world, or in reconstructing an object from its broken parts. Photographs from archaeological digs have proved useful in identifying cultural objects that made their way to major museums years later, by questionable routes. These records are evidence in current disputes between several museums in the United States and the governments of Italy and Greece. Similarly, Hurricane Katrina destroyed important specimen collections of plants and animals located in New Orleans; digital records of these collections can assist in reconstructing them and determining which specimens were unique and which might be duplicated elsewhere.

Paper catalogs stored in the same building as the artifacts or specimens they describe might be destroyed along with the objects themselves. Digital catalogs containing not only textual descriptions but elaborate digital images can be distributed and duplicated around the world. In the event of war or natural disaster, these metadata may be our only record of those artifacts, so a strong argument can be made for the anticipatory construction of cultural and scholarly metadata (Lynch in preparation).

Capacity Building for the Content Layer   Selecting, collecting, organizing, and providing access to information, whether in physical or digital form, requires considerable skill. A workforce with these skills is a prerequisite for constructing a rich and useful content layer. Building this human capacity to provide permanent access to scholarly content is among the great challenges for an e-Infrastructure. In the current environment, little motivation exists in most fields to document the data and make institutional arrangements to ensure their longevity. Scholars are in a perpetual rush to publish and to obtain funding for the next research project. Funding agencies are beginning to require plans for long-term data management in proposals, but the skill base for data management in most fields is too low to expect wide success. Similarly, the rates of contribution to document repositories remain low in most fields.

The amount of time or effort that scholars devote to information management is unlikely to increase substantially, short of a radical change in the incentive structure. Most scholars consider the time spent on creating metadata for data and publications as time not spent on their research. Inducements such as rewards for data contribution are more likely to be effective than is coercion. Tools for reliable data capture, automatic metadata creation, and data management will help. Likewise, university services can identify new publications by their faculty members, mark them up for contribution to repositories, and clear the permissions. Deposit then becomes only a matter of faculty assent, rather than another set of tasks. These are but a few examples of the ways in which better tools and services can assist in building and maintaining the content layer.

Part of the workforce capacity for building the content layer will come from the information professions. The next generation of librarians, archivists, digital asset managers, information architects, data scientists, "cybrarians," and other information professionals will work in information institutions, research teams, publishing companies, and in partnership with other stakeholders such as media and technology companies. These professionals will need to be equally comfortable with documents and data, paper and digital objects, artifacts and surrogates, and film and digital displays. Some of their educational background will come from schools of information, and some will come from the disciplines they serve. More partnerships between fields are needed to ensure the expertise required. Programs in bioinformatics, moving image archive studies, and joint master's degrees between information studies and fields such as history, management, and law are becoming more common. The demand for expertise in the management of digital collections already far exceeds the supply.

Institutional models to maintain the scholarly content of the past, present, and future also are in short supply. Some fields such as astronomy, physics, seismology, and economics have established disciplinary repositories for data or documents. Yet even these fields have uneven coverage, with astronomy focusing on data and physics on documents, for instance. The economics repository RePEc consists mostly of surrogates for documents, some of which are publicly available and others of which are in proprietary databases. Disciplinary repositories often are funded on fixed-term research contracts, which makes them part of the research enterprise rather than part of the scholarly infrastructure. The tension between investing in either research or infrastructure is implicit in discussions of repository models, but all too rarely comes to the fore. Information institutions such as libraries, archives, and museums are part of the scholarly infrastructure. Their longevity is essential for the public trust. We cannot trust in the longevity of the content without assurances that the institution holding the content will remain in business.

Rights to Preserve   Universities have continuity and are endowed with public trust, so they would seem to be the obvious institution to maintain access to the scholarly products of their faculty, research staff, and students. They are understandably reluctant to accept an unfunded mandate with large and unpredictable costs, though, and they may also be accepting liability for data loss. Furthermore, preserving digital content requires copying, which is a right assigned to the copyright owners. Universities must obtain permission to preserve and curate content that is currently under copyright. Complicating matters further are differences between countries in the intellectual property rights that inhere in databases.

Preservation rights are one of the drivers of the open access movement. Historically, libraries maintained access to content, allowing publishers to let books go out of print and dispose of remaining copies of journals, whether in print or digital form. Libraries now lease access to journals and books in digital form, and few have rights to guarantee continuing availability when contracts end or when companies or services cease to exist. Universities can capture content that is produced by their faculty members and students, but may need publishers' permission, in addition to authors' permission, to do so. The gap in responsibility and rights for permanent access to published materials is a huge concern for the continuity of the scholarly record. Publishers are reluctant to allow libraries to preserve leased material, but are not themselves promising to take permanent responsibility for maintaining online access to their products.

Even if publishers were willing to cede control of back files to universities, published materials represent a declining proportion of the world's scholarly content. Scholarly content is distributed across formal and informal communication channels around the world, and not all of it can or should be preserved. Libraries are working together as consortia to share responsibility for what they can preserve. The Internet Archive (2006) has been taking periodic snapshots of Web sites since 1996, and it partners with libraries and archives in a variety of preservation efforts. Several national libraries and university consortia are formulating strategies and policies for preserving electronic journals (Kenney 2006). These efforts are important steps forward, but coordinated national and international investments are needed to assure permanent access to essential scholarly content. Already lost are precious scientific data from NASA missions, audiotapes of disappearing languages, and artifacts of world heritage from war-torn countries. As more of the world's intellectual content is created in digital form, the risks of loss increase proportionately. Action must be taken before too many more irreplaceable records are lost forever.

Balancing the Local and the Global

The content layer should be rich, robust, and consistent so that its content can be discovered, mined, used, and preserved by present and future generations of users. The tools and services should be generalizable, scalable, and interoperable. Yet scholarly practices are not consistent, generalizable, or scalable. They tend to be local and idiosyncratic instead, varying by individual, research project, time, and context. The situation calls for ways to balance the local needs of individual scholars, students, and teams with the global requirements of a distributed, multidisciplinary, multilingual, multipurpose e-Infrastructure.

Flexible Infrastructure Design   The scholarly infrastructure must be flexible enough to serve its many stakeholders, while not optimizing so much for one community that another is greatly disadvantaged. The example of institutional repositories in chapter 5 offers such lessons. The common vision for self-archiving and for library services diverged as the systems matured and practices evolved. An e-Research infrastructure should be able to support both purposes, but negotiation may be required. Similarly, optimizing systems for individual scientific communities may be at odds with educational or other applications. For instance, dense seismic networks of sensors in populated regions generate useful scientific data that also serve early warning systems and emergency management agencies. These applications have different goals. Seismologists capture data at rates of up to five hundred samples per second, far more than emergency services require. Emergency response agencies, in contrast, must map the damage locations to maps of streets, hospitals, and other public services. Seismologists are more concerned with mapping seismic data to the geomorphology of a region than to the built environment.

Various approaches can be taken, such as multiple layers of data and documentation, gateway standards, metadata crosswalks, and other devices to bridge applications. As each new component of infrastructure is designed, continuity with the past must be considered along with the needs of present and future users.

Personal Digital Libraries   Efforts to personalize information management and discovery are among the more promising prospects for balancing local and global considerations. "Personal digital libraries" is a catchphrase for a number of different approaches to organizing the content of individuals or teams. These might be completely local and independent databases, or they might be federated, with each owner maintaining control over certain aspects of the structure, content, and access. In designing educational services for a geospatial digital library, this approach was found to balance the risks and benefits of sharing personal information resources. Geography faculty members participating in the Alexandria Digital Earth Prototype Project (ADEPT) were reluctant to contribute their teaching materials and research data to a single shared collection. An important goal of the project was to make personal collections reusable by others, so independent collections for each faculty member was not a feasible approach. The solution was to enable instructors to gather their own resources into a personal digital library. Faculty members could choose whether or not to share their personal libraries with others, and to make items visible or not in the shared collection (Borgman et al. 2004, 2005; Champeny et al. 2004; Janee and Frew 2002).

Personal digital libraries are not a universal solution to capturing research content, but they do address several of the problems identified in chapter 8. They resolve some intellectual property issues by permitting individuals or teams to maintain control of their content, at least for the time period authorized by their funding agencies. They allow researchers to use their own data for their own purposes without necessarily contributing them to the common pool. They can address documentation problems by including simple tools to capture and manage data in structures compatible with community standards. If these personal systems also support policies for data embargoes and assigning credit to originators, they may increase the likelihood that data are contributed to common pools later. The ability to document and manage one's own data was among the most attractive features of the ADEPT system, leading faculty to adopt it for other purposes such as teaching. Personal digital libraries are an architectural approach that gives individuals and teams more control over their own content, while facilitating sharing. This approach is suited to many types of research data and documents, thereby supporting interoperable, interdisciplinary collections as well (Borgman 2003; Borgman, Wallis, and Enyedy 2006).

Personalizing Discovery   Personalizing also improves the information discovery process through tailored models of searching, recommender systems, relevance feedback, or reputation management. Personalized discovery already has proven useful in relevance ranking (adjusting the rank based on individual searching patterns) and shopping (recommending products to buy). These methods have had limited application in scholarly searching because they tend to conflate relevance with quality, as Lynch (2001b) notes. Another limitation is that personalization designed for commerce tends to invade privacy.

The simplest methods of personalizing information discovery are those that are client based and infer user preferences. These enable a user's machine to build a profile over time, without requiring the user to specify detailed parameters. Client-side personalization is less effective in distributed searching, however. Server-side personal profiles can enhance the searching of collections, but risk invading privacy, which is why library-based information systems have avoided this approach. Privacy-enhancing personalizing mechanisms that involve trusted parties, encryption, and standards for interaction between personal profiles and information systems are promising approaches for building a scholarly content layer (Brusilovsky and Tasso 2004; Furner 2002; Jose 2004; Kobsa 2002; Kobsa and Schreck 2003; Lynch 2001b, 2001c; Niederee et al. 2004; Smeaton and Callan 2002; Teevan, Dumais, and Horvitz 2005).

Separating Content, Services, and Tools

The layered model of an e-Research infrastructure shown in figure 2.1 (see page 24) puts the technical infrastructure at the bottom (processors, memory, and network), the middleware as a services layer, and the content on top. Most of the middleware services are invisible to the user, involving interoperability at fairly low levels such as the exchange of e-mail or distribution of computing workload. Cutting vertically through these layers are user interfaces and tools, in what is generically called the "applications space." While this set of relationships could be drawn in many ways, the common goal is for components to work together despite the variety of providers, users, and purposes. The challenge lies in making the search process as comprehensive and transparent as possible, while respecting the boundaries of the content owners and service providers. Separating the content from the tools and services, where possible and appropriate, should ease the coordination problem.

Distributed, Heterogeneous Content   Content comes in many shapes and sizes, from many providers, for many purposes. In the simplest case, both the content and the user community are homogeneous. Interfaces, tools, and services can be tailored to the content and users. The design of individual databases, digital libraries, and repositories often is predicated on the ability to customize the content and capabilities. In the most complex case, both the content and the user community are heterogeneous. The content on the Internet includes every imaginable form, for every imaginable purpose, by every imaginable user. Scholarly content that has enduring value for research and learning is a small portion of Internet resources. The products of informal scholarly communication are more ephemeral, though some of them are worth maintaining for permanent access. No firm boundary can be drawn between scholarly and nonscholarly content, however, as almost any online transaction can be of research interest to someone.

In distributed environments, the relationship between the content, services, and tools is still more complex. Digital libraries may be distributed, not necessarily residing in any one place or on any one server. The desired content may be scattered across many collections, and consequently the services and tools must search across, rather than just within, digital libraries. People want to search in fewer places, not more, of course, and so prefer their tools to be as seamless as possible.

The range of motivations to make content available is as diverse as the content itself. Libraries, archives, museums, and other public information institutions would like their collections to reach as wide an audience as possible, and are testing multiple economic models for improving access by digitizing them. Depending on the source of funding and copyright restrictions, they may make digital content freely available, sell value-added versions (e.g., digital content with searching and display features), or exchange content with other institutions through barter agreements. Public institutions are partnering with private enterprises such as Google, Yahoo, and Microsoft to digitize portions of their resources. Similar partnerships already exist in Europe and Asia, and more are being developed. All participants in these arrangements get copies of the digital content and can offer additional services, for free or a fee, depending on the contractual terms. Government agencies are making more content available online, from statistical data to archival records, as part of digital government initiatives. Publishers and entertainment companies are finding new value in their older resources, and selling these online under a variety of formats and business models. New technologies and relationships among providers of content and services will continue to emerge.

Rethinking Resource Description   Cataloging and other means of organizing knowledge are investments to ensure that content remains discoverable, retrievable, and usable in the future. Historically, these investments were most often made in published documents and in other materials that were expected to be long lived. The publishing of books and journals continues apace, and cataloging of these resources continues. Library cataloging rules are updated regularly to reflect the new formats and methods of searching and retrieval. While the details of cataloging rules are specific to countries and languages, most rest on common principles that allow records to be exchanged. The *Anglo-American Cataloging Rules* have been widely adopted internationally, in the original and in translated and adapted versions. These rules are being restructured to accommodate digital formats and distributed environments, and renamed, after several revisions over several decades, to become "Resource Description and Access." The new rules are being posted for comment, a chapter at a time, with their full publication scheduled for 2008 (RDA 2006).

Among the notable changes for digital objects are shifts from the concept of "authorship" to a "statement of responsibility," and from describing individual works to "families of works." Under the clustering method known as FRBR (pronounced "furber"), for Functional Requirements for Bibliographic Control, whole and partial relationships can be represented, bringing together variants such as a book that later becomes a play, then a movie, and its associated scripts, music, and later remake (Tillett 2004). FRBR already is implemented in some library automation software. Searchers can follow links and graphically display relationships among results. The new rules allow links between data, documents, and variant forms to be made explicit, and thus they represent a step forward in building the value chain. Some commentators feel the rule changes are insufficiently radical, however. The IEEE Learning Technology Standards Committee, for example, criticized the Resource Description and Access draft rules for treating only fixed content, and not adequately addressing the organization of content that is dynamic, assembled on demand, and customized by users (Public Comments 2005).

Resource Description and Access and FRBR are examples of information management approaches by a community with concerns for certain kinds of information. At best, they are generic solutions for published content and other resources that can be represented in fixed forms. The content layer will consist of these and many other forms of data, documents, and objects. Learning objects pose different requirements, as does content from the entertainment industry. All may be of interest for scholars. Individual communities will construct their own information management frameworks within the bounds of the Internet's architecture, and they must somehow be knitted together.

Coherence and Control

As the variety of content, providers, tools, and services on the Internet increases, the ease of presenting a coherent view of the content layer decreases. Information seekers want a coherent, seamless, and transparent view of the content available, along with the tools and services for using that content. Content and service providers typically want to maintain control of their resources for economic and security reasons, though. All too often, coherence and control are at odds.

Generic and Specialized Tools   The relative ease of searching text across media (e.g., Web pages, documents, and descriptions as surrogates for images), disciplines, and languages belies the difficulty of searching highly specialized content. Chemists search for molecules by their chemical structure, using community-standard representations. Musicians search by notes and themes, sometimes picking out a melody on a keyboard as an input mechanism. The difficulty of building search mechanisms that are effective across media is not a new problem and is even more challenging in highly distributed, heterogeneous environments. Even within media and collections, the requirements may vary by role. Faculty members, for example, often have different requirements when searching for teaching or research purposes. Tailoring user interfaces and capabilities to the content and community remains valuable, and should not be lost in the rush toward generic services.

Data vary by research area, researcher, instrument, and project to a much greater extent that do publications. At present, individual research communities are devoting considerable effort and research funds to the development of data management and analysis tools. Funding agencies are concerned that they are paying for each field to reinvent the work of others. The next challenge is to identify transferable tools and modular components that can serve multiple fields, for both data and documents. Shareable components should lead to better interoperability among the content and services, and facilitate collaboration across disciplinary boundaries. While most researchers and funding agencies desire readily available, affordable, transferable tools, the criteria for building such tools is not yet well understood. More sociotechnical studies of scholarly practices for managing information are essential to inform the design of tools and services.

Searching, Discovery, Retrieval, and Navigation   Often the several steps from looking for information online to obtaining a useful item are combined under the concept of search. The target may be explicit (a known item) or general (information about something). In most cases, navigation to the desired content requires a discovery process to determine what exists, where, and how to get it, followed by a retrieval process to obtain items of interest. Navigation involves following a course to a goal; the path may be indirect and have dead ends. Once discovered, the item may not be retrievable because the link is broken, the item lacks a persistent identifier (e.g., a Web page produced on demand from a database), the server is down, access permission cannot be obtained, the fees are unaffordable, the fee payment cannot be accomplished (e.g., currency exchange or variations in credit card rules), or for some other reason.

Search engines attempt to make discovery and retrieval as seamless as possible by offering direct links to digital objects. This is a useful model when it works, but is not a generic solution to the coherence versus control problem. As noted above, search engines can be more comprehensive than indexing and abstracting services, directories, portals, and other information organizing mechanisms. They gain comprehensiveness at the price of context, and are single points of failure when the discovered information cannot be retrieved.

Surrogates can be used to balance coherence and control. Providers typically are willing to expose their metadata for harvesting by search engines. Harvesting enables content to be discovered without allowing computational agents to search inside proprietary databases. Once surrogates for specific content are discovered, it may be necessary to broker relationships with the providers (e.g., registration, subscriptions, service payments, micropayments, or contracts) to search inside the collections. The providers may allow computational agents to search on behalf of authorized individuals, once a relationship is established. In this way, the providers can protect the security and integrity of their resources while facilitating distributed searching across databases.

Maintaining Coherence   The coherence of the content layer will depend heavily on information organizing mechanisms such as name spaces, thesauri, ontologies, and models for metadata and data structures. These mechanisms do not take care of themselves. Some institution has to take responsibility for constructing and maintaining them. Name spaces require a set of rules for internal consistency and an agency with which to register new names, whether DOIs or bank codes. Databases must be maintained, migrated, and made accessible. Thesauri and ontologies must reflect changes in terminology in the fields they serve. Metadata models and data structures must reflect changes in data sources, instrumentation, technology, and practices, and often must adapt to interoperate with related models. Each has an institutional home. Among name spaces, the DOIs are maintained by the International DOI Foundation, the DNS by the Internet Corporation for Assigned Names and Numbers and its authorized registrars, and the ISBNs by the International ISBN Agency based at the State Library Berlin. Among thesauri and ontologies, the *Index Medicus* is maintained by the U.S. National Library of Medicine, the *Subject Headings for Engineering* by Engineering Index, Inc., the *Art and Architecture Thesaurus* by the Getty Trust, and the *Gene Ontology* by a consortium of research projects and database providers. Among metadata models, the *Dublin Core* is maintained by the Online Computer Library Center, the *Ecological Metadata Language* by a group of volunteers, and the *Sensor Modeling Language* by a consortium of public and private agencies.

These examples reflect the varied levels of control and stability in essential components of an information infrastructure. Some are maintained by national libraries, which have centuries of continuity in the stewardship of information. Others are maintained by groups of volunteers, with no clear model for long-term funding. In between are parts of the infrastructure for which private or nonprofit agencies are responsible; they may support them as long as economically feasible. Each of these components interacts with other standards and structures, including the technical layer maintained by the Internet Engineering Task Force and World Wide Web Consortium. Various other formal and de facto standards, some open and some closed, are vital to the interoperability of systems and services.

While the politics and practices of standards are well beyond the scope of this book, they are mentioned here to make explicit the importance of these invisible aspects of information infrastructure. Someone has to maintain these name spaces, thesauri, ontologies, metadata frameworks, and other elements that are indispensable for coherence. The responsibility must be clear, and with a minimal duplication of effort. Some of these components operate within communities and others work across them. Establishing the social, legal, and economic framework for relationships among these many parts of scholarly information infrastructure is requisite to constructing the whole.

Trust in Content   Last, but by no means least, are concerns for trust mechanisms. Models for managing trust in traditional relationships between authors, readers, libraries, archives, and publishers in a print world are not transferring well to the digital world. Trust in content can be manifested in many ways. It can be based in fixity, knowing that a document has not been altered. It can be based on authorship, trusting in the individual or team from which the content originated. It can be based in the responsible agency, such as the parent organization that issued the document or data, rather than in the individuals who authored them. Or it can be based in the agency that selected the information, whether a library, archive, publisher, or blogger. Trust can be placed in the colleague or friend who recommended some form of information object. Concerns about trust in content also vary by situation. When scholars are seeking evidence on which to base their own work, the standards for trust are high. When they are browsing for provocative ideas, the standards for trust may be a bit lower. When they are seeking entertainment, they may not care who authored an amusing story or game, when, or why. These typify the many considerations for trusting in content.

As digital content becomes the primary form of scholarly discourse, the need for trust mechanisms will grow. In the present social environment, security matters are driving many technology decisions. Decisions made now will determine what is possible in the future. Trust is an inherently social construct that varies widely by culture, context, and time. Individual responsibility prevails in some cultures and collective responsibility in others, for example. Authorship and identity are essential aspects of trust in most scholarly endeavors, but anonymity can be critical in settings where freedom of speech is at risk. We must be careful to allow social norms to operate and change over time and circumstances, lest we embed a narrow, current, and ethnocentric trust framework into the information infrastructure.

Conclusions

This is an opportune moment to examine the nature of scholarship in the digital age. Enough experience exists to identify both the opportunities and the threats arising from changes in the technology and policy associated with distributed access to information. General plans are in place for building a technical framework to support information-intensive, data-intensive, distributed, multidisciplinary research and learning. New social and legal frameworks to facilitate scholarship are being constructed in response to these opportunities and threats.

The devil is usually in the details, and e-Research and e-Infrastructure are no exception. It is imperative that we understand more about the behavior and practice of individual scholars and learners, how they collaborate in distributed environments, and how they can take advantage of new capabilities, along with their reasons for doing so. Scholars can be collaborative, but also highly competitive. The greatest rewards go to those who make the biggest breakthroughs, and who do so first. Incentives to collaborate and to share always are balanced with those to compete and to protect one's sources and ideas. Technology will not change these social characteristics. Nevertheless, technology and policy together can encourage either cooperation or competition. Building tools to share data will not cause people to share, but tools that simplify capturing and sharing data, in combination with policies that reward scholars for doing so, are likely to change behavior. Effective policies would reflect the competitive aspects of scholarship—for example, by placing embargoes on data for time periods agreed on by each community. Policies also can reflect collaborative aspects—for instance, by requiring that deposited data meet the best practices standards for documentation as set by the community.

Programs on cyberinfrastructure, e-Science, e-Social Science, e-Humanities, e-Infrastructure, and similar names are inherently about an information infrastructure for scholarship. Much more attention has been paid to the technical infrastructure than to the information it will contain. Yet the information will far outlive the technology, and scholarly content has more enduring value than most other kinds of information. Scholarly journals, books, and proceedings are the cumulative record that enables each generation to stand on the shoulders of the giants who came before. Long after today's e-mail conversations, blogs, games, and commercial transactions are purged and forgotten, research data on the environment, surveys on social mores, records of archaeological digs, and economic indicators will be of incalculable value.

The printed records of scholarship, both data and documents, can survive through benign neglect. Most are stable enough to be readable or useful for decades or centuries with adequate temperature and moisture controls. Digital records, however, cannot survive by benign neglect. Active curation is required to migrate them to new formats, and to add metadata reflecting changes in form, custody, and rights. Appraisal and selection are required to determine what is worth saving and migrating, and what can be discarded and when. Significant investments must be made in scholarly digital content if it is to be useful for a minimum of fifty years, following research library and archival practice. Technology and policy for scholarly information must be based on "real-time" periods of use and not on "Internet time."

Many of the assumptions about content and context associated with physical artifacts and print do not hold in distributed, digital environments. Rather than being in fixed form, which is a premise of most copyright and trust arrangements, digital objects often are malleable, mutable, and mobile. Relationships between authors, readers, publishers, libraries, universities, and funding agencies are shifting in response to the proliferation of dissemination venues, technologies, and economic models, and to changes in the intellectual property laws associated with digital content.

One can only predict or invent the future based on the knowledge available today. With a view from here, several directions appear promising. First and foremost is the need to invest in content, with the goal of building an infrastructure *for* information. The content layer can itself be viewed as an infrastructure, and considerable progress is being made in the requisite standards and structures. The information commons is emerging as a social and legal framework for facilitating scholarship while balancing the interests of stakeholders.

Second is the need for balancing local and global approaches to the design of tools and services. Engineers and economists may consider building a generic set of tools and services for all disciplines, languages, countries, and cultures to be an attractive solution. Any system that attempts to be all things to all people, however, usually serves none of them well. At the other extreme is the duplication of effort involved in designing tailored tools for each community, application, project, and research team. The present situation tends toward the tailored extreme. Determining which tools can be generic, which can be modular, and which must be tailored requires a much deeper understanding of scholarly practices within and between fields than we currently have. A primary goal of this book is to frame research questions about practices, incentives, disincentives, and solutions for an e-Infrastructure and how those questions may vary by discipline and situation.

Third are the architectural approaches to information infrastructure such as separating the content, services, and tools, and balancing the requirements for coherence and control. No single entity controls the scholarly infrastructure, or the Internet, for that matter. Solutions must be modular, so that multiple players can contribute content and offer tools and services. Providers understandably want to control their resources and brand their products. Users would like as simple and coherent a view of the information universe as possible. These requirements often conflict. Solutions also must be flexible enough to accommodate changes in technology, policy, knowledge, and practices.

The diffuse governance of the scholarly communication system is both its blessing and its curse. When the interests of the many stakeholders are in balance, the system works well. When they are out of balance, as is the present case, some players are advantaged disproportionately and others are disadvantaged. Essential components of the infrastructure—such as agencies that maintain name spaces, thesauri and ontologies, and metadata structures—are largely invisible, and so can be neglected and lost. Often the invisible must be made visible before society can remedy any problems through norms, laws, and market mechanisms.

The scholarly communication system has many stakeholders, each competing within its own domain. Scholars compete with each other for publication, research grants, jobs, students, awards, and readers of their work. Universities compete for scholars, students, staff, grants, gifts, and budgets from governments. Publishers compete for authors, contracts with libraries, and sales to readers. Funding agencies compete for research proposals and funding sources. As these entities compete with each other in their own domain, they interact in unpredictable ways, in what Willian H. Dutton (1999) has called an "ecology of games." Difficult as it is to predict what may happen within each of these games, no one can predict the outcome of the many possible combinatorics of those interactions.

Larry Lessig's (1999, 2001, 2004) cautions about the social consequences of technical architectures should be borne in mind as we shape the next generation of the scholarly information infrastructure. Over time, the mechanisms that societies use to regulate behavior in the "real world" swing from left to right, from permissive to restrictive, and ultimately are self-correcting. In the technological world, architecture can trump all of these mechanisms. Computer code can enable behavior that is not socially acceptable, and can prevent behavior that is socially acceptable and legal. People who would never steal from someone's file cabinet can appropriate data they find on an open server and claim it as their own. Scholars who wish to display a copyrighted image in a classroom may find themselves unable to do so because of digital rights management software. As we debate the complex technical issues associated with information, such as managing trust, identity, location, and intellectual property, we must remember that these are social issues first and technical issues second. We are investing in a scholarly content layer for users who have not yet been born. How will they view the decisions we make now?

References

Note: The dates for Web sites reflect the most recent updates that could be identified when the sites last were visited. The dates for online documents reflect the version retrieved.

@LIS : Alliance for the Information Society. (2006). Visited <http://ec.europa.eu/comm/europeaid/projects/alis/index_en.htm on 7 July 2006>.

Abbate, J. (1999). *Inventing the Internet.* Cambridge, MA: MIT Press.

Abbott, A. (1988). *The System of Professions: An Essay on the Division of Expert Labor.* Chicago: University of Chicago Press.

About the UK e-Science Programme. (2006). Research Councils UK. <http://www.rcuk.ac.uk/escience/> (accessed August 17, 2006).

Access to and Retention of Research Data: Rights and Responsibilities. (2006). Council on Government Relations. <http://206.151.87.67/docs/CompleteDRBooklet.htm> (accessed September 28, 2006).

Agre, P. E. (2000). Imagining the wired university. Paper presented at the Symposium on the Future of the University, University of Newcastle, September 2000. <http://dlis.gseis.ucla.edu/pagre> (accessed August 2004; no longer online).

Agre, P. E. (2003). Information and Institutional Change: The Case of Digital Libraries. In *Digital Library Use: Social Practice in Design and Evaluation*, ed. A. P. Bishop, N. Van House, and B. P. Buttenfield, 219–240. Cambridge, MA: MIT Press.

All Species Foundation. (2004). <http://www.all-species.org/> (accessed September 28, 2006).

Allen, T. J. (1969). Information Needs and Uses. In *Annual Review of Information Science and Technology*, ed. C. A. Cuadra and A. W. Luke, 4:3–29. Chicago: Encyclopedia Britannica.

Alsos Digital Library for Nuclear Issues. (2006). <http://alsos.wlu.edu/> (accessed September 28, 2006).

Ananiadou, S., Chruszcz, J., Keane, J., McNaught, J., and Watry, P. (2005). The National Centre for Text Mining: Aims and objectives. *Ariadne* 42 (January). <http://www.ariadne.ac.uk/issue42/ananiadou/intro.html> (accessed September 18, 2006).

Anderson, C. (2004). The long tail. *Wired Magazine* 12 (10). <http://wired.com/wired/archive/12.10/tail_pr.html> (accessed September 17, 2006).

Anderson, C. (2006). *The Long Tail: Why the Future of Business Is Selling Less of More*. New York: Hyperion.

Anderson, I. (2004). Are you being served? Historians and the search for primary sources. *Archivaria* 58: 81–129.

ARC: A Cross Archive Search Service. (2006). Old Dominion University. <http://arc.cs.odu.edu (accessed September 28 2006>.

Arms, C. R. (2003). Available and useful: OAI and the Library of Congress. *Library Hi Tech* 21 (2): 129–139.

Arrow, K. J. (1962). Economic Welfare and the Allocation of Resources for Inventions. In *The Rate and Direction of Inventive Activity: Economic and Social Factors*, ed. R. R. Nelson, 609–626. Princeton, NJ: Princeton University Press.

Arrow, K. J. (1971). Political and Economic Evaluation of Social Effects and Externalities. In *Frontiers of Quantitative Economics*, ed. M. Intrilligator. Amsterdam: North-Holland Publishing Company.

Arrow, K. J. (1974). *The Limits of Organization*. New York: Norton.

Arrow, K. J., and Capron, W. M. (1959). Dynamic shortages and price rises: The engineer-scientist case. *Quarterly Journal of Economics* 73: 292–308.

Art and Architecture Thesaurus Online. (2000). J. Paul Getty Trust. <http://www.getty.edu/research/conducting_research/vocabularies/aat/> (accessed September 17, 2006).

Artandi, S. (1973). Information concepts and their utility. *Journal of the American Society for Information Science* 24 (4): 242–245

Arthur, B. W. (1989). Competing technologies, increasing returns, and lock-in by historical events. *Economics Journal* 99: 116–131.

Arts and Humanities Data Service. (2006). <http://www.ahds.ac.uk/> (accessed September 28, 2006).

ARTstor. (2005). <http://www.artstor.org/info/> (accessed September 28, 2006).

ArXiv Endorsement System. (2004). <http://arxiv.org/help/endorsement> (accessed July 27, 2006).

ArXiv.org e-Print Archive. (2006). <http://arxiv.org/> (accessed April 27, 2006).

Arzberger, P., Schroeder, P., Beaulieu, A., Bowker, G., Casey, K., Laaksonen, L., Moorman, D., Uhlir, P., and Wouters, P. (2004a). An international framework to promote access to data. *Science* 303 (5665): 1777–1778.

Arzberger, P., Schroeder, P., Beaulieu, A., Bowker, G., Casey, K., Laaksonen, L., Moorman, D., Uhlir, P., and Wouters, P. (2004b). Promoting access to public research data for scientific, economic, and social development. *Data Science Journal* 3: 135–152.

Atkins, D. E., Droegemeier, K. K., Feldman, S. I., Garcia-Molina, H., Klein, M. L., Messina, P., Messerschmitt, D. G., Ostriker, J. P., and Wright, M. H. (2002). *Revolutionizing Science and Engineering through Cyberinfrastructure: Report of the National Science Foundation Blue-Ribbon Panel on Cyberinfrastructure, Draft 1.0.* National Science Foundation. <http://www.ultrasim.info/atkins _rpt.pdf> (accessed September 28, 2006).

Atkins, D. E., Droegemeier, K. K., Feldman, S. I., Garcia-Molina, H., Klein, M. L., Messina, P., Messerschmitt, D. G., Ostriker, J. P., and Wright, M. H. (2003). Revolutionizing science and engineering through cyberinfrastructure: Report of the National Science Foundation Blue-Ribbon Panel on Cyberinfrastructure. National Science Foundation. <http://www.nsf.gov/cise/sci/reports/atkins.pdf> (accessed September 18, 2006).

Atkinson, M., Crowcroft, J., Goble, C., Gurd, J., Rodden, T., Shadbolt, N., Sloman, M., Sommerville, I., and Storey, T. (2004). Computer challenges to emerge from e-science. Engineering and Physical Sciences Research Council. <http://www.semanticgrid.org/docs/Vision.pdf> (accessed April 30, 2006).

Audit Checklist for Certifying Digital Repositories. (2005). Research Libraries Group and National Archives and Records Administration. <http://www.rlg.org/ en/page.php?Page_ID=20769> (accessed September 28, 2006).

Australian Partnership for Advanced Computing. (2006). <http://www.apac .edu.au/> (accessed July 7, 2006).

Avram, H. D. (1976). International standards for interchange of bibliographic records in machine-readable form. *Library Resources and Technical Services* 20 (1): 25–35.

Axelrod, R. (1984). *The Evolution of Cooperation.* New York: Basic Books.

Ayres, E. L. (2004). The valley of the shadow. University of Virginia. <http://valley.vcdh.virginia.edu/> (accessed September 28, 2005).

Baca, M., ed. (1998). *Introduction to Metadata: Pathways to Digital Information.* Los Angeles: Getty Information Institute.

Baca, M., ed. (2002). *Introduction to Art Image Access: Issues, Tools, Standards, Strategies.* Los Angeles, CA: Getty Publications.

Bachula, G. (2006). Testimony on Net neutrality. EDUCAUSE Policy Office. <http://www.educause.edu/LibraryDetailPage/666?ID=EPO0611> (accessed July 8, 2006).

Bailey, C. (2005). *Open Access Bibliography: Liberating Scholarly Literature with e-Prints and Open Access Journals.* Washington, DC: Association of Research Libraries. <http://info.lib.uh.edu/cwb/oab.pdf> (accessed September 28, 2006).

Bain, J. L., and Michener, W. K. (2002). Ecological archives: ESA's electronic data archive. *Ecological Society of America Annual Meeting Abstracts* 87: 315.

Baltimore, D. (1991). David Baltimore's mea culpa. *Science* 252: 769–770.

Baltimore, D. (1996). Baltimore has his say. *Science* 274: 925.

Barcoding of Life. (2005). Paper presented at the International Conference for the Barcoding of Life, Natural History Museum, London. <http://www.nhm.ac.uk/about-us/news/2005/feb/news_3428.html> (accessed September 15, 2006).

Barnett, G. A., Fink, E. L., and Debus, M. B. (1989). A mathematical model of citation age. *Communication Research* 16 (4): 510–531.

Batalin, M. A., Rahimi, M., Yu, Y., Liu, D., Kansal, A., Sukhatme, G. S., Kaiser, W. J., Hansen, M., Pottie, G. J., Srivastava, M., and Estrin, D. (2004). Call and Response: Experiments in Sampling the Environment. In *Proceedings of the 2nd International Conference on Embedded Networked Sensor Systems*. New York: ACM Press. <http://cres.usc.edu/pubdb_html/files_upload/420.pdf> (accessed September 28, 2006).

Bates, M. J., Wilde, D. N., and Siegfried, S. (1993). An analysis of search terminology used by humanities scholars: The Getty Online Searching Project report no.1. *Library Quarterly* 63 (1): 1–39.

Bates, M. J., Wilde, D. N., and Siegfried, S. (1995). Research practices of humanities scholars in an online environment: The Getty Online Searching Project report no. 3. *Library and Information Science Research* 17 (1): 5–40.

The Bayh-Dole Act: A Guide to the Law and Implementing Regulations. (1999). Council on Government Relations, University of California. <www.cogr.edu/docs/Bayh_Dole.pdf> (accessed October 5, 2006).

Bazerman, C. (1981). What written knowledge does: Three examples of scientific discourse. *Philosophy of the Social Sciences* 11 (3): 361–387.

Bazerman, C. (1988). *Shaping Written Knowledge: The Genre and Activity of the Experimental Article in Science*. Madison: University of Wisconsin Press.

Beagrie, N. (2006). Digital curation for science, digital libraries, and individuals. *International Journal of Digital Curation* 1 (1). <www.ijdc.net> (accessed April 6, 2007).

Beazley Archive. (2006). University of Oxford. <http://www.beazley.ox.ac.uk/BeazleyAdmin/Script2/TheArchive.htm> (accessed March 31, 2006).

Becher, T. (1989). *Academic Tribes and Territories: Intellectual Enquiry and the Culture of Disciplines*. Buckingham, UK: Open University Press.

Bekaert, J., and Van de Sompel, H. (2006a). Access Interfaces for Open Archival Information Systems Based on the OAI-PMH and the OpenURL Framework for Context-Sensitive Services. In *PV 2005: Ensuring Long-term Preservation and Adding Value to Scientific and Technical Data*. Edinburgh: Royal Society. <http://www.ukoln.ac.uk/events/pv-2005/pv-2005-final-papers/032.pdf> (accessed September 28, 2006).

Bekaert, J., and Van de Sompel, H. (2006b). *Augmenting Interoperability across Scholarly Repositories*. Andrew W. Mellon Foundation. <http://msc.mellon.org/Meetings/Interop/FinalReport> (accessed August 13, 2006).

Belew, R. K. (2000). *Finding out About: A Cognitive Perspective on Search Engine Technology and the WWW.* Cambridge: Cambridge University Press.

Belkin, N. J. (1978). Information concepts for information science. *Journal of Documentation* 34: 55–85.

Benkler, Y. (2004). Commons-based strategies and the problems of patents. *Science* 305: 1110.

Berlin Declaration on Open Access to Knowledge in the Sciences and Humanities. (2003). <http://www.zim.mpg.de/openaccess-berlin/berlindeclaration.html> (accessed July 5, 2006).

Berman, F., and Brady, H. (2005). *Final Report: NSF SBE-CISE Workshop on Cyberinfrastructure and the Social Sciences.* National Science Foundation. <http://vis.sdsc.edu/sbe/reports/SBE-CISE-FINAL.pdf> (accessed April 30, 2006).

Bernal, J. D. (1959). The Transmission of Scientific Information: A User's Analysis. In *Proceedings of the International Conference on Scientific Information.* Washington, DC: National Academy of Sciences.

Besek, J. M. (2003). *Copyright Issues Relevant to the Creation of a Digital Archive: A Preliminary Assessment.* Council on Library and Information Resources. <http://www.clir.org/pubs/reports/pub112/pub112.pdf> (accessed September 28, 2006).

Bhattacharjee, Y. (2005). Celebrities: Flying high. *Science* 309: 49.

Bijker, W. E., Hughes, T. P., and Pinch, T., eds. (1987). *The Social Construction of Technological Systems: New Directions in the Sociology and History of Technology.* Cambridge, MA: MIT Press.

Biomedical Informatics Research Network. (2006). <http://www.nbirn.net/> (accessed September 19, 2006).

Biozon. (2006). Cornell University. <http://www.biozon.org/> (accessed September 28, 2006).

Bisby, F. A., Shimura, J., Ruggiero, M., Edwards, J., and Haeuser, C. (2002). Taxonomy, at the click of a mouse. *Nature* 418 (6896): 367.

Bishop, A. P. (1999). Document structure and digital libraries: How researchers mobilize information in journal articles. *Information Processing and Management* 35: 255–279.

Bishop, A. P., and Star, S. L. (1996). Social Informatics for Digital Library Use and Infrastructure. In *Annual Review of Information Science and Technology,* ed. M. E. Williams, 31: 301–401. Medford, NJ: Information Today.

Bishop, A. P., Van House, N., and Buttenfield, B. P., eds. (2003). *Digital Library Use: Social Practice in Design and Evaluation.* Cambridge, MA: MIT Press.

Bits of Power: Issues in Global Access to Scientific Data. (1997). Washington, DC: National Academy Press. <http://www.nap.edu> (accessed September 28, 2006).

The Bluebook: A Uniform System of Citation. (2005). 18th ed. Cambridge, MA: Harvard Law Review Association.

Blumler, J., and Katz, E., eds. (1974). *The Uses of Mass Communication: Current Perspectives on Uses and Gratifications Research*. Beverly Hills, CA: Sage.

Borgman, C. L. (1990a). Editor's Introduction. In *Scholarly Communication and Bibliometrics*, ed. C. L. Borgman, 10–27. Newbury Park, CA: Sage.

Borgman, C. L., ed. (1990b). *Scholarly Communication and Bibliometrics*. Newbury Park, CA: Sage.

Borgman, C. L. (1997). From acting locally to thinking globally: A brief history of library automation. *Library Quarterly* 67 (3): 215–249.

Borgman, C. L. (1999). What are digital libraries? Competing visions. *Information Processing and Management* 35 (3): 227–243.

Borgman, C. L. (2000a). *From Gutenberg to the Global Information Infrastructure: Access to Information in the Networked World*. Cambridge, MA: MIT Press.

Borgman, C. L. (2000b). The premise and promise of the global information infrastructure. *First Monday* 5 (8). <http://www.firstmonday.dk/issues/issue5_8/borgman/index.html> (accessed September 28, 2006).

Borgman, C. L. (2002). Challenges in Building Digital Libraries for the 21st Century. In *Digital Libraries: People, Knowledge, and Technology: Proceedings of the 5th International Conference on Asian Digital Libraries (ICADL 2002)*, 1–13. Singapore: Springer-Verlag.

Borgman, C. L. (2003). Personal digital libraries: Creating individual spaces for innovation. Paper presented at the NSF Workshop on Post-Digital Libraries Initiative Directions, Chatham, MA. <http://www.sis.pitt.edu/~dlwkshop/paper_borgman.html> (accessed September 19, 2005).

Borgman, C. L. (2006a). What can studies of e-learning teach us about e-research? Some findings from digital library research. *Journal of Computer Supported Cooperative Work* 15 (4): 359–383.

Borgman, C. L. (2006b). What Is New and Different about e-Research? In *Information, Communication, and New Media Studies: Networking a Multidisciplinary Field*. Oxford: Oxford Internet Institute, University of Oxford. <http://www.oii.ox.ac.uk/collaboration/?rq=specialevents/20060202> (accessed February 1, 2006).

Borgman, C. L. (Forthcoming). From the global information infrastructure to the grid: Evolving definitions of infrastructure.

Borgman, C. L., Bates, M. J., Cloonan, M. V., Efthimiadis, E. N., Gilliland-Swetland, A. J., Kafai, Y., Leazer, G. L., and Maddox, A. (1996). *Social Aspects of Digital Libraries: Final Report to the National Science Foundation; Computer, Information Science, and Engineering Directorate; Division of Information, Robotics, and Intelligent Systems; Information Technology and Organizations Program*. <http://is.gseis.ucla.edu/research/dl/index.html> (accessed September 28, 2006).

Borgman, C. L., and Furner, J. (2002). Scholarly Communication and Biblio-metrics. In *Annual Review of Information Science and Technology*, ed. B. Cronin, 36: 3–72. Medford, NJ: Information Today.

Borgman, C. L., Leazer, G. H., Gilliland-Swetland, A. J., Millwood, K. A., Champeny, L., Finley, J. R., and Smart, L. J. (2004). How geography professors select materials for classroom lectures: Implications for the design of digital libraries. In *JCDL '04: Proceedings of the 4th ACM/IEEE-CS Joint Conference on Digital Libraries (Tucson, AZ, June 7–11, 2004)*, 179–185. New York: Association for Computing Machinery.

Borgman, C. L., Moghdam, D., and Corbett, P. K. (1984). *Effective Online Searching: A Basic Text*. New York: Marcel Dekker.

Borgman, C. L., Smart, L. J., Millwood, K. A., Finley, J. R., Champeny, L., Gilliland, A. J., and Leazer, G. H. (2005). Comparing faculty information seeking in teaching and research: Implications for the design of digital libraries. *Journal of the American Society for Information Science and Technology* 56 (6): 636–657.

Borgman, C. L., Wallis, J. C., and Enyedy, N. (2006). Building digital libraries for scientific data: An exploratory study of data practices in habitat ecology. In: Proceedings of the Tenth European Conference on Digital Libraries (Alicante, Spain), 170–183. Berlin: Springer.

Borgman, C. L., Wallis, J. C., and Enyedy, N. (Forthcoming). Little science confronts the data deluge: Habitat ecology, embedded sensor networks, and digital libraries. *International Journal on Digital Libraries.*

Bourne, P. (2005). Will a biological database be different from a biological journal? *PLoS Computational Biology* 1 (3): e34. <http://dx.doi.org/10.1371/journal.pcbi.0010034> (accessed September 28, 2006).

Bowker, G. C. (2000a). Biodiversity datadiversity. *Social Studies of Science* 30 (5): 643–683.

Bowker, G. C. (2000b). Mapping biodiversity. *International Journal of Geographical Information Science* 14 (8): 739–754.

Bowker, G. C. (2000c). Work and Information Practices in the Sciences of Biodiversity. In *VLDB 2000: Proceedings of 26th International Conference on Very Large Databases*. Cairo, Egypt: Kaufmann.

Bowker, G. C. (2005). *Memory Practices in the Sciences*. Cambridge, MA: MIT Press.

Bowker, G. C., and Star, S. L. (1999). *Sorting Things Out: Classification and Its Consequences*. Cambridge, MA: MIT Press.

Boyarin, J., ed. (1993). *The Ethnography of Reading*. Berkeley: University of California Press.

Boyle, J. (2004). A natural experiment. *Financial Times, Comment, and Analysis*. <http://www.ft.com/cms/> (accessed June 29, 2006).

Boyle, J., and Jenkins, J. (2003). The Genius of Intellectual Property and the Need for the Public Domain. In *The Role of Scientific and Technical Data and Information in the Public Domain*, ed. J. M. Esanu and P. F. Uhlir, 10–14. Washington, DC: National Academies Press. <http://newton.nap.edu/catalog/10785.html#toc> (accessed September 13, 2005).

Brady, H. (2004). Testimony to the Commission on Cyberinfrastructure for the Humanities and Social Sciences. American Council of Learned Societies. <http://www.acls.org/cyberinfrastructure/cyber_meeting_notes_august.htm#brady_summary> (accessed April 20, 2006).

Braman, S., ed. (2004). *Biotechnology and Communication: The Meta-Technologies of Information*. Mahwah, NJ: Lawrence Erlbaum Associates.

Breast cancer and the e-diamond project. (2003). Oxford e-Science Centre. <http://www.e-science.ox.ac.uk/public/eprojects/e-diamond/> (accessed September 28, 2006).

British Atmospheric Data Centre. (2006). <http://badc.nerc.ac.uk/home/> (accessed September 24, 2006).

Broadband: Bringing Home the Bits. (2002). Washington, DC: National Academy Press. <http://newton.nap.edu/catalog/10235.html> (accessed September 28, 2006).

Brown, J. S., and Duguid, P. (1996). The social life of documents. *First Monday* 1 (1). <http://www.firstmonday.org/issues/issue1/documents/index.html> (accessed September 28, 2006).

Brown, M. (2005). The discovery of 2003 UB313, the 10th planet. California Institute of Technology. <http://www.gps.caltech.edu/~mbrown/planetlila/index.html#name> (accessed September 28, 2006).

Brown, R. H., Irving, L., Prabhakar, A., and Katzen, S. (1995). *The Global Information Infrastructure: Agenda for Cooperation*. National Technical Information Agency. <http://www.ntia.doc.gov/reports/giiagend.html> (accessed April 18, 2006).

Brumfiel, G. (2002). Misconduct finding at Bell Labs shakes physics community. *Nature* 419 (October 3): 419–421.

Brusilovsky, P., and Tasso, C. (2004). Preface to special issue on user modeling for Web information retrieval. *User Modeling and User-Adapted Interaction: Journal of Personalization Research* 14 (2–3): 147–157.

Buckland, M. K. (1988). *Library Services in Theory and Context*. 2nd ed. Oxford: Pergamon.

Buckland, M. K. (1991). Information as thing. *Journal of the American Society for Information Science* 42 (5): 351–360.

Buckland, M. K. (1992). *Redesigning Library Services: A Manifesto*. Chicago: American Library Association. <http://sunsite.berkeley.edu/Literature/Library/Redesigning/html.html> (accessed September 25, 2006).

Buckland, M. K. (1997). What is a "document"? *Journal of the American Society for Information Science* 48 (9): 804–809.

Budapest Open Access Initiative. (2005). Open Society Institute. <http://www.soros.org/openaccess/index.shtml> (accessed August 8, 2006).

Buneman, P. (2005). What the Web has done for scientific data and what it hasn't. Paper presented at Advances in Web-Age Information Management: 6th International Conference, Hangzhou, China.

Buneman, P., Khanna, S., and Tan, W.-C. (2000). Data Provenance: Some Basic Issues. In *Foundations of Software Technology and Theoretical Computer Science: Proceedings of the 20th Conference*, 87–93. Berlin: Springer.

Buneman, P., Khanna, S., and Tan, W.-C. (2001). Why and where: A characterization of data provenance. In *Database Theory—ICDT 2001: 8th International Conference*. (London). Berlin: Springer.

Burk, D. L. (2000). Intellectual Property Issues in Electronic Collaborations. In *Electronic Collaboration in Science*, ed. S. H. Koslow and M. F. Huerta, 15–44. Mahwah, NJ: Lawrence Erlbaum.

Bush, V. (1945a). As we may think. *Atlantic Monthly* 176 (1): 101–108.

Bush, V. (1945b). *Science—The Endless Frontier: A Report to the President on a Program for Postwar Scientific Research (reprinted 1990)*. Washington, DC: National Science Foundation.

Butler, D. (2006). Mashups mix data into global service: Is this the future for scientific analysis? *Nature* 439 (7072): 6–7.

Caldas, A. P. (2004). *The Structure of Electronic Scientific Communication: Electronic Networks, Research Collaboration, and the Discovery of Digital Knowledge Bases*. D.Phil. dissertation. Brighton, UK: Science and Technology Policy Research Unit, University of Sussex.

California Digital Library. (2006). University of California. <http://www.cdlib.org/> (accessed July 8, 2006).

Callon, M. (1986). The Sociology of an Actor-Network: The Case of the Electric Vehicle. In *Mapping the Dynamics of Science and Technology: Sociology of Science in the Real World*, ed. M. Callon, J. Law, and A. Rip, 19–34. London: Macmillan.

Callon, M. (1994). Is science a public good? *Science, Technology, and Human Values* 19 (4): 395–424.

Callon, M., Law, J., and Rip, A. (1986). How to Study the Force of Science. In *Mapping the Dynamics of Science and Technology: Sociology of Science in the Real World*, ed. M. Callon, J. Law, and A. Rip, 3–18. London: Macmillan.

Campbell, E. G., and Bendavid, E. (2003). Data-sharing and data-withholding in genetics and the life sciences: Results of a national survey of technology transfer officers. *Journal of Health Care Law and Policy* 6 (48): 241–255.

Campbell, E. G., Clarridge, B. R., Gokhale, M., Birenbaum, L., Hilgartner, S., Holtzman, N. A., and Blumenthal, D. (2002). Data withholding in academic genetics: Evidence from a national survey. *Journal of the American Medical Association* 287 (4): 473–480.

Carlson, S. (2006). Lost in a sea of science data. *Chronicle of Higher Education* 52 (42): A35–A37.

Case, D. O. (2002). *Looking for Information: A Survey of Research on Information Seeking, Needs, and Behavior.* San Diego, CA: Academic Press.

Cave, R. (1971). *The Private Press.* London: Faber and Faber.

Cave, R. (2001). *Fine Printing and Private Presses: Selected Papers.* London: British Library.

Center for Embedded Networked Sensing. (2006). <http://www.cens.ucla.edu> (accessed August 31, 2006).

Cerf, V. G., and Kahn, R. E. (1974). A protocol for packet network intercommunication. *IEEE Transactions on Communications* COM-22: 637–648.

Champeny, L., Mayer, R. E., Johnson, R. A., Borgman, C. L., Leazer, G. H., Gilliland-Swetland, A. J., Millwood, K. A., D'Avolio, L., Finley, J. R., Smart, L. J., and Mautone, P. D. (2004). Developing a digital learning environment: An evaluation of design and implementation processes. In *JCDL '04: Proceedings of the 4th ACM/IEEE-CS Joint Conference on Digital Libraries (Tucson, AZ, June 7–11, 2004)*, 37–46. New York: Association for Computing Machinery.

Check, E. (2005). Where now for stem-cell cloners? *Nature* 438 (7071): 1058–1059.

Chicago Manual of Style. (2003). 15th ed. Chicago: University of Chicago Press.

Chubin, D. E. (1976). The conceptualization of scientific specialties. *Scientometrics* 12 (5–6): 373–379.

Chudnov, D., Cameron, R., Frumkin, J., Singer, R., and Yee, R. (2005). Opening up OpenURLs with autodiscovery. *Ariadne* (43). <http://www.ariadne.ac.uk/issue43/chudnov/> (accessed September 29, 2006).

Clark, B. R. (1983). *The Higher Education System: Academic Organization in Cross-National Perspective.* Berkeley: University of California Press.

Clark, B. R. (1998). *Creating Entrepreneurial Universities: Organizational Pathways of Transformation.* Oxford: Pergamon/Elsevier Science.

Clark, B. R. (2004). *Sustaining Change in Universities: Continuities in Case Studies and Concepts.* Maidenhead, UK: Open University Press.

CODATA-CENDI Forum on the National Science Board Report on Long-Lived Digital Data Collections. (2005). U.S. National Committee on CODATA, National Research Council. <http://www7.nationalacademies.org/usnc-codata/Forum_on_NSB_Report.pdf> (accessed September 29, 2006).

Cogprints. (2006). <http://cogprints.org/> (accessed August 25, 2006).

Cohen, D. J., and Rosenzweig, R. (2005a). *Digital History: A Guide to Gathering, Preserving, and Presenting the Past on the Web.* Philadelphia: University of Pennsylvania Press.

Cohen, D. J., and Rosenzweig, R. (2005b). Web of lies? Historical knowledge on the Internet. *First Monday* 10 (12). <http://firstmonday.org/issues/issue10_12/cohen/> (accessed December 14, 2005).

Cohen, D. J., and Rosenzweig, R. (2006). *Digital History: A Guide to Gathering, Preserving, and Presenting the Past on the Web*. Center for History and New Media, George Mason University. <http://chnm.gmu.edu/digitalhistory/> (accessed August 25, 2006).

Cohen, J. E. (2003a). The Challenge of Digital Rights Management Technologies. In *The Role of Scientific and Technical Data and Information in the Public Domain*, ed. J. M. Esanu and P. F. Uhlir, 109–118. Washington, DC: National Academies Press. <http://books.nap.edu/catalog/10785.html> (accessed April 18, 2006).

Cohen, J. E. (2003b). DRM and privacy. *Communications of the ACM* 46 (4): 47–49.

Cohen, J. E. (2005a). Comment: Copyright's public-private distinction. *Case Western Reserve Law Review* 55 (4): 963–970.

Cohen, J. E. (2005b). The place of the user in copyright law. *Fordham Law Review* 64 (2): 347–374.

Cohen, J. E. (2006). Copyright, Commodification, Culture: Locating the Public Domain. In *The Future of the Public Domain*, ed. L. Guibault and P. B. Hugenholtz, 121–166. Amsterdam: Kluwen.

Cohen, J. E. (2007). Cyberspace as/and space. *Columbia Law Review* 107: 210–246.

Cohendet, P., and Meyer-Krahmer, F. (2001). The theoretical and policy implications of knowledge codification. *Research Policy* 30 (9): 1563–1591.

Cole, S. (2004). Merton's contribution to the sociology of science. *Social Studies of Science* 34 (6): 829–844.

Collaborative Large-Scale Engineering Analysis Network for Environmental Research. (2006). <http://cleaner.ncsa.uiuc.edu/home/> (accessed August 16, 2006).

Collins, H. M., and Evans, R. (2002). The third wave of science studies: Studies of expertise and experience. *Social Studies of Science* 32 (2): 235–296.

Collins, R. (2004). Three myths of Internet governance considered in the context of the UK. *Prometheus* 22 (3): 267–291.

Commission on Cyberinfrastructure for the Humanities and Social Sciences. (2006). American Council of Learned Societies. <http://www.acls.org/cyberinfrastructure/cyber.htm> (accessed April 18, 2006).

Computer Science: Reflections on the Field, Reflections from the Field. (2004). Washington, DC: National Academy Press. <http://www.nap.edu/catalog/11106.html> (accessed September 29, 2006).

Computing Research Repository. (2003). Association for Computing Machinery. <http://www.acm.org/corr/> (accessed September 29, 2006).

Conservation Commons. (2006). <http://www.conservationcommons.org/> (accessed August 15, 2006).

Copyright Act of 1976. (2000). 17 U.S. Code, Sec. 105.

Copyright Circular 1. (2000). U.S. Copyright Office. <http://www.copyright.gov/circs/circ1.html#wci> (accessed July 6, 2006).

Copyright Term Extension Act. (1998). S505, P. L. 105–298, October 27. <http://www.copyright.gov/legislation/s505.pdf> (accessed September 28, 2006).

Corrections and Clarifications. (1996). *Science* 273: 1477–1480.

Costs of Publication. (2004). In *Electronic Scientific, Technical, and Medical Journal Publishing and Its Implications: Report of a Symposium*, 9–19. Washington, DC: National Academies Press. <http://www.nap.edu/catalog/10969.html#toc> (accessed July 5, 2006).

Courant, P. N. (2006). Scholarship and academic libraries (and their kin) in the world of Google. *First Monday* 11 (8). <http://firstmonday.org/issues/issue11_8/courant/index.html> (accessed August 7, 2006).

Couzin, J., and Unger, C. (2006). Cleaning up the paper trail. *Science* 312: 38–43.

Covey, D. T. (2005). *Acquiring Copyright Permission to Digitize and Provide Open Access to Books*. Council on Library and Information Resources. <http://www.clir.org/pubs/reports/pub134/pub134col.pdf> (accessed August 8, 2006).

Covi, L. M. (2000). Debunking the myth of the Nintendo generation: How doctoral students introduce new electronic communication practices into university research. *Journal of the American Society for Information Science* 51 (14): 1284–1294.

Cox, A. (2004). *Building Collaborative e-Research Environments*. JISC, National e-Science Centre, Edinburgh. V<http://www.jisc.ac.uk/index.cfm?name=event_report_eresearch> (accessed April 18, 2006).

Cox, J., and Cox, L. (2003). *Scholarly Publishing Practice: The ALPSP Report on Academic Journal Publishers' Policies and Practices in Online Publishing*. Worthing, UK: Association of Learned and Professional Society Publishers.

Crane, D. (1971). Information Needs and Uses. In *Annual Review of Information Science and Technology*, ed. C. A. Cuadra and A. W. Luke, 6: 3–39. Chicago: Encyclopedia Britannica.

Crane, D. (1972). *Invisible Colleges: Diffusion of Knowledge in Scientific Communities*. Chicago: University of Chicago Press.

Crane, G. (2006). What do you do with a million books? *D-Lib Magazine* 12 (3). <http://www.dlib.org/dlib/march06/crane/03crane.html> (accessed August 17, 2006).

Crane, G. R., Chavez, R. F., Mahoney, A., Milbank, T. L., Rydberg-Cox, J. A., Smith, D. A., and Wulfman, C. E. (2001). Drudgery and deep thought: Designing a digital library for the humanities. *Communications of the Association for Computing Machinery* 44 (5): 35–40. <http://www.perseus.tufts.edu/Articles/cacm2000.pdf> (accessed April 18, 2006).

Creative Commons. (2006). <http://www.creativecommons.org> (accessed April 18, 2006).

Croft, W. B. (1995). What do people want from information retrieval? (The top 10 research issues for companies that use and sell IR systems). *D-Lib Magazine* 1. <http://www.dlib.org/dlib/november95/11croft.html> (accessed September 29, 2006).

Cronin, B. (1984). *The Citation Process: The Role and Significance of Citations in Scientific Communication.* London: Taylor Graham.

Cronin, B. (2003). Scholarly Communication and Epistemic Cultures. In *Scholarly Tribes and Tribulations: How Tradition and Technology Are Driving Disciplinary Change.* Washington, DC: Association of Research Libraries. <http://www.arl.org/scomm/disciplines/Cronin.pdf> (accessed September 29, 2006).

Cronin, B. (2004). Normative shaping of scientific practice: The magic of Merton. *Scientometrics* 60 (1): 41–46.

Cronin, B. (2005). *The Hand of Science: Academic Writing and Its Rewards.* Lanham, MD: Scarecrow Press.

CrossRef. (2006). <http://www.crossref.org/index.html> (accessed July 26, 2006).

Crow, R. (2002). *The Case for Institutional Repositories: A SPARC Position Paper.* Washington, DC: Scholarly Publishing and Academic Resources Coalition. <http://www.arl.org/sparc/IR/ir.html> (accessed April 18, 2006).

Cummings, J., and Kiesler, S. (2004). Collaborative research across disciplinary and institutional boundaries. National Science Foundation. <http://hciresearch.hcii.cs.cmu.edu/complexcollab/pubs/paperPDFs/cummings_collaborative.pdf> (accessed September 25, 2006).

Cuneiform Digital Library Initiative. (2006). UCLA and Max Planck Institute. <http://cdli.ucla.edu/> (accessed September 28, 2006).

Cyberinfrastructure for Education and Learning for the Future: A Vision and Research Agenda. (2005). Computing Research Association. <http://www.cra.org/reports/cyberinfrastructure.pdf> (accessed September 29, 2006).

Cyranoski, D. (2005). TV tests call into question cloner's stem-cell success. *Nature* 438 (7069): 718.

Cyranoski, D. (2006). Blow follows blow for stem-cell work. *Nature* 439 (7072): 8.

Dalbello, M. (2004). Institutional shaping of cultural memory: Digital library as environment for textual transmission. *Library Quarterly* 74 (3): 265–298.

Dalle, J.-M., David, P. A., Ghosh, R. A., and Steinmueller, W. E. (2005). Advancing Economic Research on the Free and Open Source Software Mode of Production. In *Building Our Digital Future: Future Economic, Social, and Cultural Scenarios Based on Open Standards*, ed. M. Wynants and J. Cornelia. Brussels:

Vrjie Universiteit Brussels Press. <http://siepr.stanford.edu/papers/pdf/04–03 .pdf> (accessed August 17, 2006).

Dalrymple, D. (2003). Scientific Knowledge as a Global Public Good: Contributions to Innovation and the Economy. In *The Role of Scientific and Technical Data and Information in the Public Domain*, ed. J. M. Esanu and P. F. Uhlir, 35–51. Washington, DC: National Academies Press. <http://books.nap.edu/catalog/10785.html> (accessed October 6, 2006).

Dasgupta, P., and David, P. A. (1994). Toward a new economics of science. *Research Policy* 23 (5): 487–521.

Data Central at San Diego Supercomputer Center. (2006). <http://datacentral .sdsc.edu/> (accessed April 30, 2006).

Data Documentation Initiative. (2006). University of Michigan. <http:// www.icpsr.umich.edu/DDI/> (accessed September 30, 2006).

Davenport, E., and Cronin, B. (1990). Hypertext and the conduct of science. *Journal of Documentation* 46 (3): 175–192.

Davenport, E., and Cronin, B. (2000). The Citation Network as a Prototype for Representing Trust in Virtual Environments. In *The Web of Knowledge: A Festschrift in Honor of Eugene Garfield*, ed. B. Cronin and H. B. Atkins, 517–534. Medford, NJ: Information Today.

Davenport, E., and Hall, H. (2002). Organizational Knowledge and Communities of Practice. In *Annual Review of Information Science and Technology*, ed. B. Cronin, 36: 171–227. Medford, NJ: Information Today.

David, P. A. (1985). Clio and the economics of QWERTY. *American Economic Review* 75 (2): 332–337.

David, P. A. (2001). The evolving accidental information super-highway. *Oxford Review of Economic Policy* 17 (2): 159–187.

David, P. A. (2003). The Economic Logic of "Open Science" and the Balance between Private Property Rights and the Public Domain in Scientific Data and Information: A Primer. In *The Role of the Public Domain in Scientific Data and Information*, 19–34. Washington, DC: National Academy Press. <http://siepr .stanford.edu/papers/pdf/02–30.html> (accessed September 30, 2006).

David, P. A. (2004). Towards a cyberinfrastructure for enhanced scientific collaboration: Providing its "soft" foundations may be the hardest part. Oxford Internet Institute Research Reports, University of Oxford. <http://www .oii.ox.ac.uk> (accessed April 18, 2006).

David, P. A. (2005). Creating the Information Commons for e-Science. In *Creating the Information Commons for e-Science: Toward Institutional Policies and Guidelines for Action*. Paris: United Nations Educational, Scientific, and Cultural Organization. <http://www.codataweb.org/UNESCOmtg/pres-pdavid.pdf> (accessed October 6, 2006>.

David, P. A., and Spence, M. (2003). Towards institutional infrastructures for e-science: The scope of the challenge. Oxford Internet Institute Research Reports,

University of Oxford. <http://129.3.20.41/eps/le/papers/0502/0502002.pdf> (accessed September 30, 2006).

Day, R. E. (2001). *The Modern Invention of Information: Discourse, History, and Power*. Carbondale: Southern Illinois University Press.

Dervin, B. (1976). Strategies for dealing with human information needs: Information or communication? *Journal of Broadcasting* 20 (3): 324–351.

Dervin, B. (1977). Useful theory for librarianship: Communication not information. *Drexel Library Quarterly* 13: 16–32.

Dervin, B. (1992). From the Mind's Eye of the User: The Sense-Making Qualitative-Quantitative Methodology. In *Qualitative Research in Information Management*, ed. J. Glazier and R. Powell, 61–84. Englewood, CO: Libraries Unlimited.

Dervin, B., and Nilan, M. (1986). Information Needs and Uses. In *Annual Review of Information Science and Technology*, ed. M. E. Williams, 21: 3–33. Medford, NJ: Information Today.

A Dictionary of Computing. (2006). Oxford: Oxford University Press. <http://www.oxfordreference.com/> (accessed September 28, 2006).

A Dictionary of the Internet. (2006). Oxford: Oxford University Press. <http://www.oxfordreference.com/> (accessed September 28, 2006).

Digital Curation Centre. (2006). <http://www.dcc.ac.uk/> (accessed April 18, 2006).

The Digital Dilemma: Intellectual Property in the Information Age. (2000). Washington, DC: National Academy Press. <http://www.nap.edu/books/0309064996/html/> (accessed October 5, 2006).

Digital Libraries Initiative Phase II. (1999–2004). National Science Foundation. <http://www.dli2.nsf.gov> (accessed April 18, 2006).

Digital Libraries: Universal Access to Human Knowledge. (2001). The President's Information Technology Advisory Committee, Executive Office of the President. <http://www.nitrd.gov/pubs/pitac/indcx.html> (accessed April 18, 2006).

Digital Library for Earth System Education. (2006). <http://www.dlese.org/dds/index.jsp> (accessed July 8, 2006).

The Digital Millennium Copyright Act. (1998). Pub. L. No. 105–304, 112 Stat. 2860, October 28. <www.copyright.gov/legislation/dmca.pdf> (accessed October 5, 2006).

The Digital Object Identifier System. (2006). International DOI Foundation. <http://www.doi.org> (accessed October 5, 2006).

DILIGENT: A Digital Library Infrastructure on Grid Enabled Technology. (2006). European Commission, Sixth Framework Programme. <http://www.diligentproject.org/> (accessed April 30, 2006).

Dillon, A. (1991). Readers' models of text structures: The case of academic articles. *International Journal of Man-Machine Studies* 35: 913–925.

Dillon, A. (1994). *Designing Usable Electronic Text*. London: Taylor and Francis.

Dirk, L. (1999). A measure of originality: The elements of science. *Social Studies of Science* 29 (5): 765–776.

Division of Shared Cyberinfrastructure. (2004). Directorate for Computer and Information Science and Engineering, National Science Foundation. <http://www.nsf.gov/od/lpa/news/publicat/nsf04009/cise/sci.htm> (accessed January 27, 2005).

Dobbs, D. (2006). Idea lab: Trial and error. *New York Times*, January 15. <http://www.nytimes.com/2006/01/15/magazine/15wwln_idealab.html> (accessed on January 25, 2006).

Drott, M. C. (2006). Open Access. In *Annual Review of Information Science and Technology*, ed. B. Cronin, 40:79–109. Medford, NJ: Information Today.

DSpace. (2006). DSpace Federation. <http://www.dspace.org> July 5, 2006).

Dublin Core Metadata Initiative. (2006). <http://dublincore.org/> (accessed May 7, 2006).

Duderstadt, J. J., Atkins, D. E., and Van Houweling, D. (2002). *Higher Education in the Digital Age: Technology Issues and Strategies for American Colleges and Universities*. Westport, CT: Praeger.

Duderstadt, J. J., Atkins, D. E., Brown, J. S., Fox, M. A., Gomory, R. E., Hasselmo, N., Horn, P. M., Jackson, S. A., Rhodes, F. H. T., Smith, M. S., Sproul, L., Van Houweling, D., Weisbuch, R., Wulf, W. A., and Wyatt, J. B. (2002). *Preparing for the Revolution: Information Technology and the Future of the Research*. Washington, DC: National Academies Press. <http://www.nap.edu> (accessed August 3, 2006).

Duff, W., Craig, B., and Cherry, J. (2004). Historians' use of archival sources: Promises and pitfalls of the digital age. *Public Historian* 26 (2): 7–22.

Duff, W. M., and Johnson, C. A. (2002). Accidentally found on purpose: Information-seeking behavior of historians in archives. *Library Quarterly* 72 (4): 472–496.

Duguid, P. (2005). "The art of knowing": Social and tacit dimensions of knowledge and the limits of the community of practice. *Information Society* 21 (2): 109–118.

Duke, M., Day, M., Heery, R., Carr, L. A., and Coles, J. C. (2005). Enhancing access to research data: The challenge of crystallography. Proceedings of the ACM/IEEE-CS Joint Conference on Digital Libraries (Boulder, CO), 46–55. New York: ACM.

Dutton, W. H. (1999). *Society on the Line: Information Politics in the Digital Age*. Oxford: Oxford University Press.

Dutton, W. H., Gillett, S. E., McKnight, L. W., and Peltu, M. (2003). *Broadband Internet: The Power to Reconfigure Access*. Forum Discussion Paper No.

1: Oxford Internet Institute. <http://www.oii.ox.ac.uk/resources/publications/FD1.pdf> (accessed September 30, 2006).

Earth Science Data Centers. (2006). Earth Sun System Division, Data and Services. <http://nasadaacs.eos.nasa.gov/> (accessed September 30, 2006).

Edge, D. O. (1979). Quantitative measures of communication in science: A critical review. *History of Science* 17: 102–134.

EDSITEment. (2006). National Endowment for the Humanities. <http://edsitement.neh.gov/> (accessed September 30, 2006).

Eisenstein, E. (1979). *The Printing Press as an Agent of Change: Communications and Cultural Transformations in Early-Modern Europe*. Cambridge: Cambridge University Press.

Ekman, R., and Quandt, R. E., eds. (1999). *Technology and Scholarly Communication*. Berkeley: University of California Press.

e-Learning and Pedagogy. (2006). <http://www.jisc.ac.uk/elearning_pedagogy.html> (accessed April 18, 2006).

e-Learning Strategy Unit. (2006). Department for Education and Skills. <http://www.dfes.gov.uk/elearningstrategy/> (accessed April 18, 2006).

Electronic Cultural Atlas Initiative. (2006). University of California at Berkeley. <http://www.ecai.org/> (accessed September 30, 2006).

Elkin-Koren, N. (2004). The Internet and Copyright Policy Discourse. In *Academy and the Internet*, ed. H. Nissenbaum and M. E. Price, 252–274. New York: Peter Lang.

Elliott, R. (2005). Who owns scientific data? The impact of intellectual property rights on the scientific publication claim. *Learned Publishing* 18 (2): 91–94.

Ellis, D. (1993). Modeling the information-seeking patterns of academic researchers: A grounded theory approach. *Library Quarterly* 63 (4): 469–486.

Ellis, D., Cox, D., and Hall, K. (1993). A comparison of the information-seeking patterns of researchers in the physical and social sciences. *Journal of Documentation* 19 (1): 356–369.

Ellis, D., and Oldman, H. (2005). The English literature researcher in the age of the Internet. *Journal of Information Science* 31 (1): 29–36.

Enabling Grids for e-Science. (2006). European Commission. <http://www.eu-egee.org/> (accessed April 18, 2006).

Enabling Grids for e-Science II. (2006). European Commission. <http://www.eu-egee.org/> (accessed July 7, 2006).

Encoded Archival Description. (2006). Library of Congress. <http://www.loc.gov/ead/> (accessed September 30, 2006).

Encoded Archival Description Finding Aids. (2006). Library of Congress. <http://www.loc.gov/rr/ead/> (accessed March 31, 2006).

Enserink, M. (2006a). Avian influenza: As H5N1 keeps spreading, a call to release more data. *Science* 311: 1224.

Enserink, M. (2006b). Avian influenza: Pushed by an outsider, scientists call for global plan to share flu data. *Science* 313: 1026.

Enyedy, N., and Goldberg, J. (2004). Inquiry in interaction: Developing classroom communities for understanding through social interaction. *Journal for Research in Science Teaching* 41: 862–893.

Eprints. (2006). <http://www.eprints.org/> (accessed April 18, 2006).

e-Resources for Research in the Humanities and Social Sciences. (2005). A British Academy Policy Review, British Academy. <http://www.britac.ac.uk/reports/eresources/> (accessed September 30, 2006).

Esanu, J. M., and Uhlir, P. F., eds. (2003). *The Role of Scientific and Technical Data and Information in the Public Domain.* Washington, DC: National Academies Press. <http://books.nap.edu/catalog/10785.html> (accessed September 30, 2006).

Esanu, J. M., and Uhlir, P. F., eds. (2004). *Open Access and the Public Domain in Digital Data and Information for Science: Proceedings of an International Symposium.* Washington, DC: National Academies Press. <http://books.nap.edu/catalog/11030.html> (accessed September 30, 2006).

e-Science Core Programme. (2006). Engineering and Physical Sciences Research Council. <http://www.epsrc.ac.uk/ResearchFunding/Programmes/e-Science/default.htm> (accessed April 18, 2006).

Esposito, J. J. (2003). The devil you don't know: The unexpected future of open access publishing. *First Monday* 9 (8). <http://firstmonday.org/issues/issue9_8/esposito/index.html> (accessed August 17, 2006).

ESRC National Center for e-Social Science. (2006). <http://www.ncess.ac.uk/> (accessed April 22, 2006).

Estrin, D., Michener, W. K., and Bonito, G. (2003). *Environmental Cyberinfrastructure Needs for Distributed Sensor Networks: A Report from a National Science Foundation Sponsored Workshop.* Scripps Institute of Oceanography. <http://www.lternet.edu/sensor_report/> (accessed May 12, 2006).

Europe and the Global Information Society: Bangemann Report Recommendations to the European Council. (1994). European Council. <www.regiony.nck.pl/download.php?id=73> (accessed July 15, 2006).

Explanatory Statement on the Andrew W. Mellon Foundation's Intellectual Property Policy for Digital Products Developed with Foundation Funds. (2001). Andrew W. Mellon Foundation. <http://www.mellon.org/IPPolicy.pdf> (accessed August 25, 2006).

Family Educational Rights and Privacy Act. (1974). 20 U.S.C. § 1232g; 34 CFR Part 99. <http://www.ed.gov/policy/gen/guid/fpco/ferpa/index.html> (accessed March 13, 2006).

Farb, S. (2006). Libraries, licensing, and the challenge of stewardship. *First Monday* 11 (7). <http://firstmonday.org/issues/issue11_7/farb/index.html> (accessed July 20, 2006).

Fazackerley, A. (2004). Wellcome embraces open access future. *Times Higher Education Supplement* (November 5): 5.

Feather, J. (1998). *A History of British Publishing*. London: Croom Helm.

Feather, J. (2003). Book Trade. In *International Encyclopedia of Information and Library Science*, 42–44. London: Routledge.

Felten, E. W. (2003). A skeptical view of DRM and fair use. *Communications of the ACM* 46 (4): 57–59.

Fienberg, S. E., Martin, M. E., and Straf, M. L., eds. (1985). *Sharing Research Data*. Washington, DC: National Academy Press.

Finholt, T. A. (2002). Collaboratories. In *Annual Review of Information Science and Technology*, ed. B. Cronin, 36: 73–107. Medford, NJ: Information Today.

Fisher, C. B. (2006). Clinical trials databases: Unanswered questions. *Science* 311: 180.

Fisher, W. W., and McGeveran, W. (2006). *The Digital Learning Challenge: Obstacles to Educational Uses of Copyrighted Material in the Digital Age*. Cambridge, MA: Berkman Center for Internet and Society, Harvard Law School. <http://cyber.law.harvard.edu/home/2006-09> (accessed August 16, 2006).

Forsythe, D. E. (1993). Engineering knowledge: The construction of knowledge in artificial intelligence. *Social Studies of Science* 23 (3): 445–477.

Foster, I. (2000). Internet computing and the emerging grid. *Nature* 408 (6815). <http://www.nature.com/nature/webmatters/grid/grid.html> (accessed August 17, 2006).

Foster, I. (2003). The grid: Computing without bounds. *Scientific American* 288 (4): 78.

Foster, I., and Kesselman, C., eds. (2001). *The Grid: Blueprint for a New Computing Infrastructure*. San Francisco, CA: Morgan-Kaufmann.

Foster, N. F., and Gibbons, S. (2005). Understanding faculty to improve content recruitment for institutional repositories. *D-Lib Magazine* 11 (1). <http://www.dlib.org/dlib/january05/foster/01foster.html> (accessed August 6, 2006).

Fox, B. L., and LaMacchia, B. A. (2003). Encouraging recognition of fair uses in DRM systems. *Communications of the ACM* 46 (4): 61–63.

Fox, G. (2004). Grids of grids of simple services. *Computing in Science and Engineering* 6 (4): 84–87. <http://www.archives.gov/era/pdf/it-conference-fox.pdf> (accessed August 25, 2006).

Fox, M. J., Wilkerson, P. L., and Warren, S. R. (1998). *Introduction to Archival Organization and Description*. Los Angeles: Getty Publications.

Frankel, M. S., Elliott, R., Blume, M., Bourgois, J.-M., Hugenholtz, B., Lindquist, M. G., Morris, S., and Sandewall, E. (2000). Defining and certifying electronic publication in science: A proposal to the International Association of STM Publishers. American Association for the Advancement of Science. <http://www.aaas.org/spp/sfrl/projects/epub/define.shtml> (accessed May 12, 2006).

Friedlander, A. (1995a). Emerging infrastructure: The growth of railroads. Corporation for National Research Initiatives. <http://www.cnri.reston.va.us/series.html#rail> (accessed July 5, 2006).

Friedlander, A. (1995b). Natural monopoly and universal service: Telephones and telegraphs in the U.S. communications infrastructure, 1837–1940. Corporation for National Research Initiatives. <http://www.cnri.reston.va.us/series.html#teltel> (accessed July 5, 2006).

Friedlander, A. (1996a). "In God we trust": All others pay cash. Corporation for National Research Initiatives. <http://www.cnri.reston.va.us/series.html#bank> (accessed July 5, 2006).

Friedlander, A. (1996b). Power and light: Electricity in the U.S. energy infrastructure, 1870–1940. Corporation for National Research Initiatives. <http://www.cnri.reston.va.us/series.html#power> (accessed July 5, 2006).

Friedlander, A. (2005). Communications and content: Radio technologies in the U.S. infrastructure, 1865–1976. Corporation for National Research Initiatives. <http://www.cnri.reston.va.us/series.html#radio> (accessed July 5, 2006).

Friedly, J. (1996). How congressional pressure shaped the "Baltimore Case." *Science* 273 (5277): 873–875.

Frischer, B. (2004). Testimony to the Commission on Cyberinfrastructure for the Humanities and Social Sciences. American Council of Learned Societies. <http://www.acls.org/cyberinfrastructure/cyber_meeting_notes_october.htm#frischer_summary> (accessed August 6, 2006).

Frischer, B., and Stinson, P. (2002). Scientific verification and model-making methodology: Case studies of the virtual reality models of the house of Augustus (Rome) and Villa of the Mysteries (Pompeii). Heritage, New Technologies, and Local Development, Ename Center, Ghent. <http://www.cvrlab.org/research/research.html#publications> (accessed July 20, 2006).

Furner, J. (2002). On recommending. *Journal of the American Society for Information Science and Technology* 53 (9): 747–763.

Furner, J. (2003). Little book, big book: Before and after *Little science, gig science*: A review article, part I. *Journal of Librarianship and Information Science* 35 (2): 115–125.

Gadd, E., Oppenheim, C., and Probets, S. (2003). The intellectual property rights issues facing self-archiving: Key findings of the RoMEO project. *D-Lib Magazine* 9 (9). <http://www.dlib.org/dlib/september03/gadd/09gadd.html> (accessed August 25, 2006).

Galison, P. (1997). *Image and Logic: A Material Culture of Microphysics.* Chicago: University of Chicago Press.

Garson, L. R. (2004). Communicating original research in chemistry and related sciences. *Accounts of Chemical Research* 37 (3): 141–148.

Garvey, W. D. (1979). *Communication: The Essence of Science.* New York: Pergamon.

Garvey, W. D., and Griffith, B. C. (1964). Scientific information exchange in psychology. *Science* 146 (3652): 1655–1659.

Garvey, W. D., and Griffith, B. C. (1966). Studies of social innovations in scientific communication in psychology. *American Psychologist* 21 (11): 1019–1036.

Garvey, W. D., and Griffith, B. C. (1967). Scientific communication as a social system. *Science* 157 (3792): 1011–1016.

Garvey, W. D., and Griffith, B. C. (1971). Scientific communication: Its role in the conduct of research and the creation of knowledge. *American Psychologist* 20 (1): 349–362.

GÉANT. (2005). European Commission. <http://www.geant.net> (accessed August 25, 2006).

GÉANT2. (2005). European Commission. <http://www.geant.net> (accessed August 25, 2006).

Genome Canada Data Release and Sharing Policy. (2005). <http://www.genomecanada.ca/xcorporate/policies/DataReleasePolicy.pdf> (accessed September 30, 2006).

Geosciences Network. (2006). <http://www.geongrid.org/> (accessed August 16, 2006).

Geser, G., and Pereira, J., eds. (2004a). *Virtual Communities and Collaboration in the Heritage Sector.* Vol. 5. European Commission.

Geser, G., and Pereira, J., eds. (2004b). *Resource Discovery Technologies for the Heritage Sector.* Vol. 6. European Commission.

Ghosh, R. A., ed. (2005). *CODE: Collaborative Ownership and the Digital Economy.* Cambridge, MA: MIT Press.

Giaretta, D. (2005). DCC approach to digital curation. Digital Curation Center. <http://dev.dcc.rl.ac.uk/twiki/bin/view/Main/DCCApproachToCuration> (accessed July 31, 2006).

Gibaldi, J. (1988). *MLA Style Manual and Guide to Scholarly Publishing* 2nd ed. New York: Modern Language Association of America.

Gieryn, T. F. (1999). *Cultural Boundaries of Science: Credibility on the Line.* Chicago: University of Chicago Press.

Gilliland-Swetland, A. J. (2000). *Enduring Paradigm, New Opportunities: The Value of the Archival Perspective in the Digital Environment.* Council on Library and Information Resources. <http://www.clir.org/pubs/reports/pub89/contents.html> (accessed May 7, 2006).

Ginsparg, P. (2001). Creating a global knowledge network. Paper presented at the Second Joint ICSU Press–UNESCO Expert Conference on Electronic Publishing in Science, Paris. <http://people.ccmr.cornell.edu/~ginsparg/blurb/pg01unesco.html> (accessed May 12, 2006).

Global Earth Observation System of Systems. (2006). <http://www.epa.gov/geoss/> (accessed April 30, 2006).

Goble, C., and Wroe, C. (2005). The Montagues and the Capulets. *Comparative and Functional Genomics* 5 (8): 623–632.

Godby, C. J., Young, J. A., and Childress, E. (2004). A repository of metadata crosswalks. *D-Lib Magazine* 10 (12). <http://www.dlib.org/dlib/december04/godby/12godby.html> (accessed May 22, 2006).

Godfray, H. C. J. (2002a). Challenges for taxonomy: The discipline will have to reinvent itself if it is to survive and flourish. *Nature* 417 (6884): 17–19.

Godfray, H. C. J. (2002b). How might more systematics be funded? *Antenna* 26 (1): 11–17. <http://www.cpb.bio.ic.ac.uk/staff/godfray/antenna_article.pdf> (accessed September 30, 2006).

Godfray, H. C. J., and Knapp, S. (2004). Taxonomy for the twenty-first century: Introduction. *Philosophical Transactions of the Royal Society of London Series B-Biological Sciences* 359 (1444): 559–569.

Goldsmith, J. L., and Wu, T. (2006). *Who Controls the Internet? Illusions of a Borderless World.* Oxford: Oxford University Press.

Government Response: Scientific Publications—Free for All? Tenth Report of Session 2003–2004. (2005). House of Commons, Science and Technology Committee, United Kingdom Parliament. <http://www.publications.parliament.uk/pa/cm200304/cmselect/cmsctech/1200/1200.pdf> (accessed July 5, 2006).

Grant Policy Manual. (2001). National Science Foundation. <http://www.nsf.gov/publications/> (accessed July 5, 2006).

Gray, J., Liu, D. T., Nieto-Santisteban, M., Szalay, A., DeWitt, D., and Heber, G. (2005). Scientific data management in the coming decade. *CT Watch Quarterly* 1 (1). <http://www.ctwatch.org/quarterly/articles/2005/02/scientific-data-management/> (accessed August 25, 2006).

Greenberg, D. (1998). Camel Drivers and Gatecrashers: Quality Control in the Digital Library. In *The Mirage of Continuity: Reconfiguring Academic Information Resources for the 21st Century*, ed. B. L. Hawkins and P. Battin, 105–116. Washington, DC: Council on Library and Information Resources and the Association of American Universities.

Gross, R. A. (2002). Forum: Historians and guns. *William and Mary Quarterly* 59 (1): 203–204.

G-7 Information Society Conference. (1995). <http://europa.eu.int/ISPO/intcoop/g8/i_g8conference.html> (accessed July 20, 2006).

Guedon, J.-C. (1994). *Why Are Electronic Publications Difficult to Classify? The Orthogonality of Print and Digital Media.* Directory of Electronic Journals,

Newsletters, and Academic Discussion Lists, Association of Research Libraries. <http://www.ifla.org/documents/libraries/cataloging/guej1.txt> (accessed August 6, 2006).

Gunsalus, C. K., Bruner, E. M., Burbules, N. C., Dash, L., Finkin, M., Goldberg, J. P., Greenough, W. T., Miller, G. A., and Pratt, M. G. (2006). Mission creep in the IRB world. *Science* 312: 1441.

Guthrie, K. M. (2001). Archiving in the digital age: There's a will, but is there a way? *EDUCAUSE Review* 36 (November–December): 56–65. <http://www.educause.edu/pub/er/erm01/erm016w.html> (accessed July 15, 2006).

Hammond, T., Hannay, T., Lund, B., and Scott, J. (2005a). Social bookmarking tools (I): A general review. *D-Lib Magazine* 11 (4). <http://www.dlib.org/dlib/april05/hammond/04hammond.html> (accessed July 20, 2006).

Hammond, T., Hannay, T., Lund, B., and Scott, J. (2005b). Social bookmarking tools (II): A case study—Connotea. *D-Lib Magazine* 11 (4). <http://www.dlib.org/dlib/april05/lund/04lund.html> (accessed July 20, 2006).

Handle System. (2006). Corporation for National Research Initiatives. <http://www.handle.net> (accessed July 5, 2006).

Harhoff, D., Henkel, J., and Hippel, E. V. (2003). Profiting from voluntary information spillovers: How users benefit by freely revealing their innovations. *Research Policy* 32: 1753–1769.

Harnad, S. (1991). Post-Gutenberg galaxy: The fourth revolution in the means of production of knowledge. *Public-Access Computer Systems Review* 2 (1): 39–53. <http://www.ecs.soton.ac.uk/~harnad/Papers/Harnad/harnad91.postgutenberg.html> (accessed September 30, 2006).

Harnad, S. (1995). The post-Gutenberg galaxy: How to get there from here. *Information Society* 11 (4): 285–292.

Harnad, S. (1998). Learned inquiry and the Net: The role of peer review, peer commentary, and copyright. *Learned Publishing* 11 (4): 183–192. <http://cogprints.org/1694/00/harnad98.toronto.learnedpub.html> (accessed July 30, 2006).

Harnad, S. (2000). Ingelfinger over-ruled: The role of the Web in the future of refereed medical journal publishing. *Lancet Perspectives* 256 (December supplement): s16. <http://cogprints.org/1703/00/harnad00.lancet.htm> (accessed September 30, 2006).

Harnad, S. (2001). The self-archiving initiative. *Nature Web Debates* 26 (April). <http://www.ecs.soton.ac.uk/~harnad/Tp/nature4.htm> (accessed September 30, 2006).

Harnad, S. (2005a). Fast-forward on the green road to open access: The case against mixing up green and gold. *Ariadne* 42. <http://www.ariadne.ac.uk/issue42/> (accessed August 7, 2006).

Harnad, S. (2005b). The green and gold roads to maximizing journal article access, usage, and impact. *Haworth Press* (occasional column) 42. <http://eprints.ecs.soton.ac.uk/11093/> (accessed August 7, 2006).

Harnad, S. (2005c). The implementation of the Berlin Declaration on Open Access: Report on the Berlin 3 neeting held 28 February–1 March 2005, Southampton, UK. *D-Lib Magazine* 11 (3). <http://www.dlib.org/dlib/march05/harnad/03harnad.html> (accessed September 30, 2006).

Harnad, S., and Brody, T. (2004). Comparing the impact of open access (OA) vs. non-OA articles in the same journals. *D-Lib Magazine* 10 (6). <http://www.dlib.org/dlib/june04/harnad/06harnad.html> (accessed September 30, 2006).

Hart, M. S. (1992). History and philosophy of Project Gutenberg. <http://www.gutenberg.org/about/history> (accessed August 17, 2006).

Hawkins, B. L. (1998). The Unsustainability of the Traditional Library and the Threat to Higher Education. In *The Mirage of Continuity: Reconfiguring Academic Information Resources for the 21st Century*, ed. B. L. Hawkins and P. Battin, 129–153. Washington, DC: Council on Library and Information Resources and the Association of American Universities.

Hawkins, B. L., and Battin, P., eds. (1998). *The Mirage of Continuity: Reconfiguring Academic Information Resources for the 21st Century*. Washington, DC: Council on Library and Information Resources and the Association of American Universities.

Hayles, N. K. (2005). *My Mother Was a Computer: Digital Subjects and Literary Texts*. Chicago: University of Chicago Press.

Hellman, E. (2003). OpenURL: Making the link to libraries. *Learned Publishing* 16 (3): 177–181.

Hemlin, S., and Rasmussen, S. B. (2006). The shift in academic quality control. *Science, Technology, and Human Values* 31 (2): 173–198.

Hermanowicz, J. C. (2003). Scientists and satisfaction. *Social Studies of Science* 33 (1): 45–73.

Hey, J. (2004). Targeting academic research with Southampton's institutional repository. *Ariadne* (40). Retrieved from http://www.ariadne.ac.uk/issue40/hey/intro.html on 17 August 2006.

Hey, T. (2004). An open letter to the computer science community. *Grid Today*. <http://www.gridtoday.com/04/0920/103823.html> (accessed January 26, 2005).

Hey, T. (2005). Tony Hey on the need for Web services standards. *Grid Today* 4 (1). <http://www.gridtoday.com/05/0110/> (accessed April 30, 2006).

Hey, T., and Trefethen, A. (2003). The Data Deluge: An e-Science Perspective. In *Grid Computing: Making the Global Infrastructure a Reality*. New York: Wiley. <http://www.rcuk.ac.uk/escience/documents/report_datadeluge.pdf> (accessed January 20, 2005).

Hey, T., and Trefethen, A. (2005). Cyberinfrastructure and e-science. *Science* 308: 818–821.

Higginbotham, B. B., and Bowdoin, S. (1993). *Access versus Assets*. Chicago: American Library Association.

Higgins, D., Berkley, C., and Jones, M. B. (2002). Managing heterogeneous ecological data using Morpho. In *Proceedings of the 14th International Conference on Scientific and Statistical Database Management*. Piscataway, NJ: IEEE Computer Society.

Higher Education Research Institute. (2006). University of California at Los Angeles. <http://www.gseis.ucla.edu/heri/heri.html> (accessed September 30, 2006).

Hilborn, R., and Mangel, M. (1997). *The Ecological Detective: Confronting Models with Data*. Princeton, NJ: Princeton University Press.

Hilgartner, S. (1998). Data Access Policy in Genome Research. In *Private Science*, ed. A. Thakray, 202–218. Oxford: Oxford University Press.

Hilgartner, S., and Brandt-Rauf, S. I. (1994). Data access, ownership, and control: Toward empirical studies of access practices. *Knowledge* 15: 355–372.

Hine, C. (1995). Representations of information technology in disciplinary development: Disappearing plants and invisible networks. *Science Technology and Human Values* 20 (1): 65–85.

Hine, C. (2000). *Virtual Ethnography*. London: Sage.

Hine, C. (2002). Cyberscience and social boundaries: The implications of laboratory talk on the Internet. *Sociological Research Online* 7 (2): 79–99.

Hine, C. (2006). Computerization Movements and Scientific Disciplines: The Reflexive Potential of e-Science. In *New Infrastructures for Knowledge Production: Understanding e-Science*, ed. C. Hine. Hershey, PA: Idea Group Publishing.

Hodge, G., and Frangakis, E. (2005). Digital preservation and permanent access to scientific information: The state of the practice. International Council for Scientific and Technical Information and CENDI, U.S. Federal Information Managers Group. <http://cendi.dtic.mil/publications/04-3dig_preserv.html> (accessed September 30, 2006).

Hollerith Census Machine. (2006). Computer History Museum. <http://www.computerhistory.org/exhibits/highlights/hollerith.shtml> (accessed September 30, 2006).

Hovy, E. (2003). Using an ontology to simplify data access. *Communications of the ACM* 46 (1): 47–49.

Hughes, T. P. (1994). Technological Momentum. In *Does Technology Drive History? The Dilemma of Technological Determinism*, ed. M. R. Smith and L. Marx, 101–113. Cambridge, MA: MIT Press.

Hughes, T. P. (2004). *Human-Built World: How to Think about Technology and Culture*. Chicago: University of Chicago Press.

Humanities Advanced Technology and Information Institute. (2006). University of Glasgow. <http://www.hatii.arts.gla.ac.uk/> (accessed August 26, 2006).

Huysman, M., and Wulf, V. (2005). The role of information technology in building and sustaining the relational base of communities. *Information Society* 21 (2): 81–89.

Iacono, S., and Kling, R. (1996). Computerization Movements and Tales of Technological Utopianism. In *Computerization and Controversy: Value Conflicts and Social Choices*, ed. R. Kling, 85–105. San Diego, Academic Press.

I-Conference. (2006). Ann Arbor, Michigan <http://iconference.si.umich.edu> (accessed July 21, 2006).

Incorporated Research Institutions for Seismology. (2006). <http://www.iris.edu> (accessed September 30, 2006).

Ingelfinger, F. (1969). Definition of "sole contribution." *New England Journal of Medicine* 281: 676–677.

Ingwersen, P. (1998). The calculation of Web impact factors. *Journal of Documentation* 54 (2): 236–243.

Ingwersen, P., and Jarvelin, K. (2005). *The Turn: Integration of Information Seeking and Retrieval in Context*. Dordrecht, Netherlands: Springer.

Institute for Advanced Technology in the Humanities. (2006). University of Virginia. <http://www.iath.virginia.edu> (accessed August 6, 2006).

Integrated Taxonomic Information System. (2006). <http://www.itis.usda.gov/index.html> (accessed August 6, 2006).

International Dunhuang Project. (2006). British Library. <http://idp.bl.uk/> (accessed September 30, 2006).

International ISBN Agency. (2006). <http://www.isbn-international.org/en/index.html> (accessed January 18, 2006).

International Standard Serial Number. (2006). <http://www.isbn-international.org/en/revision.html> (accessed January 18, 2006).

International Union of Biological Sciences Taxonomic Databases Working Group. (2006). <http://www.tdwg.org/standards.html> (accessed December 15, 2006).

International Virtual Observatory Alliance. (2006). <http://www.ivoa.net/> (accessed September 30, 2006).

Internet Archive. (2006). <http://www.archive.org/details/millionbooks> (accessed September 30, 2006).

The Internet's Coming of Age. (2001). Washington, DC: National Academy Press. <http://www.nap.edu/catalog/9823.html#toc> (accessed October 5, 2006).

ISBN Standard Revision. (2006). <http://www.isbn-international.org/en/revision.html> (accessed January 18, 2006).

Jacobs, N., ed. (2006). *Open Access: Key Strategic, Technical, and Economic Aspects*. Oxford, UK: Chandos.

Janee, G., and Frew, J. (2002). The ADEPT digital library architecture. In *Second ACM/IEEE-CS Joint Conference on Digital Libraries* (Portland, OR), 342–350. New York: ACM Press.

Jirotka, M., Procter, R., Hartswood, M., Slack, R., Simpson, A., Coopmans, C., Hinds, C., and Voss, A. (2005). Collaboration and trust in healthcare innovation: The eDiaMoND case study. *Computer Supported Cooperative Work* 14: 369–398.

Jose, J. M. (2004). Personalization Techniques in Information Retrieval. In *Resource Discovery Technologies for the Heritage Sector*, ed. G. Geser and J. Pereira, 6: 22–26. European Commission.

JSTOR: The Scholarly Journal Archive. (2006). <http://www.jstor.org/> (accessed 17, August 2006).

Kaghan, W. N., and Bowker, G. C. (2001). Crossing boundaries and building bridges: Irreductionist "frameworks" for the study of sociotechnical systems. *Journal of Engineering and Technology Management* 18: 253–269.

Kahin, B., and Varian, H., eds. (2000). *Internet Publishing and Beyond: The Economics of Digital Information and Intellectual Property*. Cambridge, MA: MIT Press.

Kaiser, J. (2004a). NIH proposes 6-month public access to papers. *Science* 305: 1584.

Kaiser, J. (2004b). Zerhouni plans a nudge towards open access. *Science* 305: 1386.

Kaiser, J. (2005). Resurrected influenza virus yields secrets of deadly 1918 pandemic. *Science* 310 (5745): 28–29.

Kaiser, J. (2006a). Courts ruled no forum for data-quality fights. *Science* 311: 1536.

Kaiser, J. (2006b). Bill would require free public access to papers. *Science* 312: 828.

Kanfer, A. G., Haythornthwaite, C., Bruce, B. C., Bowker, G. C., Burbules, N. C., Porac, J. F., and Wade, J. (2000). Modeling distributed knowledge processes in next-generation multidisciplinary alliances. *Information Systems Frontiers* 2 (3–4): 317–331.

Kaput, J., and Hegedus, S. (2002). Exploiting classroom connectivity by aggregating student constructions to create new learning opportunities. *Proceedings of the 26th Annual Conference of the International Group for the Psychology of Mathematics Education*. Norwich, UK: University of East Anglia.

Karasti, H., Baker, K. S., and Halkola, E. (2006). Enriching the notion of data curation in e-Science: Data managing and information infrastructuring in the Long-Term Ecological Research (LTER) Network. *Journal of Computer Supported Cooperative Work* 15: 321–358.

Kay, A. (1971). The best way to predict the future is to invent it. <http://www.smalltalk.org/alankay.html> (accessed March 21, 2006).

Keep the Net Neutral. (2006). *Los Angeles Times*, March 6, B10.

Kellner, D. (2004). Technological transformation, multiple literacies, and the re-visioning of education. *eLearning* 1 (1). <http://www.wwwords.co.uk/ELEA/> (accessed September 30, 2006).

Kelly, K. (2006). Scan this book! *New York Times Magazine*, May 14, 42–49, 64, 71.

Kennedy, D. (2003). Research fraud and public policy. *Science* 300: 393.

Kennedy, D. (2004). Praise, for a change. *Science* 304: 1077.

Kenney, A. R. (2006). Surveying the e-journal preservation landscape. *ARL Bimonthly Report* (245). <http://www.arl.org/newsltr/245/preserv.html> (accessed June 29, 2006).

Kenney, A. R., McGovern, N. Y., Martinez, I. T., and Heidig, L. J. (2003). Google meets eBay: What academic librarians can learn from alternative information providers. *D-Lib Magazine* 9 (6). <http://www.dlib.org/dlib/june03/kenney/06kenney.html> (accessed September 30, 2006).

Kerr, R. A. (2005). Discovery of Pluto contender contested in planetary court. *Science* 309: 1972–1973.

King, C. J., Harley, D., Earl-Novell, S., Arter, J., Larence, S., and Perciali, I. (2006). *Scholarly Communication: Academic Values and Sustainable Models*. Berkeley: Andrew W. Mellon Foundation, Center for Studies in Higher Education, University of California. <http://cshe.berkeley.edu/publications/publications.php?id=230> (accessed July 28, 2006).

Kircz, J. G. (1998). Modularity: The next form of scientific information representation? *Journal of Documentation* 54 (2): 210–235.

Kircz, J. G., and Roosendaal, H. E. (1996). Understanding and shaping scientific information transfer. Paper presented at UNESCO Expert Conference on Electronic Publishing in Science, UNESCO House, Paris. <http://www.kra.nl/Website/Artikelen/unesco1996.htm> (accessed September 30, 2006).

Klein, J. T. (1993). Blurring, Cracking, and Crossing: Permeation and the Fracturing of Discipline. In *Knowledges: Historical and Critical Studies in Disciplinarity*, ed. E. Messer-Davidow, D. R. Shumway, and D. Sylvan, 185–211. Charlottesville: University Press of Virginia.

Klein, J. T. (1996). *Crossing Boundaries: Knowledge, Disciplinarities, and Interdisciplinarities*. Charlottesville: University Press of Virginia.

Kline, R., and Pinch, T. (1999). The Social Construction of Technology. In *The Social Shaping of Technology*, ed. D. MacKenzie and J. Wajcman. 113–115. Maidenhead, UK: Open University Press.

Kling, R. (1999). What is social informatics and why does it matter? *D-Lib Magazine* 5 (1). <http://www.dlib.org/dlib/january99/kling/01kling.html> (accessed September 30, 2006).

Kling, R. (2004). The Internet and Unrefereed Scholarly Publishing. In *Annual Review of Information Science and Technology*, ed. B. Cronin, 38: 591–631. Medford, NJ: Information Today.

Kling, R., and Callahan, E. (2003). Electronic Journals, the Internet, and Scholarly Communication. In *Annual Review of Information Science and Technology*, ed. B. Cronin, 37: 127–177. Medford, NJ: Information Today.

Kling, R., and Covi, L. (1995). Electronic journals and legitimate media in the systems of scholarly communication. *Information Society* 11 (4): 261–271.

Kling, R., and McKim, G. (1999). Scholarly communication and the continuum of electronic publishing. *Journal of the American Society for Information Science* 50: 890–906.

Kling, R., and McKim, G. (2000). Not just a matter of time: Field differences and the shaping of electronic media in supporting scientific communication. *Journal of the American Society for Information Science* 51 (14): 1306–1320.

Kling, R., McKim, G., and King, A. (2003). A bit more to it: Scholarly communication forums as socio-technical interaction networks. *Journal of the American Society for Information Science* 54 (1): 47–67.

Kling, R., Spector, L. B., and Fortuna, J. (2004). The real stakes of virtual publishing: The transformation of e-biomed into PubMed Central. *Journal of the American Society for Information Science* 55 (2): 127–148.

Knapp, S., Bateman, R. M., Chalmers, N. R., Humphries, C. J., Rainbow, P. S., Smith, A. B., Taylor, P. D., Vane-Wright, R. I., and Wilkinson, M. (2002). Taxonomy needs evolution, not revolution: Some changes are clearly necessary, but science cannot be replaced by informatics. *Nature* 419 (6907): 559.

Knorr-Cetina, K. (1999). *Epistemic Cultures: How the Sciences Make Knowledge*. Cambridge, MA: Harvard University Press.

Knowledge Network for Biocomplexity. (2006). University of California at Santa Barbara. <http://knb.ecoinformatics.org/index.jsp> (accessed September 30, 2006).

Kobsa, A. (2002). Personalized hypermedia and international privacy. *Communications of the ACM* 45 (5): 64–67.

Kobsa, A., and Schreck, J. (2003). Privacy through pseudonymity in user-adaptive systems. *ACM Transactions on Internet Technology* 3 (2): 149–183.

Korfhage, R. R. (1997). *Information Storage and Retrieval*. New York: Wiley.

Kranich, N. (2004). *The Information Commons: A Public Policy Report*. Free Expression Policy Project, Brennan Center for Justice, New York University, School of Law. <http://www.fepproject.org/policyreports/InformationCommons.pdf> (accessed September 30, 2006).

Krieger, K. (2006). Life in silico: A different kind of intelligent design. *Science* 312 (5771): 189–190.

Kuhn, T. (1962). *The Structure of Scientific Revolutions*. Chicago: University of Chicago Press.

Kurtz, M. J., Eichhorn, G., Accomazzi, A., Grant, C., Demleitner, M., Henneken, E., and Murray, S. S. (2005). The effect of use and access on citations. *Information Processing and Management* 41 (6): 1395–1402.

Kurtz, M. J., Eichhorn, G., Accomazzi, A., Grant, C., Demleitner, M., Murray, S. S., Martimbeau, N., and Elwell, B. (2005). The bibliometric properties of article readership information. *Journal of the American Society for Information Science and Technology* 56 (2): 111–128.

Lagoze, C. (2001). The open archives initiative: Building a low-barrier interoperability framework. Proceedings of the First ACM/IEEE-CS Joint Conference on Digital Libraries (Roanoke, VA), 24–28. New York: ACM.

Lamb, R., and Davidson, E. (2005). Information and communication technology challenges to scientific professional identity. *Information Society* 21 (1): 1–24.

Lamb, R., and Johnson, S. (2004). A special issue on social aspects of digital information in perspective. *Journal of Digital Information* 5 (4). <http://jodi.ecs.soton.ac.uk/> (accessed September 30, 2006).

Lamont, M., and Molnar, V. (2002). The study of boundaries in the social sciences. *Annual Review of Sociology* 28 (1): 167–195. <http://arjournals.annualreviews.org/loi/soc> (accessed October 1, 2006).

Lanham, R. A. (1993). *The Electronic Word: Democracy, Technology, and the Arts*. Chicago: University of Chicago Press.

Larsen, R., and Wactlar, H. (2003). *Knowledge Lost in Information: Report of the NSF Workshop on Research Directions for Digital Libraries*. University of Pittsburgh. <http://www.sis.pitt.edu/~dlwkshop/report.pdf> (accessed September 30, 2006).

Latour, B. (1987). *Science in Action: How to Follow Scientists and Engineers through Society*. Cambridge, MA: Harvard University Press.

Latour, B. (1988). Drawing Things Together. In *Representation in Scientific Practice*, ed. M. Lynch and S. Woolgar, 19–68. Cambridge MA: MIT Press.

Latour, B. (1993). *We Have Never Been Modern*. Trans. C. Porter. Cambridge, MA: Harvard University Press.

Latour, B., and Woolgar, S. (1979). *Laboratory Life: The Social Construction of Scientific Facts*. Beverly Hills, CA: Sage Publications.

Latour, B., and Woolgar, S. (1986). *Laboratory Life: The Construction of Scientific Facts*. 2nd ed. Princeton, NJ: Princeton University Press.

Lave, J., and Wenger, E. (1991). *Situated Learning: Legitimate Peripheral Participation*. Cambridge: Cambridge University Press.

Lavoie, B., and Dempsey, L. (2004). Thirteen ways of looking at . . . digital preservation. *D-Lib Magazine* 10 (7–8). <http://www.dlib.org/dlib/july04/lavoie/07lavoie.html> (accessed August 4, 2006).

Lavoie, B., Silipigni-Connaway, L., and Dempsey, L. (2005). Anatomy of aggregate collections: The example of Google print for libraries. *D-Lib Magazine* 11 (9). <http://www.dlib.org/dlib/september05/lavoie/09lavoie.html> (accessed October 1, 2006).

Lawrence, S. (n.d.). Free online availability substantially increases a paper's impact. *Nature* Web Debates. <http://www.nature.com/nature/debates/e-access/Articles/lawrence.html> (accessed May 9, 2005).

A Leaflet on Open Access. (2005). JISC Committee for Support of Research. <http://www.jisc.ac.uk/uploaded_documents/JISC-BP-OpenAccess-v1-Final.pdf> (accessed July 5, 2006).

Lesk, M. (1990). *Image Formats for Preservation and Access: A Report of the Technology Assessment Advisory Committee*. Council on Library and Information Resources. <http://www.clir.org/pubs/abstract/pub5.html> (accessed August 7, 2006).

Lesk, M. (2005). *Understanding Digital Libraries*. 2nd ed. San Francisco: Morgan Kaufmann.

Lessig, L. (1999). *Code and Other Laws of Cyberspace*. New York: Basic Books.

Lessig, L. (2001). *The Future of Ideas: The Fate of the Commons in a Connected World*. New York: Random House.

Lessig, L. (2004). *Free Culture: How Big Media Uses Technology and the Law to Lock Down Culture and Control Creativity*. New York: Penguin. <http://www.free-culture.cc/freeculture.pdf> (accessed October 1, 2006).

Levien, R., Austein, S. R., Borgman, C. L., Casey, T., Dubberly, H., Faltstrom, P., Halvorsen, P.-K., Jenkins, M., Klensin, J. C., Mueller, M. L., Nelson, S., Partridge, C., Raduchel, W., and Varian, H. R. (2005). *Signposts in Cyberspace: The Domain Name System and Internet Navigation*. Washington, DC: National Academies Press. <http://www.nap.edu> (accessed October 1, 2006).

Lewis-Beck, M., Bryman, A. E., and Liao, T. F., eds. (2003). *Sage Encyclopedia of Social Science Research Methods*. Thousand Oaks, CA: Sage.

Lexicon of Greek Personal Names. (2006). University of Oxford. <http://www.lgpn.ox.ac.uk/> (accessed March 31, 2006).

Libecap, G. D. (2003). State regulation of open-access, common-pool resources. University of Arizona and National Bureau of Economic Research. <http://www.icer.it/docs/wp2003/Libecap19-03.pdf> (accessed October 1, 2006).

Library Copyright Alliance. (2005). <http://www.copyright.gov/orphan/comments/OW0658-LCA.pdf> (accessed October 1, 2006).

Licklider, J. C. R. (1965). *Libraries of the Future*. Cambridge, MA: MIT Press.

Lievrouw, L. A. (1988). Four programs of research in scientific communication. *Knowledge in Society* 1 (2): 6–22.

Lievrouw, L. A. (1990). Reconciling Structure and Process in the Study of Scholarly Communication. In *Scholarly Communication and Bibliometrics*, ed. C. L. Borgman, 59–69. Newbury Park, CA: Sage.

Lievrouw, L. A. (1995). Constructing Research Narratives and Establishing Scholarly Identities: Properties and Propositions. In *Interaction and Identity*, ed. H. B. Mokros, 5: 215–235. New Brunswick, NJ: Transaction.

Lievrouw, L. A. (2002). Determination and Contingency in New Media Development: Diffusion of Innovations and Social Shaping Perspectives. In *The Handbook of New Media*, ed. L. Lievrouw and S. Livingston, 183–199. London: Sage.

Lievrouw, L. A. (2004). Biotechnology, Intellectual Property, and the Prospects for Scientific Communication. In *Biotechnology and Communication: The Meta-Technologies of Information*, ed. S. Braman, 145–172. Mahwah, NJ: Lawrence Erlbaum Associates.

Lievrouw, L. A., and Livingstone, S., eds. (2002). *The Handbook of New Media*. London: Sage.

Line, M. (1993). Changes in the use of literature with time: Obsolescence revisited. *Library Trends* 41 (4): 665–663.

Litman, J. (2001). *Digital Copyright*. Amherst, NY: Prometheus Books.

Liu, A. (2004). *The Laws of Cool: Knowledge Work and the Culture of Information*. Chicago: University of Chicago Press.

Liu, X., Brody, T., Harnad, S., Carr, L., Maly, K., Zubair, M., and Nelson, M. L. (2002). A scalable architecture for harvest-based digital libraries: The ODU/Southamptom experiments. *D-Lib Magazine* 8 (11). <http://www.dlib.org/dlib/november02/liu/11liu.html> (accessed October 1, 2006).

Livingstone, D. N. (2003). *Putting Science in Its Place: Geographies of Scientific Knowledge*. Chicago: University of Chicago Press.

Lloyd, S., Jirotka, M., Simpson, A. C., Highnam, R. P., Gavaghan, D. J., Watson, D., and Brady, J. M. (2005). Digital mammography: A world without film? *Methods of Information in Medicine* 44 (2): 168–171.

Long-Lived Digital Data Collections: Enabling Research and Education for the 21st Century. (2005). National Science Board. <http://www.nsf.gov/nsb/documents/2005/LLDDC_report.pdf> (accessed October 1, 2006).

Lord, P., and Macdonald, A. (2003). *e-Science Curation Report—Data Curation for e-Science in the UK: An Audit to Establish Requirements for Future Curation and Provision*. JISC Committee for the Support of Research. <http://www.jisc.ac.uk/uploaded_documents/e-scienceReportFinal.pdf> (accessed October 1, 2006).

Loring, J. F., and Campbell, C. (2006). Intellectual property and human embryonic stem cell research. *Science* 311: 1716–1717.

Lyman, P. (1996). What is a digital library? Technology, intellectual property, and the public interest (special issue on books, bricks, and bytes). *Daedalus, Journal of the American Academy of Arts and Sciences: Proceedings of the American Academy of Arts and Sciences* 125 (4): 1–33.

Lyman, P., and Varian, H. R. (2003). How much information 2003? <http://www.sims.berkeley.edu/how-much-info-2003> (accessed October 1, 2006).

Lynch, C. A. (1994). The integrity of digital information: Mechanics and definitional issues. *Journal of the American Society for Information Science* 45 (10): 737–744.

Lynch, C. A. (2001a). The battle to define the future of the book in the digital world. *First Monday* 6 (6). <http://www.firstmonday.dk/issues/issue6_6/lynch/index.html> (accessed October 1, 2006).

Lynch, C. A. (2001b). Personalization and recommender systems in the larger context: New directions and research questions. Paper presented in the Joint DELOS-NSF Workshop on Personalization and Recommender Systems in Digital Libraries, ACM SIGIR Forum, Dublin, Ireland. <http://www.ercim.org/publication/ws-proceedings/DelNoe02/> (accessed March 21, 2006).

Lynch, C. A. (2001c). When documents deceive: Trust and provenance as new factors for information retrieval in a tangled web. *Journal of the American Society for Information Science and Technology* 52 (12): 12–17.

Lynch, C. A. (2002). The afterlives of courses on the network: Information management issues for learning management systems. *EDUCAUSE Center for Applied Research: Research Bulletin* 2002 (23).

Lynch, C. A. (2003a). Institutional repositories: Essential infrastructure for scholarship in the digital age. *ARL Bimonthly Report*: 1–7. <http://www.arl.org/newsltr/226/ir.html> (accessed October 1, 2006).

Lynch, C. A. (2003b). Life after graduation day: Beyond the academy's digital walls. *EDUCAUSE Review* 38 (5): 12–13.

Lynch, C. A. (2004). Preserving digital documents: Choices, approaches, and standards. *Law Library Journal* 96 (4): 609–617 <http://www.aallnet.org/products/pub_llj_v96n04.asp> (accessed July 30, 2006).

Lynch, C. A. (2006). Open Computation: Beyond Human-Reader-Centric Views of Scholarly Literatures. In *Open Access: Key Strategic, Technical, and Economic Aspects*, ed. N. Jacobs. Oxford, UK: Chandos. <http://www.cni.org/staff/cliffpubs/opencomputation.htm> (accessed December 15, 2006).

Lynch, C. A. (In preparation). *Anticipatory Digitization of Cultural Artifacts*.

Lynch, C. A., and Garcia-Molina, H. (1995). *Interoperability, Scaling, and the Digital Libraries Research Agenda*. IITA Digital Libraries Workshop. <http://www.diglib.stanford.edu/diglib/pub/reports/iita-dlw/main.html> (accessed October 1, 2006).

Lynch, C. A., and Garcia-Molina, H. (2002). Retrospective: The 1995 interoperability, scaling, and the digital libraries research agenda report. Paper presented at the DLI2/IMLS/NSDL Principal Investigators Meeting, Portland, Oregon. <http://www.dli2.nsf.gov/dli2pi2002/program.html> (accessed February 4, 2005).

Lynch, C. A., and Lippincott, J. K. (2005). Institutional repository deployment in the United States as of early 2005. *D-Lib Magazine* 11 (9). <http://www.dlib.org/dlib/september05/lynch/09lynch.html> (accessed October 1, 2006).

Lynch, M., and Woolgar, S., eds. (1988). *Representation in Scientific Practice*. Cambridge, MA: MIT Press.

Lyon, L. (2003). e-Bank UK: Building the links between research data, scholarly communication, and learning. *Ariadne* (36). <http://www.ariadne.ac.uk/issue36/lyon/intro.html> (accessed October 1, 2006).

Machlup, F., and Mansfield, U., eds. (1983). *The Study of Information: Interdisciplinary Messages*. New York: Wiley.

MacKenzie, D., and Wajcman, J., eds. (1999). *The Social Shaping of Technology*. 2nd ed. Maidenhead, UK: Open University Press.

MacLean, D., ed. (2004). *Internet Governance: A Grand Collaboration*. New York: United Nations ICT Task Force.

Management's Discussion and Analysis. (2005). National Science Foundation. <http://www.nsf.gov/pubs/2006/nsf0601/pdf/05a.pdf> (accessed July 20, 2006).

Marchionini, G., and Crane, G. (1994). Evaluating hypermedia and learning: Methods and results from the Perseus project. *ACM Transactions on Information Systems* 12 (1): 5–34.

Marine Organisms Database. (2005). Marine Biological Laboratory. <http://www.mbl.edu/marine_org/> (accessed October 1, 2006).

Markoff, J., and Wyatt, E. (2004). Google is adding major libraries to its database. *New York Times*, December 14. <http://www.nytimes.com/> (accessed October 1, 2006).

Marris, E. (2005). Chemistry society goes head to head with NIH in fight over public database. *Nature* 435: 718–719.

Marshall, E. (2005). Will DNA bar codes breathe life into classification? *Science* 307: 1037.

Maskus, K. E., and Reichman, J. H. (2004). The globalization of private knowledge goods and the privatization of global public goods. *Journal of International Economic Law* 7 (2): 279–320.

Mason, E. (1971). The great gas bubble prick't; or, computers revealed—by a gentleman of quality. *College and Research Libraries* 32 (3): 183–196.

Mass Digitization: Implications for Information Policy. (2006). Report from Scholarship and Libraries in Transition: A Dialogue about the Impacts of Mass Digitization Projects, National Commission on Libraries and Information Science symposium, University of Michigan, March 10–11. <http://www.nclis.gov/digitization/MassDigitizationSymposium-Report.pdf> (accessed July 29, 2006).

McCook, A. (2006). Is peer review broken? *Scientist* 20 (2): 26.

McCray, A. T. (1993). Representing Biomedical Knowledge in the UMLS Semantic Network. In *High-Performance Medical Libraries: Advances in Information Management for the Virtual Era*, ed. N. C. Broering, 31–44. Westport, CT: Meckler.

Meadows, A. J. (1974). *Communication in Science*. London: Butterworths.

Meadows, A. J. (1998). *Communicating Research*. San Diego, CA: Academic Press.

Meadows, A. J. (2001). *Understanding Information*. Munich: K. G. Saur.

Mellon International Dunhuang Archive. (2006). <http://www.artstor.org/info/collections/mida.jsp> (accessed October 1, 2006).

Menzel, H. (1966). Information Needs and Uses. In *Annual Review of Information Science and Technology*, ed. C. A. Cuadra and A. W. Luke, 1: 41–69. New York: Wiley Interscience.

Merton, R. K. (1961). Singletons and multiples in scientific discovery. *Proceedings of the American Philosophical Society* 105 (5): 470–486.

Merton, R. K. (1963a). Ambivalence of scientists. *Bulletin of the Johns Hopkins Hospital* 112 (2): 77–97.

Merton, R. K. (1963b). The Mosaic of the Behavioral Sciences. In *The Behavioral Sciences Today*, ed. B. Berelson, 247–272. New York: Basic Books.

Merton, R. K. (1968). The Matthew effect in science. *Science* 159: 56–63.

Merton, R. K. (1969). Behavior patterns of scientists. *American Scientist* 57 (1): 1–23.

Merton, R. K. (1970). Behavior patterns of scientists. *Leonardo* 3 (2): 213–220.

Merton, R. K. (1972). Insiders and outsiders. *American Journal of Sociology* 77 (July): 9–47.

Merton, R. K. (1973a). The Normative Structure of Science. In *The Sociology of Science: Theoretical and Empirical Investigations*, ed. N. W. Storer, 267–278. Chicago: University of Chicago Press.

Merton, R. K. (1973b). *The Sociology of Science: Theoretical and Empirical Investigations*. Chicago: University of Chicago Press.

Merton, R. K. (1984). Scientific fraud and the fight to be first. *Times Literary Supplement* (4257): 1265.

Merton, R. K. (1988). The Matthew Effect in science II: Cumulative advantage and the symbolism of intellectual property. *ISIS* 79 (299): 606–623.

Merton, R. K. (1994). Scientists competitive behavior is not peculiar to our competitive age. *Scientist* 8 (15): 12–14.

Merton, R. K. (1995). The Thomas theorem and the Matthew effect. *Social Forces* 74 (2): 379–422.

Merton, R. K. (2000). On the Garfield Input to the Sociology of Science: A Retrospective Collage. In *Web of Knowledge: A Festschrift in Honor of Eugene Garfield*, ed. B. Cronin and H. B. Atkins, 435–448. Medford, NJ: Information Today, Inc.

Merton, R. K., and Lewis, R. (1971). Competitive pressures (I): The race for priority. *Impact of Science on Society* 21 (2): 151–161.

Metadata Encoding and Transmission Standard. (2006). Library of Congress. <http://www.loc.gov/standards/mets/> (accessed October 1, 2006).

Monastersky, R. (2005). The number that's devouring science. *Chronicle of Higher Education* 52 (8): A12–A17.

Morrison, K. (1988). Some Researchable Recurrences in Science and Situated Science Inquiry. In *The Interactional Order*, ed. D. Helm et al., 141–157. New York: Irvington.

Mullins, N. C. (1968). The distribution of social and cultural properties in informal communication networks among biological scientists. *American Sociological Review* 42: 552–562.

Murray-Rust, P. (2005). Open data! Paper presented at the Joint Infrastructure Systems Committee Annual Meeting. <http://www.dspace.cam.ac.uk/handle/1810/31316> (accessed October 2, 2006).

Murray-Rust, P., Mitchell, J. B. O., and Rzepa, H. S. (2005). Chemistry in bioinformatics. *BMC Bioinformatics* 6 (June 7): article 141.

Murray-Rust, P., and Rzepa, H. S. (2004). The next big thing: From hypermedia to datuments. *Journal of Digital Information* 5 (1): article 248. <http://jodi.tamu.edu/Articles/v05/i01/Murray-Rust/> (accessed October 1, 2006).

Murray-Rust, P., Rzepa, H. S., Tyrrell, S. M., and Zhang, Y. (2004). Representation and use of chemistry in the global electronic age. *Organic and Biomolecular Chemistry* 2 (22): 3192–3203.

Name Authority Cooperative Program. (2006). Program for Cooperative Cataloging, Library of Congress. <http://www.loc.gov/catdir/pcc/naco/> (accessed April 3, 2006).

NASA's Earth Science Data Resources. (2004). NASA, Earth Science Enterprise. <http://outreach.eos.nasa.gov/broch.html> (accessed December 15, 2006).

Nash, V., Dutton, W. H., and Peltu, M. (2004). *Innovative Pathways to the Next Level of e-Learning*. Oxford Internet Institute Forum Discussion Papers, University of Oxford. <http://www.oii.ox.ac.uk/resources/publications/OIIFD2_200409.pdf> (accessed October 3, 2006).

National Centre for Text Mining. (2006). <http://www.nactem.ac.uk/> (accessed October 3, 2006).

National Earthquake Engineering Simulation Cyberinfrastructure Center. (2006). <http://it.nees.org/> (accessed October 3, 2006).

National Ecological Observatory Network. (2006). <http://neoninc.org/> (accessed October 3, 2006).

National Science Digital Library. (2006). National Science Foundation. <http://www.nsdl.org> (accessed October 3, 2006).

Nature Peer Review Trial and Debate. (2006). *Nature*. <http://www.nature.com/nature/peerreview/index.html> (accessed June 29, 2006).

Neelameghan, A., and Tocatlian, J. (1985). International cooperation in information systems and services. *Journal of the American Society for Information Science* 36 (3): 153–163.

Nelson, R. R. (1959). The simple economics of basic scientific research. *Journal of Political Economy* 67: 323–348.

Nelson, T. H. (1987). *Computer Lib: Dream Machines*. Redmond, WA: Tempus Books of Microsoft Press.

Nelson, T. H. (2004). A cosmology for a different computer universe: Data model, mechanisms, virtual machine, and visualization infrastructure. *Journal of Digital Information* 5 (1). <http://jodi.tamu.edu/Articles/v05/i01/Nelson/> (accessed October 3, 2006).

Nentwich, M. (2003). *Cyberscience: Research in the Age of the Internet*. Vienna: Austrian Academy of Sciences Press.

Nentwich, M. (2004a). Qualitative aspects of quantitative measurements in the age of cyberscience. Paper presented at the AOIR-ASIST 2004 workshop the Web as a Mirror of Scientific and Technical Achievements: Issues in Access and Measurement and the preconference workshop at the Association of Internet Researchers conference, Brighton, England. <http://www.cybermetrics.wlv.ac .uk/AoIRASIST/NentwichASISTAoIR04_shortpaper.pdf> (accessed October 3, 2006).

Nentwich, M. (2004b). Quality control in academic publishing: Challenges in the age of cyberscience. *Poiesis and Praxis: International Journal of Ethics of Science and Technology Assessment* 3 (3): 181–198.

Network of Expertise in Long-Term Storage of Digital Resources. (2006). <http://www.langzeitarchivierung.de> (accessed October 3, 2006).

Networked Computer Science Technical Reference Library. (2006). <http:// www.bath.ac.uk/library/info/notes/ncstrl.html> (accessed October 3, 2006).

Networked Digital Library of Theses and Dissertations. (2006). Virginia Technological University. <http://www.ndltd.org/> (accessed August 31, 2006).

Niederee, C., Stewart, A., Mehta, B., and Hemmje, M. (2004). A multidimension, unified user model for cross-system personalization. Paper presented in the Environments for Personalized Information Access Workshop, Gallipoli, Italy. <http://www.di.uniba.it/avi2004/e4pia/> (accessed October 3, 2006).

NIH Public Access Policy. (2005). National Institutes of Health. <http:// publicaccess.nih.gov/publicaccess_manual.htm> (accessed March 28, 2006).

NIMS: Networked Infomechanical Systems. (2006). <http://www.cens.ucla.edu/ portal/nims> (accessed October 3, 2006).

NISO/ALPSP Working Group on Versions of Journal Articles. (2006). National Information Standards Organization; Association of Learned and Professional Society Publishers. <http://www.niso.org/committees/Journal_versioning/ JournalVer_comm.html#docs> (accessed July 5, 2006).

Normile, D. (2004). Summit pledges global data sharing. *Science* 304: 661.

Normile, D., Vogel, G., and Couzin, J. (2006). Cloning: South Korean team's remaining human stem cell claim demolished. *Science* 311 (5758): 156–157.

NSF's Cyberinfrastructure Vision for 21st Century Discovery. (2006). NSF Cyberinfrastructure Council, National Science Foundation. <http://www.nsf.gov/ od/oci/ci_v5.pdf> (accessed February 24, 2006).

OAIster. (2006). <http://oaister.umdl.umich.edu/o/oaister/> (accessed October 3, 2006).

Odlyzko, A. M. (1995). Tragic loss or good riddance: The impending demise of traditional scholarly journals. *International Journal of Human-Computer Studies* 42 (1): 71–122.

Odlyzko, A. M. (1997a). The economics of electronic journals. *First Monday* 2 (8). <http://www.firstmonday.org/issues/issue2_8/odlyzko/index.html> (accessed October 3, 2006).

Odlyzko, A. M. (1997b). Silicon dreams and silicon bricks: The continuing evolution of libraries. *Library Trends* 46 (1): 152–167.

Odlyzko, A. M. (2001). Internet pricing and the history of communications. *Computer Networks: The International Journal of Computer and Telecommunications Networking* 36 (5–6): 493–517.

Odlyzko, A. M. (2002). The rapid evolution of scholarly communication. *Learned Publishing* 15 (1): 7–19.

Odlyzko, A. M. (2003). The many paradoxes of broadband. *First Monday* 8 (9). <http://www.firstmonday.dk/issues/issue8_9/odlyzko/index.html> (accessed October 3, 2006).

Olsen, F. (2002). Historian resigns after report questions his gun research. *Chronicle of Higher Education* (November 8): A17.

Olson, G. M. (2005). Long-distance collaborations in science: Challenges and opportunities. Keynote talk presented at the First International Conference on e-Social Science, Manchester, UK.

Olson, G. M., and Olson, J. S. (2000). Distance matters. *Human-Computer Interaction* 15 (2–3): 139–178.

Online Qualitative Data Resources: Best Practice in Metadata Creation and Web Standards (2005). National Centre for e-Social Science Workshop, London. <http://www.esds.ac.uk/qualidata/news/eventdetail.asp?ID=1441> (accessed November 25, 2005).

Open Source Definition. (2006). Open Source Initiative. <http://www.opensource.org/osd.html> (accessed October 3, 2006).

OpenURL and CrossRef. (2006). <http://www.crossref.org/02publishers/16openurl.html> (accessed October 3, 2006).

Oppenheim, C., Greenhalgh, C., and Rowland, F. (2000). The future of scholarly journal publishing. *Journal of Documentation* 56 (July): 361–398.

Osterlund, C., and Carlile, P. (2005). Relations in practice: Sorting through practice theories on knowledge sharing in complex organizations. *Information Society* 21 (2): 91–107.

Pafford, J. H. P. (1935). *Library Co-operation in Europe*. London: Library Association.

Paisley, W. J. (1968). Information Needs and Uses. In *Annual Review of Information Science and Technology*, ed. C. A. Cuadra and A. W. Luke, 3: 1–30. Chicago: Encyclopedia Britannica.

Paisley, W. J. (1984). Communication in the Communication Sciences. In *Progress in the Communication Sciences*, ed. B. Dervin and M. Voigt, 5: 1–44. Norwood, NJ: Ablex.

Paisley, W. J. (1990). The Future of Bibliometrics. In *Scholarly Communication and Bibliometrics*, ed. C. L. Borgman, 281–299. Newbury Park, CA: Sage.

Paskin, N. (2003). DOI: A 2003 progress report. *D-Lib Magazine* 9 (6). <http://www.dlib.org/dlib/june03/paskin/06paskin.html> (accessed October 3, 2006).

Paskin, N. (2005). Digital object identifiers for scientific data. *Data Science Journal* 4 (1): 1–9.

Paterson, R. K. (2005). The "caring and sharing" alternative: Recent progress in the International Law Association to develop draft cultural material principles. *International Journal of Cultural Property* 12: 62–77.

Perry, J. W., Kent, A., and Berry, M. M. (1956). *Machine Literature Searching.* New York: Interscience.

Perseus Digital Library. (2006). Tufts University. <http://www.perseus.tufts.edu/> (accessed April 22, 2006).

Pettigrew, K. E., Fidel, R., and Bruce, H. (2001). Conceptual Frameworks in Information Behavior. In *Annual Review of Information Science and Technology*, ed. B. Cronin, 35. 43 78. Medford, NJ: Information Today.

Phelps, T. A., and Wilensky, R. (2004). Robust Hyperlinks: Cheap, Everywhere, Now. In *Digital Documents: Systems and Principles*, 2023: 28–43.

Polanyi, M. (1966). *The Tacit Dimension.* Garden City, NY: Doubleday.

Polsby, N. W. (1998). Social science and scientific change: A note on Thomas S. Kuhn's contribution. *American Review of Political Science* 1: 199–210.

Pon, R., Batalin, M. A., Gordon, J., Rahimi, M. H., Kaiser, W., Sukhatme, G. S., Srivastava, M., and Estrin, D. (2005). Networked infomechanical systems: A mobile wireless sensor network platform. *IEEE/ACM Fourth International Conference on Information Processing in Sensor Networks (IPSN-SPOTS)* (April): 376–381. <http://cres.usc.edu/pubdb_html/files_upload/450.pdf> (accessed April 30, 2006).

Pool, R. (1989). Will new evidence support cold fusion? *Science* 246: 206.

Pool, R. (1990). Cold fusion: Only the grin remains. *Science* 250: 754–755.

Popper, K. (1972). *Objective Knowledge: An Evolutionary Approach.* Oxford: Oxford University Press.

Porter, M. E. (1985). *Competitive Advantage: Creating and Sustaining Superior Performance.* New York: Free Press.

Powell, A. (2004). The JISC Information Environment and Google. UKOLN. <http://www.ukoln.ac.uk/distributed-systems/jisc-ie/arch/ie-google/ie-google.pdf> (accessed October 3, 2006).

Poynder, R. (2006). Clear blue water. <http://www.eprints.org/community/blog/index.php?/archives/43-Clear-blue-water.html> (accessed June 29, 2006).

PREMIS: Preservation Metadata. (2006). Library of Congress. <http://www
.loc.gov/standards/premis/> (accessed August 16, 2006).

Price, D. J. d. S. (1963). *Little Science, Big Science.* New York: Columbia
University Press.

Price, D. J. d. S. (1975). *Science since Babylon.* New Haven, CT: Yale
University Press.

Pritchard, S. M., Carver, L., and Anand, S. (2004). *Collaboration for Knowledge
Management and Campus Informatics.* University of California at Santa Barbara.
<http://www.library.ucsb.edu/informatics/informatics/documents/UCSB_Campus
_Informatics_Project_Report.pdf> (accessed July 5, 2006).

Project Gutenberg. (2006). <http://www.gutenberg.org> (accessed October 4,
2006).

Project MUSE. (2006). Johns Hopkins University Press. <http://muse.jhu.edu/>
(accessed October 3, 2006).

Protein Data Bank. (2006). <http://www.rcsb.org/pdb/> (accessed October 4,
2006).

Public Comments on Resource Description and Access. (2005). IEEE Learning
Technology Standards Committee. <http://cybertrails.org/P14ALA26.HTM>
(accessed October 4, 2006).

Public Library of Science. (2006). <http://www.plos.org> (accessed October 4,
2006).

Public Proofs: Science, Technology, and Democracy. (2004). Society for Social
Studies of Science and the European Association for the Study of Science and
Technology 2004 Meeting, Paris. <http://www.csi.ensmp.fr/WebCSI/4S/index
.php> (accessed October 4, 2006).

Publication Business Models and Revenue. (2004). In *Electronic Scientific,
Technical, and Medical Journal Publishing and Its Implications: Report of a
Symposium,* 20–39. Washington, DC: National Academies Press. <http://www
.nap.edu/catalog/10969.html> (accessed October 3, 2006).

Publication Manual of the American Psychological Association. (2001). 5th ed.
Washington, DC: American Psychological Association.

PubMed Central. (2006). National Institutes of Health. <http://www
.pubmedcentral.nih.gov/> (accessed October 4, 2006).

Quandt, R. E. (2003). Scholarly materials: Paper or digital? *Library Trends* 51
(3): 349–375.

*A Question of Balance: Private Rights and the Public Interest in Scientific and
Technical Databases.* (1999). Washington, DC: National Academy Press.
<http://www.nap.edu> (accessed September 28, 2006).

Quinones, S. (2006). Enlisting a posse of scientists. *Los Angeles Times,* May 20,
A1, A16–17.

Quotations Book. (2005). Answers.com. <http://www.answers.com/topic/
dressler-fritz-r-s#copyright> (accessed on 23 December 2006).

Rajasekar, A., and Moore, R. (2001). Data and Metadata Collections for Scientific Applications. In *HPCN 2001: Proceedings of the 9th International Conference on High-Performance Computing and Networking*, 72–80. New York: Springer.

Rayward, W. B. (1991). The case of Paul Otlet, pioneer of information science, internationalist, visionary: Reflections on biography. *Journal of Librarianship and Information Science* 23 (3): 135–145.

Rayward, W. B. (1994). Visions of Xanadu: Paul Otlet (1868–1944) and hypertext. *Journal of the American Society for Information Science* 45 (4): 235–250.

Rayward, W. B., and Buckland, M. K. (1992). Paul Otlet and the prehistory of hypertext. *Proceedings of the ASIS Annual Meeting* 29: 324–324.

RCUK Position Statement on Dissemination of and Access to Research Outputs. (2005). Research Councils UK. <http://www.rcuk.ac.uk/access/2005statement.pdf> (accessed July 5, 2006).

RDA: Resource Description and Access. (2006). Joint Steering Committee for Revision of the Anglo-American Cataloging Rules. <http://www.collectionscanada.ca/jsc/index.html> (accessed March 20, 2006).

Reference Model for an Open Archival Information System. (2002). Recommendation for Space Data System Standards, Consultative Committee for Space Data Systems Secretariat, Program Integration Division (Code M-3), National Aeronautics and Space Administration. <http://public.ccsds.org/publications/archive/650x0b1.pdf> (accessed October 4, 2006).

Reichman, J. H., and Uhlir, P. F. (2003). A contractually reconstructed research commons for scientific data in a highly protectionist intellectual property environment. *Law and Contemporary Problems* 66 (1–2): 315–462.

Report of the Investigation Committee on the Possibility of Scientific Misconduct in the Work of Hendrik Schon and Coauthors. (2002). Bell Laboratories. <http://www.lucent.com/news_events/pdf/summary.pdf> (accessed October 4, 2006).

Research Assessment Exercise. (2006). <http://www.rae.ac.uk/> (accessed October 4, 2006).

Research Papers in Economics. (2006). University of Connecticut. <http://www.repec.org/> (accessed August 25, 2006).

Rethinking How We Provide Bibliographic Services for the University of California. (2005). Bibliographic Services Task Force, University of California. <http://libraries.universityofcalifornia.edu/sopag/BSTF/Final.pdf> (accessed March 10, 2006).

Reuters. (2006). Moonwalk tape misplaced, NASA says. *Los Angeles Times*, August 15, A13.

Ribes, D., and Bowker, G. C. (forthcoming). Ontologies and the machinery of difference: Towards a sociology of knowledge representation. *Journal of the Association of Information Systems*.

RieussetLemarie, I. (1997). P. Otlet's Mundaneum and the international perspective in the history of documentation and information science. *Journal of the American Society for Information Science* 48 (4): 301–309.

Rockman, I. F. (2004). *Integrating Information Literacy into the Higher Education Curriculum: Practical Models for Transformation.* San Francisco: Jossey-Bass.

Rogers, E. M. (1995). *Diffusion of Innovations.* 4th ed. New York: Free Press.

Roosendaal, H. E., and Geurts, P. (1997). Forces and functions in scientific communication: An analysis of their interplay. Paper presented at the Cooperative Research Information Systems in Physics conference, Oldenburg, Germany. <http://www.physik.uni-oldenburg.de/conferences/crisp97/roosendaal.html> (accessed October 4, 2006).

Ross, S., Donnelly, M., and Dobreva, M. (2004). *DigiCULT: Emerging Technologies for the Cultural and Scientific Heritage Sector.* DigiCULT Technology Watch Report, European Commission. <http://www.digicult.info/downloads/twr_2_2004_final_low.pdf> (accessed October 4, 2006).

Ross, S., Donnelly, M., Dobreva, M., Abbott, D., McHugh, A., and Rusbridge, A. (2005). *Core Technologies for the Cultural and Scientific Heritage Sector.* DigiCULT Technology Watch Report 3, European Commission. <http://www.digicult.info/downloads/TWR3-lowres.pdf> (accessed October 4, 2006).

Ruben, B. D. (1992). The communication-information relationship in system-theoretic perspective. *Journal of the American Society for Information Science* 43 (1): 15–27.

Rusbridge, C. (2006). Excuse me. . . . Some digital preservation fallacies? *Ariadne* (46). <http://www.ariadne.ac.uk/issue46/rusbridge/> (accessed August 15, 2006).

Ryle, G. (1949). *The Concept of Mind.* London: Hutchinson.

Saltzer, J. H., Reed, D. P., and Clark, D. D. (1984). End-to-end arguments in system design. *ACM Transactions on Computer Systems* 2 (4): 277–288. <http://web.mit.edu/Saltzer/www/publications/endtoend/endtoend.pdf> (accessed October 4, 2006).

Samuelson, P. (2003). DRM [and, or, vs.] the Law. *Communications of the ACM* 46 (4): 41–45.

Sanders, T. (1998). *Into the Future: On the Preservation of Knowledge in the Electronic Age.* Council on Library and Information Resources. 60 minutes. <http://www.clir.org/pubs/film/future/order.html> (accessed August 16, 2006).

Scheiner, S. M. (2004). Experiments, observations, and other kinds of evidence. In *The Nature of Scientific Evidence: Statistical, Philosophical, and Empirical Considerations,* ed. M. L. Taper and S. R. Lele, 51–66. Chicago: University of Chicago Press.

Schiffman, L. H. (2002). The many battles of the scrolls. *Journal of Religious History* 26 (2): 157–178.

Schnase, J. L., Lane, M. A., Bowker, G. C., Star, S. L., and Silberschatz, A. (1997). Building the Next-Generation Biological Information Infrastructure. In *Nature and Human Society: The Quest for a Sustainable World*, ed. P. H. Raven and T. Williams, 291–300. Washington, DC: National Academy Press. <http://darwin.nap.edu/books/0309065550/html> (accessed October 4, 2006).

Schottlaender, B. (1998). Electronic publishing course, University of California, Los Angeles, with C. L. Borgman.

Schroder, P. (2003). Digital Research Data as Floating Capital of the Global Science System. In *Promise and Practice in Data Sharing*, ed. P. Wouters and P. Schroder, 7–12. Amsterdam: NIWI-KNAW. <www.virtualknowledgestudio.nl/> (accessed October 4, 2006).

Schwartz, M. F., Emtage, A., Kahle, B., and Neuman, B. C. (1992). A comparison of Internet discovery approaches. *Computing Systems* 5 (4): 461–493.

Schwartz Cowan, R. (1985). How the Refrigerator Got Its Hum. In *The Social Shaping of Technology*, ed. D. MacKenzie and J. Wajcman, 201–218. Maidenhead, UK: Open University Press.

Science Commons. (2006). A Project of Creative Commons. <http://sciencecommons.org/about/index.html> (accessed October 6, 2006).

Scientific Publications: Free for All? Tenth Report of Session 2003–2004. (2004). House of Commons, Science and Technology Committee, United Kingdom Parliament. <http://www.publications.parliament.uk/pa/cm200304/cmselect/cmsctech/399/39902.htm> (accessed October 4, 2006).

Scopus FAQ. (2006). Elsevier. <http://www.info.scopus.com/faq/> (accessed March 31, 2006).

Scopus in Detail. (2006). Elsevier. <http://www.info.scopus.com/detail/what/> (accessed March 31, 2006).

Seife, C. (2005). Tabletop accelerator breaks "cold fusion" jinx but won't yield energy, physicists say. *Science* 308: 613.

Selected Resources on Orphan Works. (2005). <http://www.arl.org/info/frn/copy/orphanedworks/resources.html> (accessed May 4, 2005).

Semantic Web Activity: W3C. (2006). <http://www.w3.org/2001/sw/> (accessed October 4, 2006).

Shankar, K. (2002). *Scientists, Records, and the Practical Politics of Infrastructure.* Ph.D. dissertation. Los Angeles: Information Studies, University of California, Los Angeles.

Shannon, C., and Weaver, W. (1949). *The Mathematical Theory of Communication.* Urbana: University of Illinois Press.

Shapiro, C., and Varian, H. (1999). *Information Rules: A Strategic Guide to the Network Economy.* Cambridge, MA: Harvard Business School Press.

Shatz, D. (2004). *Peer Review: A Critical Inquiry.* Lanham, MD: Rowman and Littlefield.

Shepard's Citations Service. (2006). Lexis-Nexis. <http://www.lexisnexis.com/shepards/> (accessed January 14, 2006).

SHERPA/RoMEO: Publisher Copyright Policies and Self-Archiving. (2006). SHERPA Project. <http://www.sherpa.ac.uk/projects/sherparomeo.html> (accessed October 3, 2006).

Shneiderman, B. (2003). *Leonardo's Laptop: Human Needs and the New Computing Technologies.* Cambridge, MA: MIT Press.

Shneiderman, B., and Kearsley, G. (1989). *Hypertext Hands-On! An Introduction to a New Way of Organizing and Accessing Information.* Reading, MA: Addison-Wesley.

Shortliffe, E. H., Atkins, D. E., Bloom, F., Ginsburg, J., Lynch, C., Mackie-Mason, J., Okerson, A., and Waltham, M. (2004). *Electronic Scientific, Technical, and Medical Journal Publishing and Its Implications: Report of a Symposium.* Washington, DC: National Academies Press. <http://books.nap.edu/> (accessed October 7, 2006).

Siegfried, S., Bates, M. J., and Wilde, D. N. (1993). A profile of end-user searching behavior by humanities scholars: The Getty Online Searching Project report no. 2. *Journal of the American Society for Information Science* 44 (5): 273–291.

Sloan Digital Sky Survey. (2006). <http://www.sdss.org/> (accessed August 15, 2006).

Small, H. (2004). On the shoulders of Robert Merton: Towards a normative theory of citation. *Scientometrics* 60 (1): 71–79.

Smeaton, A., and Callan, J. (2002). Joint DELOS-NSF workshop on personalization and recommender systems in digital libraries. *ACM SIGIR Forum* 35 (1): 7–11 (accessed March 21, 2006).

Smith, D. A., Mahoney, A., and Crane, G. (2002). Integrating harvesting into digital library content. Proceedings of the Second ACM/IEEE-CS Joint Conference on Digital Libraries (Portland, OR), 183–184. New York: ACM.

Smith, M., Rodgers, R., Walker, J., and Tansley, R. (2004). DSpace: A Year in the Life of an Open Source Digital Repository System. In *Eighth European Conference on Digital Libraries.* Bath, UK: Springer.

Social Informatics Web Site. (2006). Indiana University. <http://rkcsi.indiana.edu/> (accessed October 4, 2006).

Social Informatics Workshop. (2006). Center for Research on Information Technology and Organizations, University of California, Irvine. <http://www.crito.uci.edu/si/> (accessed October 4, 2006).

Solomon, P. (2002). Discovering Information in Context. In *Annual Review of Information Science and Technology*, ed. B. Cronin, 36: 229–264. Medford, NJ: Information Today.

Sonnenwald, D. H. (2006). Collaborative Virtual Environments for Scientific Collaboration: Technical and Organizational Design Frameworks. In *Avators at*

Work and Play, ed. R. Schroeder and A. Axelsson, 63–96. London: Springer Verlag.

Sonnenwald, D. H. (2007). Scientific Collaboration. In *Annual Review of Information Science and Technology*, ed. B. Cronin, 41: 643–681. Medford, NJ: Information Today.

Specification for the Second Phase Nodes. (2004). ESRC National Centre for e-Social Science. <http://www.esrcsocietytoday.ac.uk/ESRCInfoCentre/opportunities/Commissioning_updates/index36.aspx> (accessed October 4, 2006).

Stallman, R. M. (2002). *Free Software, Free Society: Selected Essays of Richard M. Stallman*. Boston: Free Software Foundation.

Staples, T., Wayland, R., and Payette, S. (2003). The Fedora project: An open-source digital object repository management system *D-Lib Magazine* 9 (4). <http://www.dlib.org/dlib/april03/staples/04staples.html> (accessed October 4, 2006).

Star, S. L. (1983). Simplification in scientific work: An example from neuroscience research. *Social Studies of Science* 13: 205–228.

Star, S. L., ed. (1995). *Ecologies of Knowledge: Work and Politics in Science and Technology*. Albany: State University of New York Press.

Star, S. L. (1999). The ethnography of infrastructure. *American Behavioral Scientist* 43 (3): 377–391.

Star, S. L., Bowker, G. C., and Neumann, L. J. (2003). Transparency beyond the Individual Level of Scale: Convergence between Information Artifacts and Communities of Practice. In *Digital Library Use: Social Practice in Design and Evaluation*, ed. A. P. Bishop, N. Van House, and B. P. Buttenfield, 241–270. Cambridge, MA: MIT Press.

Star, S. L., and Griesemer, J. (1989). Institutional ecology, "translations," and boundary objects: Amateurs and professionals in Berkeley's Museum of Vertebrate Zoology, 1907–1939. *Social Studies of Science* 19 (3): 387–420.

Star, S. L., and Ruhleder, K. (1996). Steps toward an ecology of infrastructure: Design and access for large information spaces. *Information Systems Research* 7 (1): 111–134.

Stephan, P. E. (1996). The economics of science. *Journal of Economic Literature* 34 (3): 1199–1235.

Stephan, P. E. (2004). Robert K. Merton's perspective on priority and the provision of the public good knowledge. *Scientometrics* 60 (1): 81–87.

Stephenson, J. (2006). Stem cell research probed. *Journal of the American Medical Association* 295 (3): 265–265.

Stokes, D. (1997). *Pasteur's Quadrant: Basic Science and Technological Innovation*. Washington, DC: Brookings Institution Press.

Stone, S. (1982). Humanities scholars: Information needs and uses. *Journal of Documentation* 38 (4): 292–313.

Strong, D. F., and Leach, P. B. (2005). *National Consultation on Access to Scientific Research Data: Final Report.* Canada Institute for Scientific and Technical Information, National Research Council Canada. <http://ncasrd-cnadrs.scitech.gc.ca/NCASRDReport_e.pdf> (accessed October 3, 2006).

Strong, G. (2006). Digital Libraries Course, University of California, Los Angeles, with C. L. Borgman.

Style Manuals and Citation Guides. (2006). Duke University Libraries. <http://www.lib.duke.edu/reference/style_manuals.html> (accessed February 15, 2006).

Suchman, L. A. (1987). *Plans and Situated Actions: The Problem of Human-Machine Communication.* Cambridge: Cambridge University Press.

Suleman, H., Atkins, A., Goncalves, M. A., France, R. K., Fox, E. A., Chachra, V., Crowder, M., and Young, J. (2001). Networked digital library of theses and dissertations. Bridging the gaps for global access—Part 1: Mission and progress. *D-Lib Magazine* 7 (9). <http://www.dlib.org/dlib/september01/suleman/09suleman-pt1.html> (accessed October 4, 2006).

Survey Research Center. (2005). University of California at Berkeley. <http://srcweb.berkeley.edu/> (accessed May 24, 2005).

Survey Research Center. (2006). Institute for Social Research, University of Michigan. <http://www.isr.umich.edu/src/> (accessed October 4, 2006).

Sutton, C. (2003). UCLA develops mobile sensing system for enriched monitoring of the environment. University of California at Los Angeles. <http://www.engineer.ucla.edu/stories/2003/nims.htm> (accessed October 4, 2006).

Svenonius, E. (2000). *The Intellectual Foundation of Information Organization.* Cambridge, MA: MIT Press.

Szalay, A. (2006). eScience and physics data. Paper presented at Microsoft Research Faculty Summit, Redmond, WA, July.

Száva-Kováts, E. (2002). Unfounded attribution of the "half-life" index-number of literature obsolescence to Burton and Kebler: A literature science study. *Journal of the American Society for Information Science and Technology* 53 (13): 1098–1105.

Tansley, H., Bass, M., and Smith, M. (2003). DSpace as an Open Archival Information System: Current Status and Future Directions. In *Research and Advanced Technology for Digital Libraries, 7th European Conference ECDL.* Heidelberg, Germany: Springer-Verlag.

Taper, M. L., and Lele, S. R., eds. (2004). *The Nature of Scientific Evidence: Statistical, Philosophical, and Empirical Considerations.* Chicago: University of Chicago Press.

Taubes, G. (1990). Cold fusion conundrum at Texas A&M. *Science* 248: 1299–1304.

Teevan, J., Dumais, S. T., and Horvitz, E. (2005). Personalizing search via automated analysis of interests and activities. In *Proceedings of the 28th Annual*

International ACM SIGIR Conference on Research and Development in Information Retrieval. (Salvador, Brazil), 449–456. New York: ACM.

Tenopir, C. (2003). Electronic publishing: Research issues for academic librarians and users. *Library Trends* 51 (4): 614–635.

Tenopir, C., and King, D. W. (1998). Designing the future of electronic journals with lessons learned from the past: Economic and use patterns of scientific journals. Proceedings of the IEEE: Socioeconomic Dimensions of Electronic Publishing (SeDEP) Workshop (Santa Barbara, CA), 11–17. Los Alamitos, CA: IEEE.

Tenopir, C., and King, D. W. (2000). *Towards Electronic Journals: Realities for Scientists, Librarians, and Publishers.* Washington, DC: Special Libraries Association.

Tenopir, C., and King, D. W. (2002). Reading behaviour and electronic journals. *Learned Publishing* 15: 259–265.

Tenopir, C., and King, D. W. (2004). *Communication Patterns of Engineers.* Hoboken, NJ: Wiley.

Text Encoding Initiative. (2006). <http://www.tei-c.org/> (accessed October 4, 2006).

Thelwall, M. (2006). Interpreting social science link analysis research: A theoretical framework. *Journal of the American Society for Information Science and Technology* 57 (1): 60–68.

Thelwall, M., Vaughan, L., and Bjorneborn, L. (2005). Webometrics. In *Annual Review of Information Science and Technology*, ed. B. Cronin, 39: 81–135. Medford, NJ: Information Today.

Thesaurus Linguae Graecae. (1972–). University of California, Irvine. <http://repositories.cdlib.org/escholarship/> (accessed October 5, 2006).

Thompson, J. B. (2005). *Books in the Digital Age.* Cambridge, UK: Polity.

Tibbo, H. R. (2003). Primarily history in America: How U.S. historians search for primary materials at the dawn of the digital age. *American Archivist* 66 (Spring–Summer): 9–50.

Tillett, B. (2004). What is FRBR? A conceptual model for the bibliographic universe. Library of Congress. <http://www.loc.gov/cds/FRBR.html> (accessed March 10, 2006).

Toms, E. G., and Duff, W. (2002). "I spent 1 1/2 hours sifting through one large box . . .": Diaries as information behavior of the archives user: Lessons learned. *Journal of the American Society for Information Science and Technology* 53 (14): 1232–1238.

Toy, J. (2002). The Ingelfinger rule: Franz Ingelfinger at the *New England Journal of Medicine*, 1967–1977. *Science Editor* 25 (6): 195–198.

Tragedy of the Commons? (2003). *Science* 302: 1906–1929.

Traweek, S. (1992). *Beamtimes and Lifetimes: The World of High Energy Physicists.* 1st Harvard University Press pbk. ed. Cambridge, MA: Harvard University Press.

Traweek, S. (2004). Generating High-Energy Physics in Japan. In *Pedagogy and Practice in Physics*, ed. D. Kaiser. Chicago: University of Chicago Press.

Traweek, S., and Nakayama, S. (2005). Digital archives and oral history at Japanese physics laboratories. Japan Society for the Promotion of Science <http://www.history.ucla.edu/traweek/> (accessed October 5, 2006).

Uhlir, P. F. (2006). The Emerging Role of Open Repositories as a Fundamental Component of the Public Research Infrastructure. In *Open Access: Open Problems*, ed. G. Sica. Monza, Italy: Polimetrica. UK Data Archive. (2006). <http://www.data-archive.ac.uk/about/about.asp> (accessed October 5, 2006).

UK e-Science Centres. (2006). <http://www.nesc.ac.uk/centres/> (accessed October 5, 2006).

Union List of Artists' Names Online. (2000). J. Paul Getty Trust. <http://www.getty.edu/research/conducting_research/vocabularies/ulan/> (accessed October 5, 2006).

United Nations Working Group on Internet Governance. (2005). Secretariat of the Working Group on Internet Governance. <http://www.wgig.org/> (accessed October 5, 2006).

Universal Bibliographic Control and International MARC. (2003). International Association of Library Associations. <http://www.ifla.org/VI/3/ubcim.htm> (accessed October 5, 2006).

Unsworth, J., Courant, P., Fraser, S., Goodchild, M., Hedstrom, M., Henry, C., Kaufman, P. B., McGann, J., Rosenzweig, R., and Zuckerman, B. (2005). Only connect: Reintegrating the human record and reconnecting scholarship with public life. Report of the Commission on Cyberinfrastructure for the Humanities and Social Sciences. American Council of Learned Societies. <http://www.acls.org/cyberinfrastructure/cyber.htm> (accessed October 17, 2005).

Unsworth, J., Courant, P., Fraser, S., Goodchild, M., Hedstrom, M., Henry, C., Kaufman, P. B., McGann, J., Rosenzweig, R., and Zuckerman, B. (2006). *A Shared Human Record: The Report of the American Council of Learned Societies' Commission on Cyberinfrastructure for Humanities and Social Sciences.* American Council of Learned Societies. <http://www.acls.org/cyberinfrastructure/cyber.htm> (accessed July 20, 2006).

Update: Apollo 11 Tapes. (2006). <http://www.nasa.gov/mission_pages/apollo/apollo_tapes_prt.htm> (accessed August 16, 2006).

US, Russia, China link up to form a global ring network for advanced science and education cooperation. (2003). <http://www.icair.org/pr/dec03/gloriad.html> (accessed July 7, 2006).

Usability Research Challenges in e-Science. (2005). UK e-Science Usability Task Force, University of Nottingham. <www.cs.nott.ac.uk/~tar/UTF.pdf> (accessed October 5, 2006).

Van de Sompel, H., and Beit-Arie, O. (2001a). Generalizing the OpenURL framework beyond references to scholarly works. *D-Lib Magazine* 7 (7–8). <http://www.dlib.org/dlib/july01/vandesompel/07vandesompel.html> (accessed October 5, 2006).

Van de Sompel, H., and Beit-Arie, O. (2001b). Open linking in the scholarly information environment: Using the OpenURL framework. *D-Lib Magazine* 10 (9). <http://www.dlib.org/dlib/march01/vandesompel/03vandesompel.html> (accessed April 27, 2005).

Van de Sompel, H., Hammond, T., Neylon, E., and Weibel, S. L. (2006). Request for comments 4452: The "info" URI scheme for information assets with identifiers in public namespaces. Internet Engineering Task Force. <http://www.rfc-archive.org/getrfc.php?rfc=4452> (accessed October 5, 2006).

Van de Sompel, H., Hochstenbach, P., and Beit-Arie, O. (2000). OpenURL syntax description. <http://www.exlibrisgroup.com/sfx_openurl_syntax.htm> (accessed October 5, 2006).

Van de Sompel, H., Nelson, M. L., Lagoze, C., and Warner, S. (2004). Resource harvesting within the OAI-PMH framework. *D-Lib Magazine* 10 (12). <http://www.dlib.org/dlib/december04/vandesompel/12vandesompel.html> October 5, 2006.

Van de Sompel, H., Payette, S., Erickson, J., Lagoze, C., and Warner, S. (2004). Rethinking scholarly communication: Building the system that scholars deserve. *D-Lib Magazine* 10 (9). <http://www.dlib.org/dlib/september04/vandesompel/09vandesompel.html> (accessed October 5, 2006).

Van de Sompel, H., Young, J. A., and Hickey, T. B. (2003). Using the OAI-PMH ... differently. *D-Lib Magazine* 9 (7–8). <http://www.dlib.org/dlib/july03/young/07young.html> (accessed October 5, 2006).

Van House, N. A. (2003). Digital Libraries and Collaborative Knowledge Construction. In *Digital Library Use: Social Practice in Design and Evaluation*, ed. A. P. Bishop, N. Van House, and B. P. Buttenfield, 271–296. Cambridge, MA: MIT Press.

Van House, N. A. (2004). Science and Technology Studies and Information Studies. In *Annual Review of Information Science and Technology*, ed. B. Cronin, 38: 3–86. Medford, NJ: Information Today.

van Raan, A. F. J. (2000). The Pandora's Box of Citation Analysis—Measuring Scientific Excellence: The Last Evil? In *The Web of Knowledge: A Festschrift in Honor of Eugene Garfield*, ed. B. Cronin and H. B. Atkins, 301–319. Medford, NJ: Information Today.

van Schewick, B. (2007). Towards an economic framework for network neutrality regulation. *Journal on Telecommunications and High Technology Law* 5. <http://ssrn.com/abstract=812991> (accessed October 5, 2006).

Varian, H. (2000). Versioning Information Goods. In *Internet Publishing and Beyond: The Economics of Digital Information and Intellectual Property*, ed. B. Kahin and H. R. Varian, 190–202. Cambridge, MA: MIT Press.

Vaughan, D. (1999). The role of the organization in the production of techno-scientific knowledge. *Social Studies of Science* 29 (6): 913–943.

Vaughn, L., and Shaw, D. (2005). Web citation data for impact assessment: A comparison of four science disciplines. *Journal of the American Society for Information Science and Technology* 56 (10): 1075–1087.

Vitiello, G. (2004). Identifiers and identification systems. *D-Lib Magazine* 10 (1). <http://www.dlib.org/dlib/january04/vitiello/01vitiello.html> (accessed October 5, 2006).

Waltham, M. (2005). Open access: The impact of legislative developments. *Learned Publishing* 18: 101–114.

Warburg, F. (1959). *An Occupation for Gentlemen*. London: Hutchinson.

Waters, D. J. (2006). Managing digital assets in higher education: An overview of strategic issues. *ARL Bimonthly Report* 244 (February): 1–10. <http://www.arl.org/newsltr/244/assets.html> (accessed October 5, 2006).

Watson, P. (2003). Databases and the grid. In *Grid Computing: Making the Global Infrastructure a Reality*, ed. F. Berman, G. Fox, and A. J. G. Hey, 363–384. New York: Wiley.

The Web of Life: A Strategy for Systematic Biology in the United Kingdom. (2006). <http://www.nhm.ac.uk/hosted_sites/uksf/web_of_life/index.htm> (accessed October 5, 2006).

The Web's Worst New Idea. (2006). *Opinion Journal from the Wall Street Journal*, May 18. <http://www.opinionjournal.com/editorial/feature.html?id=110008391> (accessed July 8, 2006).

Weibel, S. L. (1995). Metadata: The foundations of resource description. *D-Lib Magazine* 1 (1). <http://www.dlib.org/dlib/July95/07weibel.html> (accessed January 16, 2006).

Weinberg, A. M. (1961). Impact of large-scale science on the United States. *Science* 134: 161–164.

Wellcome Trust Policy on Access to Bioinformatics Resources by Trust-Funded Researchers. (2001). Wellcome Trust. <http://www.wellcome.ac.uk/doc%5Fwtd002759.html> October 5, 2006).

Wellcome Trust Position Statement in Support of Open and Unrestricted Access to Published Research. (2005). Wellcome Trust. <http://www.wellcome.ac.uk/doc_WTD002766.html> (accessed October 5, 2006).

Wellcome Trust Statement on Genome Data Release. (1997). <http://www.wellcome.ac.uk/doc%5Fwtd002751.html> (accessed October 5, 2006).

Weller, A. C. (2000). Editorial peer review for electronic journals: Current issues and emerging models. *Journal of American Society for Information Science and Technology* 51 (14): 1328–1333.

Weller, A. C. (2001). *Peer Review: Its Strengths and Weaknesses*. Medford, NJ: Information Today.

Wenger, E. (1998). *Communities of Practice: Learning, Meaning, and Identity.* New York: Cambridge University Press.

Westrienen, G. V., and Lynch, C. (2005). Academic institutional repositories deployment status in 13 nations as of mid-2005. *D-Lib Magazine* 11 (9). <http://www.dlib.org/dlib/september05/westrienen/09westrienen.html> (accessed October 5, 2006).

What Are CERN's Greatest Achievements? The World Wide Web. (2006). <http://public.web.cern.ch/public/Content/Chapters/AboutCERN/Achievements/Achievements-en.html> (accessed October 5, 2006).

Wiberley, S. E. (1983). Subject access in the humanities and the precision of the humanists' vocabulary. *Library Quarterly* 53 (4): 420–433.

Wiberley, S. E. (1988). Names in space and time: The indexing vocabulary of the humanities. *Library Quarterly* 58 (1): 1–28.

Wiberley, S. E., and Jones, W. G. (1989). Patterns of information seeking in the humanities. *College and Research Libraries* 50 (6): 638–645.

Wiberley, S. E., and Jones, W. G. (1994). Humanists revisited: A longitudinal look at the adoption of information technology. *College and Research Libraries* 55 (6): 499–509.

Wiberley, S. E., and Jones, W. G. (2000). Time and technology: A decade-long look at humanists' use of electronic information technology. *College and Research Libraries* 61 (5): 421–431.

Wiener, J. (2002). How the critics shot up Michael Bellesiles's book *Arming America. Nation* 275 (15): 28–32.

Willinsky, J. (2005). The unacknowledged convergence of open source, open access, and open science. *First Monday* 10 (8). <http://firstmonday.org/issues/issue10_8/willinsky/index.html> (accessed October 5, 2006).

Willinsky, J. (2006). *The Access Principle: The Case for Open Access to Research and Scholarship.* Cambridge, MA: MIT Press.

Wiser, S. K., Bellingham, P. J., and Burrows, L. E. (2001). Managing biodiversity information: Development of New Zealand's National Vegetation Survey databank. *New Zealand Journal of Ecology* 25 (2): 1–17. <http://nvs.landcareresearch.co.nz/html/Wiser_etal_2001_screen.pdf> (accessed October 5, 2006).

Wiswesser, W. J. (1985). Historic development of chemical notations. *Journal of Chemical Information and Computer Sciences* 25 (3): 258–263.

Witten, I. H., and Bainbridge, D. (2003). *How to Build a Digital Library.* Amsterdam: Morgan Kaufmann.

Wohn, D. Y., and Normile, D. (2006). Korean cloning scandal: Prosecutors allege elaborate deception and missing funds. *Science* 312: 980–981.

Woolgar, S. (1976). Writing an intellectual history of scientific development: The use of discovery accounts. *Social Studies of Science* 6: 395–422.

Woolgar, S. (2003). *Social Shaping Perspectives on e-Science and e-Social Science: The Case for Research Support—A Consultative Study for the Economic and Social Research Council (ESRC)*. Swindon, UK: Economic and Social Research Council. <http://www.sbs.ox.ac.uk/html/faculty_area_sci_tech.asp> <www.sbs.ox.ac.uk/downloads/e-SocialScience.pdf> (accessed April 22, 2006).

World International Property Organization. (2006). <http://www.wipo.int/portal/index.html.en> (accessed October 5, 2006>.

World Wide Web Consortium. (2006). W3C. <http://www.w3.org/> (accessed October 5, 2005).

Wouters, P. (2002). *Policies on Digital Research Data: An International Survey*. Amsterdam: NIWI-KNAW.

Wouters, P. (2004). What is the matter with e-science? Thinking aloud about informatisation in knowledge creation. Paper presented at *Society for Social Studies of Science Annual Meeting, Paris, September*. <http://www.nerdi.knaw.nl> (accessed October 29, 2004).

Wouters, P., and Reddy, C. (2003). Big Science Data Policies. In *Promise and Practice in Data Sharing*, ed. P. Wouters and P. Schroder, 13–40. Amsterdam: NIWI-KNAW. <http://www.niwi.knaw.nl/en/nerdi2/group_members/paul/publ/datasharing/toonplaatje> (accessed October 5, 2006).

Wouters, P., and Schroder, P., eds. (2003). *Promise and Practice in Data Sharing*. Amsterdam: NIWI-KNAW. <http://www.niwi.knaw.nl/en/nerdi2/group_members/paul/publ/datasharing/toonplaatje> (accessed July 22, 2005).

Wouters, P., Helsten, L., and Leydesdorff, L. (2004). Internet time and the reliability of search engines. *First Monday* 9 (10). <http://www.firstmonday.org/issues/issue9_10/wouters/index.html> (accessed February 10, 2005).

Wu, T. (2005). Network neutrality, broadband discrimination. *Journal of Telecommunications and High Technology Law* 2:141. <http://ssrn.com/abstract=388863> (accessed October 5, 2006).

Wulf, W. A. (1989). The National Collaboratory: A white paper. In *Towards a National Collaboratory: Report of an Invitational Workshop*. Washington, DC: National Science Foundation.

Wulf, W. A. (1993). The collaboratory opportunity. *Science* 261: 854–855.

Yakel, E. (1992). Pushing MARC AMC to its limits: The Vatican Archives Project. *American Archivist* 55 (1): 192–201.

Yakel, E. (2005). Introduction to reference work in the digital age. *Journal of the American Society for Information Science and Technology* 56 (11): 1237–1238.

Yakel, E., and Kim, J. (2005). Adoption and diffusion of encoded archival description. *Journal of the American Society for Information Science and Technology* 56 (13): 1427–1437.

Zerhouni, E. A. (2004). NIH public access policy. *Science* 306: 1895.

Zerhouni, E. A. (2006). *Report on the NIH Public Access Policy*. Department of Health and Human Services, National Institutes of Health. <http://publicaccess.nih.gov/Final_Report_20060201.pdf> (accessed October 5, 2006).

Zhuge, H. (2004). China's e-science knowledge grid environment. *IEEE Intelligent Systems and Their Applications* 19 (1): 13–17.

Zimmerman, A. S. (2003). *Data Sharing and Secondary Use of Scientific Data: Experiences of Ecologists*. PhD dissertation. Ann Arbor: School of Information, University of Michigan.

Zimmerman, A. S. (Forthcoming). New knowledge from old data: The role of standards in the sharing and reuse of ecological data. *Science, Technology, and Human Values*.

Zook, M. (2006). The Geographies of the Internet. In *Annual Review of Information Science and Technology*, 40: 53–78. Medford, NJ: Information Today.

Zuckerman, H., and Merton, R. K. (1971a). Patterns of evaluation in sciences: Institutionalisation, structure, and functions of referee system. *Minerva* 9 (1): 66–100.

Zuckerman, H., and Merton, R. K. (1971b). Sociology of refereeing. *Physics Today* 24 (7): 28–33.

Index